I0819305

WOVEN TAPESTRY

ART *and* PRACTICE

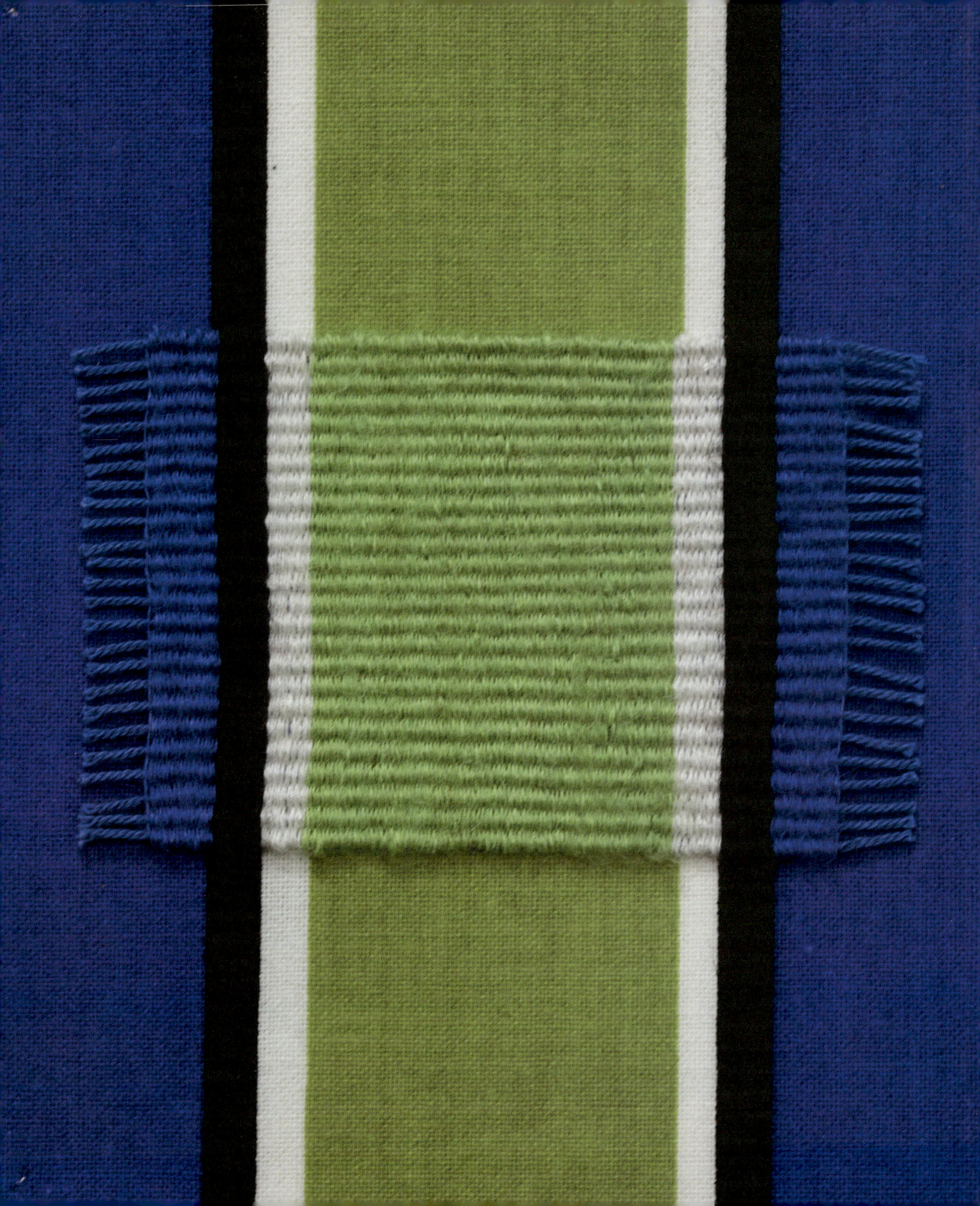

Louise Martin and Ros Bryant

WOVEN TAPESTRY

ART *and* PRACTICE

THE CROWOOD PRESS

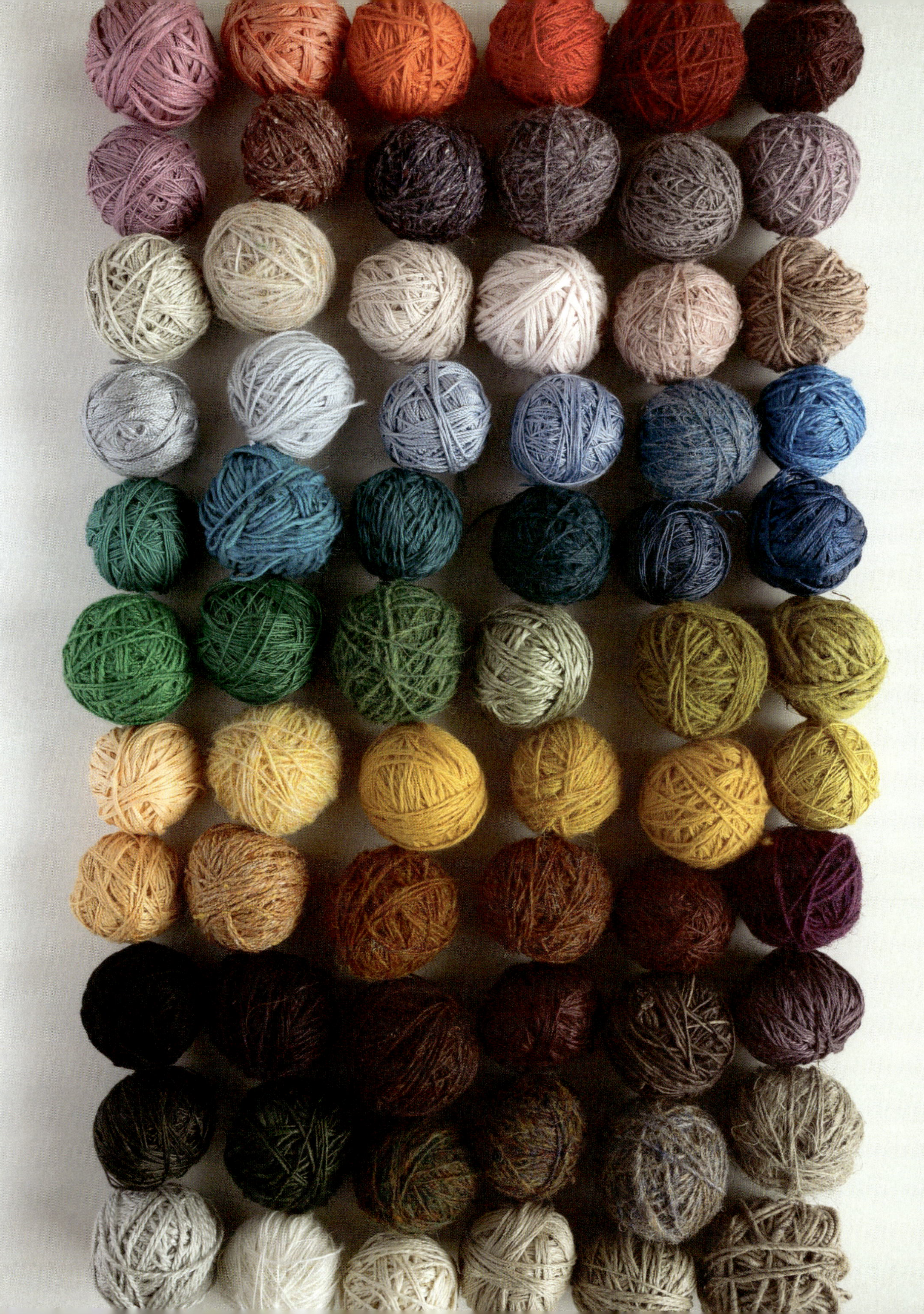

CONTENTS

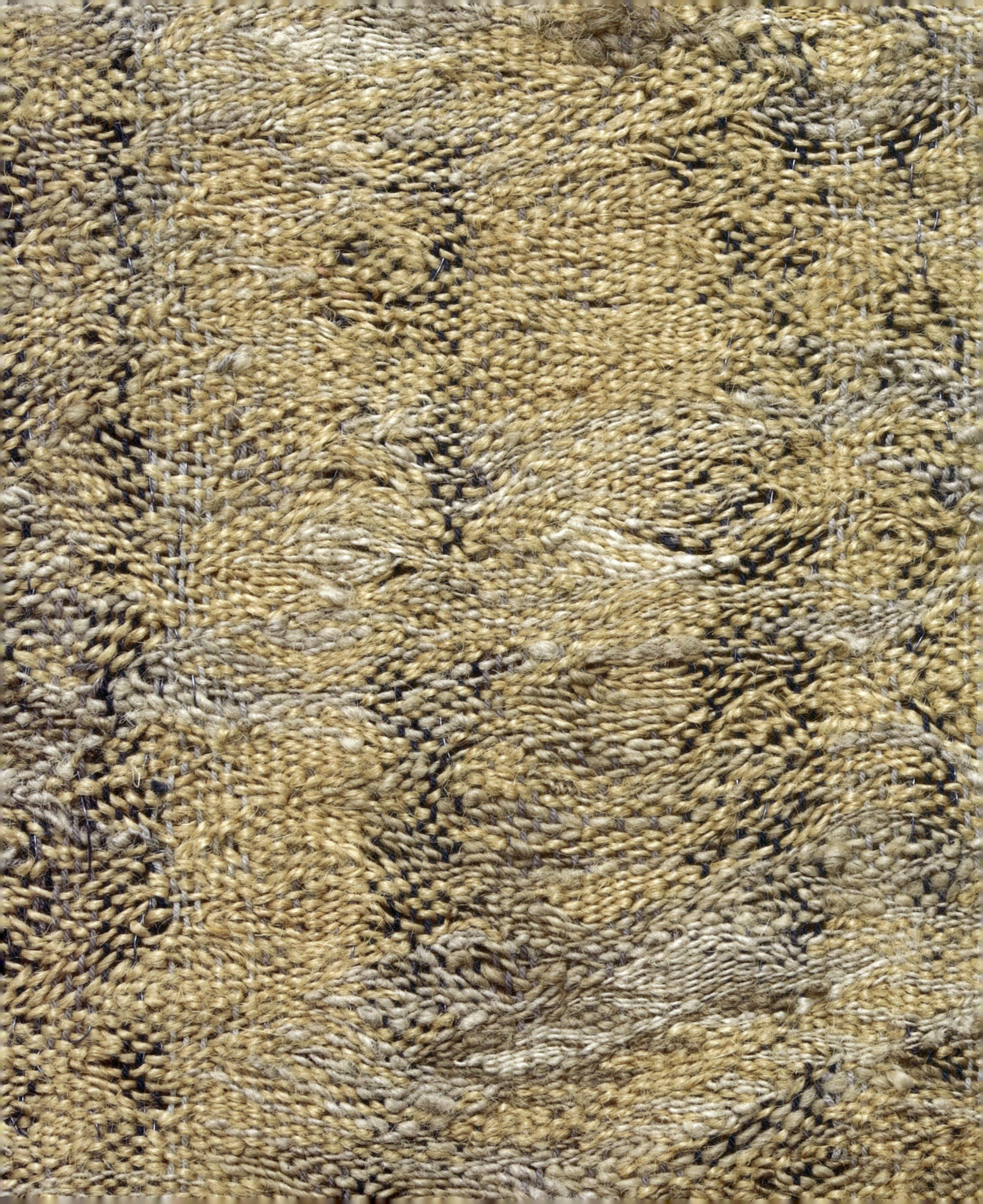

INTRODUCTION

Written from the authors' shared passion for woven tapestry, for the delight of handling yarn and for the expressive freedom it offers, this book is based on what we have each learned through a combined 50 years of making and teaching. It aims to equip the discerning learner with the means to make the creative language of woven tapestry their own.

Technique is taught in considerable detail in the belief that technical fluency is essential to creative freedom, to making work of beauty, originality and integrity. The underlying principles are fully outlined with the aim of equipping the reader with a working understanding. Specially woven samples, drawn diagrams and written explanations are used throughout including suggestions for choices of material and application of techniques. The samples, the drawn diagrams and most of the tapestries are Louise's, the words are Ros's.

As a constructed medium, woven tapestry rewards close observation and a hand sensitive to the way warp and weft hold each other. Its slow under/over rhythm allows time to respond with carefully made choices. There is a fundamental simplicity to the structure which belies the complexity of which it is capable.

The opening four chapters cover the basics of setting up, managing warp and weft and weaving simple forms. Chapters 5 and 6 move onto more complex designs and aesthetically based choices. Chapters 7 to 9 introduce further techniques, some unique to this book. The final chapter offers insights into work made by both authors and guidance on developing the reader's own creative 'voice'.

Louise's path into tapestry weaving was through seven years of study from foundation to masters. Having developed her creative voice, she deepened her technical mastery through studio work, including a ten-year commitment to the weaving of the Hunt of the Unicorn tapestries as senior weaver at Stirling Castle, Scotland, which demanded the most exacting understanding of tapestry technique.

Landscape and a sense of place have a deep influence on Louise's work – from her native Isle of Man to Mongolia, Finland, Syria, Turkey, Bangladesh, and Orkney. Her tapestries are made instinctually, in direct response to the landscape, and have been described as 'quietly powerful, deeply weaverly and intensely personal'. With minimal planning, most choices are made at the loom allowing freedom to explore the essential qualities and integrity of weave. As a teacher, she approaches technique with care and precision, encouraging close observation and sensitivity to the language of weave with the aim of students making individual and authentic work.

For Ros, a chance visit to an exhibition of contemporary art tapestry proved to be a high point in a life of discovery, and seeing the exquisite range of expression possible in woven tapestry opened up a whole new world. In pursuit of learning tapestry, she gained the support of a well-established tutor with help from Arts Council, England, and changed to part-time work. She became instrumental in forming the British Tapestry Group with the aim of promoting excellence in tapestry as an art-form. Later moving to the wide sea horizons of Orkney, she established Northlight studio where she wove and exhibited tapestries and taught large numbers of students.

There remains so much yet to be discovered in tapestry weaving – we wish you joy in your journey.

Sea of Threads detail. Woven at 11 epi. Blue and grey fine cotton and metal warp. Jute and nettle weft.

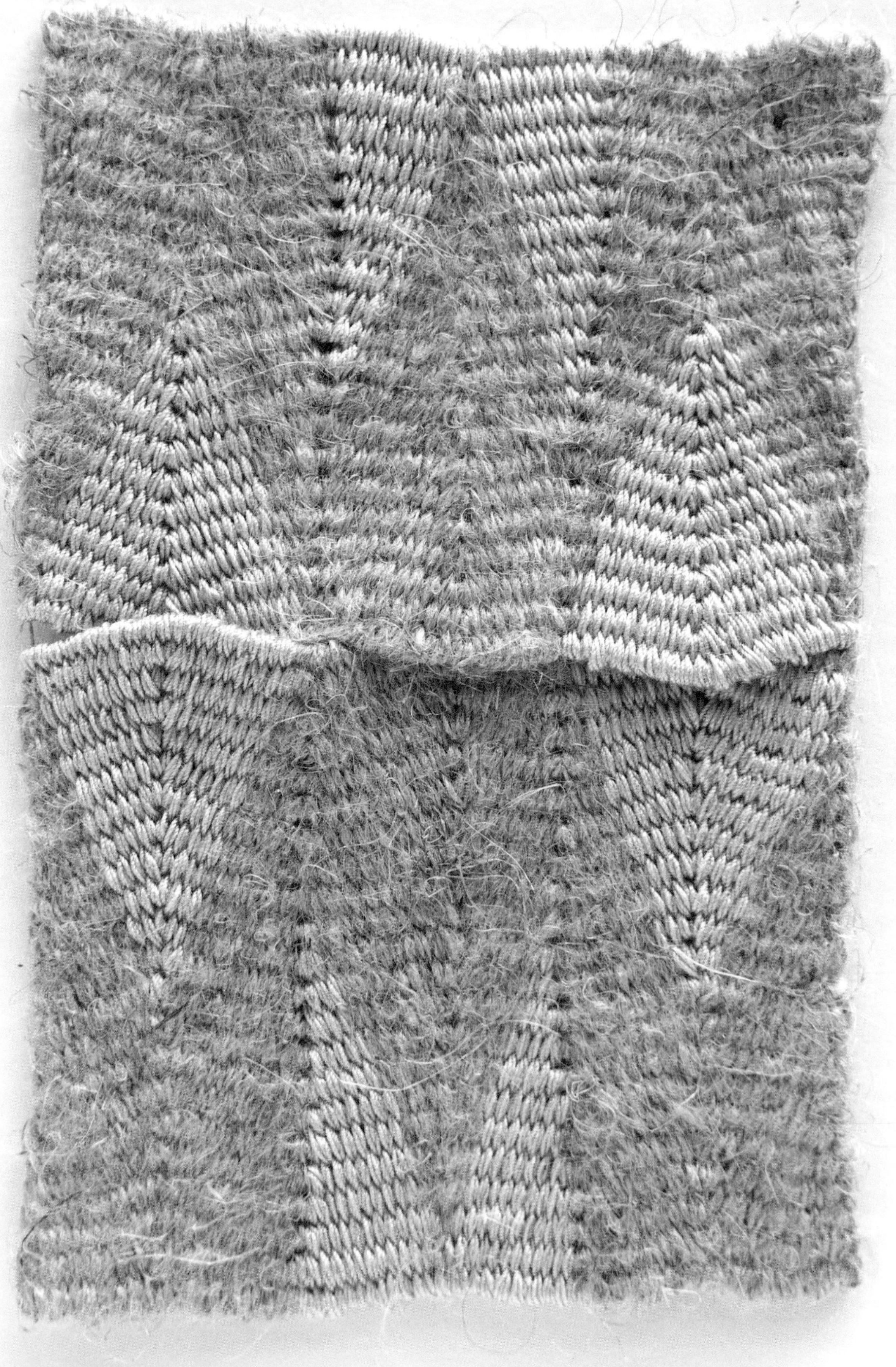

TERMS AND TECHNIQUES

These fundamental terms are defined as used within this book, with alternative terms shown in brackets. When the terms explained here are first introduced in the text, they are included in italics.

Heading cords. Two lengths of warp yarn tied around one side of the frame and woven to the other side at the start of a piece. They are pulled tight to draw the front and back warps together and secured to the other side of the frame. This forms a firm, level base to start weaving from.

Double half hitches. These are made at the start and finish of a weaving. Two half hitches are made on each warp in turn along a row to stop the weaving from unravelling once cut off the loom. This is spoken of as **knotting on or knotting off.**

Twining. Two cords or lengths of warp yarn tied to the side of the frame and twisted over each other under tension, in the space between consecutive warps. This is then tied to the other side of the frame to keep it under tension. Made at the outset of a piece, the twining draws the front and back warps level, making a flat surface.

Slip knot. Slip knots are used when tying on at the start and end of a new warp to secure whilst allowing for re-tensioning.

Frame (or loom). Any structure on which a warp may be tensioned could be considered a tapestry loom. For the purposes of this book, this will simply be a rigid rectangular wooden frame suitable for small-scale work. Larger tapestries may be woven on a floor loom, generally tubular steel and with a tensioning device, sometimes called a scaffold loom. The terms frame and loom are both used in this book.

Warp. Warp is the yarn which is wound around the frame from bottom to top, usually at regular intervals and knotted so that it remains under tension.

Warp weight. Warp comes in various thicknesses, or weights. These are often described by a 'yarn count' but since there are many different versions, we will use fine, medium and heavy.

A warp. We speak about 'putting on a warp' meaning to wind warp yarn around a frame under tension for as many times as the width of a piece requires, normally at regular intervals. A warp is the structure through which weft passes in the weaving of a tapestry. The term is also used singularly to mean an individual warp.

Warp sett (or setting). This is the spacing between warps, usually regular and established whilst putting on a warp. For the purposes of this book warp sett is measured in inches – termed epi, ends per inch. This means the number of warps in each inch. Some weavers prefer to work in ends per centimetre.

Epi/Epc. *See* warp sett.

Back warps. Warps which pass around the back of the frame.

Front warps. Warps which pass around the front of the frame.

Low warps. As the weft is woven back and forth it generally passes under and over each warp in turn. A low warp is one which the weft has just passed under. Visually this shows as a hollow in the undulating line which a weft naturally makes. Some weavers speak of hollows and hills in

Wedge weave in linen and cotton. 7 × 11cm.

place of **lows and highs**. When a weft returns and weaves the next row, it should go over the warp which it previously went under, or to put it another way, fall into the hollows left by the previous row. Each warp alternates in being high or low depending on whether the weft has gone under or over it.

High warps. A high warp is one which the weft has just passed over. Visually this shows as a hill, or what we will term a **bead**.

Wefts start, finish and pause in specific places, marked:

- ● paused weft
- X starting
- ▲ finishing

Ends. The term 'end' is used variously to mean a length of warp or weft. Most commonly it is used in describing warp settings, in the form of epi, ends per inch. An end may also be one of several weft lengths in play, or the ends of the warp remaining unwoven at the end of a piece.

Weft. Weft is the yarn which is woven back and forth from side to side by passing under and over alternate warps. Weft may be used in single strands or with several woven together in a bundle.

A weft. Usually a length of about a metre is ideal to work with; this may consist of a single strand of yarn or several in a bundle. There are generally several of these in play during the weaving of a tapestry. Each individual length is termed 'a weft'. When several wefts are in play simultaneously, they all have a direction of weave, starting and finishing points which are in a sequence with each other. This is explained in greater depth in Chapter 2, 'Managing multiple wefts – a summary'.

A bundle (or weft bundle). This is a general term for a weft made up of several strands of yarn rather than just one. The strands in a bundle may either be several of the same yarn or different yarns in the same bundle. In weaving a bundle, all the strands weave together as if one.

A mix, or weft mix. This is a weft (or weft bundle) made up of strands of different yarn. The strands in a mix may be of different fibre, colour, tone, spin or weight. They weave together as one.

Rug or carpet yarn. As recommended for the early samples, this is a fairly thick and robust wool yarn, probably of 3–4 ply.

A discontinuous weft. This refers to any weft which is woven across only part of the width of the warp, rather than the whole way from one side to the other. This is the most usual practice in woven tapestry so that typically several wefts are in use at any time, each weaving different sections of the piece. For many, discontinuous weft is a characteristic by which tapestry weaving is defined, in contrast to for example cloth weaving when the weft usually passes all the way from right to left across a piece.

Working end. The end of a weft which is being woven is referred to as the working end.

Tail end. The end which a weft starts with. It is secured by passing under two warps then back over one, the end remaining at the back of the work.

Weft weight. The thickness of a weft, either a single strand or the cumulative thickness of several strands woven together. Weft weight is best judged by pinching a yarn between thumb and finger, since some yarns compress a good deal when woven.

Plain weave (flat weave). A weave is referred to as plain when the weft travels perpendicular to the warp, passing over and under alternate warps. The weft is beaten down so that it covers the warps which are then no longer visible except as ridges where the weft passed over them. This excludes any eccentric or double weave, knotting or other techniques which alter the surface. Plain weave is considered by many to be the norm in woven tapestry.

Surface. The surface of a weave is just that, the visual, tactile and aesthetic quality of the weave. In tapestry, the surface of the weave is fundamental to its nature as a constructed medium. The endless variation and nuanced control possible are arguably amongst tapestry's greatest strengths.

Weft-faced weave. Weave in which only the weft is visible, the warps having been covered entirely by the weft. Generally considered to be the norm in tapestry, for many it is a defining characteristic.

Single weave. The weft travels under and over *each* warp in turn as it travels back and forth across a tapestry.

Double weave. Weave in which the weft passes over *two* then under *two* warps.

Eccentric weave. Weave is termed eccentric if the weft travels across the warp at an angle rather than straight across or perpendicular to the warp. This may apply to an isolated pass or may extend to include a whole tapestry.

Hatching. In which adjacent wefts alternate in either turning before or weaving across an area of hatching, which is thus built of alternating passes of each. Hatching may be used to make gradual changes of colour, tone or texture and to manage tension.
Hachure. A self-contained mark made singly with an introduced weft. Each is built of two or more passes coming to a point at the ends. Characteristic of medieval weaving, where they were used to create interim colour and shading.
Soumak/Reverse soumak. In which the weft winds around the warp rather than passing over and under, in a variety of patterns.
Turn. The weft makes a turn around one warp as it changes direction. Turns may be made either at an edge or any point along the warp. A turn may be approached either from the left or right, depending on the direction the weft is travelling.

- **High turn**. This is made when the weft goes around the warp by passing first under then back over as it turns. We would speak of the weft making a high turn.
- **Low turn**. This is the reverse and is made when the weft goes around the warp, first over then under as it turns. We would speak of the weft making a low turn.

Half pass (or row). A single row of weaving, across either the whole warp or more commonly an area within it. A half pass may travel either from right to left or left to right.
Pass. A pair of rows or half passes of weaving. One weft goes from left to right and back again or vice versa, starting and finishing on the same side. Each pass may either be woven across the whole width of the piece from one side to the other by one or by several adjacent wefts weaving in sequence with each other. Weaving is made bottom to top, layer by layer, a little like rows of bricks in a wall – the pass works rather like a course of bricks.
Bead (sometimes referred to as a stitch). The shape or mark formed as the weft passes over a warp. This varies but often somewhat resembles a grain of rice. Its shape is determined by the nature of the weft and the spacing and thickness of the warp. The bead may be described as round, flat, long or short. The shape of the bead largely determines the character of the weave at any given point and may change throughout a piece.
Beating down (or packing down). Tapping down a new section of weft, on top of the previous row (or half pass). When beaten down, the section of weft should cover the warp by falling into the hollows left by the previous row. Beating down is usually done with a fork – one from your cutlery drawer which is comfortable to handle, or a **tapestry bobbin**, generally turned in wood with a slim shaft around which the weft may be wound and a wider beating end which tapers to a point.
Filling. A weft is said to fill the warp as it is beaten down. The aim is to balance weft volume and character with the warp setting so that the warp is neither under-filled nor over-filled.
Butterfly. One way to work with a length of weft is to wind it into a butterfly. This is done by making a figure of eight around thumb and one finger, wrapping around the middle and tucking the end in.
Cartoon. A cartoon is usually a simple line drawing which gives the outlines of a design. This is used as a guide and may be secured behind the warps whilst weaving.
Couching. To make a running stitch on the reverse side of a tapestry taking in the loose ends of wefts, or once cut off the loom, the warp ends. Most often the unwoven warp is turned to the back and secured by being couched down. Wefts which finish at the edge of a piece generally need to be couched down to keep them from showing.
Sheds. A warp is set up by winding the warp yarn around the outside of the frame. Alternate warps therefore pass around at the front and back and are separated by the width of the frame.

- **Open shed.** The space made naturally as the warp goes around the thickness of the frame. When weaving in the open shed, the weft passes readily through this space, under the warps from the front of the frame, and over those from the back.
- **Closed shed.** When weaving in the closed shed, the reverse applies. There is no space naturally available. Instead, the back warps need to be picked, or pulled forwards with a finger to pass the weft behind them. In plain weave, the weft crosses the warp in the open and closed shed on alternate half passes.

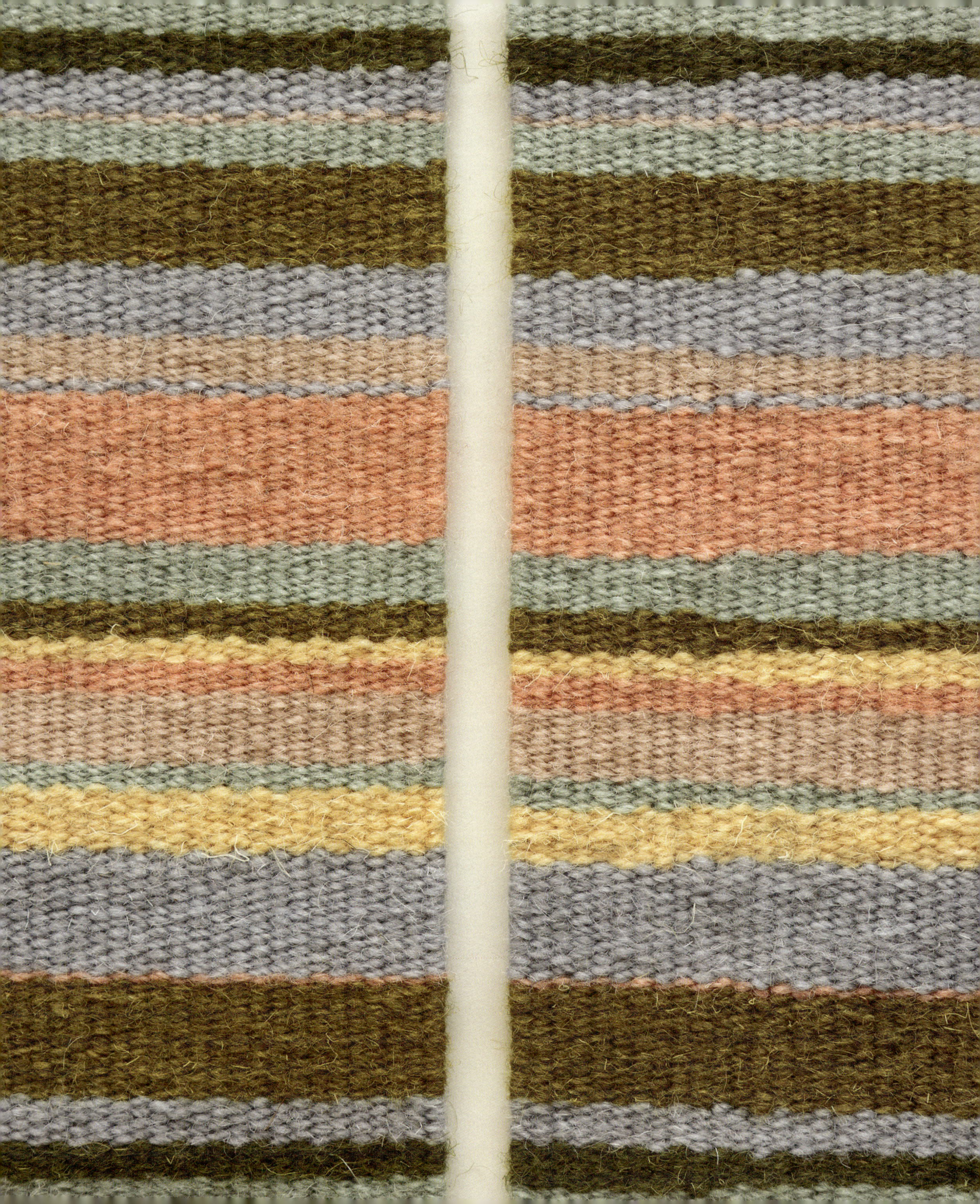

CHAPTER 1

STRIPES

WEAVING STRIPES, A FIRST EXERCISE

Stripes – bold stripes, fine stripes, yarns of many personalities set alongside each other. A simple design within which to explore the medium of woven tapestry, and to discover what works best for you. By close observation and repetition, handling *warp* and *weft* will become natural, allowing you space to think and create freely ever after.

Terms introduced in italics have been defined in Terms and Techniques.

Equipment

Tapestry weaving does not rely on a great deal of equipment, even to weave complex pieces. The tapestry *frame* or *loom* is really just that – a simple wooden frame which allows for *a warp* of any spacing to be wound on. It is sufficient for all the exercises covered in this book. To start with, a frame of 40cm × 60cm (14in × 24in) is ideal, made with 50mm × 20mm timber. Artist's stretchers reinforced at the corners also work well. G clamps are useful to clamp the frame to the edge of a table whilst warping up. Frame supports which fasten the loom to a table at variable heights can be useful but are by no means essential. Masking tape stuck along the top and bottom bar is useful to mark where the warps should land. You will need sharp scissors for cutting yarn, a permanent marker pen for marking the loom or warps and a ruler to check weaving width and height. Finally, either a table fork or a *tapestry bobbin* to *beat down* the weft; both work equally well.

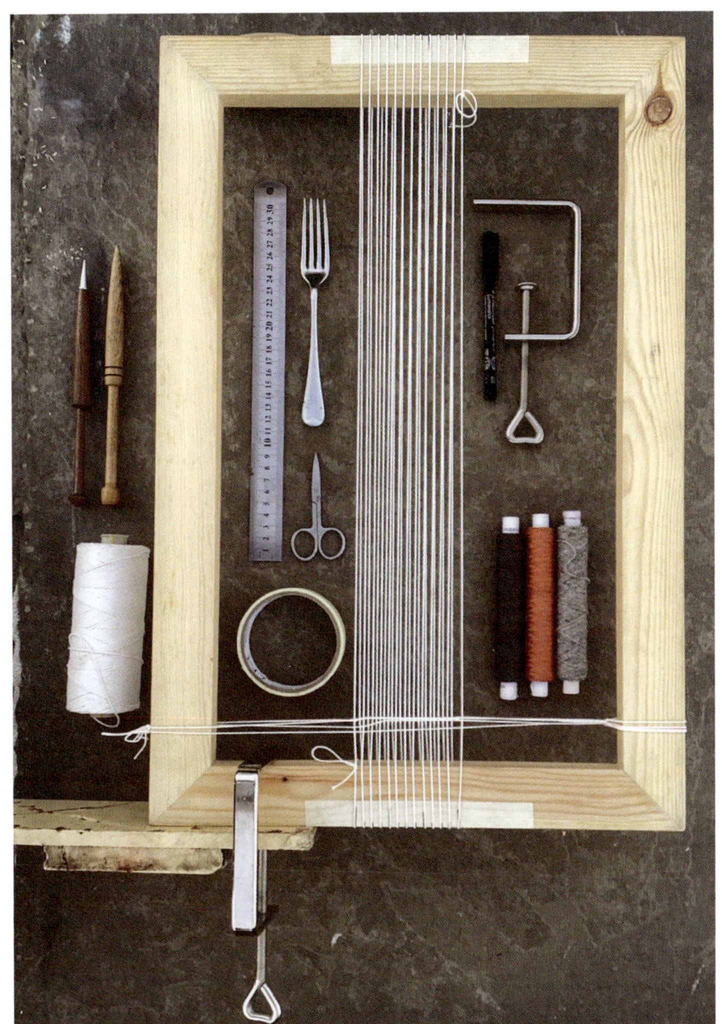

Tools and materials to get started.

Two striped samplers. 8 epi. Cotton warp, wool weft.

Materials

A medium-weight cotton tapestry warp is ideal to start with. It is very worthwhile to source good-quality warp. A good warp should have some stretch when pulled hard but should return to its length. Stretch an arm's length tight and pluck it like a string. A yarn which 'rings' is the one to choose. On the frame, a good warp should 'speak', having a slight bounce when patted.

For weft yarns there's a lifetime's choice available but wool is a forgiving start. Choose one which is quite tightly spun. As a guide, take a short length and pull – if it stretches significantly, it's not ideal. Take a ball or cone and squeeze it; if it compresses much, again it's not ideal. Many wools are designed for garment knitting for which the yarn needs to stretch and hold air. 'Tapestry wool' is designed for stitched not woven tapestry and is too soft. For tapestry weaving, a harder, less elastic yarn is better suited.

Markers

It is useful to put markers on a length of masking tape along the top and bottom bar of the loom as a guide to where the warps should be. Here a 3in section of warp at eight *ends* per inch is shown, a *sett* or spacing which is used for most of the early exercises in this book. Because of its larger size, the inch is a more convenient unit to use than the centimetre for spacing warps. It has therefore remained in common usage and is used throughout this book. The alternative in centimetres is shown here.

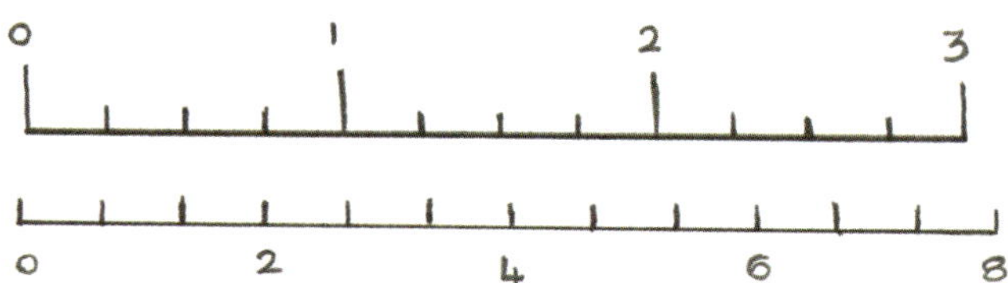

Gauge showing the marks to follow for a warp of 8 ends per inch (8 epi) with the equivalent 3 ends per cm (3 epc) below. When winding the warp around the frame each turn should fall on a mark. When the warps from the front and back of the frame are drawn together, alternate ones will fall between the marks. The samples in this chapter are all woven on a warp of 8 epi.

Looking after yourself

We believe that tapestry should be good for you and hope you will be excited to spend long hours at the loom. Here are a few ways to stay comfortable:

- **Weaving height** – keep the point at which you are weaving about belly height with your upper arms able to sit by your sides. Adjustable clamps or seating are needed to adjust your frame height as you work up a piece.
- **Seat** – the base should be level, not reclined, head and neck kept upright and relaxed.
- **Light** – bright, non-directional light is good, so that you can focus comfortably without stooping forwards.
- **Move** – at least half hourly, get up and walk about, move your upper body, rest your hands or change activity. You may find exercises designed to maintain flexibility and core strength helpful.

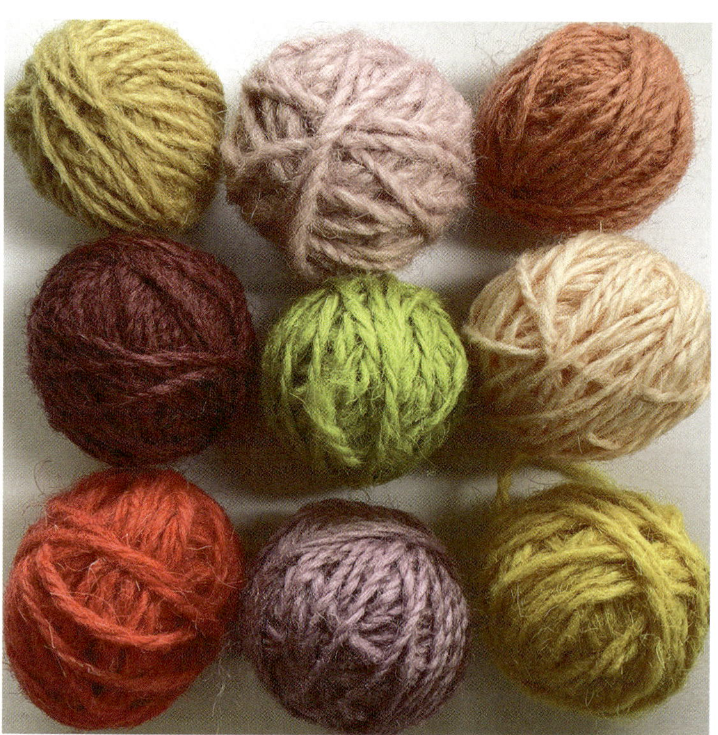

Balls of wool rug yarn are perfect for beginner weavers.

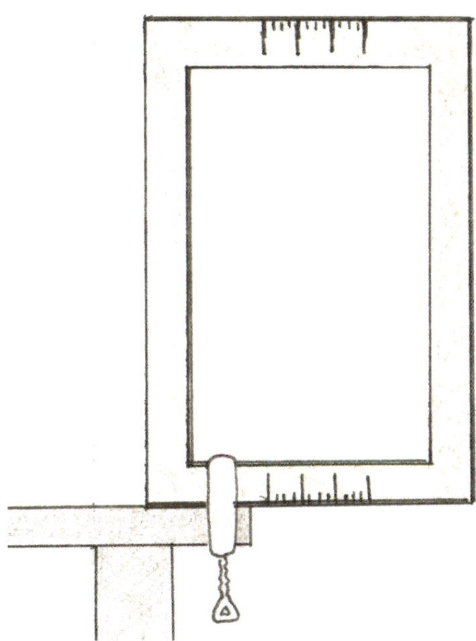

Putting on a *warp*. Stick masking tape along the bottom and top bars. Towards the centre, measure and mark a 3in strip, with marks at each quarter inch, and a bolder mark at each inch. A gauge is provided on the previous page. Clamp your frame to a table at the bottom left. Set a pair of scissors close to hand.

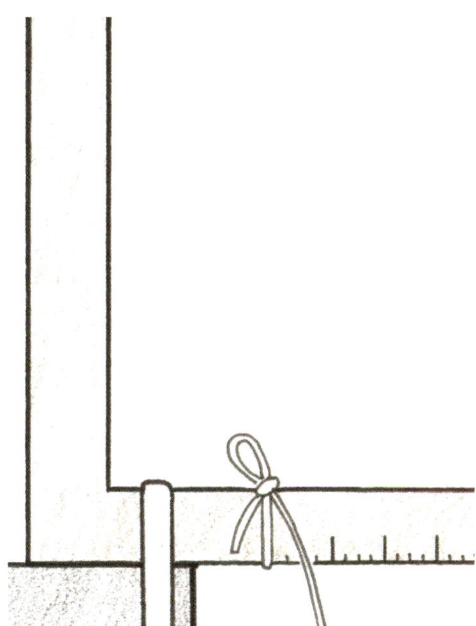

Place your medium *warp yarn* in a container on the floor and bring up the loose end. At the left-hand end of your markers, wind the *warp* round the bottom bar. Secure with a knot (preferably a slip knot to allow for re-tensioning). Knot on the **inner** edge of your frame, so that it cannot slide round under tension.

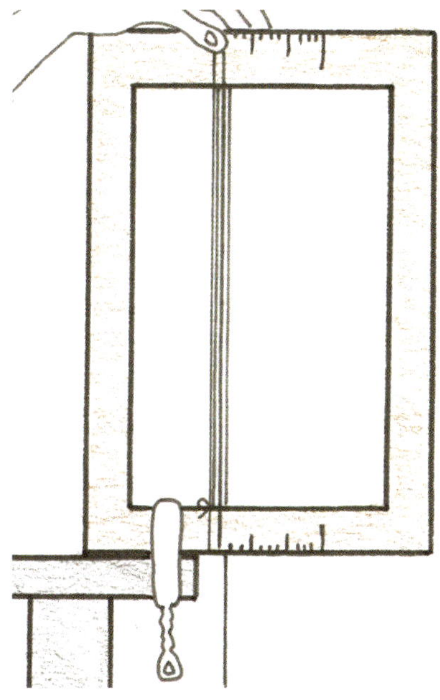

With the warp in your right hand, wind it **clockwise** around the **outside** of the loom, with each turn falling on the next mark. Keep pressing your left thumb firmly on the warp along the top bar to **hold the tension** throughout warping. Beware the warps do not cross over each other. Keep a moderate, even pull on the *warp* as you wind.

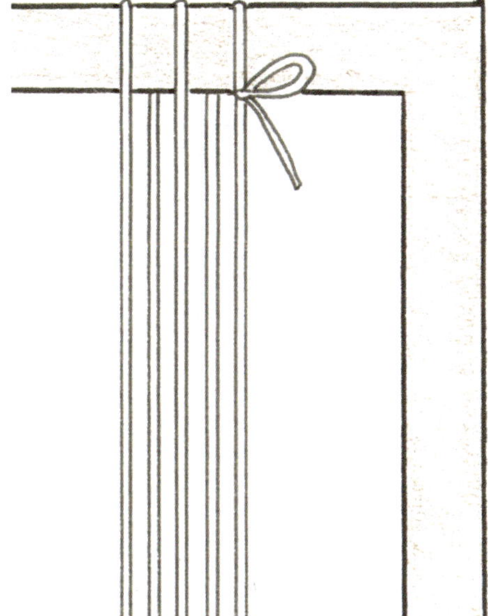

At the last marker along the **top** right of your loom, cut the warp leaving a generous 30cm (12in). Wind this tail end round the top bar, and knot it to the last warp, on the inner edge of the loom. Reposition any warps that are not on the marks. A well tensioned *warp* should 'speak' or bounce slightly when patted.

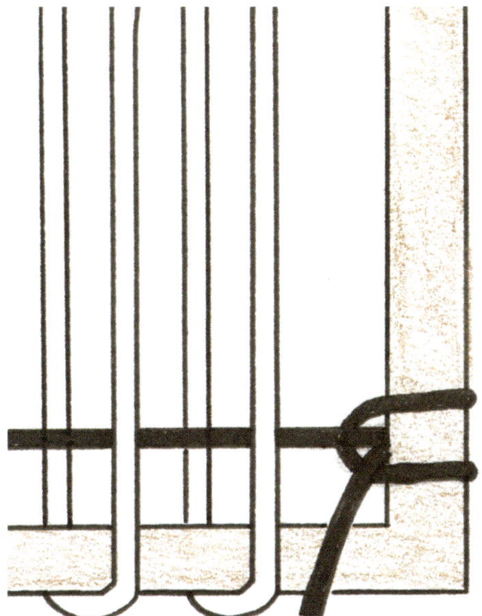

Putting on a *heading cord* to bring back and front warps together into a firm base. Cut a length of warp three times the width of your frame, fold in half. Take the folded end around the right side of your loom. Pass the cut ends through the loop, pull tight**.** Pass one cord right though the space between front and back warps (termed the *open shed*), leave it hanging at the left-hand edge.

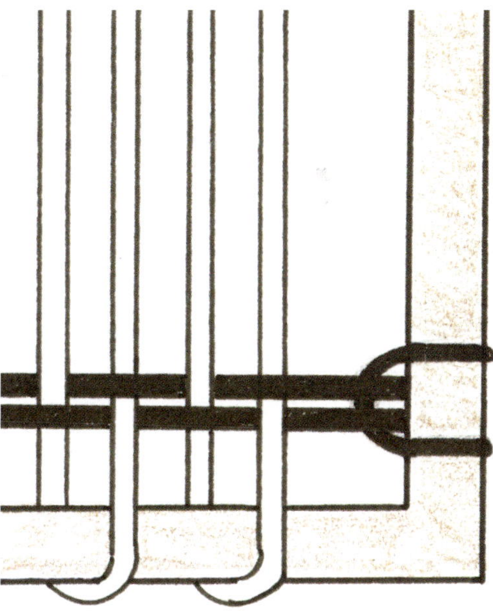

Pass the second cord over the first warp, and under (or behind) the second warp. Continue this over/under sequence across the full width of your warp. You should see that where your first cord passed underneath the warp, the second should now be passing over it, and vice versa. Take the two cords round the front and back of the left side of the frame. Pull hard till they sit tight and flat across the warps then knot together. Reset any warps which have moved from the markers.

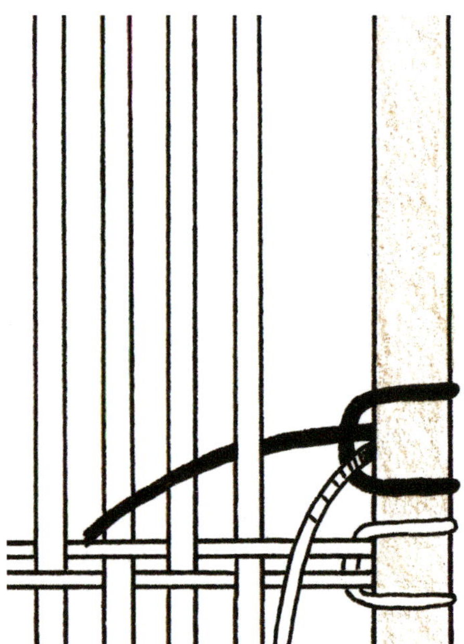

Twining, to draw the warps level, making a flat surface to begin weaving from. Take a length of warp yarn three times the width of your frame and fold in half. Pass the folded end around the right-hand side of your loom just above the heading cord. Pass the cut ends through this loop and pull up tight. Pass one length under the first warp.

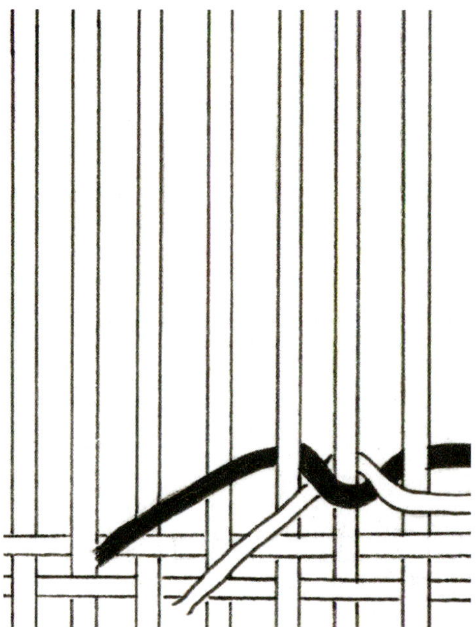

Maintain a firm pull on both cords at all times throughout the twining process. In the space between warps, take the lower cord, pass it over the other cord then under the next warp. Repeat across the whole warp, pulling tightly on alternate cords. The warps should now sit level with each other.

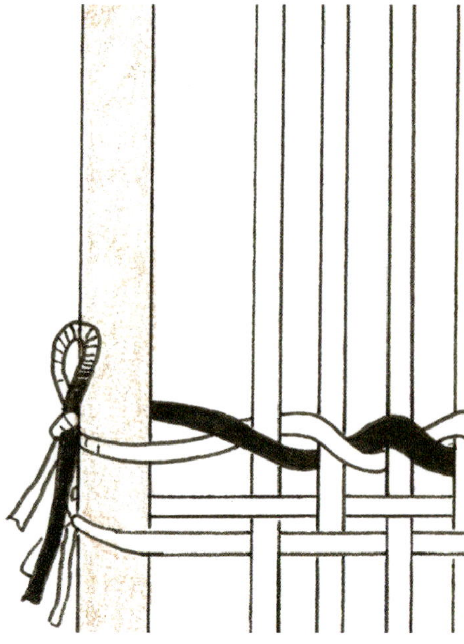

After the last warp, make a final crossover. Take the ends around the side bar bringing them together. Tie with a secure (preferably slip) knot. Look to see that the warps are evenly spaced, reposition any which are not on the markers.

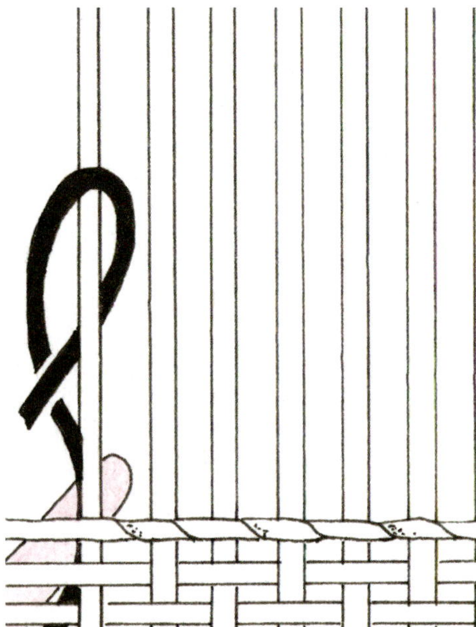

Double half hitches, to secure the weaving. Cut a 1m (3ft) length of weft yarn roughly the same thickness as your warp. *Rug or carpet wool* is a good start. Leaving about 10cm (4in) spare, hold your weft behind the first warp. Make a loop out to the left, pass over the first warp, back under it, then up into the loop.

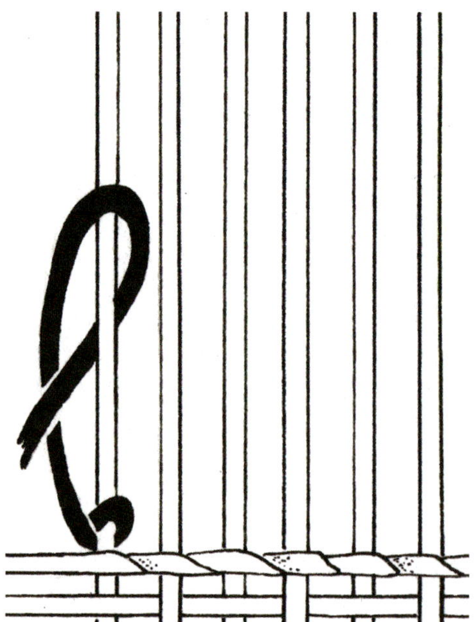

Draw the weft through and tug gently. Repeat, **on the same warp** – form a loop to the left, pass over the first warp from **left to right**, back under it from **right to left,** and up into the loop. Again, draw the weft yarn right through, then tug gently to tighten the double half hitch knot on the first warp.

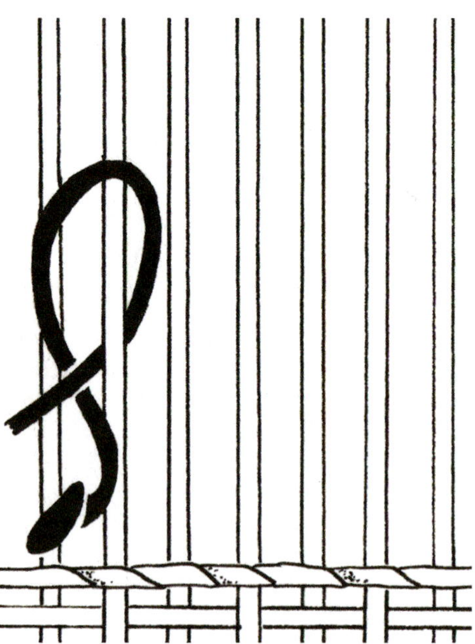

Move onto the second warp and repeat – form a loop to the left, back under the second warp, up into the loop, draw through and tug gently. Repeat, on the **same warp.** Next, move onto the third warp and do the same, form a half hitch then another on top. Work right across your warp, making **two** half hitches on **each warp.**

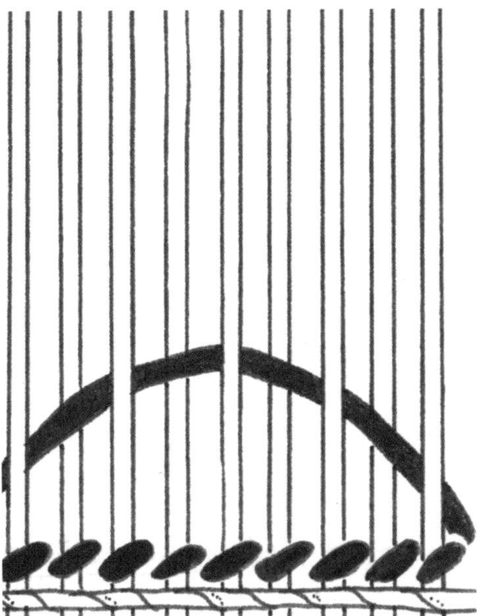

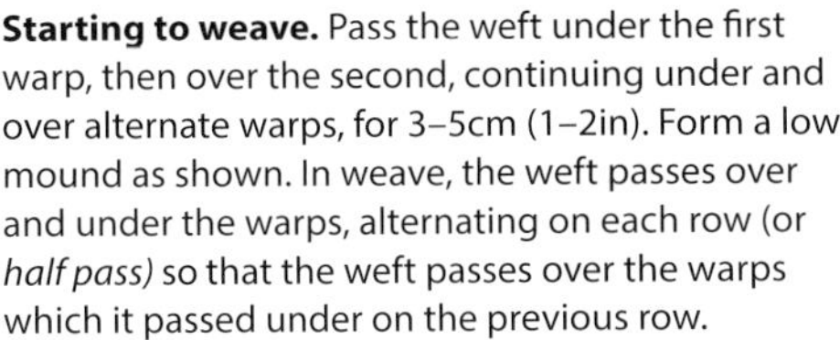

Starting to weave. Pass the weft under the first warp, then over the second, continuing under and over alternate warps, for 3–5cm (1–2in). Form a low mound as shown. In weave, the weft passes over and under the warps, alternating on each row (or *half pass)* so that the weft passes over the warps which it passed under on the previous row.

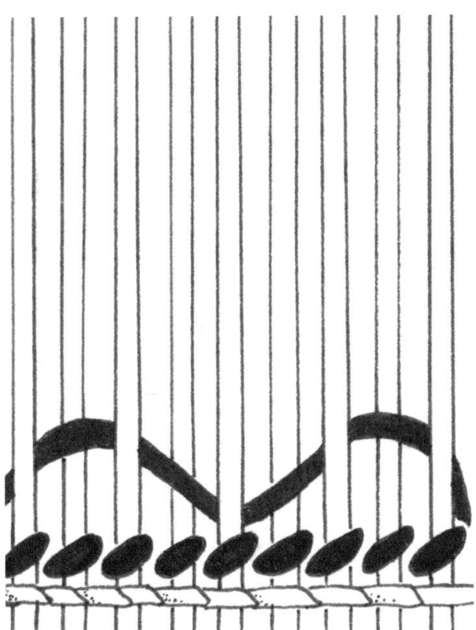

With your *fork* or *bobbin*, tap the weft down in the middle of the mound, so that it touches the row of double half hitches. This is called *beating down*. Making a mound gives extra length of weft, which will be taken up as the weft passes tightly over and under the warp.

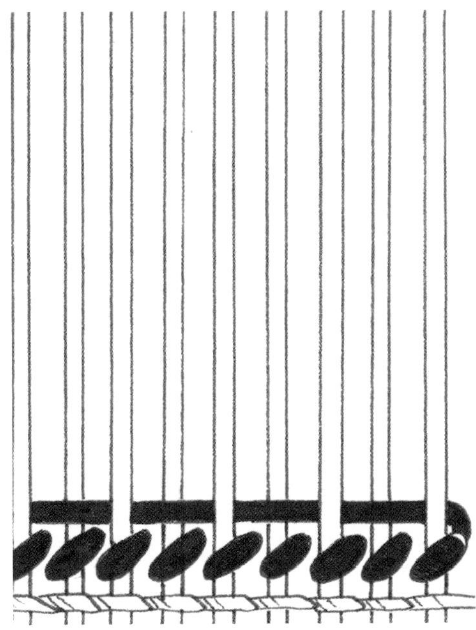

Next beat down the rest of the mound, so that this first part row or half pass sits snugly on top of the double half hitches. Beating down from the middle of the mound outwards allows the extra weft length to be evenly distributed. Without forming a mound, the weft would be too tight, resulting in the warps being pulled together.

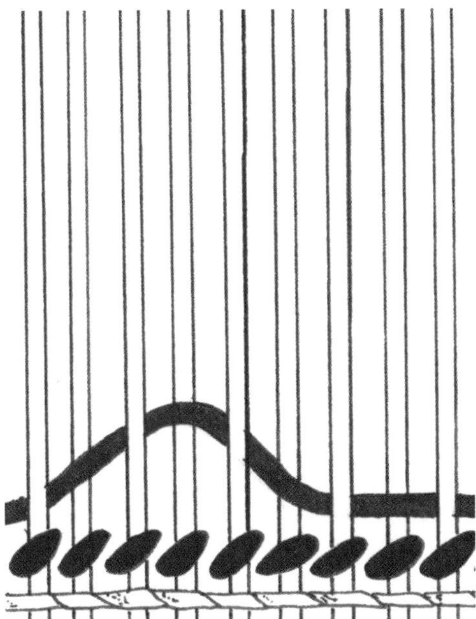

Pass the weft over and under the next 3–5cm (1–2in) of warps taking care to remain in sequence. Form a mound and beat down as before – this is vital to ensure you put in sufficient length of weft to allow it to go over and under the warps freely. Continue, making mounds and beating down across to the other side of your warp.

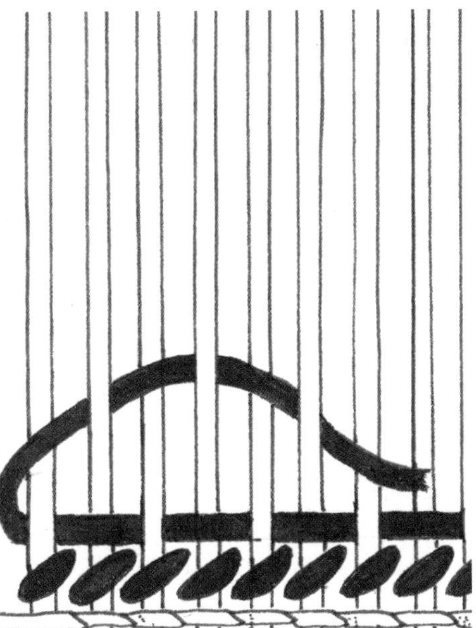

Turn after the edge warp and continue weaving. End your mound at a **different** warp to the previous row. There is a tendency for the weaving in one direction not to match the other. Try to look out for this and replicate your action in both directions. Make sure, as you become more confident, **not** to stop forming mounds before beating down.

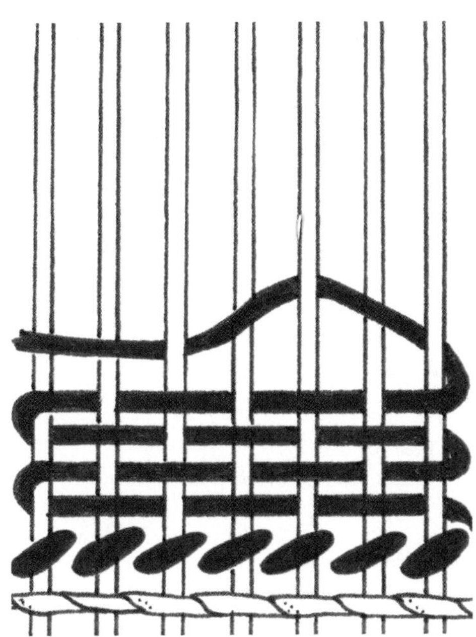

Look carefully – as the weft passes ***over*** a warp, it forms what is termed a ***bead.*** This should always fall into the ***hollow*** in the previous row, made as the weft passed ***under*** the warp. If the warp shows through, check that you haven't got out of sequence. A common cause is passing under more than one warp at a time.

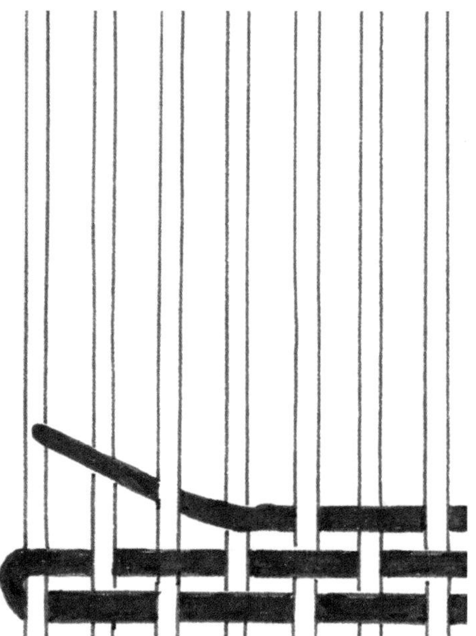

Finishing a weft. Finish weaving when you come to the **left**-hand edge of your warp, stop at the last warp which you would expect to be going **over**. (If you have warped up as shown, this will be the **second to last** warp.)

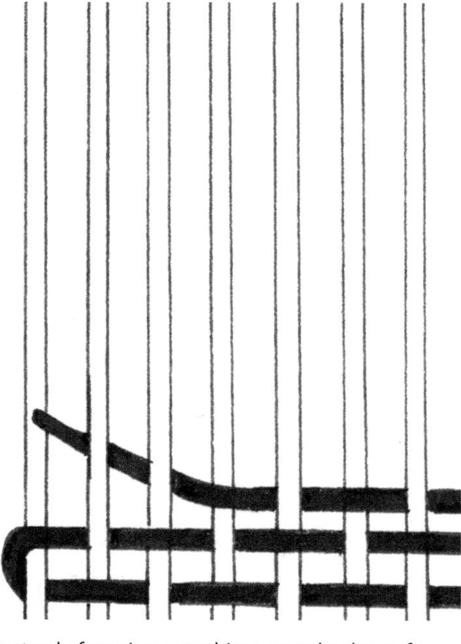

Instead of passing over this warp, take the weft end **under,** so that you have passed **under two consecutive** warps.

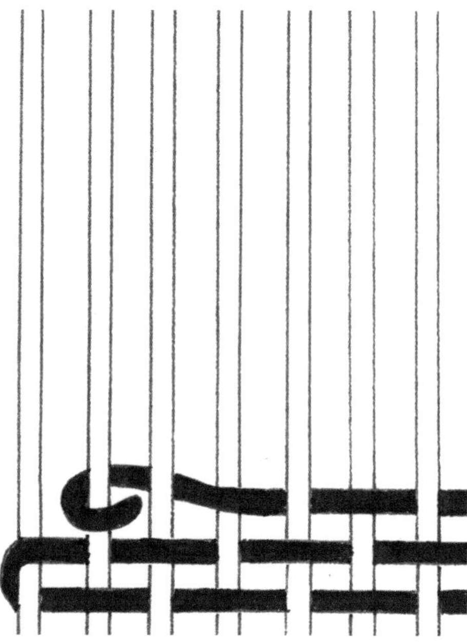

Next take the weft end **back over** the **second** of the two warps which you passed under – raise the last row and push the end through to the back, **between** the two warps, **below** the last row of weaving. Draw through and beat down. This sequence of **passing under two warps**, **back over one** is used whenever starting or finishing any weft.

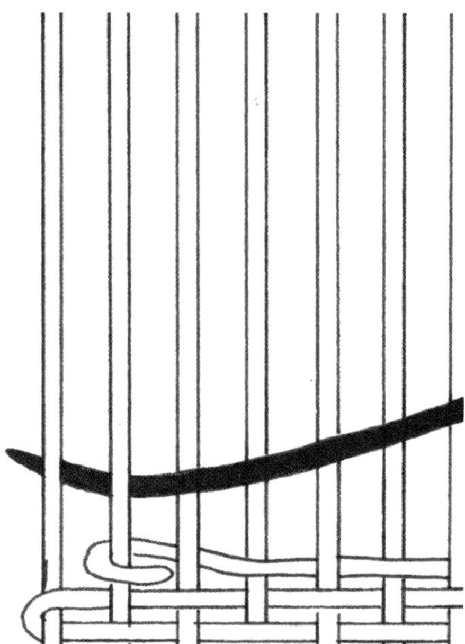

Starting. Take a different coloured weft yarn, of about 50cm (20in) in length. Lay it along the front of your weaving. Take the **left-hand end** and pass it under the last **two** warps on the left-hand edge. Notice that when starting a new weft, the end is inserted in the **opposite direction** to the way it is to be woven – in effect the *tail end* is put in **backwards**.

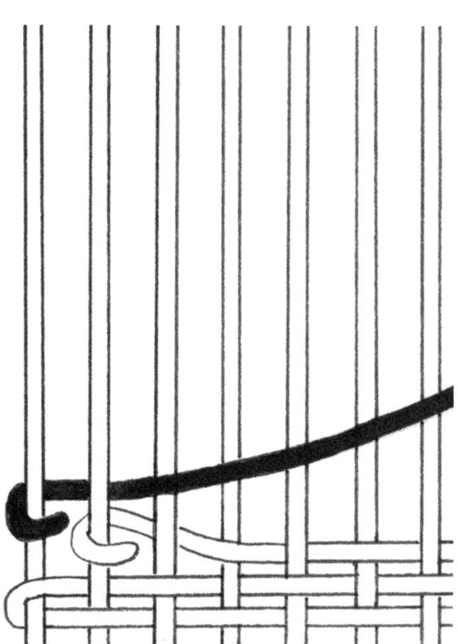

Pass the end back over the left-hand edge warp, push the short end through to the back of the weaving between the first and second warps, below your new row. Draw through to the back leaving about 10cm (4in) spare and beat down. Pick up the other end ready to continue weaving, being careful not to pull on it.

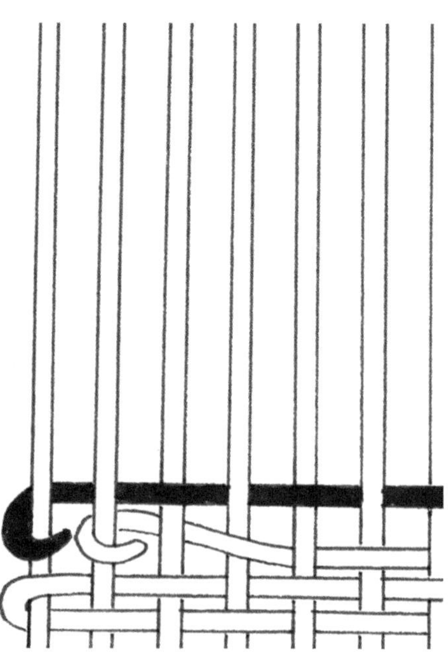

The weft continues, passing over the next warp. **Look** carefully to be sure that the weft always passes **over** the warps which it passed **under** on the previous row. Several warps may be lifted at the same time (termed 'picking'). Best to pick with the left index finger when weaving left to right, and your right index finger when heading right to left.

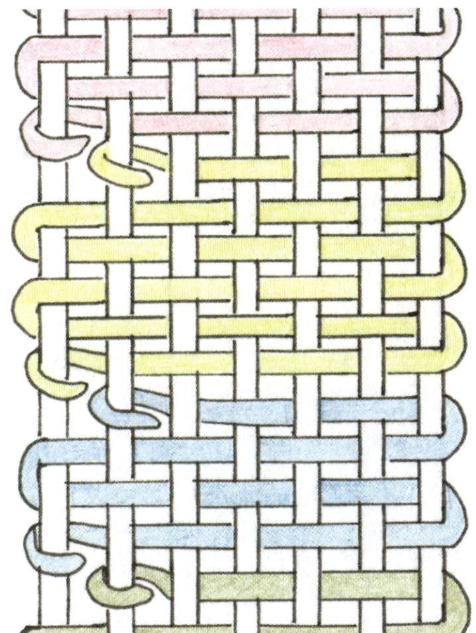

Finishing a sample. Keep weaving up your stripes sample, choosing differing wefts, looking closely to make sure of your under/over sequence, and learning to beat down evenly. Stop weaving with at least 20cm (8in) of warp still unwoven, otherwise the warp will become too tight to weave well. Stop at the left edge of your warp with about 60cm (24in) of weft left.

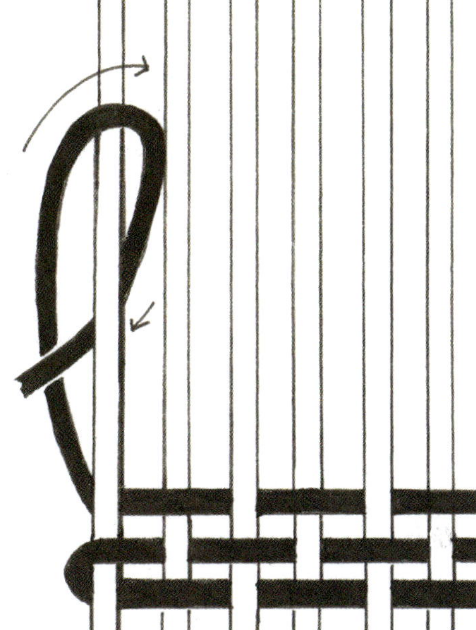

Double half hitches. These ensure your weaving does not unravel once cut off the loom and are the same as the knot you started with. Make a loop of weft to the left side, pass over the first warp, then back under it, bring the end up through the loop, draw through then **repeat**, pull to tighten. Continue, making two half hitches on every warp.

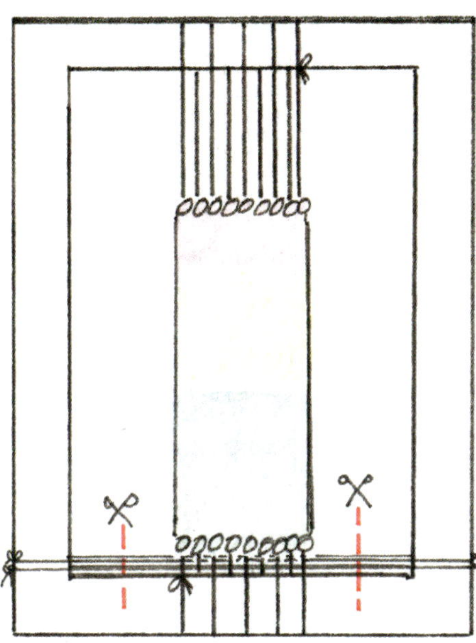

Your first sample is complete! Your weft ends should have been taken through to the back rather than remaining on the front face of the weaving. Cut the heading and twining cords at either side of the weaving and pull them out.

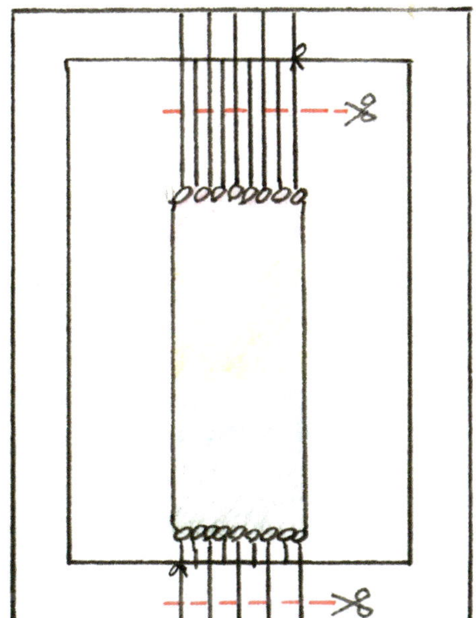

Cutting off. Hold the tapestry with one hand and cut the warps towards the top edge of your loom. Then cut through the warps along the bottom bar of your loom and lift the completed sample away. Cutting off is always a transition; released from tension a tapestry relaxes and may appear smaller, but is ready for finishing and mounting.

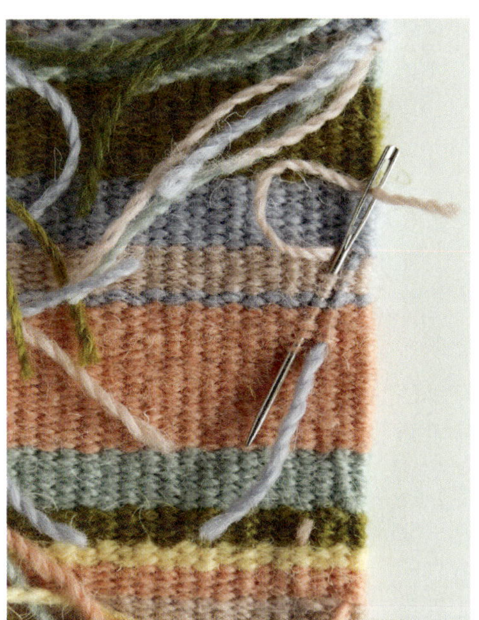

Sewing the weft ends in. On the reverse side, sew in any ends at the edge of the sample by threading each into a large-eyed needle and making two or three stitches into the weft on the back surface of the weaving. Trim to about 1cm. Ends which have finished part way across the sample may simply be trimmed.

Sewing the warp ends in, by *couching* to the reverse side. Fold back the unwoven lengths of warp. With sewing thread, make a running stitch passing over each warp close to the top of the weaving, just catching the back of the weaving. Repeat 1cm or so further down. The stitches should not show through to the front, nor pucker up the weaving.

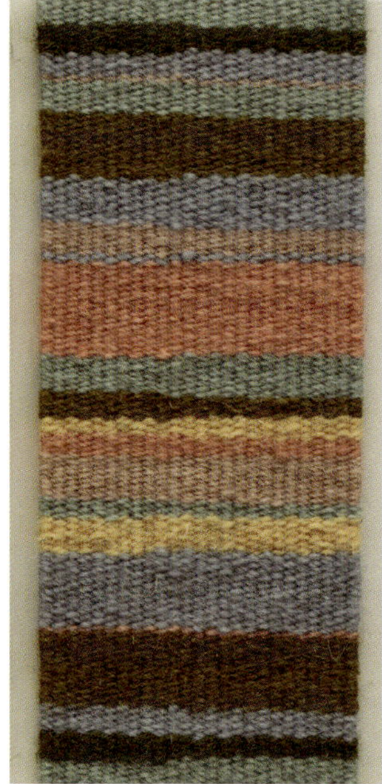

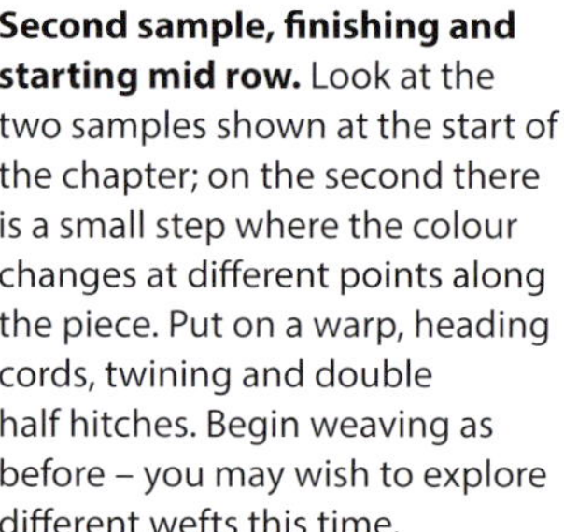

Second sample, finishing and starting mid row. Look at the two samples shown at the start of the chapter; on the second there is a small step where the colour changes at different points along the piece. Put on a warp, heading cords, twining and double half hitches. Begin weaving as before – you may wish to explore different wefts this time.

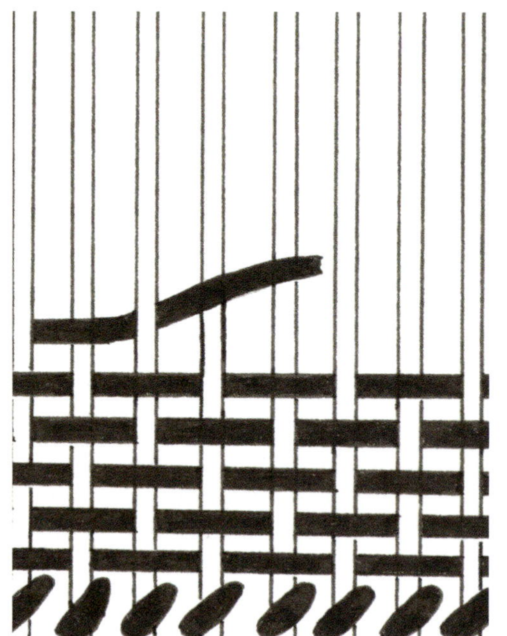

On a row going from left to right, stop somewhere near the **middle** with about 10cm (4in) of weft left. Stop weaving having just passed under a warp, then, instead of passing over the next, **pass under a second warp.**

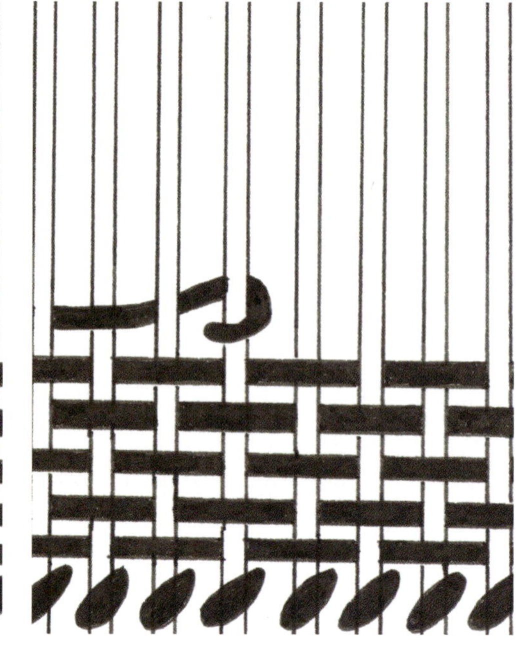

Raise up the weft, then take the end **backwards, over** the last warp below the row you are weaving. Draw it neatly through to the back without pulling tight, then beat down. The finished end should now be at the reverse side of the weaving. Cut another length of weft of about 50cm (20in).

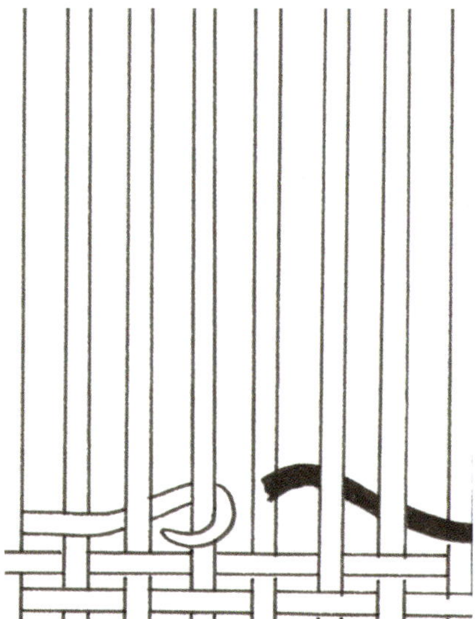

Ignore the next warp to the right, as you would expect to be weaving under it in the over/under sequence. Take the tail end of the new length of weft in your right hand and pick up the next two warps with the left. Pass the end of the weft from right to left behind the two warps.

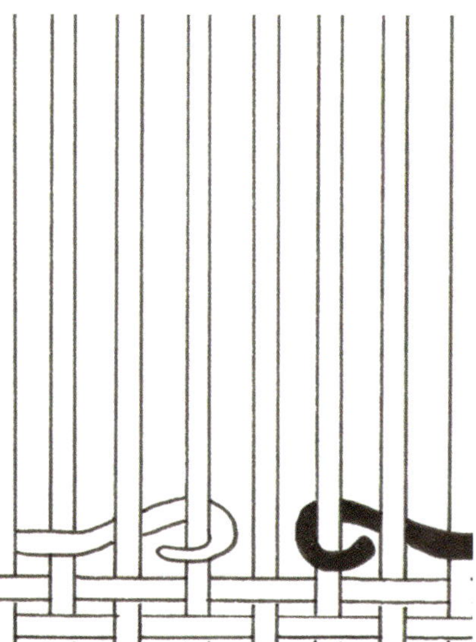

Push the weft a little way up the warp, take the new tail end **back over** the left-hand of the two warps, then tuck it underneath to the reverse side of the weaving, down between the two warps. **It should appear that one warp has been left out –** this will be covered in the next row.

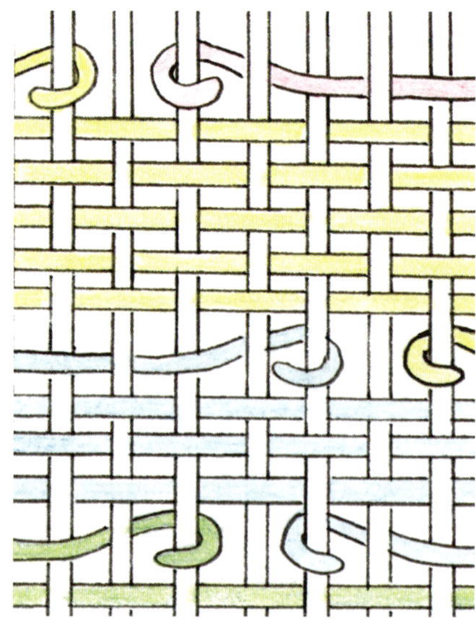

Choose a different point to stop and start each new weft as you continue weaving stripes of different colour and yarn. Although the diagram shows the weft stopping from the left and starting from the right, it is equally possible to start and stop from either direction, in which case the process would simply be reversed.

COMMON PROBLEMS

Weaving in the wrong shed

This occurs when the under/over sequence of the weave is interrupted so that on two or more **consecutive** *rows*, the weft passes either over or under the same warps.

Common causes

- Going under, or over (less likely as the mistake is more obvious) more than one warp at a time.
- Starting a new weft length without leaving a warp between finishing and starting.
- Not going under two warps (then back over one) when starting or finishing.
- Starting a new weft at a different place to where the previous weft finished.

Signs

- The warp is likely to show through, even after the weft has been beaten down.

Putting it right

Once in the wrong *shed*, the only real way to put your weaving right is to take it back to the point when the weft failed to cover the warp. This should show the reason you got in the wrong shed. It may seem frustrating when tapestry is slow to make to then take it back out, but a mistake in the shed will remain wrong for the whole row and be locked in once you weave on up your piece. It is surprisingly easy to weave on past mistakes, so it is worth getting used to always actively checking. There are times when an experienced weaver may choose to alter the shed, but at the outset, it is best to learn how to stay in the right shed.

Weaving in the wrong shed.

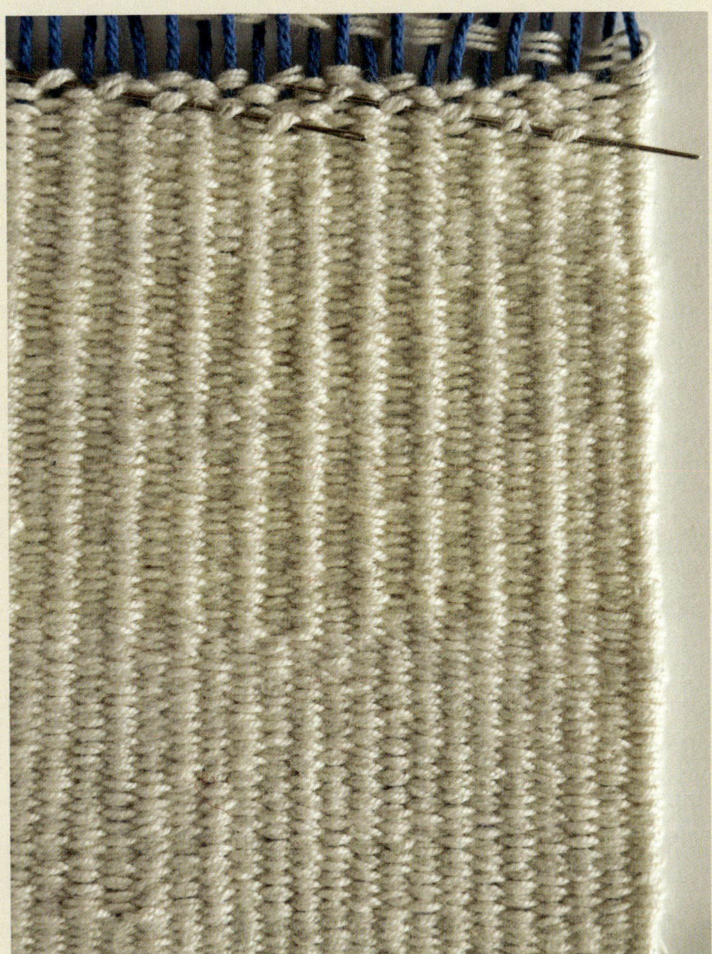

Ribbing.

Ribbing

One common problem with the *surface* is that it may develop ridges, with alternate warps sitting forwards or back instead of level with each other. Unlike getting in the wrong shed, this is a problem that develops gradually and takes careful observation to notice it happening early on.

Common causes

- Putting too little weft in the open shed. Because it is easier to pass the weft through the open shed, it is tempting to go through more warps at a time or fail to make a high enough mound before beating down.
- Conversely, too much weft in the closed shed has the same effect but is less likely to happen. Either way, look to see that you are putting the same length of weft in both the open and closed sheds.
- Making the warp either too tight or too slack.
- Weaving closer than 20cm (8in) from the top edge of your frame. The warp then becomes too tight, and the front and *back warps* too far apart because of the thickness of the frame. Putting in an extra row of *twining* to the top edge can help by drawing these together – but will also tighten the warp.
- Weaving with your work positioned too high so that you are not relaxed.

Putting it right

As soon as you notice signs of ribbing, act immediately, since once it begins it will become worse. Take a long, thin needle. In the area of ribbing, just below the point you have woven up to, insert it over the warps which are coming forwards and under the ones going back, as if you were sewing. Use additional needles to cover the whole area that shows ribbing. This forces the backward warps forwards, and the forward ones back. Leave these in place and continue to weave for another 2cm (1in). Put in less weft on rows when passing over the warps that had become raised, and extra weft when passing over the wefts that are sitting back. You should see that the *bead* is becoming equal again and the surface of your weave flatter. The needles can then be removed.

Pulling in - managing weft tension

Signs

When warping, take care that all the warps are regularly spaced. As weaving progresses, the warps may wander. Especially common is for the warps towards the middle of your piece to pull in so that they become too close together, with the result that your piece gradually becomes narrower. Often assumed to be the actual edges pulling in, this is seldom the case. It is usual for weavers, experienced and otherwise, to need to observe constantly and adjust the warp spacing.

Common causes

The most common cause is not putting in enough length of weft to allow it to go around the warps when beaten down. This happens most commonly in the open shed. Avoiding pulling in is the reason for making a mound before beating down. Pulling on the weft or turning too tightly, including in the middle, can also cause the warps to draw together. Some weft yarns will need extra care when weaving, particularly non-elastic, or tightly spun yarns.

Putting it right

Observe the warp spacing constantly so that you notice warps pulling in as soon as possible. When you notice the warps pulling together, make an extra high mound on both the open and closed sheds in the area where they have become too close together, and beat down very firmly to push the warps apart again. Make the usual sized mounds in the unaffected areas. Allow extra weft length when turning, so that there is a space between the weft and the edge warp. Continue until the warp spacing becomes even again, then keep watching. When weaving, try to make the action identical in both directions. It is usual to have a natural variation which is best overcome. This is based on the assumption that a weaver will be aiming for a rectangular piece to remain parallel-sided, and warps equally spaced. However, once you have learned to control warp spacing, you may choose to use it to shape pieces, expose areas of warp, or make open areas in ways that are unique to the creative language of weave.

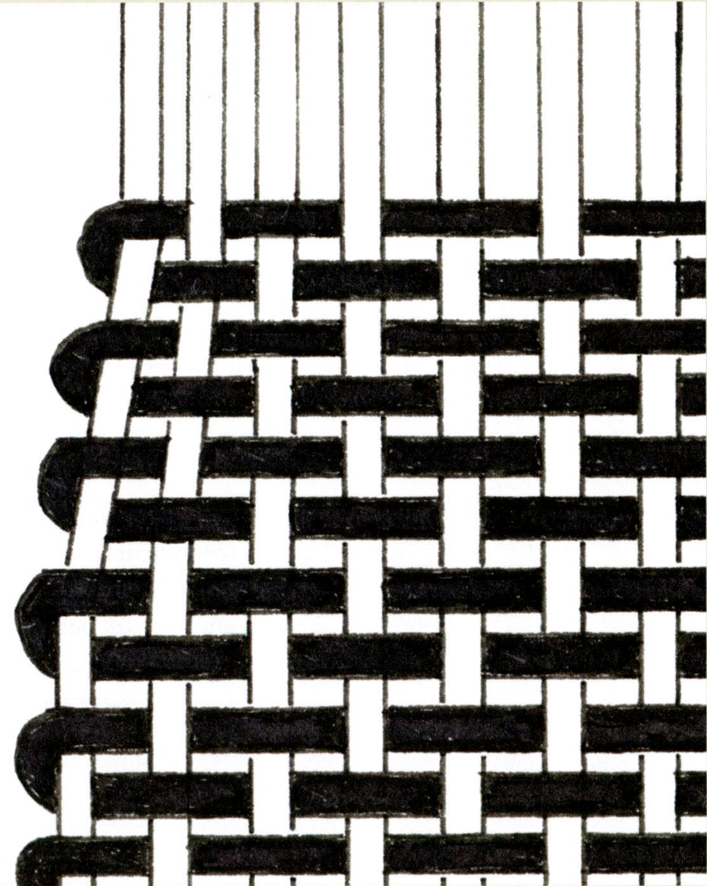

Pulling in. See how the left-hand edge of the weaving has gone inwards, and that the warps at the edge have drawn closer together. If you have an edge pulled in as much as illustrated, it is best taken back to the point where the pulling in began. Observing the spacing of the warps during weaving is the best way to see the problem of pulling as it develops.

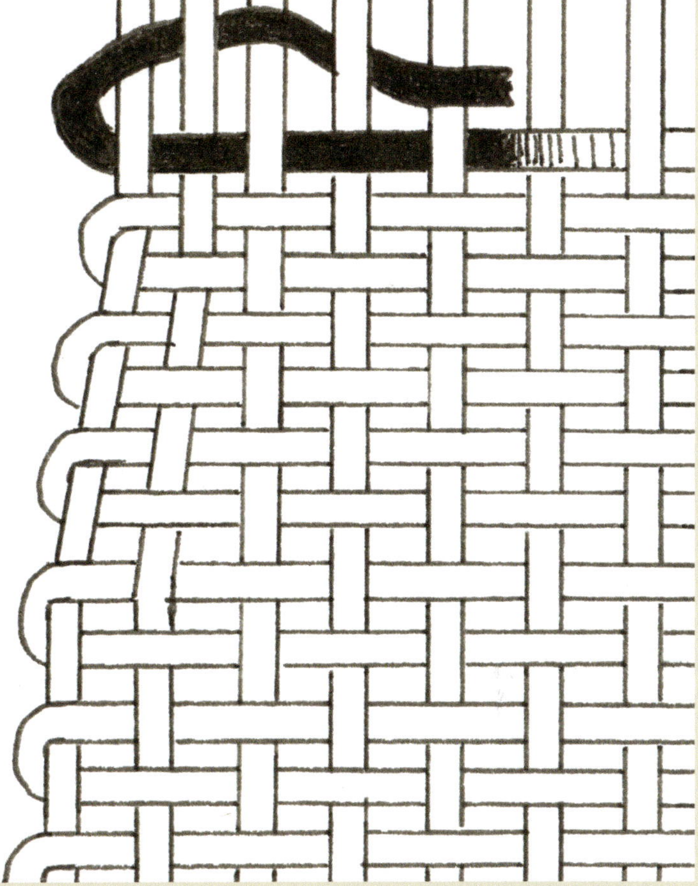

If the pulling in is less severe, it may be corrected. Make a slack turn and form a higher mound in the area which is pulled in, for several rows. Beat down the mound extra hard to force the warps back apart. You may also push the edge warps outward at the top edge of your frame, putting them back on the markers once corrected.

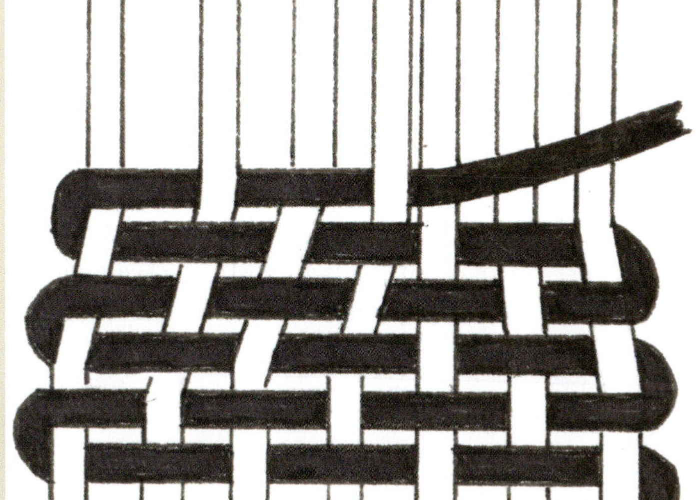

Pulling in mid row. See how the warps are pulled closer together part way along the weaving. The edge of the weaving has drawn in as a consequence, but notice that it is only further along the piece that the warps have drawn together, not at the edge. This is where the problem originates and where to correct it.

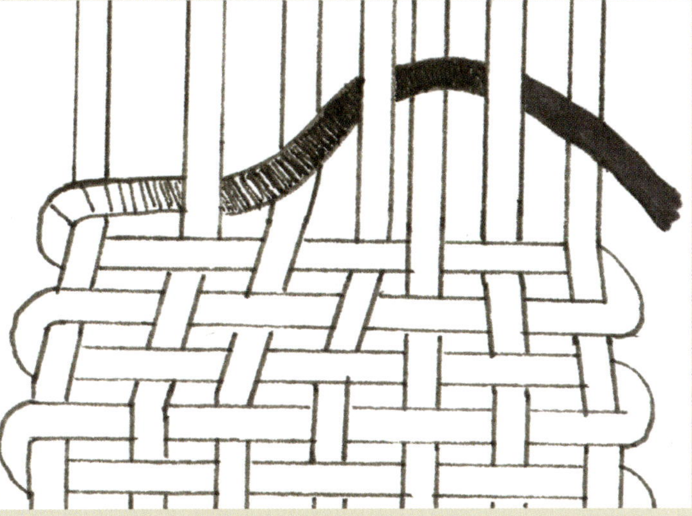

Pulling in mid row may be corrected by making a higher mound in the area where the warps have pulled together. The mound should then be beaten down extra hard, so that initially it will bulge slightly from the surface but will have the effect of forcing the warps back apart. Continue for several rows till the warps are evenly spaced once more.

WARP *SETTING* AND *WEIGHT*

Warps may be positioned at a wide range of spacing, termed the *warp setting or sett* which is generally measured in numbers of *ends* – meaning warps to the inch, epi, or to the centimetre, epc. The gauges here are to scale and may be used as a guide to marking up. Having made long marks at each inch, the gauges show the number of turns round the frame needed in between each 1 inch mark to give the required ends per inch.

The nearest equivalent for ends per centimetre is shown with long marks at either 2 or 1cm spacing. The short marks then show the number of marks needed in between to give the required ends per cm. For the even number warp settings, marks at each centimetre can be made, but this doesn't work for the odd numbers of epc where marks of 2cm are needed. This complexity is the reason why inches have remained in common usage, and is the choice for the purposes of this book.

When warping up, the warp should fall on each mark. Once the front and back warps are drawn together there will be one falling between each mark which then gives the desired warp setting. Make sure the warps all fall on the markers at both the top and bottom of the loom, and check again after putting on the header band and twining, both of which can put the warps off their marks. Watching to make sure warps remain aligned with the marks whilst weaving is important, as it can warn the weaver that, for example, that the piece is starting to pull in.

In practice warps do move very slightly both twisting and moving side to side constantly during weaving. We talk a lot in this book about observing as you weave. One of the reasons for this is that the relationship between warp and weft is an ever-changing one. An experienced weaver constantly adjusts the amount of weft put in, how it is beaten down and how the turns are made.

The examples in the early chapters of this book mostly use a setting of 8 epi and are printed more or less at scale. This fairly coarse setting means the warps are relatively easy to handle, and the detail easy to observe, especially when woven with a single warp strand as recommended. Weavers quite quickly find their own comfortable setting; however, weaving at different settings is well worth experimenting with at any stage of learning.

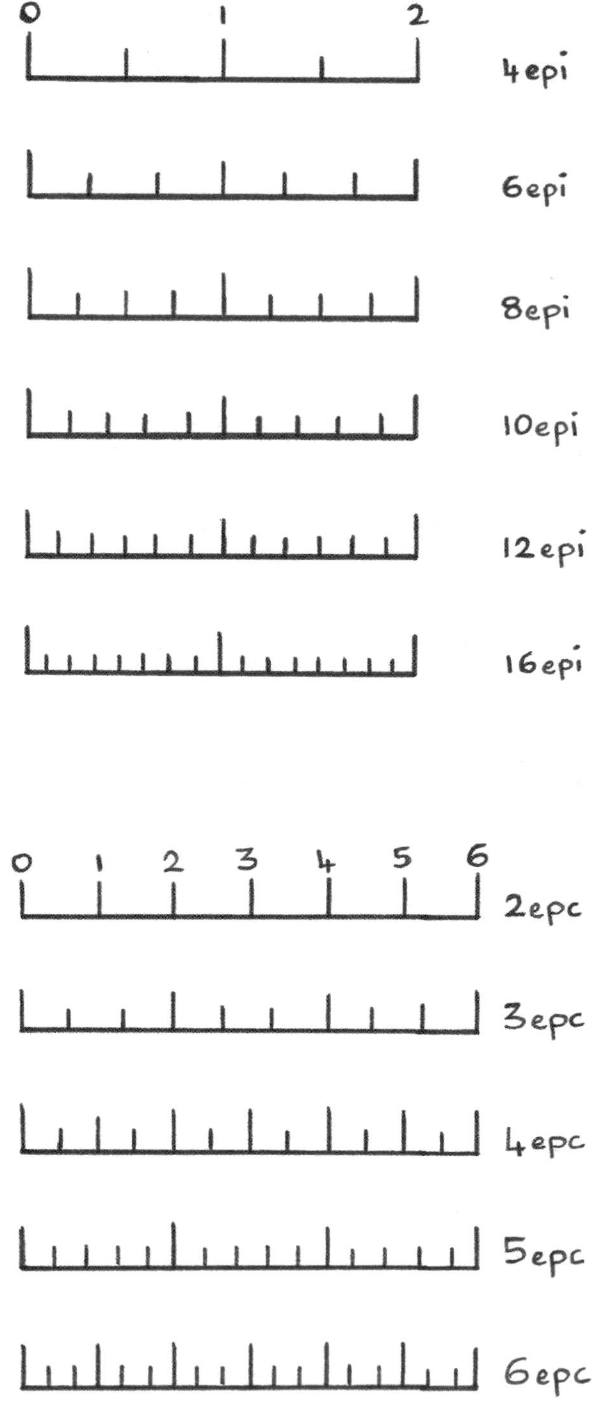

Warp settings. These gauges are to scale and may be used as reference for warping in ends per inch [epi] or ends per centimetre [epc].

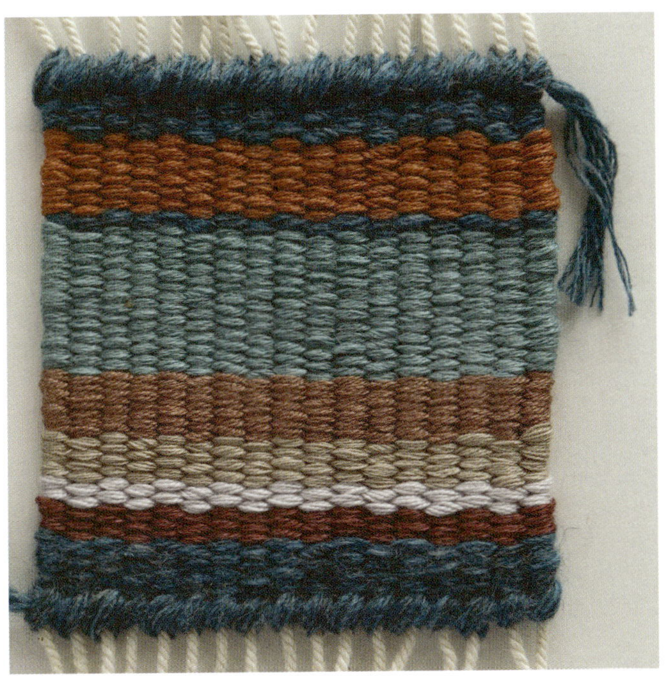

4 epi, 17 warps, heavy warp, 10 strands in the weft bundle.

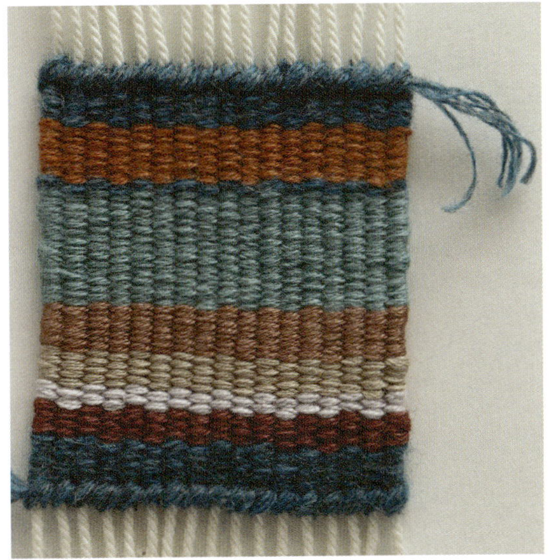

8 epi, 17 warps, medium warp, 6 strands in the weft bundle.

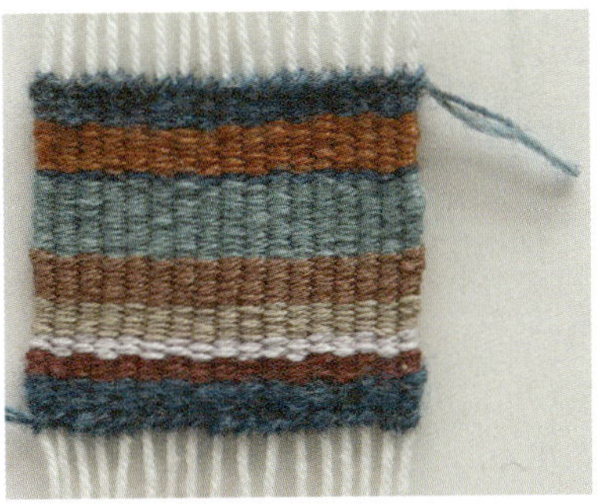

12 epi, 17 warps, medium warp, 2 strands in the weft bundle.

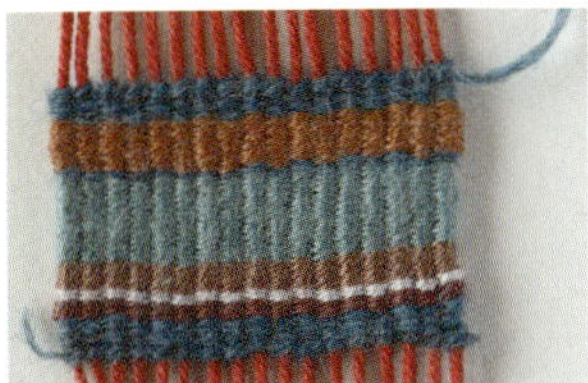

16 epi, 17 warps, fine warp, single strand in the weft bundle.

These four samples all have the same number of warps and are photographed to scale. The first and largest has 17 warps sett at 4 epi. The smallest also has 17 warps, this time finer warps, and sett at 16 epi. Apart from having a coloured warp, the weft for the smallest sample is just a single strand. The same weft yarn has been used for all the samples, increasing in number to ten strands for the largest.

Looking at the exposed warp ends, you will see that there are three different thicknesses of warp used. All are cotton; the first is heavy warp, the second medium and the last two are fine. There is a range of settings at which each weight of warp will work, assuming the weft type and volume are also adjusted to suit. There is in fact a great deal of flexibility possible in the relationship between warp weight and setting which will have both practical implications and offer endless aesthetic possibilities.

Choice of warp setting may also be influenced by the design of a piece. A design with a lot of fine detail is likely to demand a finer warp setting, although there is a great deal of complexity and choice possible without having to weave too fine.

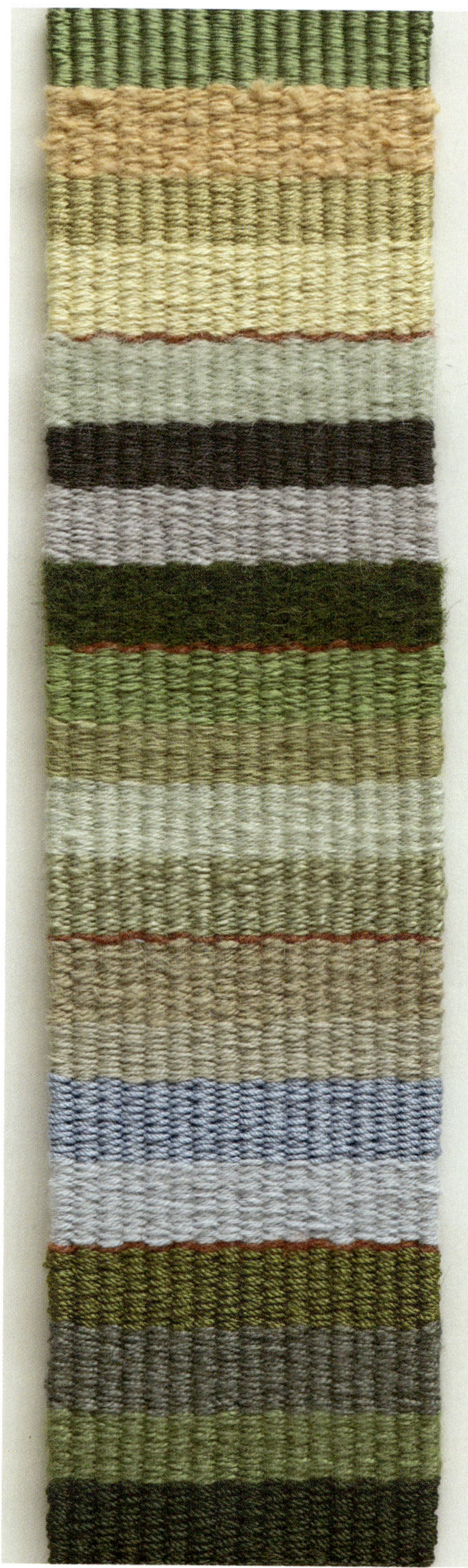

See how the weft fibres look once woven. From top to bottom; silk, wool, linen, cotton, rayon with a pass of red weft to separate each section.

Qualities to look for in weft yarn

Staple – this refers to the length of fibre from which the yarn is spun. It is often possible to pull out a single fibre to check this. Spinning longer staple fibres tends to make a more muscular, less malleable yarn, in which case less volume may be needed to beat down. Shorter fibres may protrude from the woven surface giving a hairy, woolly or fuzzy surface.

Spin – this refers to the degree to which the fibres have been spun together. This can be checked by twisting a short length back in the reverse direction to the spin. A more tightly spun yarn will have a harder texture and beat down less readily.

Ply – most yarns are made by plying. This involves spinning together two or more previously spun strands in the reverse direction to which they were spun. The number of strands can be checked by twisting the yarn back in the reverse direction, when it should then separate. A plied yarn tends to be rounder, often thicker and more compressible. A yarn which has not been plied at all is termed a single.

Stranding – a yarn may consist of several strands which are simply wound together onto a cone or hank without being plied together. When woven they tend to be quite biddable and lay flatter than if plied, giving a smooth surface. It is possible to separate the individual strands to use singly or combined in mixes.

Thickness – you will have observed by now that there is a range of possible thicknesses for a given weft or weft bundle. A single thick yarn will weave very differently to several thinner ones, even of the same type. Squeeze the yarn to check how it is likely to compress when beaten down; if a ball of yarn feels very soft it is unlikely to weave well.

Weft fibre groups

Silk

The cultivation of silk was China's best kept secret for more than 1,500 years. It is the finest known natural fibre, able to produce cloth of exceptional warmth and lightness with a lustre and luxurious drape second to none. For the tapestry weaver, silk yarn offers a wide range of effects. The high lustre of the green and gold stripes is given by using very fine yarns, the low volume of which also allows the roundness of the underlying warp to be strongly evident despite the weft fully covering it. In between is a very different wild – or tussah – silk. Here, the silkworm has been allowed to hatch and break the cocoon into very short lengths. The resulting slubbed yarn weaves to a soft, almost chalky-looking surface which nevertheless has an underlying sheen.

Wool

Historically the yarn of choice for woven tapestry, partly because of its ability to last. Wool beats down readily, favouring designs based on complex imagery. Depending on the breed of sheep, wool fibres may be of varying length, coarseness and hair content, and with curl and crimp, producing yarns that can vary considerably. Here, the middle two have a less hairy and brighter, more lustrous surface. The darker one has been blended with nylon which adds strength. Relatively short staple and naturally curly or crimped, wool yarn tends to have the most loft. Knitting yarn is best avoided as it gives an ill-defined weave – look instead for a harder spun worsted yarn.

Linen

Linen yarns weave beautifully, although they are quite robust, often needing less weft volume than expected. Apart from the most highly spun yarns, linen holds particularly well when beaten down and offers the weaver precise control of marks and surface. Linen is one of several yarns spun from bast fibres separated from the stems of tall grass-like plants, in this case the flax plant. The first fibres in the combing process make a heavy yarn of irregular thickness, called tow. The remainder may be combed into very fine, long, lustrous fibres.

Cotton

Cotton yarn is spun from the short fibres in the plant's seed head, or boll, and tends to give a softer, less lustrous yarn. It is usually plied to give strength, and so tends to be quite a round yarn. Cotton is readily available in a great range of yarns, from fine sewing cotton, stranded embroidery 'silk', yarns produced for cloth weaving, to softer knitting yarns all of which will offer possibilities worth exploring. The top example is Cottolin, cotton and linen fibres combined and spun together into a blended yarn combining the qualities of both. The sky-blue strip is woven with a tightly spun crochet cotton giving a pronounced bead and a lustre produced by a process called mercerising.

Rayon

This term refers to the chemical process by which cellulose material is reduced to a resin from which a yarn is extruded, which is then spun and plied as with any fibre. The raw material is most often wood pulp but may also be bamboo or cotton. The resulting yarns are generally strong, lustrous and soft to handle. It is often found as part of a blended yarn, as with fully synthetic fibres such as nylon and polyester, all of which have qualities worth exploring. Rayons tend to cover the warp quite readily, often giving an attractive sheen, although they can be rather slithery to handle.

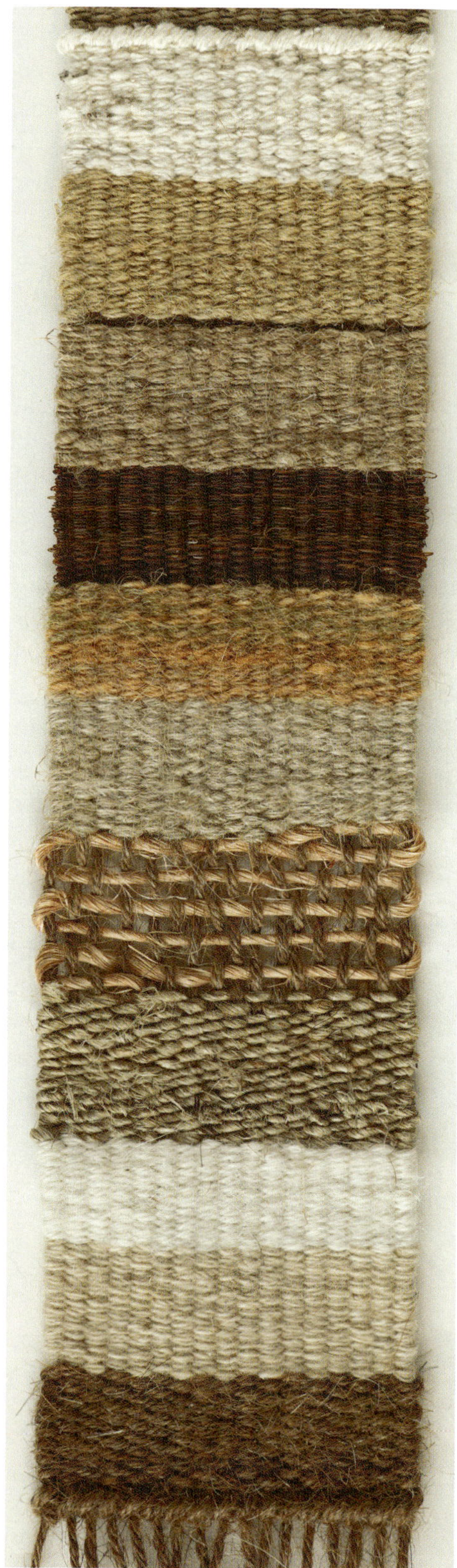

More weft yarn possibilities, from the top – wild or tussah silk, jute, nettle, horsehair, hand-spun, linen, sisal, hemp, alpaca, cashmere and camel.

More weft yarn possibilities

The warp used here is camel, which is a mix of hair and finer undercoat. Both the colour and hair fibres come through the weft in places.

Wild or tussah silk

This has curiously contradictory qualities, hand spun from short lengths of highly lustrous fibre – the surface is both chalky, lustrous and slubbed. A bundle of six strands of a fine single-ply yarn have been woven together. Wild silk beats down readily, with a characteristic 'squeak' when handled.

Jute

Known as the 'golden yarn' for its silky sheen, jute is nevertheless a very robust fibre and surprisingly coarse to handle. It does not beat down easily – here two thick strands of single ply woven together allows a little of the dark warp to show through.

Nettle

Robust but less so than jute and hemp, and with less of a sheen, it comes in a beautiful range of natural ecrus. As with other bast fibres, it tends to contain slubs, so it is best to hold the warps apart when drawing it through. Its muscularity will mean using less weft if the warp is to be fully covered, and it will need to be beaten down quite hard.

Horsehair

Hair fibres are often springy and slithery to handle. Here, six strands have been woven together showing a sumptuous dark brown colour with natural 'highlights'. Being hard and wiry, the roundness of the warp shows through, as do the actual warps when lit from behind.

Hand-spun

Vegetable-dyed wool. The 'imperfections' of hand-spun can be a gift to weavers, giving a lovely random surface texture which would not be possible by conscious control. The variable, soft mellow colours of vegetable dyes can add further subtle interest and depth, especially if woven in a reasonably large area.

Linen

This bundle of five single-ply strands has beaten down fully. Another ecru from a wide natural range, this mix has a soft, slightly chalky quality. Though robust, linen tends to be more malleable than many bast fibres and beats down readily to give a clear bead.

Sisal

Springy and very robust. This yarn is thicker than the warp with the consequence that the warp remains exposed when beaten down, even leaving space between each row of weave, giving a basket-like quality.

Hemp

A single but tightly spun, springy yarn giving a wonderfully pronounced bead with the appearance of slanting diagonally. Dark sections in the yarn appear in the weave adding depth and subtle variation to the colour. This robust yarn needs to be beaten down firmly to conform to the warp and turn at the edges.

Alpaca

A native of Peru, the alpaca's fine, thick coat is adapted to survival in a mountain environment. It has a natural colour range, from dark chocolate to bright creamy white and makes a deliciously soft, almost soapy-feeling yarn.

Cashmere

A Himalayan goat with an exceptionally fine, wavy undercoat, producing woven fabric of similarly cold-resisting ability. Beautifully soft to handle, this bundle of four single-ply yarns has woven readily to give a clean, clear bead.

Camel

Weft and warp here are of the same tightly spun four-ply yarn, naturally combining soft undercoat and hairy kemp. It has woven with a definite bead and a hairy surface which appears much softer than it feels to touch.

Alternative wefts

There is no rule about what material may be used as weft – it is simply a case of try them out, some will work more easily than others but there is a whole world of physical and aesthetic qualities to explore.

Wire

A coloured stainless-steel wire. Because of its hardness, it shows the ridges of the warp underneath. In this sample we have used a fairly thick, dark mohair warp. Wire does not compress when being beaten down, so tends not to cover the whole warp. Here the dark colour shows through, especially when held up to the light. This is a rigid but malleable weave which could be bent into three-dimensional forms once off the loom.

Paper yarn, three ply

By plying several twisted strips together, a rounder, generally more pliant yarn has been produced. Being quite tightly spun, this paper yarn does not compress much when beaten down, so, as you will see, the dark warp shows through in places. It has produced a firm, hard-feeling weave with a very visible and clear bead.

Mohair

A fine goat-hair fibre which is very soft and short. It is generally spun on a core of some sort, often cotton, so that it holds together. The mohair fibres are trapped in the core but also protrude freely from it, giving the soft, fuzzy surface more familiar in fabrics and knitwear. In this sample it gives a double-layered weave, the bead and even some of the warp showing through the deep, hairy surface layer.

Greaseproof paper

Cut into strips about 1cm wide. As they are beaten down, the paper scrunches up, giving an angular, 'dry' looking surface. The warp shows through in places and the weave is quite hard. Paper clearly comes in many types, any of which could be experimented with. Soft, thinner paper such as newspaper will beat down more easily than for example photographic paper, which would sit in the warp as a strip.

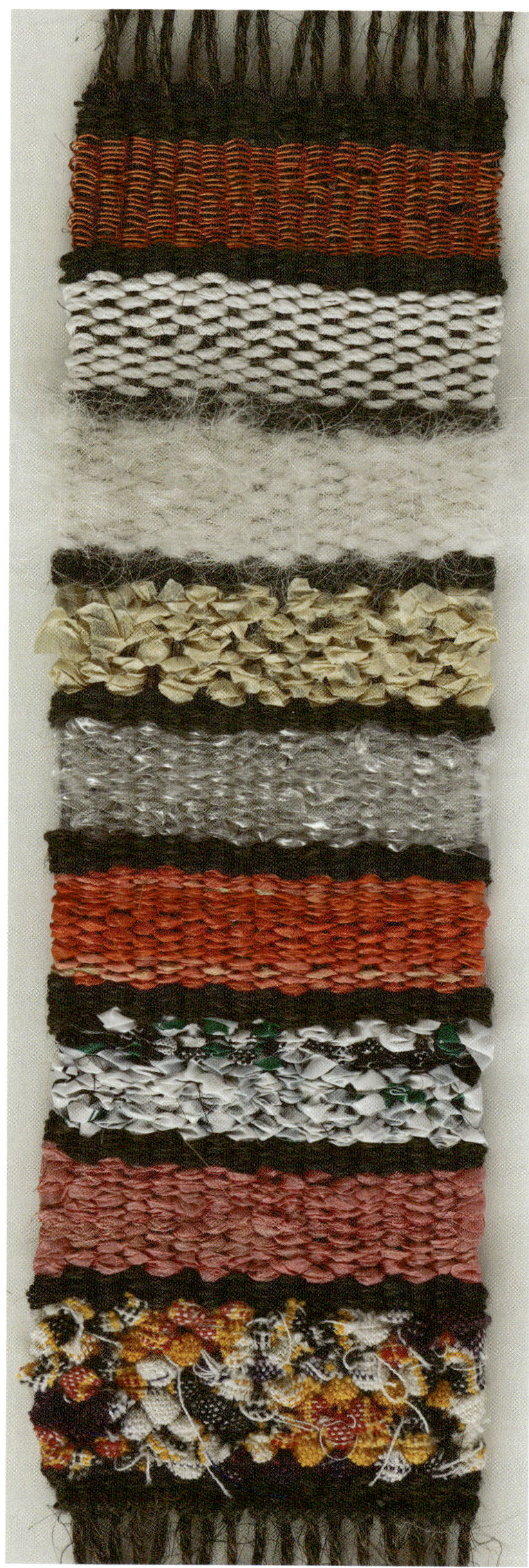

More weft yarn possibilities, from the top – wire, paper yarn, mohair, greaseproof paper, clear plastic, raffia, plastic bag, tissue paper and fabric, dark brown horsehair warp.

Clear plastic

This plastic is from a food bag cut into strips of about 1cm wide. As with the greaseproof, this plastic sheet scrunches up when beaten down to give an irregular but lustrous surface. Because it is clear, it allows the dark colour of the warp to show through, especially when held up to the light. A surface such as this would also respond differently to directional lighting.

Raffia

A plant fibre stripped from the underside of raffia palm leaves, it tends to come in variable width strips which can be pared down further. In this case stained red, it naturally has variable straw colour. Raffia is hard and non-elastic, causing the warps to show through in places. It has an almost gooey quality which makes it stay in place well once beaten down, giving a slippery, almost soapy-feeling surface, and a mat-like handle once off the loom.

Plastic bag

A fairly thin carrier bag with print, cut into 5–10mm wide strips. This plastic is slightly stretchy, and so has beaten down quite firmly to cover the warp entirely. The white, green and black areas of the bag show in the weave, sometimes in lines, other times as dots of colour. It has produced a quite spongy, pliable weave.

Tissue paper

Cut into 1cm strips. As with the greaseproof, the tissue has been woven without any attempt to spin it. Consequently it scrunches up to give a quite variable and hard-looking surface. Being quite thin, it has beaten down to cover the warp almost entirely whilst the weave remains quite soft and flexible.

Fabric

Thin cotton cut into 1cm strips. The fabric is of a fairly open weave and has a woven-in pattern. Of all the wefts shown in this sample, this is the thickest and most spongy surface. Because of its softness it has beaten down to cover the warp entirely giving a thick, rounded bead in which the colours and even the weave of the cotton fabric remain evident. Because the edges of the cloth strips are fraying, there are random fibres sitting on the surface.

Weft lengths, bobbins and butterflies

In general for small scale work, we recommend working with a weft length of about 50–100cm as being the simplest and most workable option. Shorter lengths would mean multiple changes, while longer lengths take time to pull through and may become fuzzy in the process. In later chapters we move on to weaving with a bundle of weft yarns; a loose length allows these to beat down differently as yarns do, and makes it easy to change strands along the way.

Tapestry bobbins, typically wooden and sometimes metal-tipped, are useful in small scale work to beat down the mounds of weft. Their main use is in larger scale work on a vertical loom where the weft is wound round the shaft, and the bobbin left hanging at the front of the work between uses. For work on a small loom, an ordinary dining fork works just as well.

Butterflies, made by winding a figure-of-eight round two fingers then securing round its middle, are another possibility. Their main use is again in large scale work, this time on a horizontal loom where the butterflies rest on the surface between uses.

WEFTS

Checking weft thickness

To check what thickness of weft works well for a warp sett, simply take a short length and weave a centimetre square. If the volume is suitable it should beat down, covering the warps, and hold itself when woven. At the turns, the weft should occupy **half** of the space available **between the warps**.

Bundles

It is usual to use wefts in *bundles* – a *mix* of several yarns often of varying colour, weight and fibre. The only possible way to know how any mix may behave is to weave it.

If the weft – either a single strand or a bundle – doesn't fill **half the space** between warps there will be a little gap formed at each turn. If it fills more than half the space, it is too thick and would lead to the surface bulging or the width of the weaving increasing.

Besides changes in the mix, each weaver's *tension* will vary so it's worth checking a mix by first trying a very small square. It will help you to get to know yarns or other weft materials intimately and make personal and subtly refined choices.

Weavers usually make small adjustments to the way they turn to suit the way each mix behaves. You may choose to turn by either leaving a little extra weft or by hugging the warp – but beware not to pull tight as this will draw the warps together.

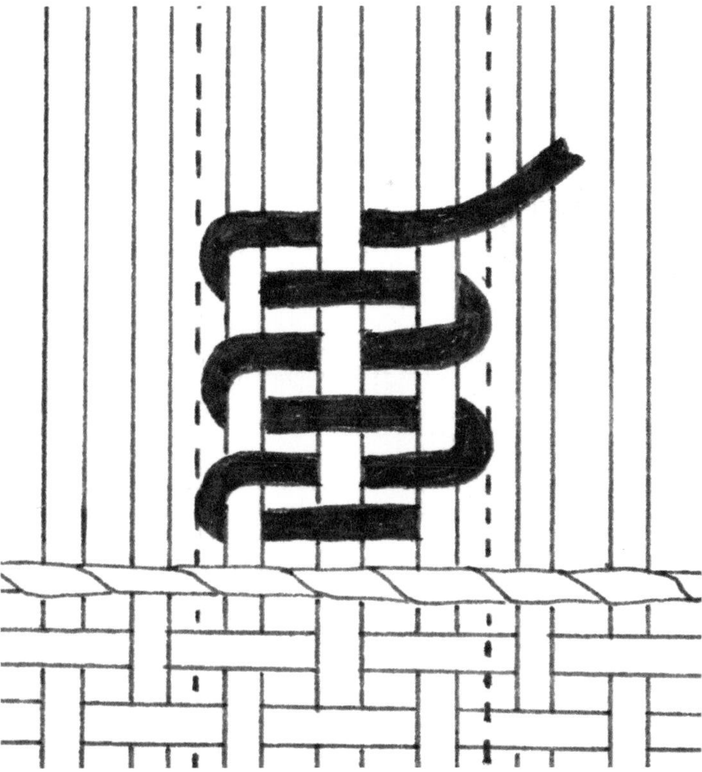

How to check if your weft is the right thickness for your sett.

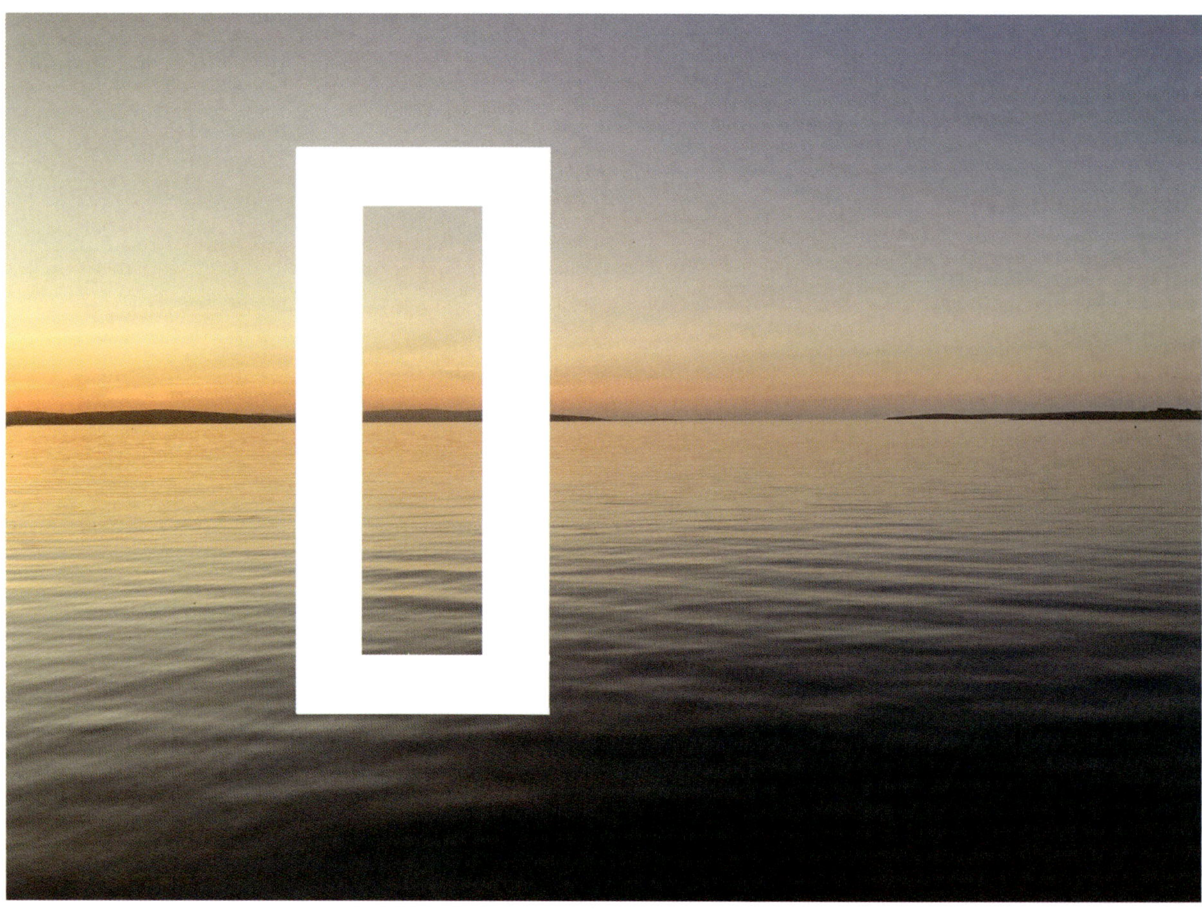

Image taken from Kirkwall harbour seen through a viewfinder.

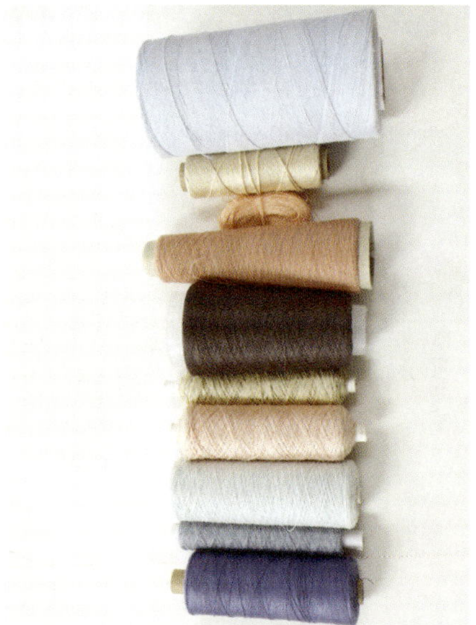

Yarns colour matched from the image.

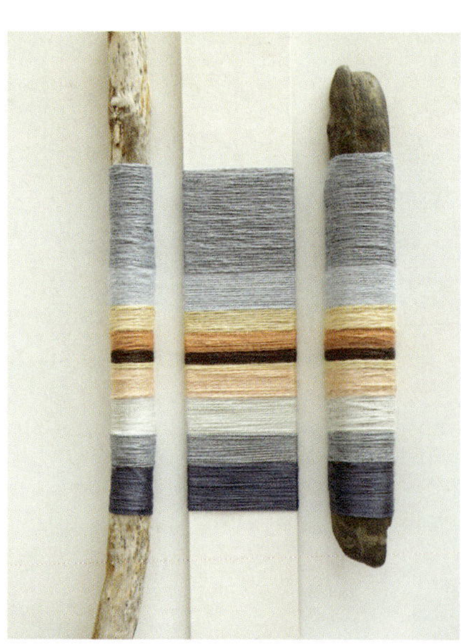

Yarns wrapped around card, stone and driftwood.

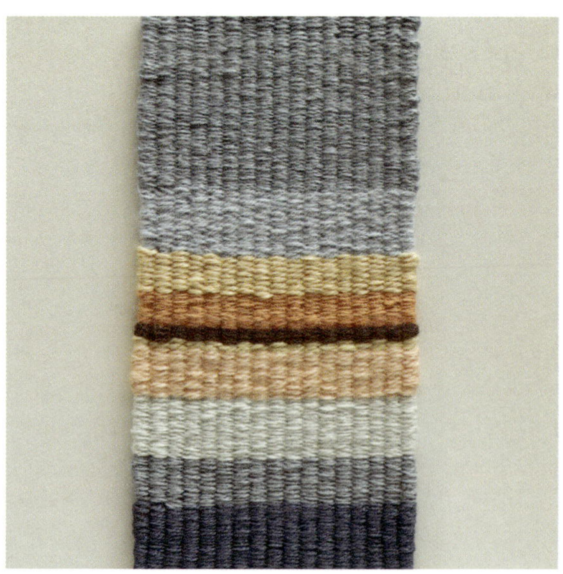

The chosen yarns woven.

WEAVING FROM LIFE – A WAY TO SEE THE WORLD IN WEAVE

If you have worked through the exercises in this chapter, we hope you will have become comfortable handling warp and weft, and acquainted with a few of the infinite number of yarn combinations. Here is a quick and simple exercise in observing a landscape, interpreting what you see directly into yarn and then into weave.

When designing for tapestry, it is often the case that more is less. Whilst tapestry is capable of complex imagery, a design formed of large areas can work equally well and allow the qualities of the yarns chosen to come through.

Choose a landscape which you either know and love – or aspire to. It is possible to work from an image but much preferable is working direct from life, either out of a window, or if you are lucky enough to have the weather, by working outside.

Viewfinder

To make a viewfinder, take an A4 sheet of stiff card and cut a 3cm × 10cm (1in × 4in) slot in the middle. Hold it up, either close or at arm's length. Look through it at a section of the landscape, moving the viewfinder up and down, forwards and backwards, left or right till you find a satisfying position for the view. Look for the main areas in the landscape; assuming you have made the window tall and narrow, these will fall into horizontal stripes. Try to focus on the large areas and not get distracted by details within them. Observe the qualities of different sections – is their colour bright or subdued, mixed or uniform, do they reflect the light or are they translucent, are they soft, dry, gritty, lush…?

Choosing yarns

Before starting to weave a piece, it is worth spending time in choosing the weft yarns. This means that once started the weaving can flow more easily, giving you time to look closely at the weave as it develops. Having observed the qualities found in your landscape, take time to look at as many different yarns as you have available. Through experience you will gather a library of yarns whose qualities you get to know. Fortunately, tapestry weaving does not require great quantities of yarn, so a small cone may last for a considerable time. Besides looking at colour, look at how the texture and lustre might correspond to what you see in the landscape.

Wrapping

Cut a piece of card or any other rigid material about 3cm × 10cm (1in × 4in) – the piece cut out to make a viewfinder will serve, or a found object such as the driftwood used here can also work. Prop up your viewfinder somewhere you can look through it. Starting from the bottom, choose individual yarns or combinations of yarns which most correspond to what you see. Cut a length of about 60cm (24in). Holding it at the back, wrap closely round your card to form a stripe. Continue with each section, leaving a 10cm (4in) length of each yarn or mix loose. A piece of masking tape may be used to secure each yarn at the back. The yarns you choose will look different in a wrap to how they looked on a cone and will give the closest approximation of how they will look once woven.

Weave

Put on a warp about 3in wide as before. Taking the same yarn as the first in your wrapping, weave a stripe. Continue weaving stripes of each of your wrapping yarns. Observe how the appearance of a yarn alters when woven, how closely their properties describe what you observed from life and how they have their own personalities.

As a quick and direct way of recording observations from life without the need for paper media, this is a useful exercise for beginners and experienced weavers alike.

Keep looking

If you are weaving your way through this book, we hope that you will have begun to see how the natural tension of weft yarn held in the warp works, and what a feast of texture and colour is available in yarn. The next few chapters will introduce you to weaving simple forms. We will explain the principles of weave and introduce the enormous creative potential it offers. We would encourage the weaver at this point to be patient with themselves and to persevere. The most important thing to remember in learning is to keep looking. Looking to see that the wefts are working as illustrated, looking to see that the warp remains evenly spaced, looking to see how the warp holds the weft.

Although the making of tapestry is a slow art, even for the experienced weaver, the need to keep seeing, feeling and reacting to the weave as it grows absorbs all the time available. The continuous under/over rhythm of weft passing through warp can promote a mental space in which to think and feel more deeply and ultimately to create.

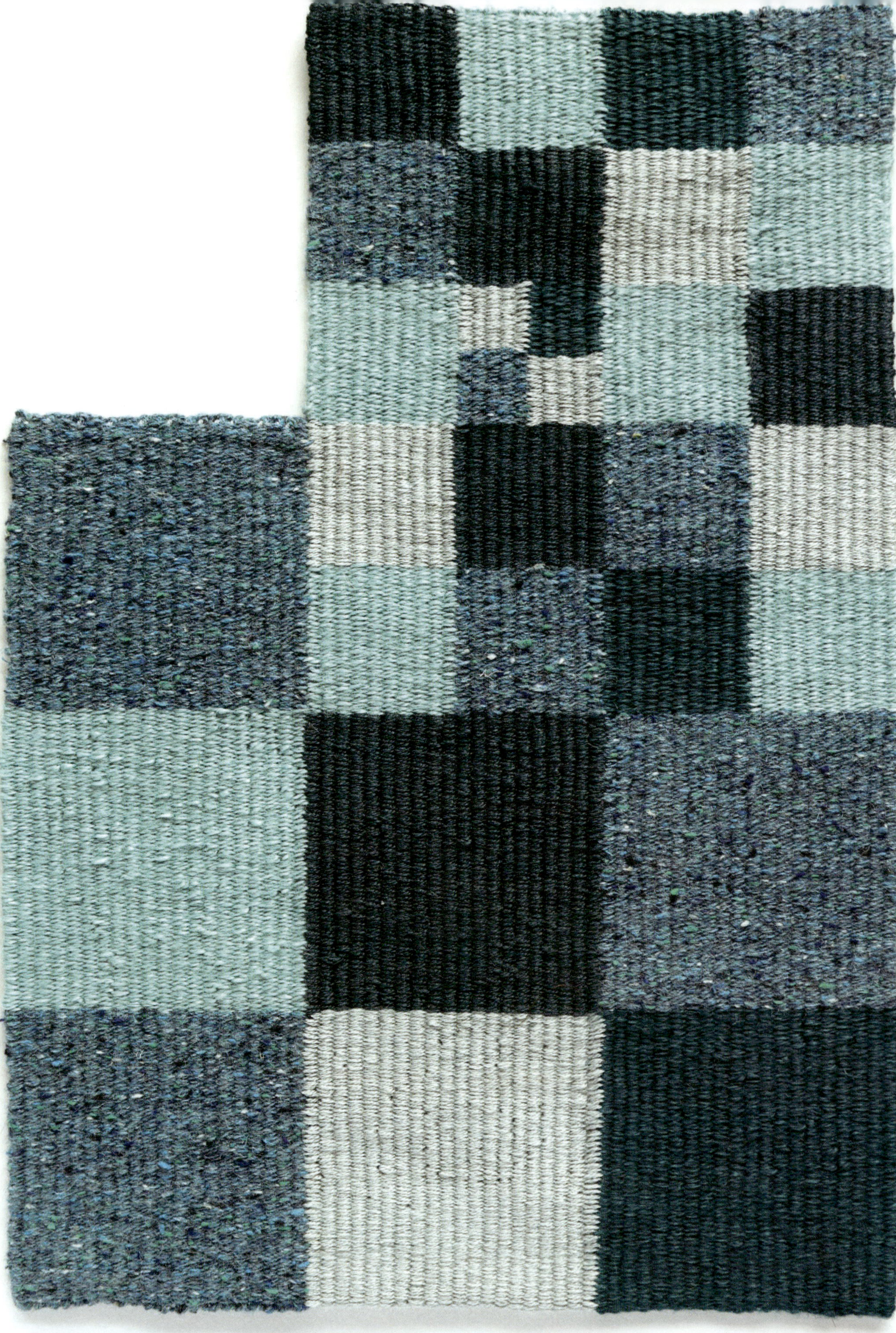

CHAPTER 2

SQUARES

Squares as a form fall very naturally into the grid of warp and weft, frequently appearing in ethnic and folk weaves from for example Scandinavia, Africa, the Middle East and South America.

We will now be weaving with increasing numbers of wefts across a piece, which is the norm in tapestry. This is termed a *discontinuous weft* and is often considered to be the characteristic which defines tapestry from other forms of weaving in which a single weft passes all the way from one side of the warp to the other. Multiple wefts allow for the complex imagery, pattern and shading which can be achieved in tapestry, as opposed to cloth.

With several wefts in play, they must all weave as if they are one continuous weft to maintain the fundamental over/under rhythm of the weave. This means that there is a sequence to follow which will become familiar through the exercises, and which is summarised at the end of the chapter. Learning to manage multiple wefts does take time and close attention. The reward of careful learning at this stage is being able to weave fluently with as many wefts as you choose to weave with in future, so it's worth persevering.

The term 'weft' will be used to mean a yarn used to weave a particular area. If the yarn runs out before the area is complete, we'll demonstrate how to continue with more of the same yarn – referring to this new piece as a 'weft length' rather than a new weft, since it continues within the same area of weave.

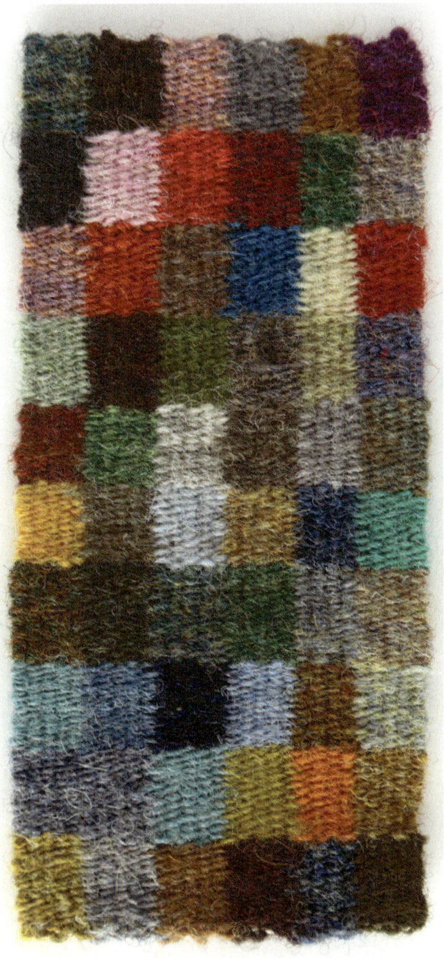

Interlocked rectangles woven in wool, 6 x 13cm.

Interlocked squares. 10 epi. Grey cotton 12/6 warp, linen and silk weft.

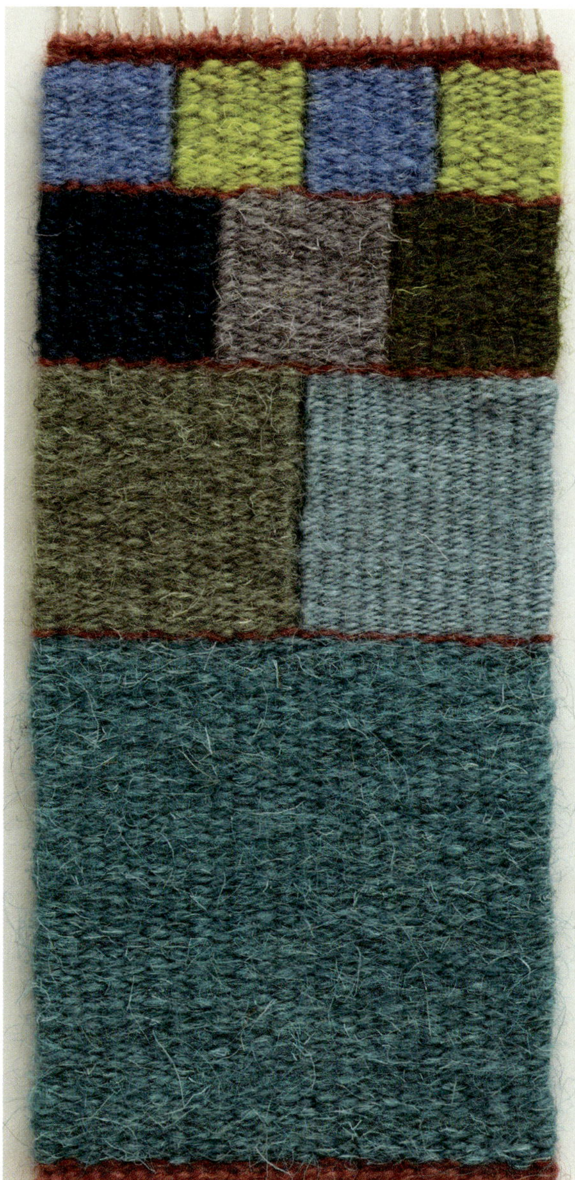

Weaving spares with slits, 3in wide, 8 epi, 24 warps. Cotton medium [12/9] warp, wool rug yarn weft.

WEAVING SQUARES WITH SLITS

In this sample, the squares have been woven one by one adjacent to each other, with naturally occurring *slits* left in between. Later in the chapter we will introduce the alternative of *interlocking* adjacent squares, a more complex technique with a different aesthetic and practical uses.

Weaving with increasing numbers of wefts has an effect on the tension. There is less tendency for the warps to be drawn together, pulling the edges of the weaving inwards. Turns should be made snugly but without pulling the warps out of alignment. Through experience you will learn to make frequent but subtle adjustments. Most importantly, remember to keep observing your warps, to see that they remain parallel and evenly spaced.

This sample has 24 warps (rather than the 23 warps in the first chapter sample). This number was chosen since it is divisible by two, three and four, allowing for two, three and four squares to be woven in a row. Using an even number means the warp starts and finishes at the same edge of the frame.

Please note, the number of *passes* (or rows) drawn on the diagrams will not correspond to the actual number of passes you will need to weave. This will be influenced by the thickness and type of the wefts you choose and how hard you beat down.

The samples in Chapters 1 to 5 have all been woven using a single strand of fairly robust wool *rug yarn* as weft, and a medium-weight cotton tapestry warp. There are no 'standard' weft yarns, but at this stage it would be good to find a rug yarn which is available in several different colours.

If the warp and weft you have chosen are working together well, the weft should be held snugly in place by the warp when *beaten down*. Remember always to put the weft six to eight warps at a time, forming a mound and beating it down before continuing. The weft should not feel sloppy or bounce back out. You may wish to weave a small square first to test your weft, taking it back out afterwards.

ONE SQUARE

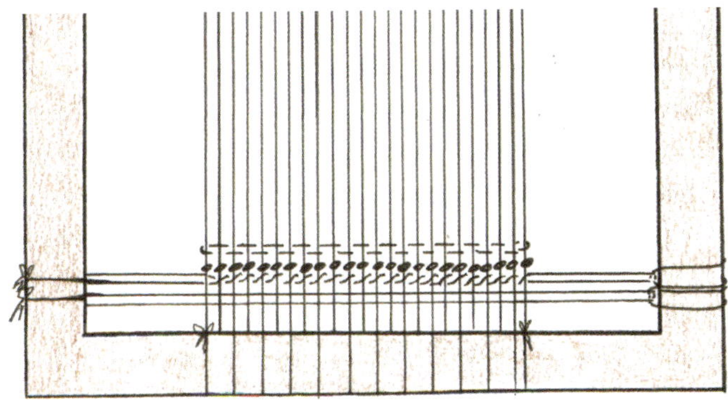

Warping up. Put on a warp of 24 ends set at 8 ends per inch (*epi*) following the instructions given in Chapter 1. Note, the warp will now start and finish at the bottom of the frame. Put on heading cords, twining, a row of *double half hitches,* plus one *full pass* as shown in Chapter 1. Finish as illustrated at the right-hand edge, by passing the weft under warps 23 and 24 and back over 24 taking the remaining length neatly through to the back.

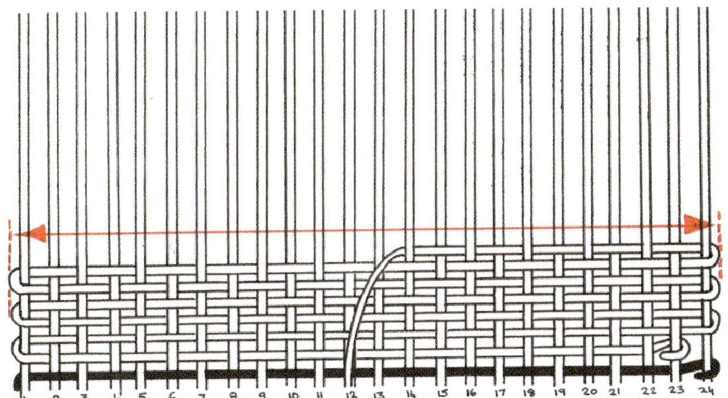

Starting a weft. Take one weft yarn and cut a 1m (40in) length. Start on warp 23 (by passing the tail end under warps 22 and 23, then back over 23). Weave a couple of *passes*, pause in the middle of the row. Measure the width, as marked by the red dotted line to the sides of the image, including the width of the weft as it turns around the edge warps. A detailed summary of how to start and finish wefts is included at the end of this chapter.

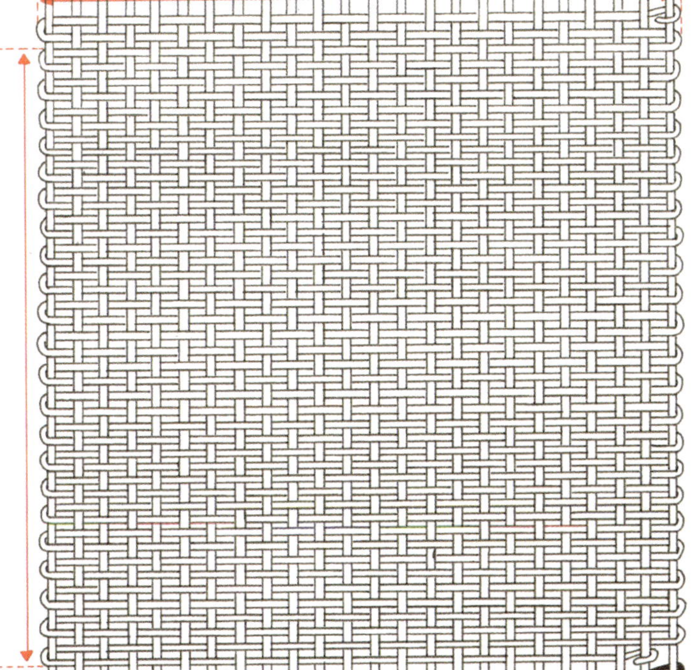

Continuing to weave and finishing. Continue weaving from side to side right across the warp**,** making sure to form short mounds as shown in Chapter 1. When the height equals the starting width, weave one extra pass – this is generally needed because the top few rows will pack down further. Finish the square on warp 24 by passing first under 23 and 24, then back over 24, taking the weft through to the back below your last row of weaving. Cut off, leaving about 10cm (4in) spare so that the end may be sewn in later.

Running out of a weft length. As you weave this first square, your metre or so length of weft will probably run out. If so, finish part way along a row rather than at the edge where it is easier to observe what warp to finish and start on. A weft must always finish on a warp which was low in the previous row, which you will recognise as a hollow made as the weft passed underneath the warp. Note, there is always a warp remaining in between finishing one weft length and starting another. This is the same whichever direction the finishing yarn comes from.

TWO SQUARES

Managing the tension at turns

If the tension is working well, the two squares should sit neatly side by side. If the slit gapes or pulls apart, the tension may be too tight or the weft may be too thin. If the two edges push forwards or even overlap, your tension is probably too slack or your weft yarn may be too thick. To check the weight of your weft, weave a 1cm square as described in Chapter 1, taking it back out afterwards. Alternatively, put a narrow section of warp on to one side of your loom to sample wefts on.

As you turn around the edge warp on either side of the square, the weft should 'hug' the warp, turning snugly but without pulling in. Inserting the right amount of weft length across the square will also influence the way they sit together. Be careful to keep forming short mounds and beating them down from the middle. Tension may vary a good deal from one weaver to another and still work fine. Keep checking your warps to make sure that they remain parallel and evenly spaced. As you weave with increasing numbers of wefts, you will need to make frequent subtle adjustments to your weaving tension.

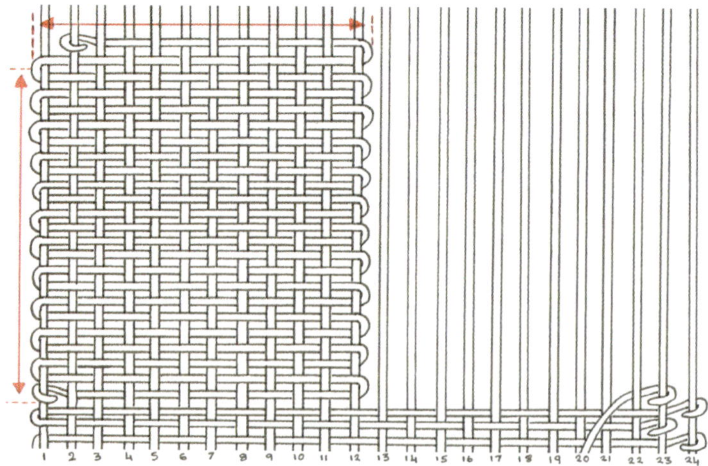

Two squares. Weave one pass in a contrasting-coloured weft across the width of the piece. Select two more wefts of similar weight but different colour. Start one at the right-hand side, by passing the tail end left to right under warps 22 and 23, then back over 23. Leave this weft hanging for now. Start the second weft at the left-hand edge by passing the tail end right to left under warps 2 then 1, then back over 1. Weave, turning on warp 12 till height equals width. Add an extra pass. Finish on the second warp. To weave just a section of the warp and leave the other half unwoven may seem strange, but to weave the whole of an area in one go where possible is the most convenient way.

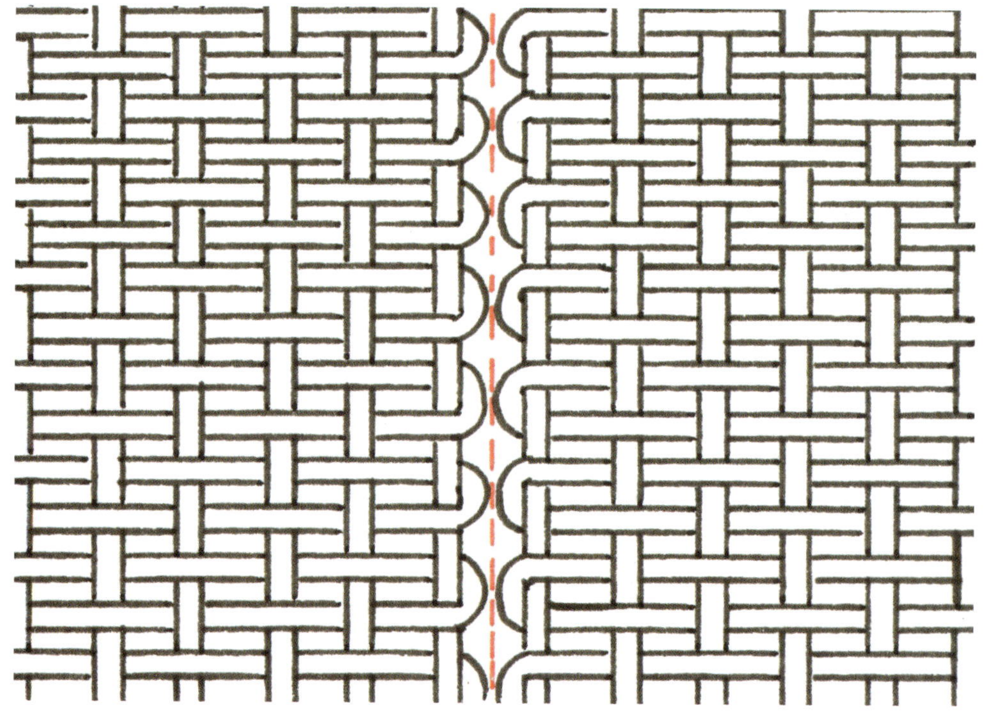

Turns. Notice how the weft turns at the inner edge of the block. It should occupy half the space between warps and be snug without pulling the warps to one side. As you weave the neighbouring block, the space occupied by the turn will become more evident, as illustrated. Each turn should occupy half the space between two warps, the weaving to either side of the slit should lie neatly together, not gape or kick forwards. Turns should always occupy half the space between warps.

Two squares completed

Here are the two squares now completed alongside each other, meeting with a slit in between and divided from the previous full-width square by a pass woven in red. Notice, on the first of these two squares, the weft finished to the left-hand side, one warp in from the edge having started on the edge warp. In both cases, the warp on which the weft started and finished was a *low warp* in the previous row. A low warp is one which the weft passes under, or behind.

To weave the right-hand square, pick up the weft you left hanging at the right-hand side. Continue to weave your second square turning round warp 13. At this point you will meet the turn at the edge of the already completed square. As you weave, a slit will develop between the two squares.

Continue as before, until the height equals the width, then make an extra pass. Finish on warp 24, at the same side as the weft started. Take a contrasting colour and weave a full pass right across the warp to secure the slit.

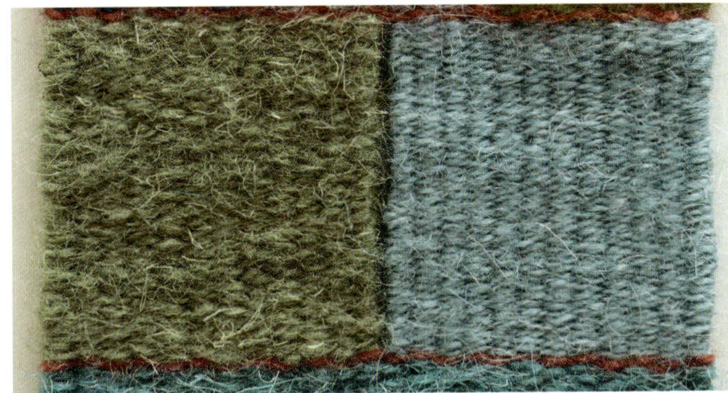

Two squares of twelve warps woven.

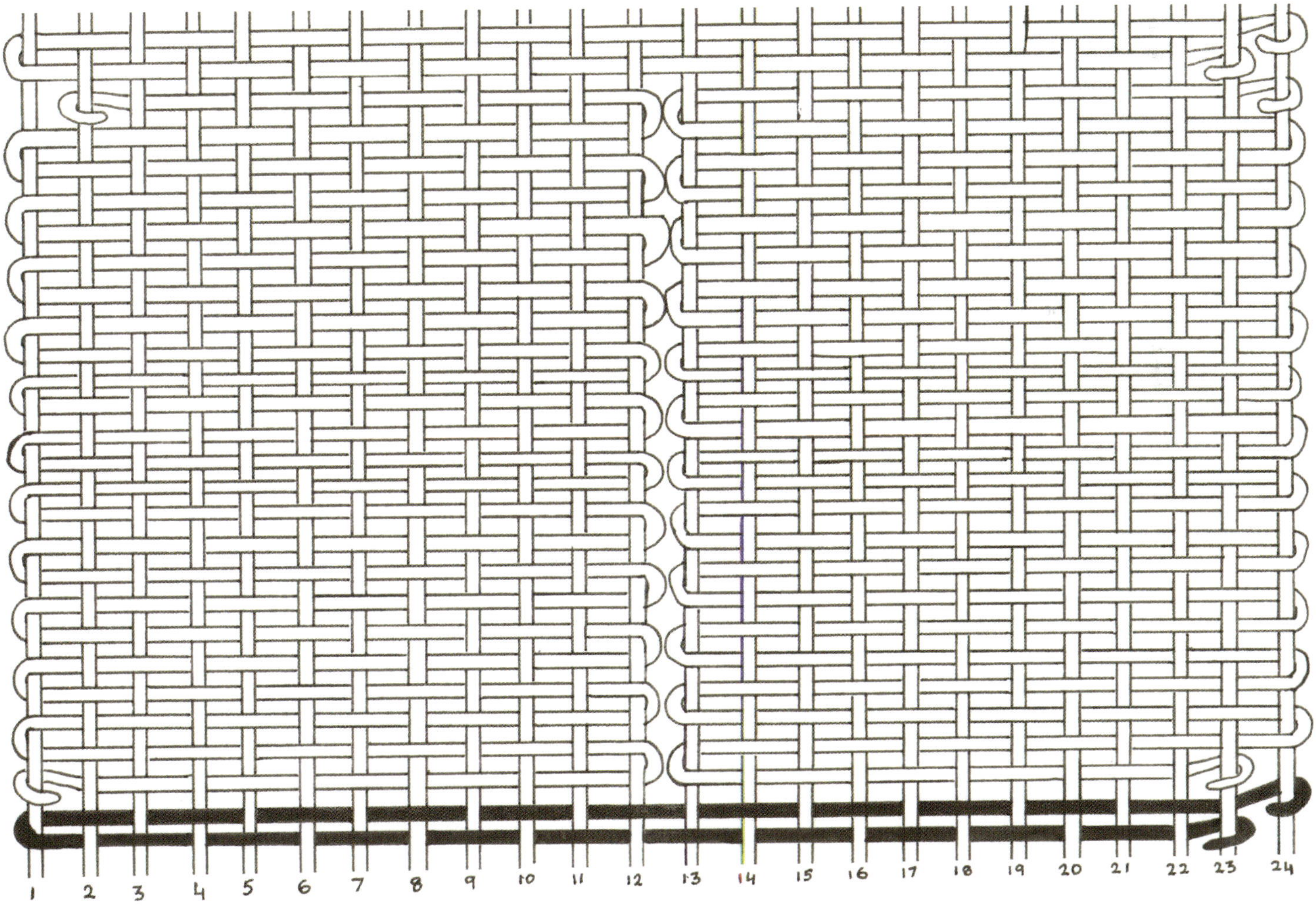

1 2 3 4 5 6 7 8 9 10 11 12 13 14 15 16 17 18 19 20 21 22 23 24

Two squares of twelve warps drawn

THREE SQUARES

Select three equal weight wefts of contrasting colour and cut about a metre length of each. Start one weft at the left-hand edge – passing the *tail end* under the first two warps, right to left, then back over the first. Weave to warp 8, turn and weave as before till height equals width. Add an extra pass.

Next start the middle weft on 15, by passing the tail end under warps 14 and 15 and back over 15. Weave to the left to meet the first square, pause. Start the last weft by passing the tail end under 18 and 17, then back over 17. Weave to the right-hand side, pause. The techniques for starting and finishing are more fully illustrated later in this chapter in the summary. Picking up the middle weft, weave a square turning on 9 and 16, and finish on 16. Finally pick up the third weft and weave a square turning on 17 and 24, finishing on 18, adjacent to where the middle square was finished, checking the height and adding an extra pass to each square. Weave a contrasting pass all the way across to join the three squares and to check they all remain in the correct shed.

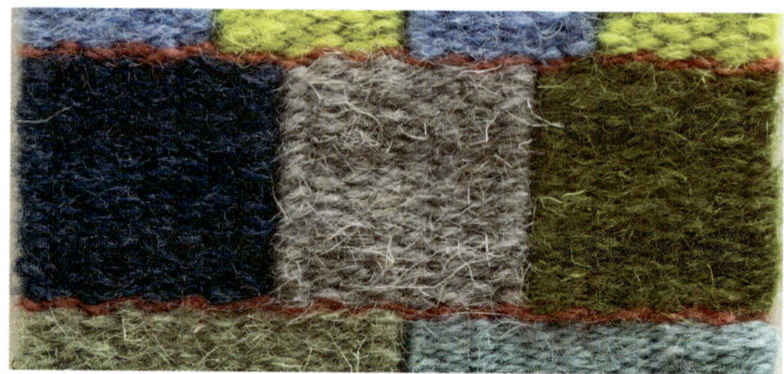

Three squares of eight warps each woven.

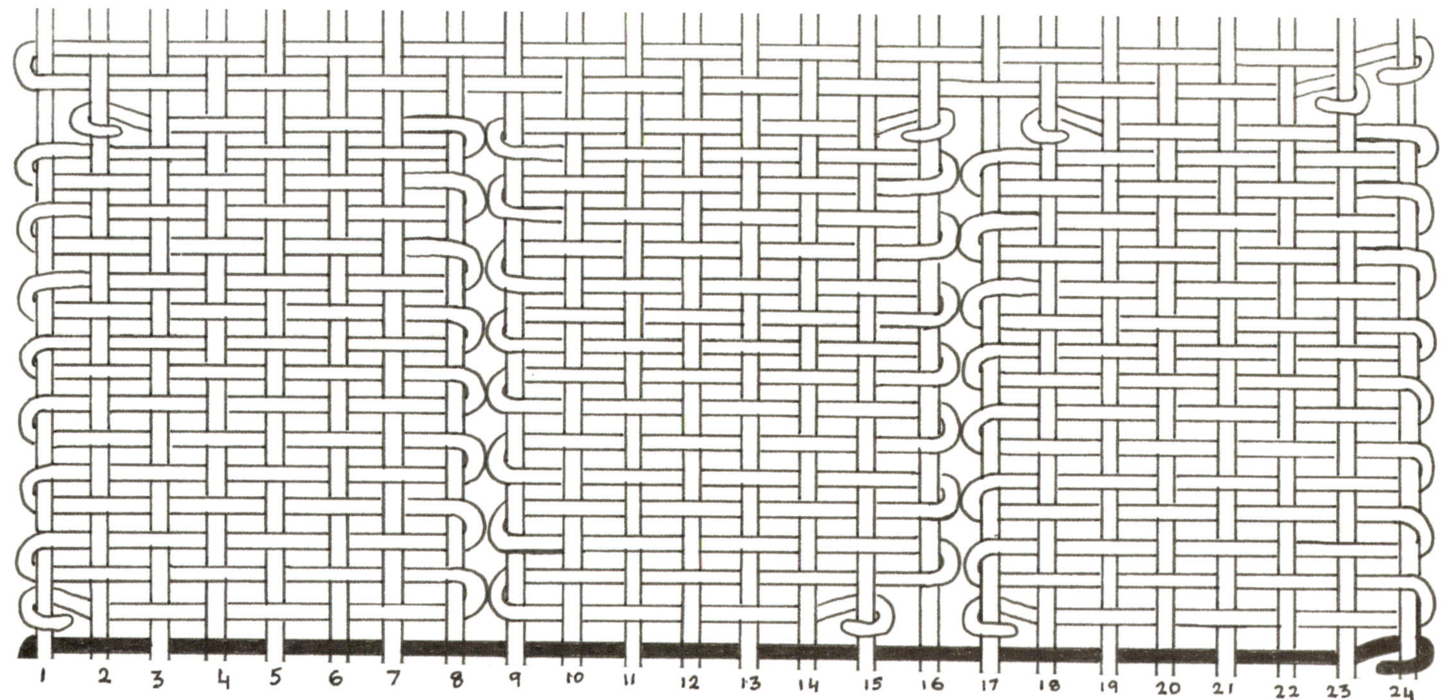

Three squares of eight warps each drawn.

FOUR SQUARES

Taking four weft lengths, start them on warps 1, 11, 13 and 23 as illustrated. Weave the first square, turning on warp 6, till height equals width, adding an extra pass as before, and finishing on warp 2. Weave the second square, turning on 7 and 12, finishing on 12. Weave the third square turning on 18 and 13, finishing on 14. And finally weave the fourth square, turning on 19 and 24, and finishing on 24. Weave a pass and a half all the way across to join the squares. Finally, add a row of *double half hitches* to secure the weaving once cut off the frame.

You may now see a pattern – adjacent wefts always pass back and forth in opposing directions to their neighbours. Wefts start at their tail ends, with one warp left between and hang ready to weave away from each other.

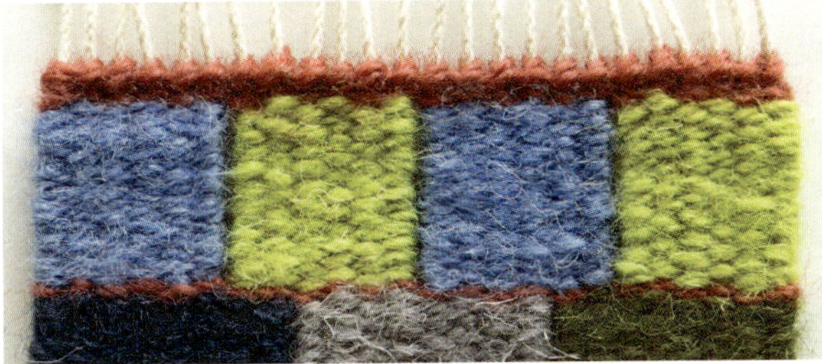

Four squares of six warps woven.

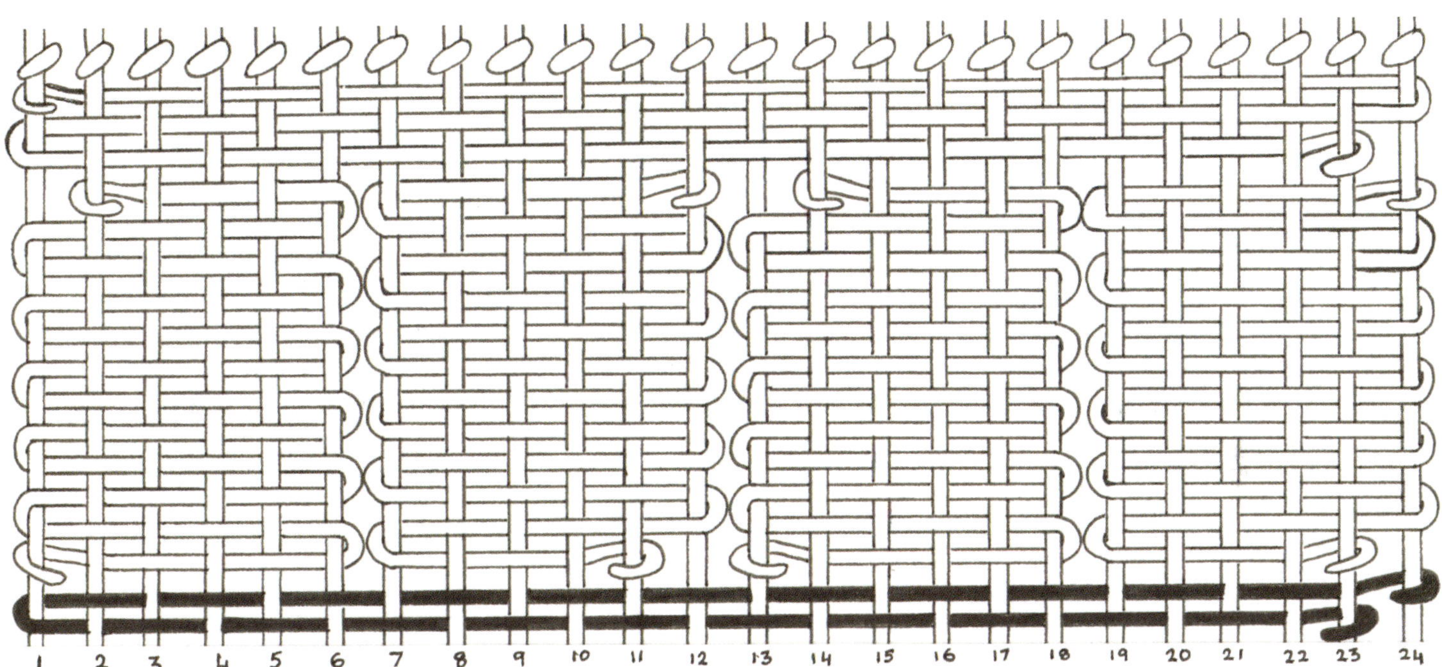

Four squares drawn of six warps each.

INTERLOCKING

Interlocking is an alternative to slits when adjacent areas of weave meet vertically. This exercise will show how to weave the same two to four squares as before, but this time the joins between them are interlocked.

If you look closely, you should see how the interlocked join is quite different in appearance to a slit. The line between is slightly more diffuse, and you'll see that the wefts from adjacent squares alternate a little like a zip. In an interlock, the shape of the bead is long and narrow when compared to the rounder beads made along a row of weaving. The interlocked join sits flat in the surface of the weave, very firm and robust.

The process when weaving an interlock is quite different to weaving with slits. The wefts for each square will be set up at the start, as in the earlier exercise 24 warps at 8 epi. This time, however, all the squares will be woven simultaneously, row by row, moving back and forth across the full width of the piece, picking up each weft in sequence.

To make the interlock, one weft links with its neighbouring weft by passing under it as it turns round the warp. This is an action which could best be described as 'scooping it up'. There is always one of the two wefts which should lead in making this action. To find the right one, look at the position of the two wefts. One weft will hang between the two warps where the interlock is to be made – this is the one which remains in place whilst the other makes a turn around it. The weft which should lead in making the interlock is always the one which passed over a warp immediately before. Approaching the interlock from above, the leading weft turns by passing first under the neighbouring weft then under the warp. The two wefts should lie so that this is an easy action to make. Although it is physically possible to take the wefts around each other the opposite way, you'll find that this is an awkward action and gives a clumsy-looking result – so, if it feels right, it should indeed be right.

Learning this technique takes patience but with time you should become fluent, and it will feel quite natural.

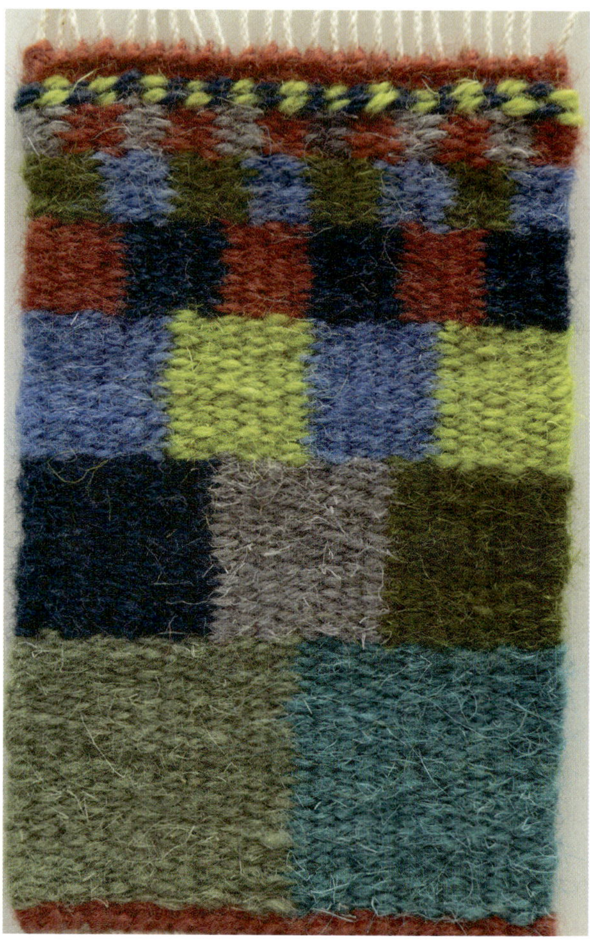

Weaving interlocked squares, 3in wide, 8 epi, 24 warps. Cotton medium [12/9] warp, wool rug yarn weft.

Interlocking two squares, of 12 warps each, 1-12, 13-24

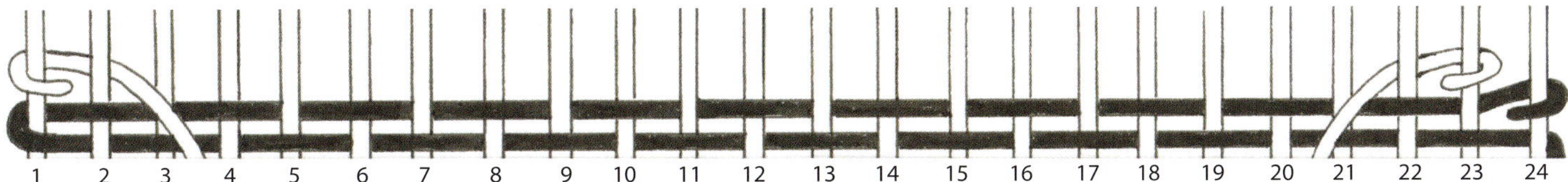

Put on another warp as for the last exercise, 24 warps set at 8 epi, finishing at the bottom of the frame. Put on heading cords, twining, a row of double half hitches then weave one full pass, as for previous samples. Choose two weft yarns of similar weight and cut a metre (40in) of each. Start one on the first warp. Take the second weft and start it on warp 23 as shown.

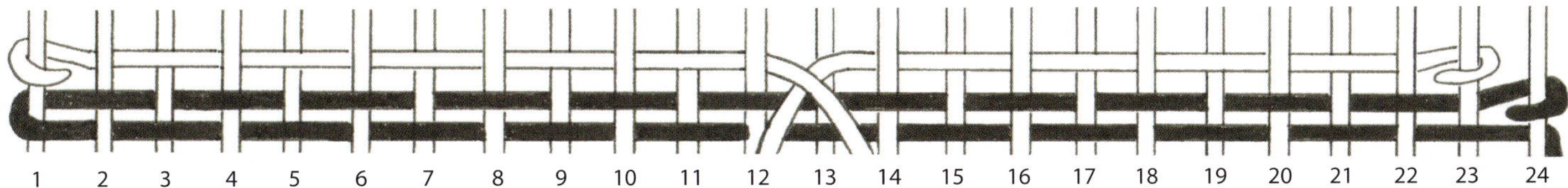

Weave the left-hand weft to the right and leave it hanging ready to be interlocked with in the space between 12 and 13, at the front of the weaving. Usually wefts are paused out of the way of their neighbours, but in interlocking they have to come together, ready to turn around each other.

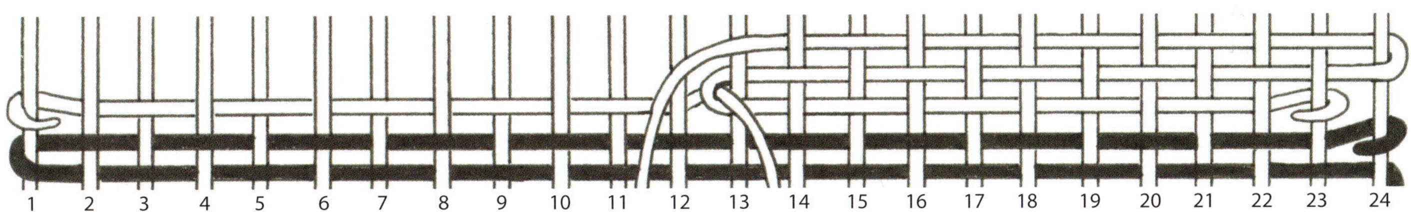

Pick up the right-hand weft, weave to warp 13 where the left-hand weft was left hanging. Pass over 13, then as you turn, **go around the left-hand weft as well, in an action that can best be described as 'scooping it up'.** Continue to weave the right-hand weft, first to the right then back to the left, leaving the weft hanging between 12 and 13.

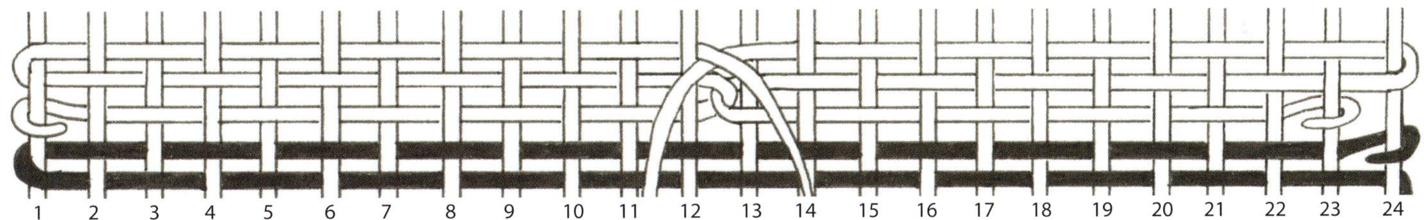

Take the left-hand weft and weave a pass, out to the left-hand edge and back to the middle, leave it hanging between 12 and 13. Next, pick up the right-hand weft, make a turn, again scooping up the left-hand weft which was left hanging. Continue to the right, turn at the edge and return to the point of interlocking on the previous row; pause.

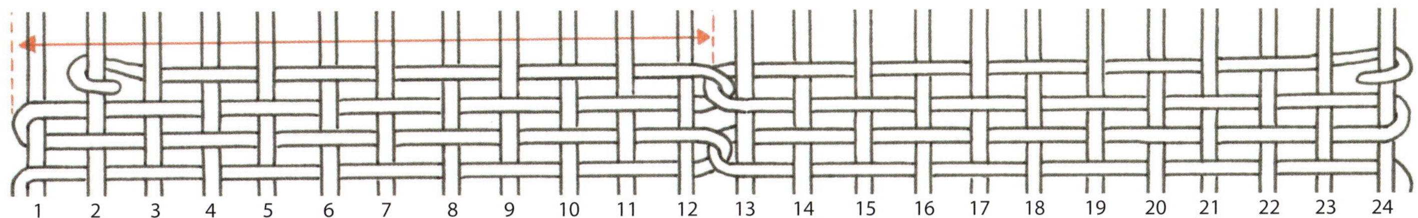

Continue this alternating sequence till the height of each square equals its width, weave an extra pass on each, finish at the edges, on warps 2 and 24. There is no need to weave a connecting pass between layers of squares as there is no slit to secure when interlocking.

Interlocking three squares, of 8 warps each, on warps 1-8, 9-16, 17-24

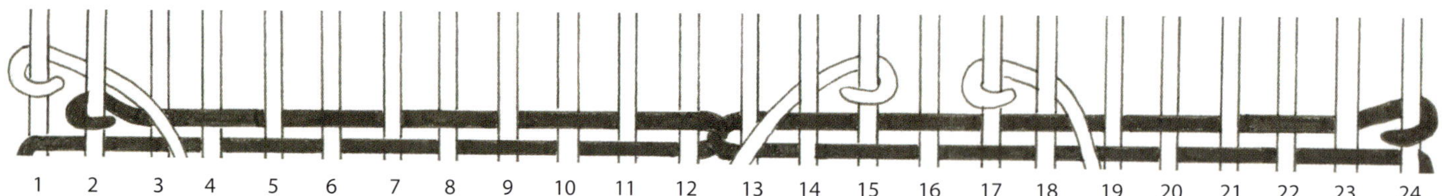

Cut three wefts of contrasting colour but equal weight. Start the first weft on the first warp. Start the second on warp 15, by passing the tail end under 14 and 15, back over 15 through to the back. Leave it hanging ready to be woven to the left. Start the third weft on warp 17 using the same 'under two warps back over one' pattern as for all starts and finishes. This weft should be left hanging ready to weave to the right. If in doubt about how to start, *see* the summary at the end of this chapter.

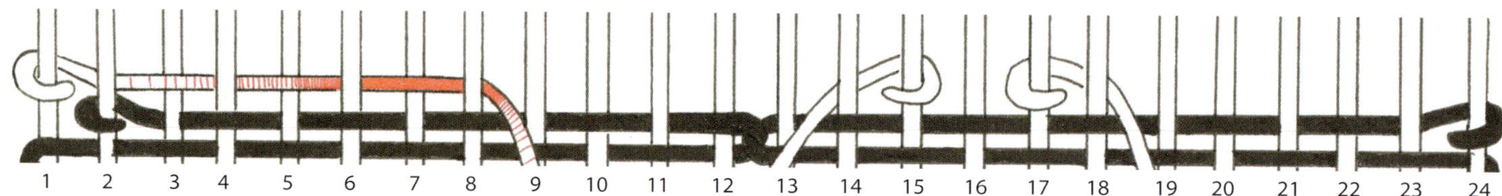

Pick up the left-hand weft, and weave along to the space between the warps 8 and 9. Leave it hanging there. This action is illustrated by the length of weft coloured red.

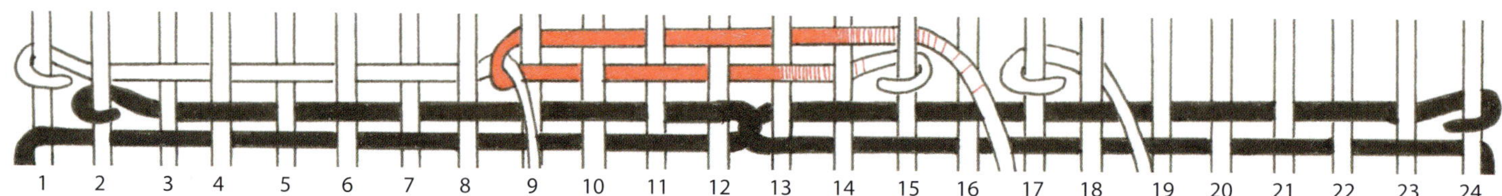

Pick up the middle weft and weave to the left to meet the first in the space between 8 and 9. Turn by scooping up the left-hand weft where you left it hanging, pass under 9 and continue weaving to the right. Leave the middle weft hanging between 15 and 16.

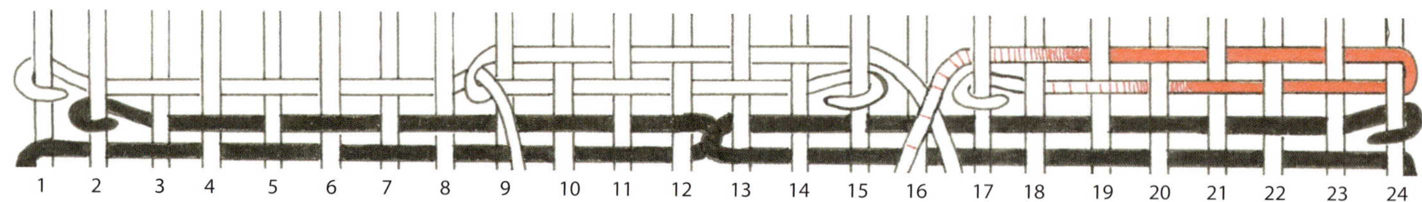

Pick up the third weft, weave to the right-hand edge then return to meet the middle weft.
You may see that this weft made a whole pass before pausing, whereas the middle weft only wove one way (a *half pass*) before being paused.

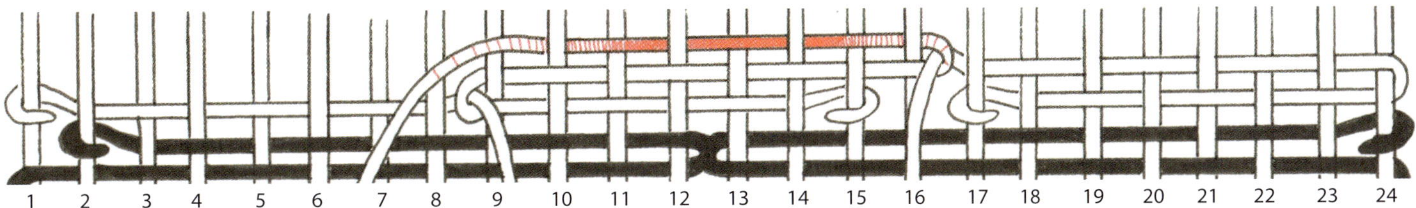

Pick up the middle weft (since this is the one which passed over the last warp before the interlock). Turn by scooping up the right-hand weft, passing under the warp to weave back to the left, pausing at 9 alongside the paused left-hand weft.

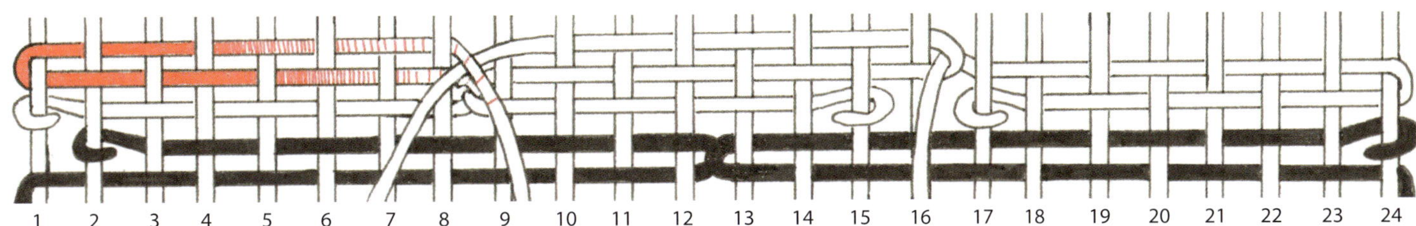

Pick up the first weft, weave to the left-hand edge, turn on warp 1 and weave to the right. Pause between 8 and 9. Be careful of the tension at the interlocks. Take care not to pull on the weft as it turns around the other – it is easy to pull to one side at this point. The interlock should happen centrally within the space between warps, not to one side or the other. Also look to see that the warps are all still parallel, and evenly spaced.

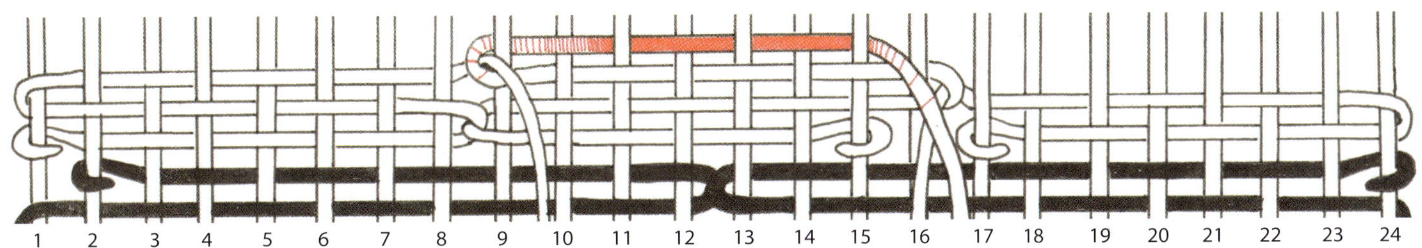

Pick up the middle weft. Make the turn by scooping up or passing under the left-hand weft, and under the warp. Weave a half pass and pause after warp 15. You may now notice that the middle weft can only weave half a pass before interlocking with its neighbour on either side. The outer two wefts can go out to the edge and return in a full pass before interlocking.

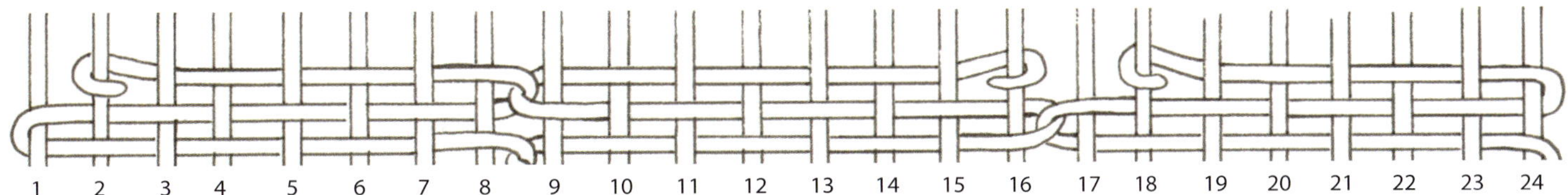

Repeat the previous four steps in sequence, weaving each square till the height equals the width. Weave one extra pass on each of the three squares. Finish on warps 2, 16 and 18. When first learning interlocking, the process may feel fiddly and slow. With practice, working with the wefts in sequence will flow seamlessly.

Interlocking four squares of 6 warps each, 1-6, 7-12, 13-18, 19-24

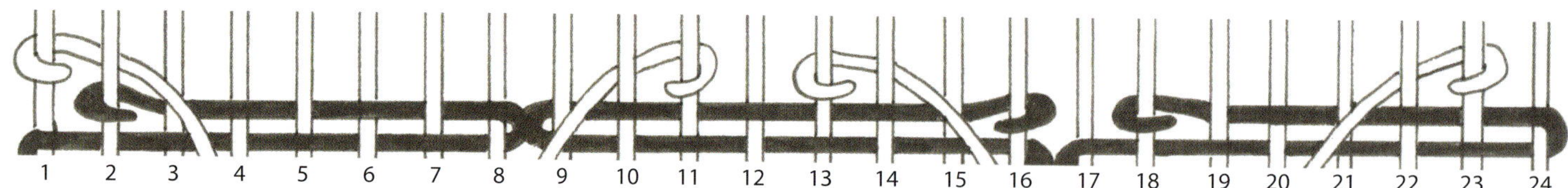

First check that your previous row ended correctly. All the wefts should pass under and over the warps in sequence. If unsure, weave a length of weft all the way across – it should fall into all the hollows left by the previous row. If this doesn't happen, check that each weft finished in the correct position. As we move onto weaving four squares, the points at which you previously interlocked can now be disregarded. Take four equal weight wefts, and start them on warps 1, 11, 13 and 23. These should all be low warps. Each weft should lie ready to weave in the opposing direction to its neighbour. Leave them all hanging.

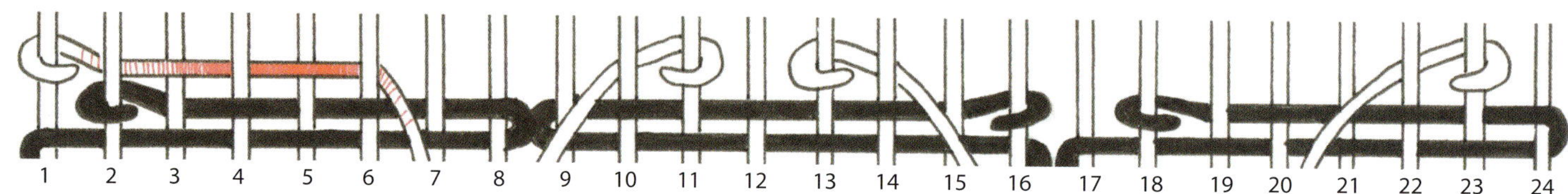

Pick up the left-hand weft, weave to the right, pause after warp 6. In this sample we have chosen to start the first square from the left-hand edge, with additional wefts being added from the right-hand edge when increasing the number of squares. The important thing to note is that adjacent wefts either start together (alongside each other) or start apart (at opposite sides of the adjacent squares). Likewise, wefts either finish together (with a warp left in between), or finish apart. **Never one of each.**

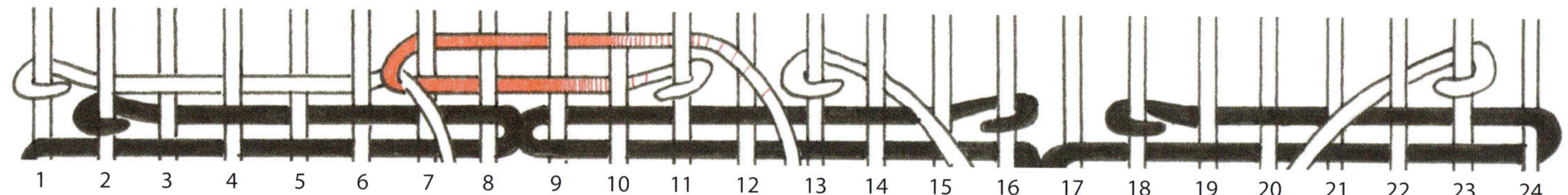

Pick up the second weft. Weave a half pass to the left, to meet the first weft between warps 6 and 7. Scoop up the first weft before turning round warp 7 and weaving back to warp 12. Leave the second weft lying over warp 12. A reminder – if you should choose the wrong weft to lead with, you will find it an awkward manoeuvre producing a clumsy-looking turn which won't sit smoothly on the surface. The weft which leads by gathering up its neighbouring weft is always the one that passed over a warp immediately before the interlock.

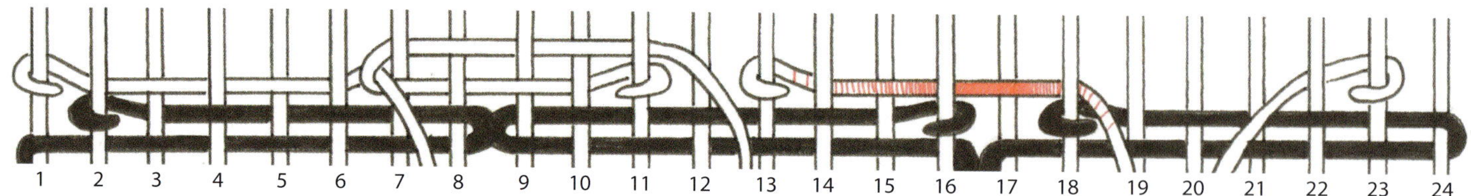

Pick up the third weft and weave to warp 18. Leave the third weft hanging in the space between warps 18 and 19 ready to be scooped up by the fourth weft. You will see that this weft has passed under warp 18 immediately before the point of interlocking, which means that this is the weft which will be gathered or scooped up by its neighbouring weft. The weft which does the scooping up must always be the one which passed over not under the warp immediately before.

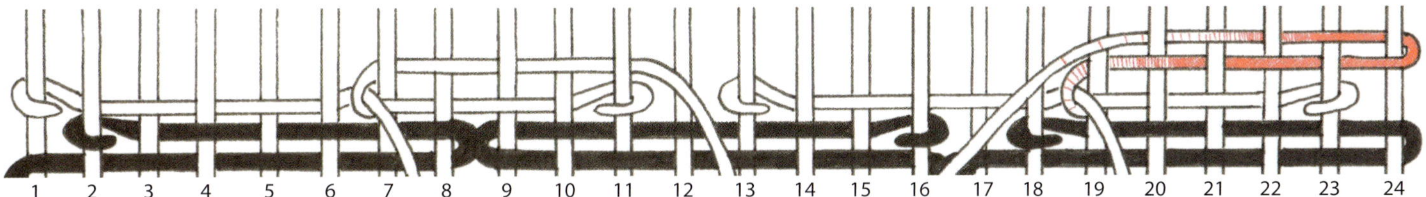

Next pick up the fourth weft which will weave the final square on the right-hand side. Pass over warp 19, scoop up the third weft, turn around warp 19 and continue weaving to the right-hand edge. Then make a turn, by gathering up the third weft where you just paused it and passing back under 19 to continue weaving to the right-hand edge. Turn and weave back to warp 19 leaving this weft lying over warp 19 ready to make an interlock at the next pass.

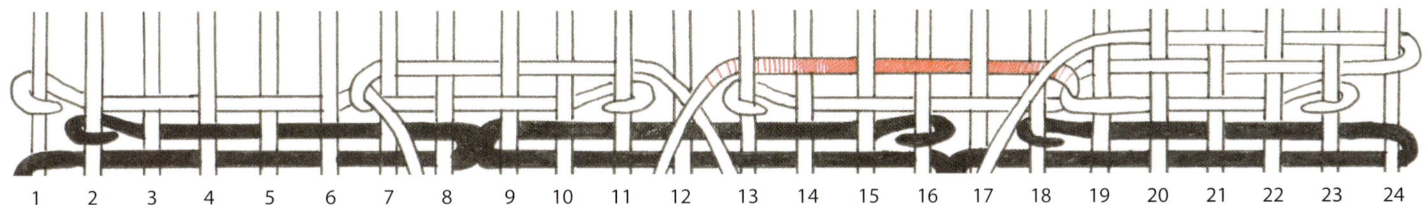

Return to the third weft which was interlocked with the fourth in the previous pass. Turn, passing back over warp 18 and weave to the left. Pass under 13 and leave the third weft hanging between warps 12 and 13 where the next interlock will be made. This weft now has to wait, because it passed under not over the last warp.

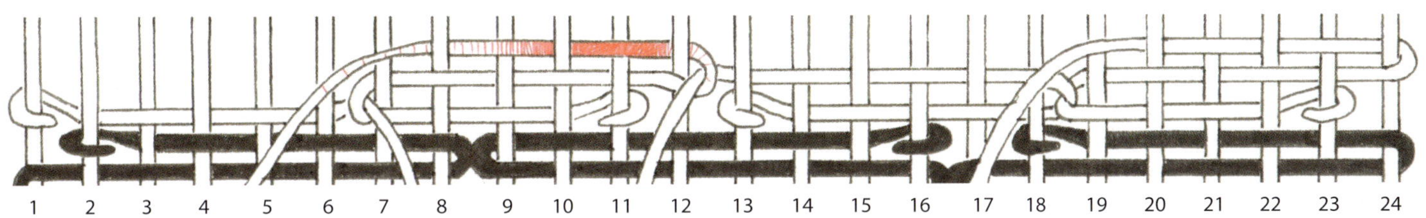

There should be two wefts hanging together between 12 and 13, pick up the second weft, which came from the left. Scoop up the neighbouring weft which came from the right. Turn, passing the second weft back under warp 12 and weave to the left as far as the next point of interlocking between warps 6 and 7. Notice that this second weft leads each time, interlocking at either end of each half turn with its neighbouring weft. You may now see the pattern emerging. Alternate wefts lead at the interlock, so that the order of leading and scooped-up wefts remains the same for each pass. The wefts which pass over the warp immediately before the interlock are always the ones which will lead when interlocking with the neighbouring weft.

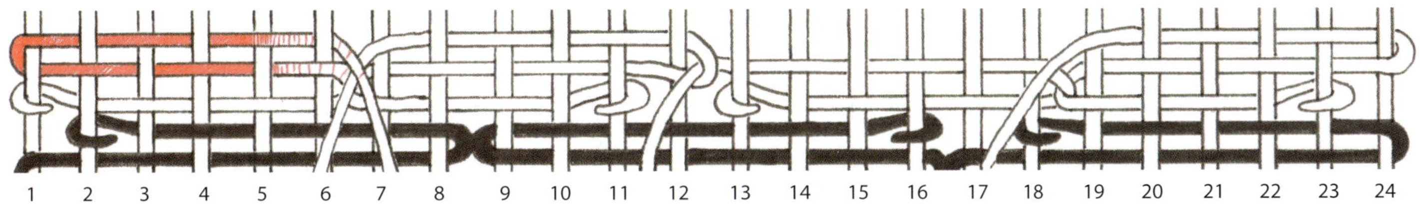

Pick up the first weft and weave a pass, returning to the space between 6 and 7. Note that you should be keeping in *shed*, i.e. passing over and under alternate warps, always making sure the weft falls into the hollow left by the previous row, or to put it another way, covers the warp left uncovered on the previous row. Unfortunately, if the wefts have got out of shed the only way to correct this is to take them back to the point the error began.

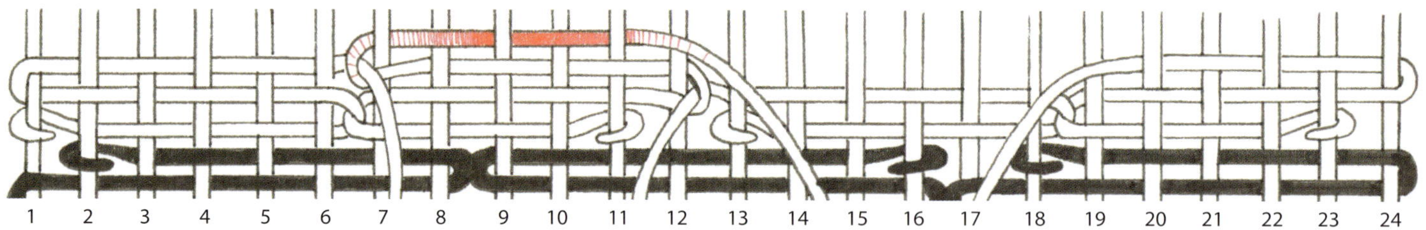

Between warps 6 and 7, where the first two wefts should be hanging, pick up the second weft. Make a turn, gathering up the first weft, and passing under warp 7 to return to the right. Pass this weft over 12 and leave it hanging between 12 and 13 ready to make the next interlock once the third weft has been woven up to the same level.

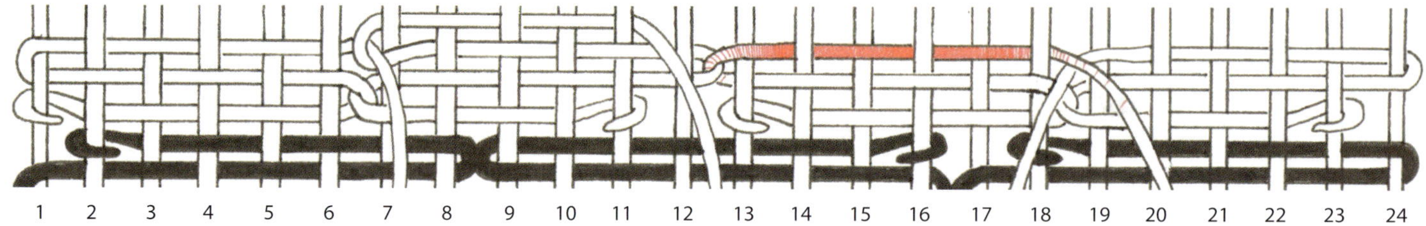

Pick up the third weft, weave half a pass to the right as far as warp 18, pause. Continue weaving, repeating the sequence in six steps as follows – weft 4 – full pass, weft 3 – half pass, weft 2 – half pass, weft 1 – full pass, weft 2 – half pass, weft 3 – half pass and so on. Notice the two outer wefts make a full pass, the inner two only a half pass each time. Keep repeating this sequence until the height of each square equals its width then weave an extra full pass on each square. Check that all the squares are in sequence – you may find it useful to weave a length of weft right across the piece to check, removing it afterwards.

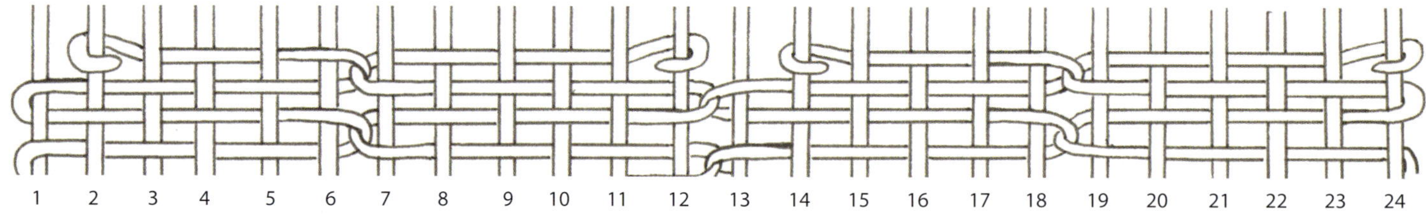

Finishing. Working from left to right, finish the first weft on warp 2 and the second on 12, at the opposing edge of the square to the first. Finish the third weft on 14, which should be alongside the second weft, with a warp left in between, and facing in the opposing direction. Finish the right-hand weft on 24. The weft for each square should finish at the same side as it started from. You can check this by looking at the back of the weaving. You may wish to move on to weaving six squares following the same principles. Finally make a row of double half hitches to finish.

Technical notes on interlocking

All wefts which are to be interlocked are woven simultaneously. The wefts should all be set up at the start. In order that adjacent wefts follow the same under/over sequence, it is essential to get the right warp on which to start and finish, and they should weave in opposing directions. This is explained more fully at the end of the chapter from 'Managing Multiple Wefts' onwards.

Wefts are woven in a regular pattern. For example, in a row of four wefts, the order of weaving moves side to side from weft 1, 2, 3, 4 – 3, 2, 1, 2 and so on. The wefts at the edges will weave a full pass from the point of interlocking out to the edge and back. The wefts mid row will only weave a *half pass* before meeting their neighbouring weft and interlocking. Beware – the weft you have just woven is not necessarily the one with which to lead when interlocking. The weft which leads is always the one which passed over the warp just before the point of interlocking. Having passed over the warp, the leading weft scoops up the neighbouring weft which was left hanging ready. The leading weft then makes a turn by going around or scooping up the other weft, then back under the warp.

To lead with the wrong weft would be an awkward action making a clumsy-looking interlock. If the action of interlocking does not lie flat, check in case you are leading with the wrong weft. The right action feels natural and easy.

COLOURS FROM A LANDSCAPE, IN SQUARES

Squares of contrasting colour and tone can form the basis of a simple but dynamic design. Choose a landscape which has colours within it that you find interesting or attractive. This could be an actual remembered or imagined landscape. It may be taken from life, photographed or portrayed in another medium. You may choose to look at the whole landscape for colours, or to focus on a small detail.

The image here is from a Westray beach, showing the colours of lichens growing on the rocks above the high-tide mark. Cut 20–30 square colour 'tiles'. You may wish to make copies of your image to cut up, or maybe colour wash your own paper for this. Setting aside the actual image, use your tiles to make a mosaic, enjoying the movement of colour and tone across the piece rather than trying to replicate the original image. Stick down the tiles and use this design as the *cartoon* for your woven piece.

In choosing weft yarns, try not to be too concerned about exact matches. Yarns will have a different aesthetic to colour on paper anyway. Developing a library can happen over time as you get to know your yarns and which ones you love, or don't. For now, take care to choose wefts of reasonably similar weight – though it is possible to use two or three finer yarns woven together. Some of the yarns in this woven sample are of solid colours, whilst others have a speckled appearance. For example, the mid-grey squares were woven with a yarn which had a mix of greys and flecks of colour.

Once you are happy with your selection, put on a warp of 24 (or any number which is divisible by the number of squares in a row you intend to weave). You may choose to weave your squares either with slits between, or with interlocks, or a mixture of both. Revisit the exercises in this chapter to check on the practical steps.

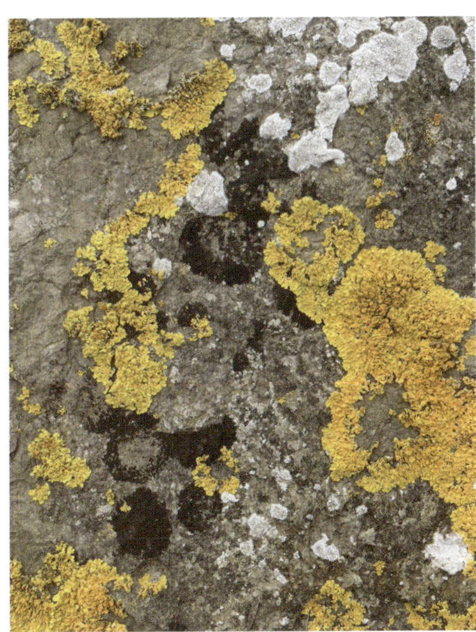

Lichen on stone.

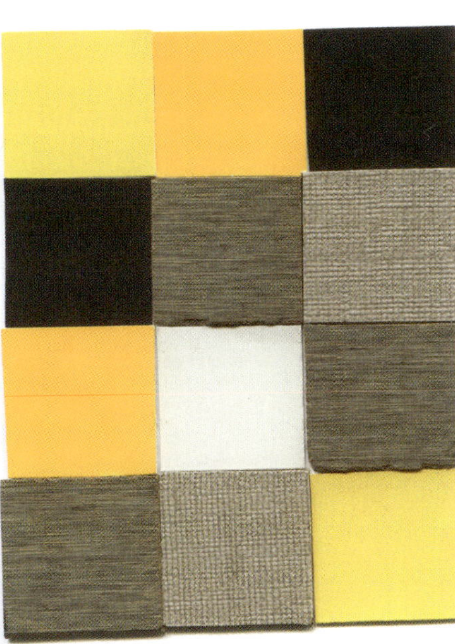

Colours collaged using squared paper.

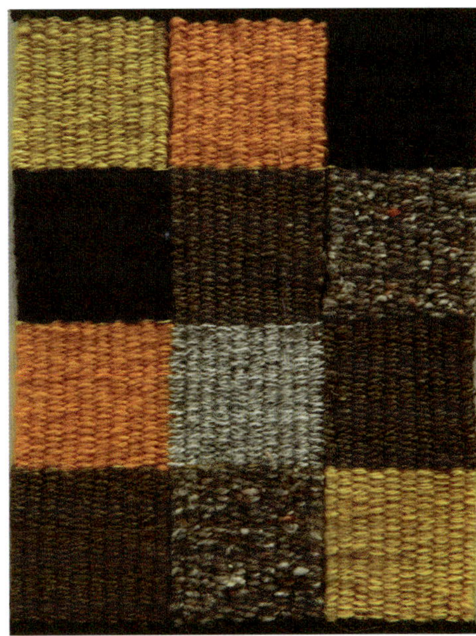

Colours woven in squares.

MANAGING MULTIPLE WEFTS

Managing multiple wefts; a summary

If you have been following the exercises so far, we would hope that you have become familiar with how *a weft* looks as it passes over and under alternate warps, nestling into the hollows left by the previous row. Your hands will know the way the warp grips the weft as each row answers to the last in the sequence of under and over. This creates the strength and essential character of weave. As with all norms, this may be experimented with to exciting effect once you are fluent with the basics.

A length of weft yarn will have two ends – the one with which it is started is termed the tail end. The other end which leads as it weaves and with which it finishes is termed the *working end.* The aim is to maintain an unbroken sequence of wefts passing under and over the warp throughout a piece.

In starting or finishing a weft, there are two things to consider. First, which side of an area to start or finish at. Then on exactly which warp. The choice of which side to start and finish at becomes more complex as the number of different shapes or areas to be woven in a design increases. These choices will be explained in subsequent chapters. The principle, however, remains the same – neighbouring wefts must travel in opposing directions. The drawings on the next page illustrate this.

The choice of exactly which warp to start on is explained in detail on the next page. The main principle is that a weft must always start on the next warp in the row which is due to be covered in the over/under sequence.

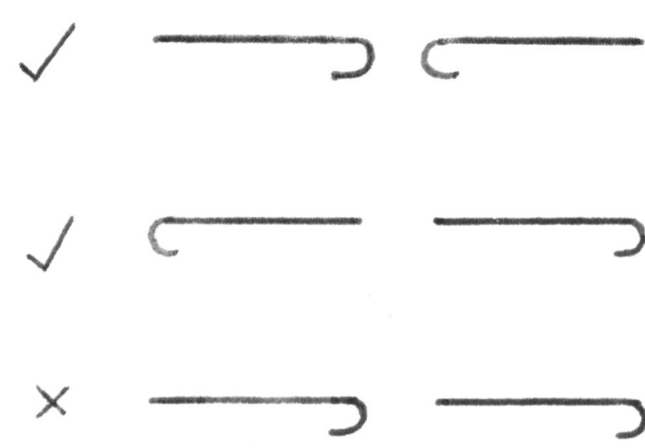

Adjacent wefts must always travel in opposing directions. They need to be started so that they weave away from or towards each other, never in the same direction. Here are two ways to achieve this:
Top – neighbouring wefts may start with their tail ends together.
Middle – neighbouring wefts may start with their tail ends at opposite edges of the warp.
Bottom – this will **not** work, notice that the tail end is adjacent to the working end of the other.
The practice to remember here is – **'two tail ends or two working ends, never one of each'**.

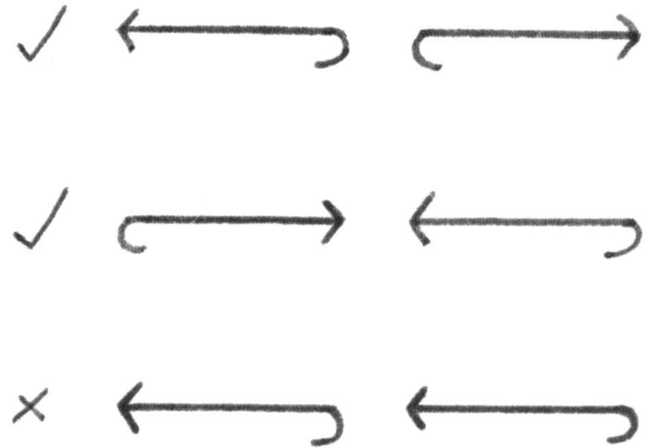

Here the arrows have been added to show the direction the weft will travel in. You should see that in the correct examples, the two wefts travel in the opposite direction to each other.
Top – two wefts started mid row should weave out to the sides.
Middle – two wefts started at the edges weaving inwards towards each other.
Bottom – this will **not** work; one weft started in the middle, the other at the edge will mean that they both then travel in the **same** direction.

STARTING AND FINISHING MULTIPLE WEFTS

These illustrations follow the layout of the samples in this chapter but would work for any design of two or more areas regardless of the shape, although there may then be choices about the order in which they need to be woven which will be explained in the next chapter.

You may now observe a common pattern which is essential to maintaining the under/over sequence – wefts start and finish either **adjacent** to each other, or at **opposing** sides of the area, in this case a square. Neighbouring wefts always travel in the **opposite** direction to each other. In effect, multiple wefts work in a sequence of alternating pairs, except at the edge where a single weft may be introduced or taken away. It is not possible to add or to remove a single weft mid row, only a pair. In later chapters we will see how this may be managed in more complex designs.

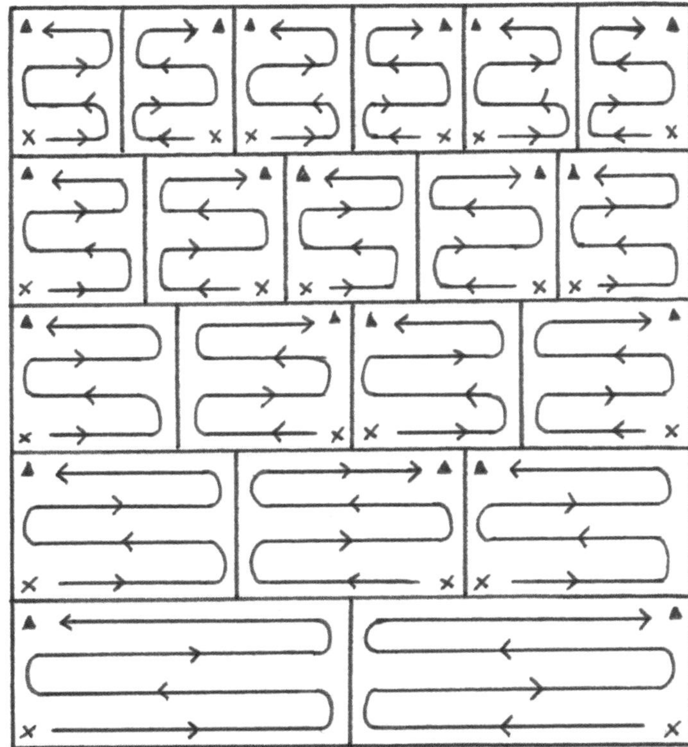

Setting up a row of two to six wefts. Please read from the bottom upwards – the way a tapestry is woven! For each weft you will see the starting point marked 'x', and the finishing point with a *triangle*. The direction of weave is marked by arrows. In the row of two squares, the wefts have both started at the outside edge and travel inwards towards each other, finishing back out at the edges.
Next, three squares. The pattern for the left-hand pair is the same as when weaving two adjacent squares. There is an additional weft added to the right-hand side which starts on the left and weaves to the right.
Four squares – notice, the first three are as for the previous row, with another weft introduced from the right-hand side. This time, it has started on the right and travels inwards towards its immediate neighbour. The same principle is applied to finishing wefts, so that if a weft started on the left it will finish on the left, and likewise for the right.

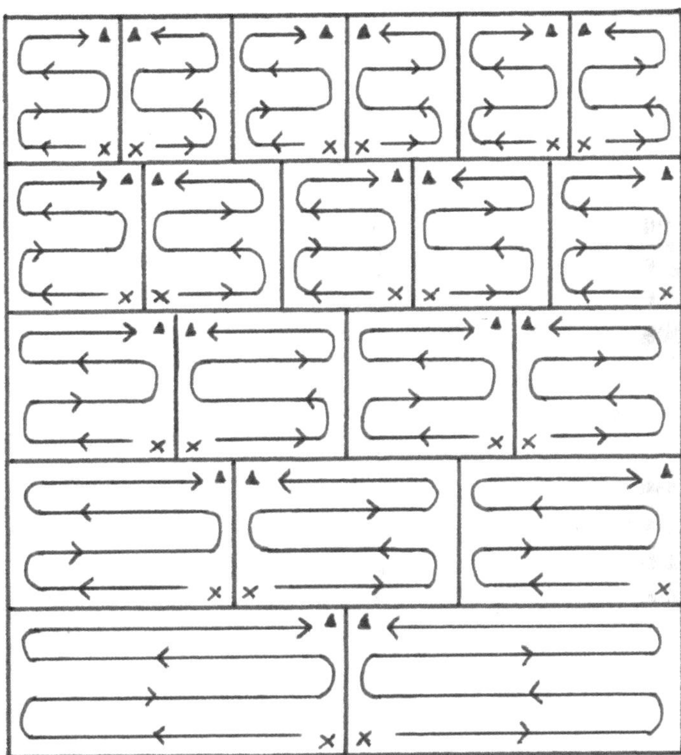

The alternative way to set up two to six and more wefts. This illustration shows the same sequence of two to six squares except that the two wefts on the first row start with their tail ends **together**, instead of at opposite edges of the blocks. This is the only correct alternative to the previous example where the tail ends were to the outer edges. Once started, they follow the same sequence as for the previous sample.
Either of these two options would mean that adjacent wefts will all work together continuously, without breaking the essential under/over sequence.
Note – when setting up an odd number of wefts in a row, one must start from the edge. When setting up an even number of wefts to set up, you may choose to start them in pairs either from in the middle or to one side.

SAMPLERS SHOWING INTERLOCKED SQUARES

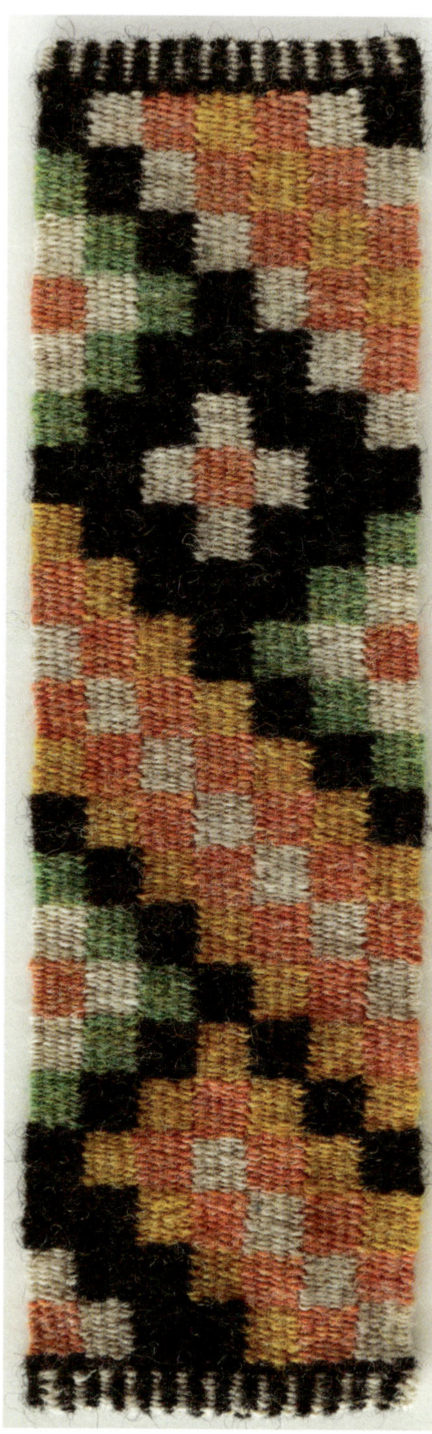

12 epi. Fine cotton (12/6) warp, worsted wool weft. Interlocked sample inspired by a Norwegian coverlet. The weaving begins and ends with pick and pick, which is explained in Chapter 6.

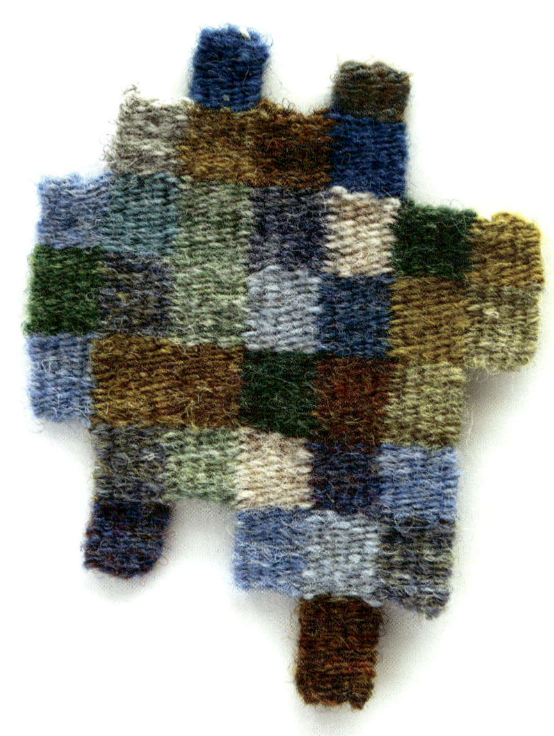

12 epi, Fine cotton (12/6) warp, worsted wool weft. Shaped tapestry sampling the colours of sea and land.

THINGS TO REMEMBER WHEN STARTING AND FINISHING A WEFT WITHIN A ROW

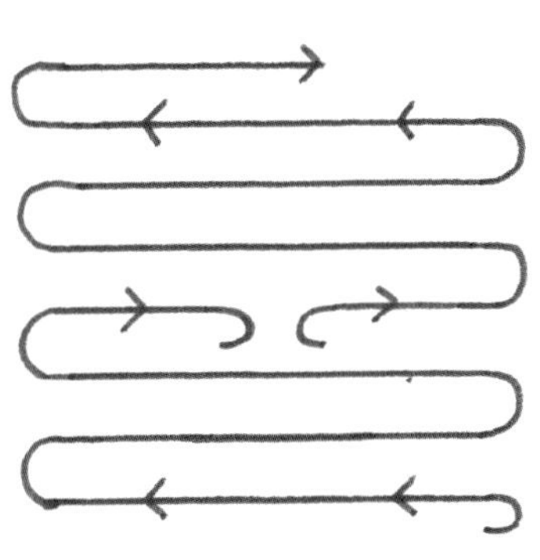

Starting a new length of weft after running out mid row. A new length of weft must continue from the point where the last one finished and travel in the same direction as if the two were continuous. Choosing to replace a weft length mid row makes seeing what warps to use simpler. Weft ends left at the edges need to be sewn down afterwards to keep them from protruding out to the sides, whereas those finished in the middle often do not.

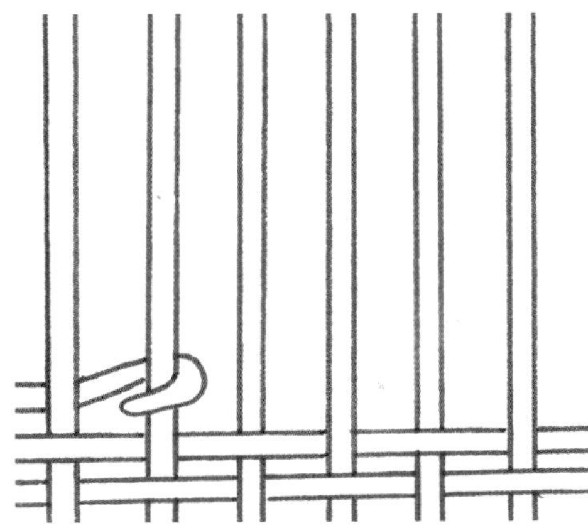

A finishing weft. To finish, choose a warp which the weft was due to pass *over* in the current row (this will be a low warp). Instead of going over, pass under it, then back over, pushing remaining weft length through to the back beneath the row you are weaving. It is now held in place and may be either sewn in or trimmed to 2cm once the piece is finished. A weft may finish on any low warp in the row but never on a high.

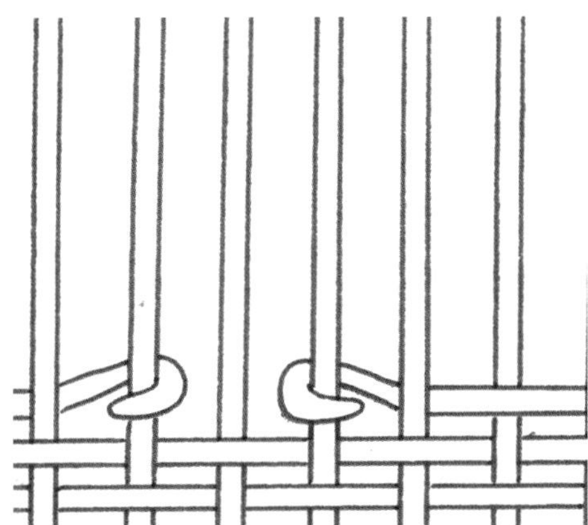

A starting weft. Note, the weft has started on the next warp which was due to have been covered if the row had simply continued. You will see that there is a warp remaining between the points of finishing and starting. The weft will cover this warp in the next row. When starting a weft, the tail end needs to be inserted in the opposite direction to the one in which the weft is to weave.

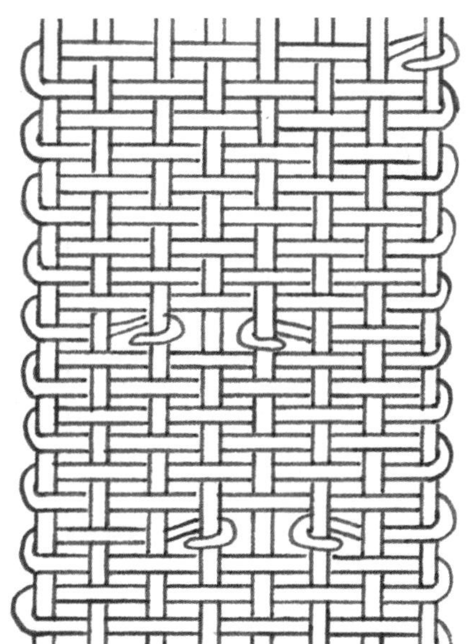

Finishing a weft length and starting a new one mid weave. Note – the wefts all start and finish on low warps and with a warp left in between. The new weft length then continues, following the over/under sequence. Wefts always finish on a low warp regardless of the direction from which the finish is approached. In the diagram you may see that the lower finish is approached from the left, the upper from the right. This may take a little time to become natural.

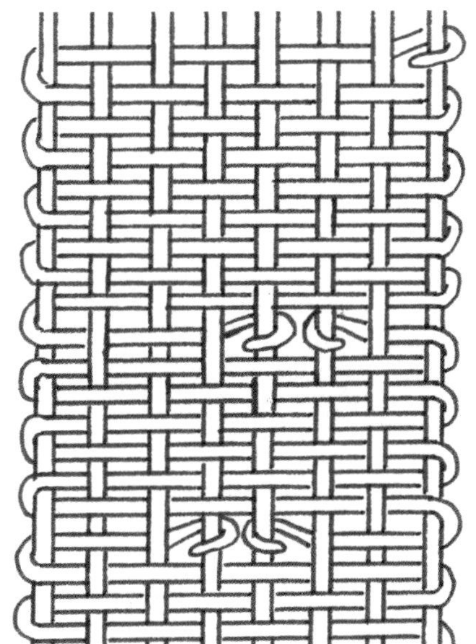

How not to start or finish mid row. Here the new weft has started immediately adjacent to the finishing one, **without** a warp left in between. The consequence is immediately visible, since the new weft passes over and under the same warps as in the preceding row. You may notice that the warp still shows through as you beat down the weft. This weft will remain out of sequence with the wefts on either side until corrected. It is best to find out why and take it back.

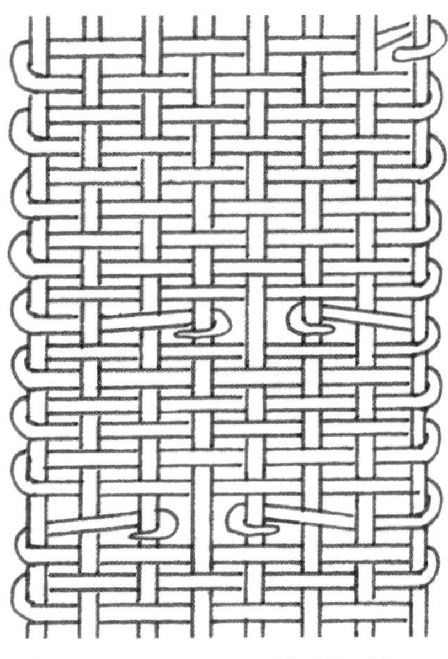

Another way not to start and finish mid row. Although a warp has been left between wefts finishing and starting, the start and finish have been made on high warps instead of low ones. By taking the ends over a high warp, a second bead is made on the same warp as in the previous row, instead of nestling into the hollow left by a low weft as it should. The warp left in between will now remain uncovered for three consecutive rows and is likely to show through.

STARTING TWO NEW WEFTS

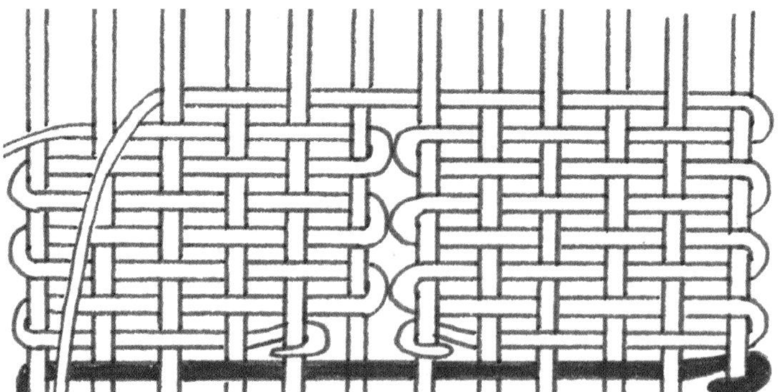

The right way. Both wefts begin on low warps, with a warp left in between (this warp becomes part of the left-hand square in the next row, when the left-hand weft turns on it). You will see that from the start, both wefts weave in sequence with their preceding row. The two adjacent squares will weave in sequence with each other which can be demonstrated by weaving the right-hand weft over the left-hand block, as shown. It falls readily into the hollows left by the previous row.

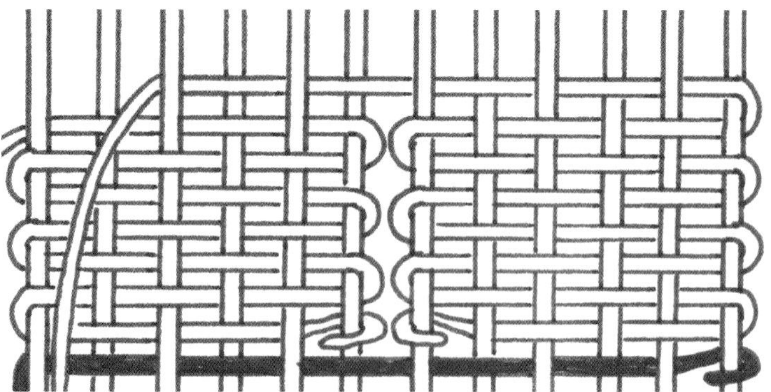

A wrong way. Two wefts started without leaving a warp in between. The problem can be seen immediately on the bottom left where the weft falls into the same highs and lows as the preceding row. As the squares are woven the interrupted sequence may not be obvious, until the weft from the right-hand square is passed over the left. Here you will see that again, the weft is falling wrongly – or out of *shed*. It is passing under and over the same warps as the previous row. Whilst weaving, if you wish to check whether or not areas remain in sequence, weave a length of weft across the whole piece. It will fall wrongly in any areas that are out of sequence.

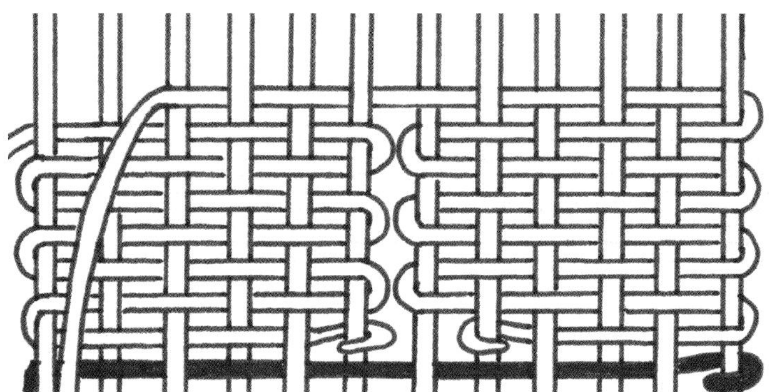

Another wrong way: two wefts started on high warps, although there is a warp left in between. The interruption to the sequence is immediately evident since both sides are falling into the same under and over sequence as the previous row. Initially the warps are likely to show through when this pass is beaten down. As the weaving proceeds, all appears fine, and the right-hand weft can weave over the left-hand square. There would however be difficulties with neighbouring areas of weave to either side once trying to continue weaving up the piece.

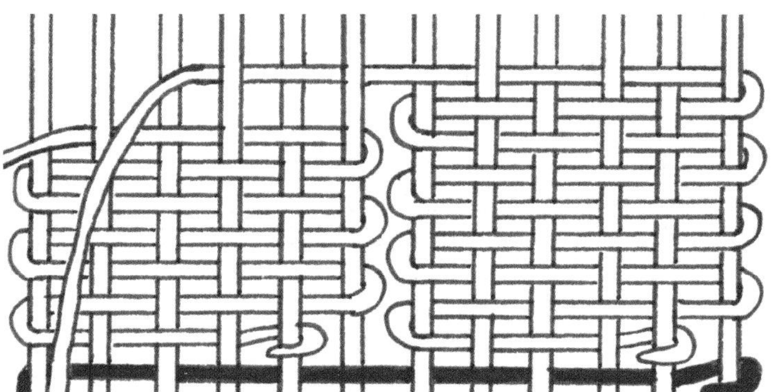

Another wrong way: two wefts both started at the same side. Here the wefts for both squares have been started to the right-hand side. Initially this error does not show in the weave, but the weaver would become aware that the two wefts are now travelling in the same direction, instead of opposing directions as they should. When the weft from one square tries to weave over the top of the other, it will now fall under and over the same warps as in the previous row. Any of the above errors once noticed are best corrected by taking the weaving back to the point they occurred. Although taking a tapestry back may feel frustrating, to continue weaving a weft once out of sequence will only cause repeated problems as your piece progresses.

HOW TO START A WEFT CORRECTLY AT THE EDGES

Take care to choose a low warp – one which the weft has passed under, never a high warp which the weft has passed over to start a new weft on. This may be either the edge warp or the next one in. There are two choices, and only one that will work.

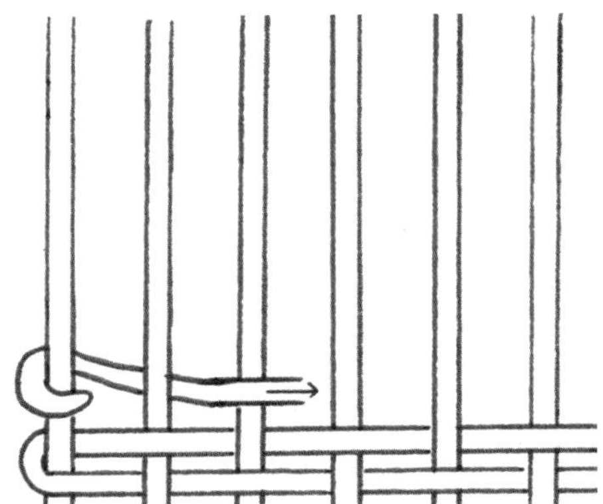

Starting on the left when the first warp is a low warp. To see which warp to begin on, look at the previous row to see which warp needs to be covered first in the current row. The first warp was a low in the preceding row, so it will now need to be covered – this low warp is therefore the one to start on. The tail end of the new weft has been passed in reverse under the first two warps then back over the edge warp.

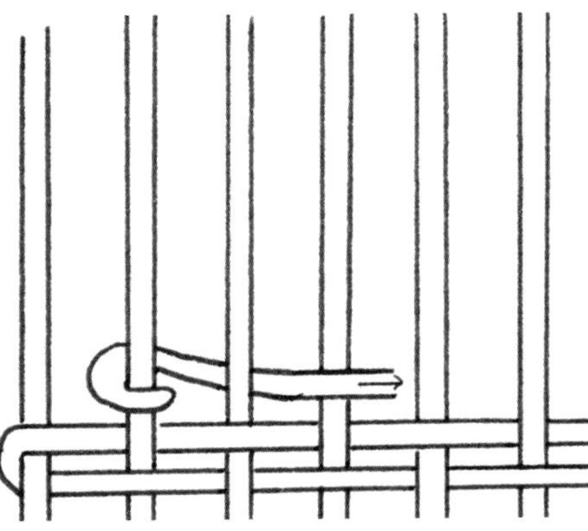

Starting on the left when the first warp is a high warp. Look at the last completed row to see which warp was a low – you will see that the weft turned by passing first under then over the left-hand warp – making a high turn. It passed under the next warp along. This second warp is the one which needs to be covered in the present row and so is the correct warp to start on. The tail end of the new weft has passed in reverse under the third and second warps, then back over the second.

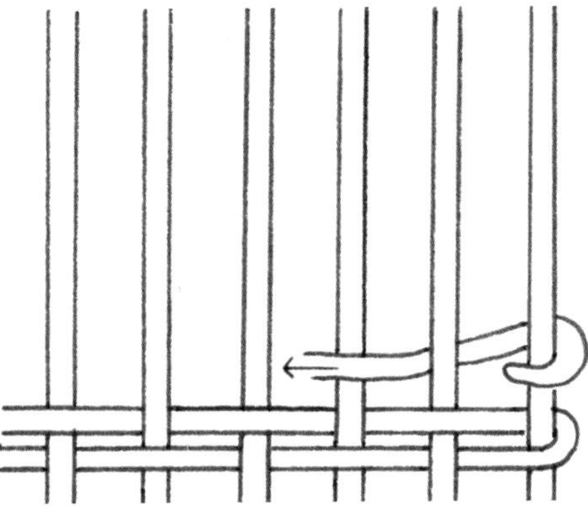

Starting on the right-hand side when the edge warp is a low warp. Look at the direction your new row will weave in and find the first warp which should be covered. In this case it is the right-hand edge warp, which you should see is a low. In the previous row, the weft made a low turn, meaning that it turned by passing first over, then under the warp. This means that it needs to be covered in this row and is therefore the warp to start on. The tail end of the starting weft has passed backwards under the last two warps and back over the right-hand one.

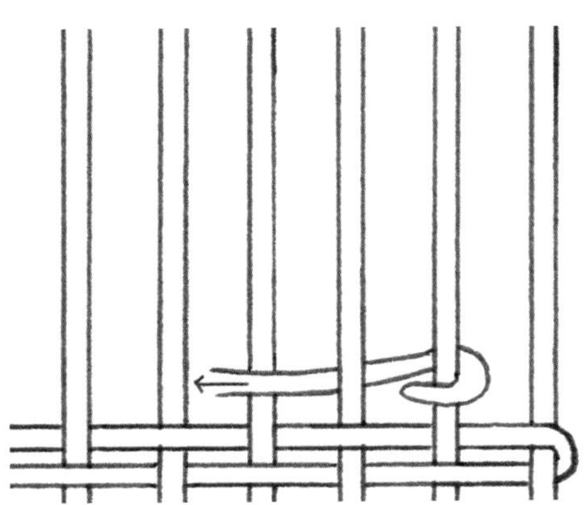

Starting at the right-hand side when the edge warp is a high warp. Look at the previous row to find the first warp which was left uncovered – this is the next warp in from the edge. On the edge warp, the weft passed first under then over the warp, therefore it is a high turn and should **not** be chosen as the warp to start on. This right-hand edge warp will be covered in the next row of weaving. The starting weft passed backwards under the third and second warps from the right-hand edge, then back over the second from the edge. The edge warp appears to have been missed out but will be covered in the next row.

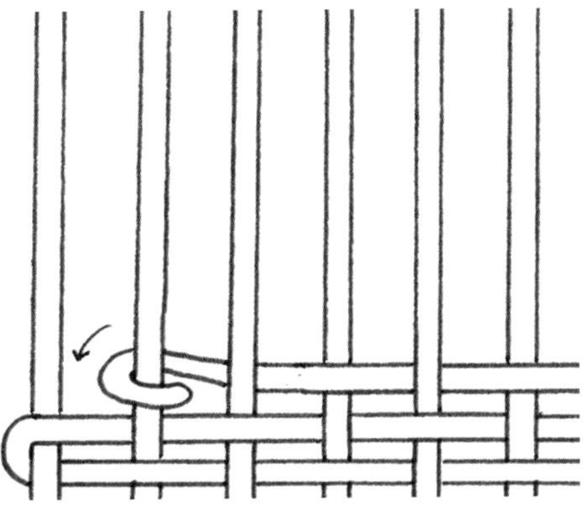

Finishing a weft on the left when the edge warp is a high. As when starting a weft, look for the last warp in the row which needs to be covered in the under/over sequence. You will see that this is the second from the left. Note, in the previous row, the weft passed first under then over the warp, making it a high turn, and not suitable for finishing on. The working end of the weft which is to finish has passed under the third and second warps then back over the second before being taken through to the back below the last row of weaving.

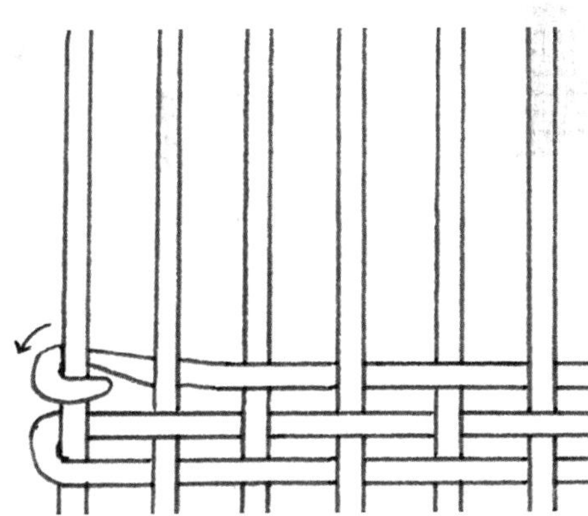

Finishing a weft on the left when the edge warp is a low. Look to see which is the last warp in the row that needs to be covered. You should see that this is now the left-hand edge warp which is a low turn since it passed first over and then under the edge warp on the previous row. This is therefore the warp to finish on. The finishing weft has passed under the last two warps, before passing back over the left-hand one and being taken through to the back below the last row of weaving.

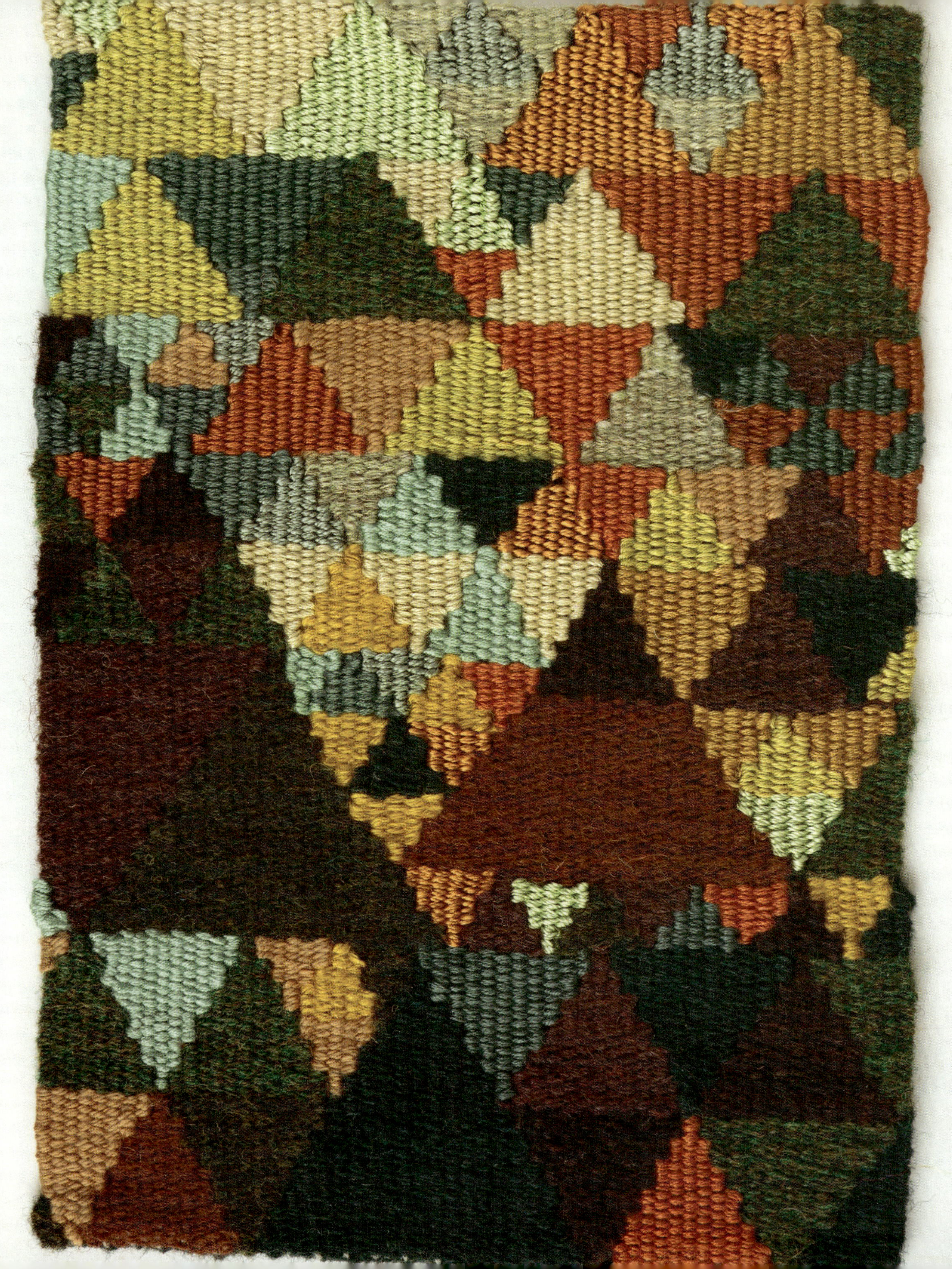

CHAPTER 3

TRIANGLES

The quality of a diagonal line in tapestry weave has a very distinctive and uniquely dynamic aesthetic quality.

Looking at this sample, you may see that the steeper the angle, the more stepped in appearance it becomes. The quality of line is also influenced by the choice to turn on either a low or high warp at the point of stepping back. As the name suggests a *low turn* is lower and produces a less pronounced step than a *high turn*.

There are several new techniques used in weaving this sample which will be explained. Firstly, to form a diagonal means reducing or stepping back to a set pattern. To form shallow angles, each pass may reduce by several warps. For example, minus two (written as -2) means the pass reduces, or steps back by two warps. To form a steep angle on the other hand will require several passes to be made to each warp before stepping back. So for example, plus three (written simply as +3) means make three passes to the warp before stepping back.

In the case of a shape with diagonal sides, one area of weave inevitably overlays another. This means making choices about the order in which areas need to be woven. This then affects where wefts need to start and finish and the direction they will weave in. Since triangles come to a point, there is also the question of how to weave on a single warp.

As with previous chapters, once the principles have become familiar, they may become the foundation for complex and highly individual choices.

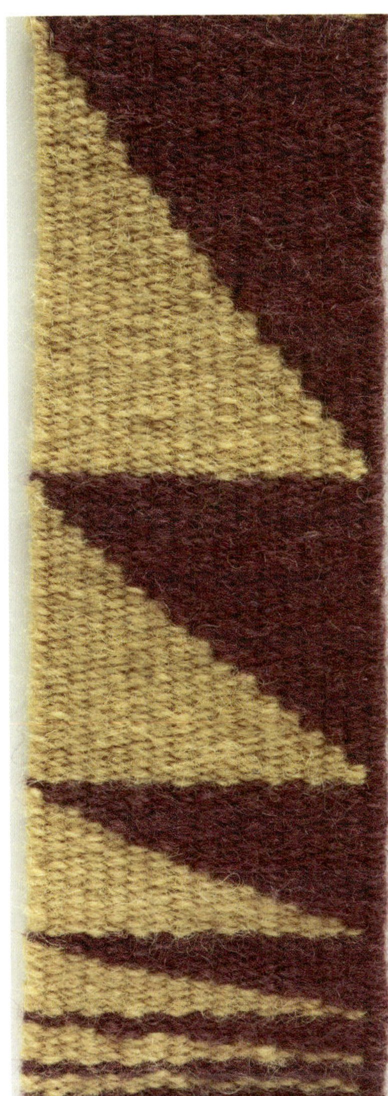

Sampler showing triangles starting at one edge, 2in wide, using 17 warps at 8 epi.

Woven at 11 epi. 12/6 fine cotton warp, cotton, wool, rayon, linen and silk weft.

TRIANGLES STARTING AT ONE EDGE

Here are the first three triangles from the sample, with differing shallow angles. At this warp setting, the line visibly undulates as the weft passes over and under the warps.

Graphing out is a technique used to work out the stepping sequence needed. Each pass is represented by a horizontal row of squares. Each warp is represented by a vertical line. Here we have chosen a warp of 17 because, allowing for a spare warp at the right-hand edge, the remaining 16 is divisible by two, four and eight which allows for the different angles to be formed.

The suggested starting point for each weft is marked 'x', and the finishing point with a small triangle with an arrow indicating the direction of weave. A paused weft is marked with a dot. These positions will ensure that all the wefts follow the same under/over sequence. The drawing shows that the longer the steps are made, the shallower the slope. To make a straight diagonal line, the stepping sequence must remain the same for its entire length. Also marked are the seven areas in the order in which they need to be woven.

This warp of 17 at 8 epi has been set up with header bands and twining as explained in Chapter 1, finishing with a row of double half hitches to secure the weft once cut off the loom. The warp is a medium-weight cotton and weft the same rug yarn as for the previous chapters.

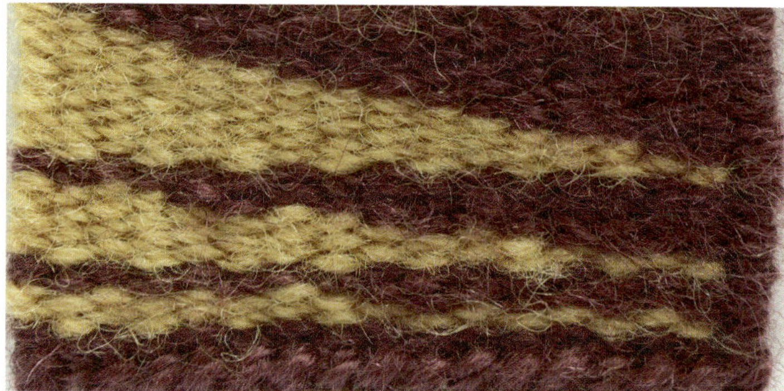

First three triangles from the sampler.

Graphing out the triangles.

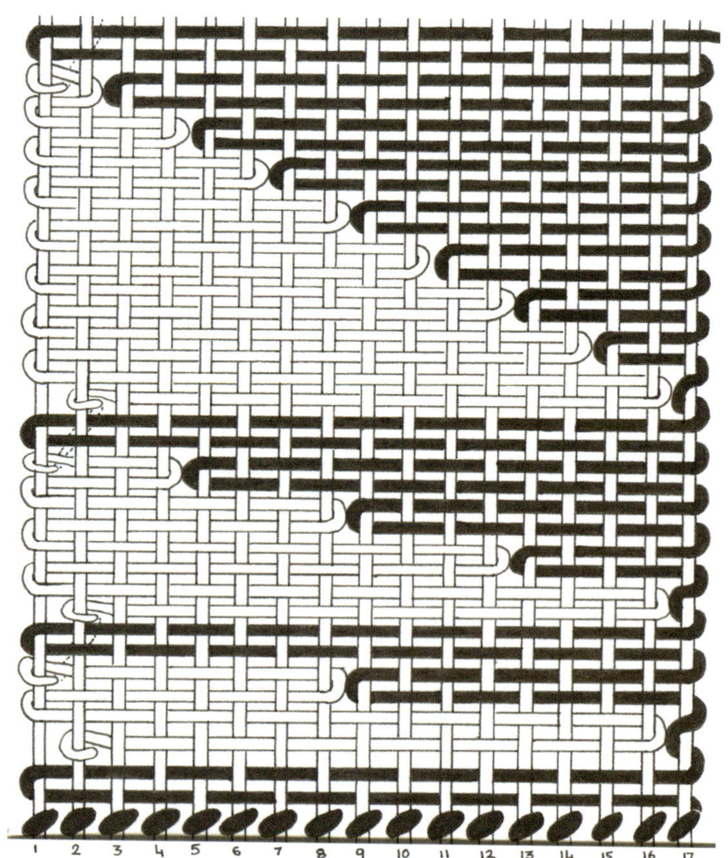

Weaving the first three triangles.

Looking from the bottom up, the weft used for *knotting on* weaves a pass then pauses at the right-hand side. Wefts always start on the first warp in the row which was uncovered in the previous row, so the warp for area 2 starts on the second and not the first warp. If unsure, *see* Chapter 2, 'Managing multiple wefts, a summary'. All the triangles in this sample begin and finish to the left for simplicity.

To form the first triangle, the weft turns on warp 16, then the next pass steps back by eight turning on warp 8. This is termed -8, in other words stepping back by eight warps. Notice, when finishing, this weft has passed through to the back ready to be *floated* up to start the next triangle. Next the darker weft is picked up and takes a turn once round the right-hand edge warp, then returns to meet the turn of the triangle already woven. We speak of this area (3) as '*filling*' or making the answering or negative form. This weft should pass over the layers of the already woven triangle, covering the warps previously left uncovered.

Next the second triangle, area 4, may be woven. The weft left hanging at the back after weaving area 2 is shown *floated up* at back of the piece. It is brought back through to the front to weave area 4 rather than starting a new weft. As for area 2, it weaves to the second last warp, then steps back by four warps at each subsequent pass, termed -4. Four passes are now needed to reach the top, finishing on the first warp and left hanging at the back. Again, the darker weft weaves the infill.

The last triangle (6) is formed, stepping back by two warps each pass (-2), taking eight passes to reach the top of this steeper slope. Finally, area 7 infills making a full pass to finish.

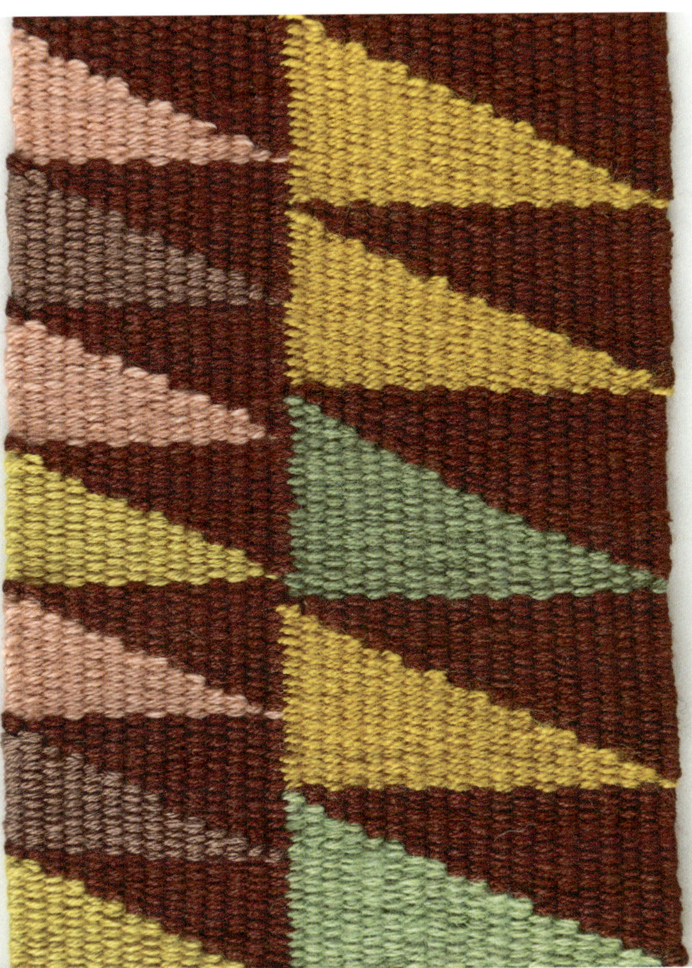

Interlocked triangles woven in cotton and linen. 8 x 12cm.

The fourth triangle

Continuing to work up the sample, this triangle now reduces by one warp on each pass. You may note that this diagonal looks more stepped than the previous slightly shallower one. This is because by turning on each warp, the turns now alternate between highs and lows. Looking closely at the line, you may see that alternate steps are slightly higher.

Here the weaving sequence is *graphed out*, showing each pass represented as a horizontal row of squares. Each pass reduces by one warp, represented by a vertical line. Now the triangle will take 16 passes to reach the top, and the infill likewise. Again, the suggested point to start is marked 'x'. The point to finish is marked by a small triangle, and a pause marked by a dot. An arrow shows the direction of weave. As before we suggest following these closely to ensure staying in shed until the principles become familiar and natural. Note that the height of the triangle in the drawn diagrams does not represent the actual height once woven. This will vary according to warp spacing, weft thickness and fibre.

First a pass of the darker weft has been woven to separate this triangle from the previous one. The weft pauses to the right-hand side. The triangle area 8 is formed, starting on the second warp, weaving to the right as far as the second last warp, then stepping back by one warp at every subsequent pass. Since weave is based on a grid, this stepped appearance is one of the characteristics which distinguishes it from, for example, a drawn line. The dividing pass between triangles is again shown, after which the weft pauses at the right-hand side.

Stepping by one warp each pass, this triangle comes to a single warp at the top. To weave round a single warp securely we suggest taking the weft under then back over as if to finish, then making a single half hitch – the same knot as used to secure a piece at the start and finish. The weft is then taken through to the back and the paused background weft picked up to infill area 9.

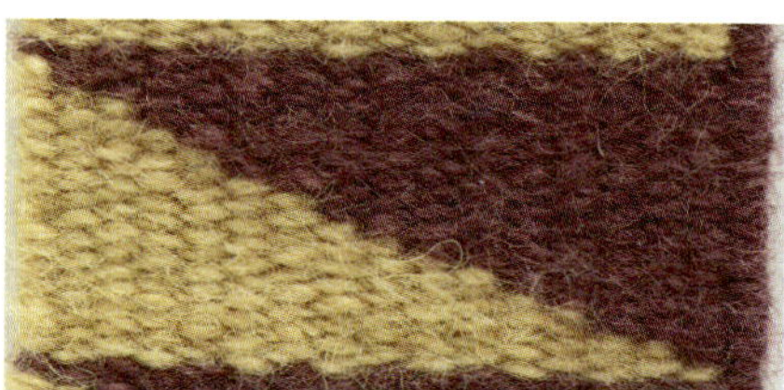

The fourth triangle in the sampler.

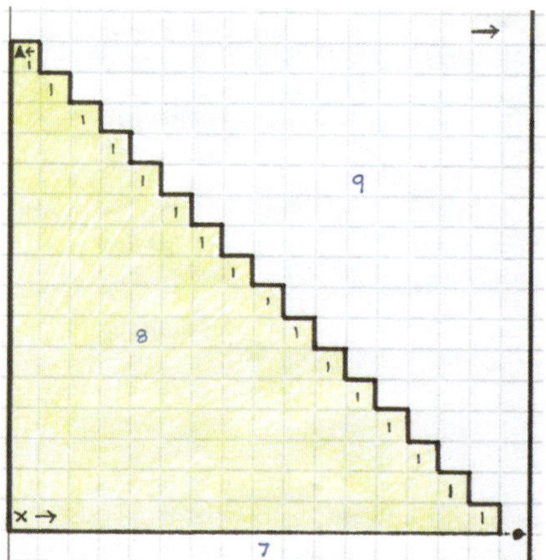

Graphing out the fourth triangle.

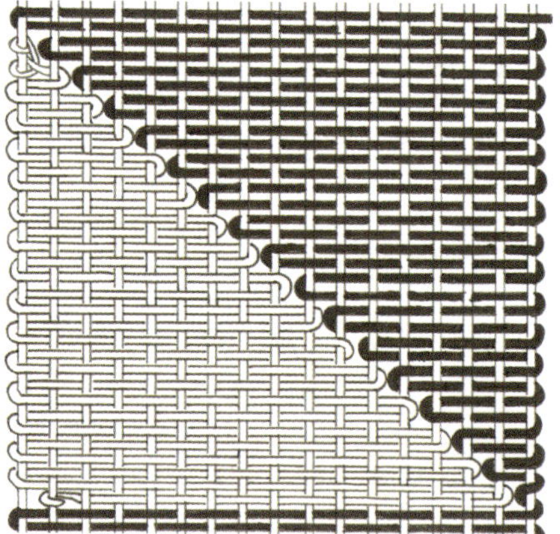

Weaving diagram for the fourth triangle.

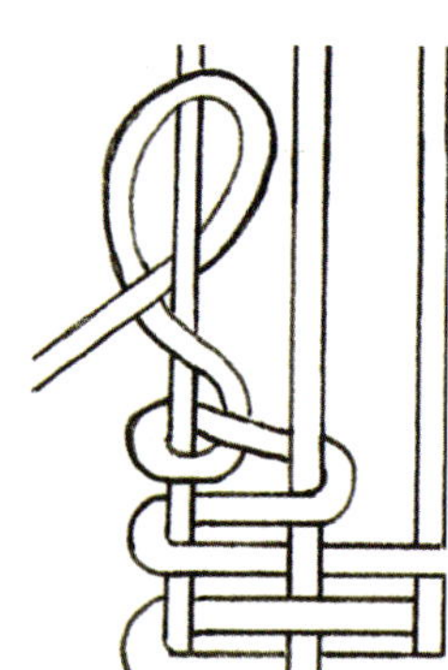

Half hitch to create a point.

Fifth triangle

Continuing working up the sample, here is the second to last triangle, forming a roughly 45-degree angle. The actual angle will also be influenced by the warp sett and *weft weight*. You may see that alternate steps are not quite equal in height because the weft has made high and low turns alternately.

A line in tapestry, or a meeting of two areas as in this case, will always show the quality of the underlying grid on which weave is formed. In tapestry a line is made, not drawn, and the structure creates its aesthetic quality.

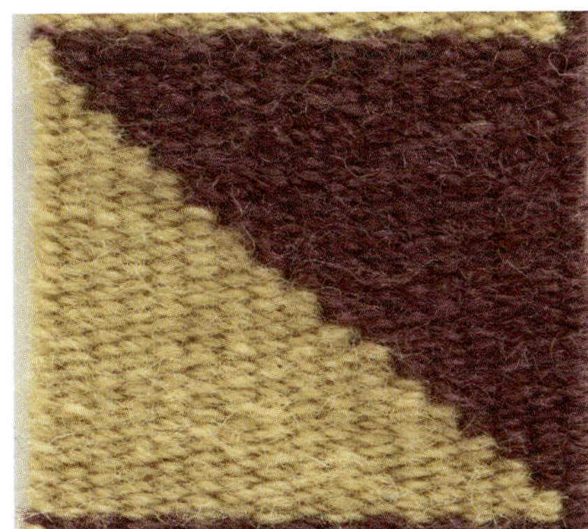
Fifth triangle in the sampler.

Graphing out the fifth triangle

Here is the same triangle drawn out on squared paper showing the stepping sequence.

Each horizontal row represents a pass as before, and each vertical line a weft – you will see that the weft makes two passes to each warp before stepping back by one warp. This is termed +2, meaning two weft turns to each warp before stepping back by one warp.

As before the term 'stepping back' is applied to forming a shape, in this case the yellow triangle, area 10. The infill simply meets the turns made by the formed triangle rather than being given a numbered sequence.

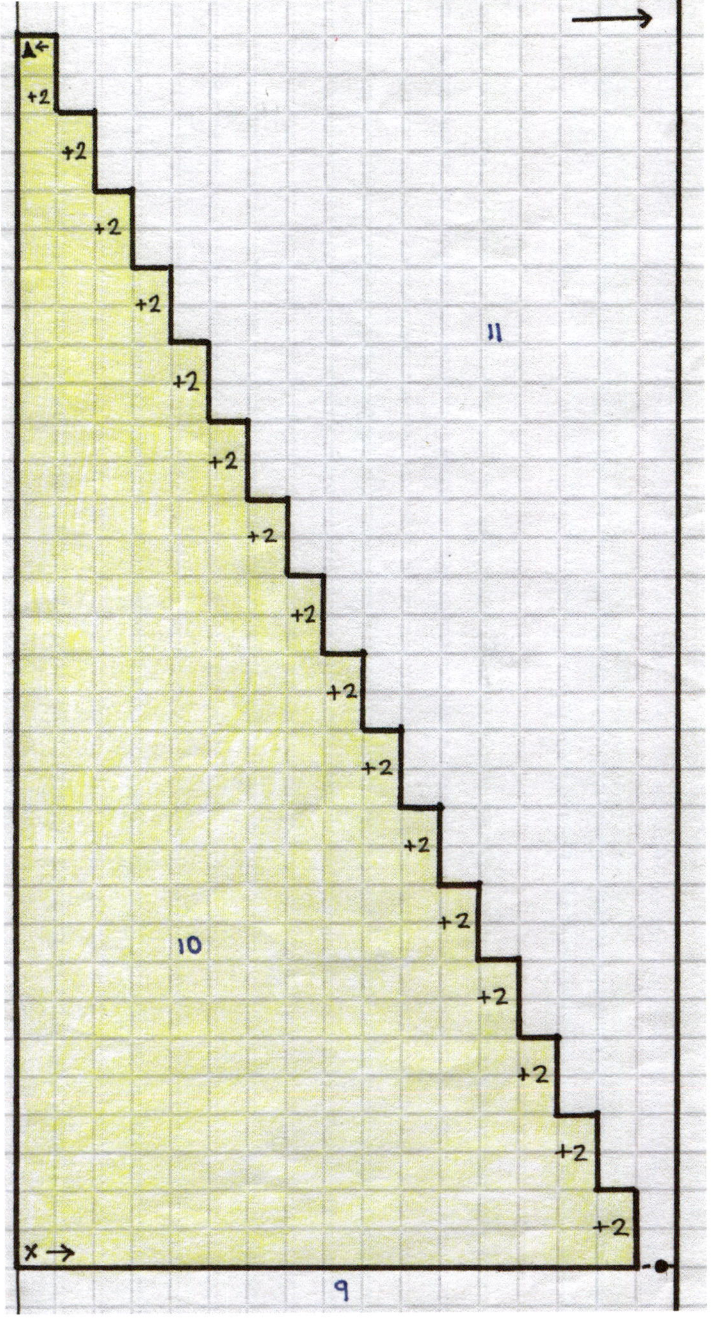

Graphing out the fifth triangle.

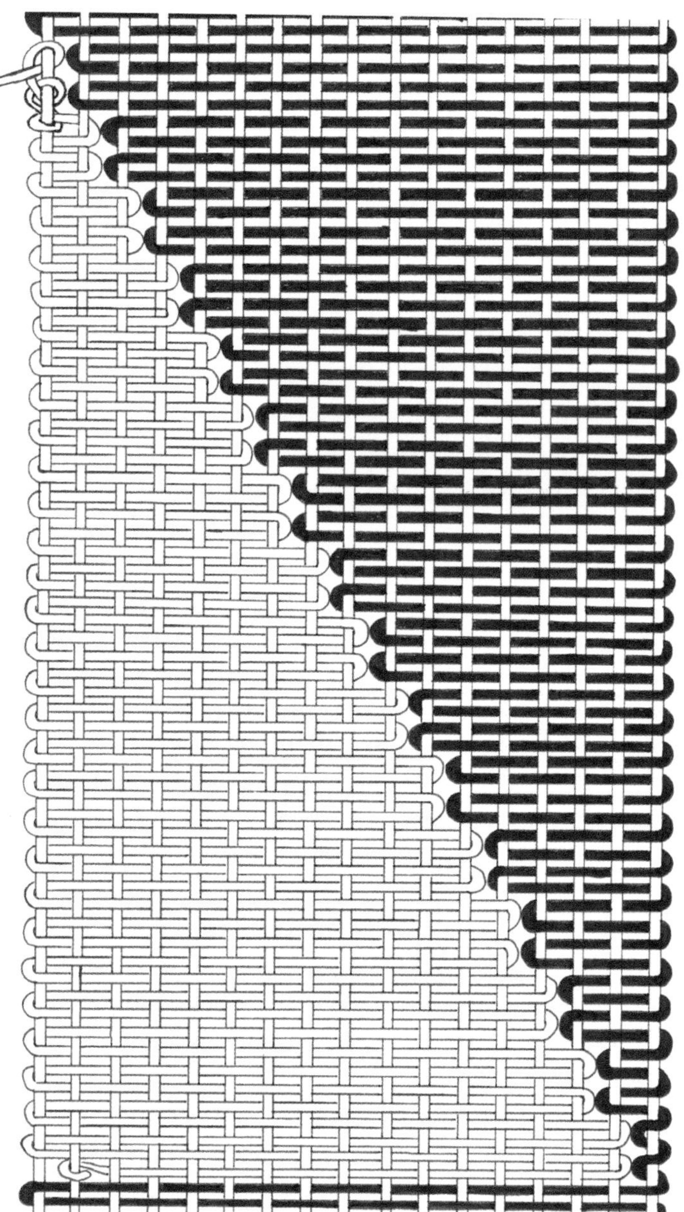

Weaving diagram of the fifth triangle.

Weaving diagram, fifth triangle

Again the weft starts on the second warp in from the left and extends to the sixteenth. It makes two passes to each warp before stepping back by one. The triangle will now take 32 passes to complete.

Again finishing on a single warp at the top point, the weft is first tucked in as for a finish, then given two half hitches in the same way as starting or finishing a piece. Finally the infill, area 11, may be woven.

The final triangle on the sample has not been illustrated, but you may wish to continue and weave it. It varies from this triangle only in being +3 in place of +2, so that you would weave three passes to each warp before stepping back by one warp. The finishing point would then be made by adding three half hitches.

The whole sample is finished by taking a pass right across, then a row of double half hitches to secure.

TRIANGLES INSET WITHIN A PIECE AND CHOOSING HIGH AND LOW TURNS

Viewed from the bottom up are two triangles of the same incline, the first turning on *high warps*, the second on low, showing the difference in smoothness.

A warp of 17 has been chosen so that there is a central warp on which the middle pair of triangles ends and starts. If the size of your loom allows, this sample may continue from the last, as the warp number, weight and sett are the same. Beware never to try weaving further than three-quarters of the way up your frame, otherwise the warp may become unworkably tight and the warps too widely separated by the thickness of the top bar.

For designs involving multiple and more complex shapes, planning is increasingly helpful. Starting from the bottom, each area is numbered in order of weave. The underlying areas are always woven before any overlying areas, and with the largest possible areas woven in one go. Also, by observing the progress of the first green weft, you will see that it pauses five times on its way up the right-hand side but is actually continuous from start to finish. Each of the bottom two triangles is woven with the weft starting at the edge. Areas 6 and 7, 9 and 10, 12 and 13 are woven by pairs of wefts started and finished alongside each other. The continuous weft extends from the right side across the piece to weave dividing passes and to finish. To form the 14 areas of this sample, only three separate wefts have been used; two green and one yellow.

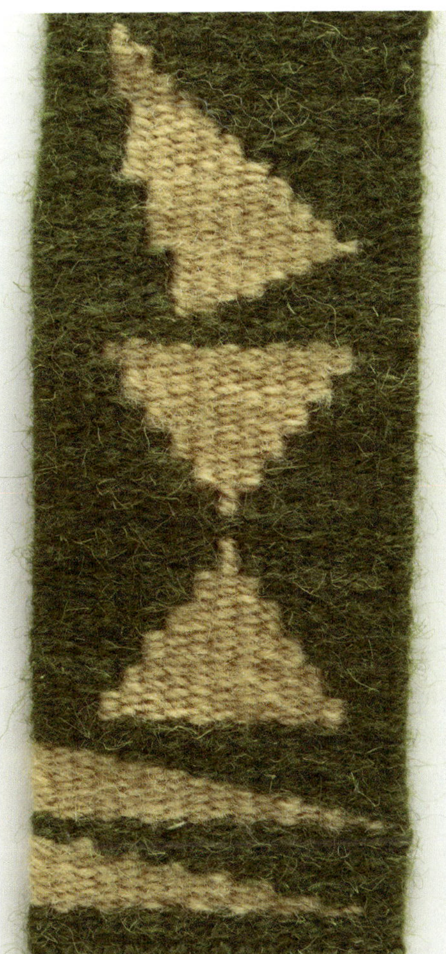

Triangles sampler. 17 warps, 8 epi.

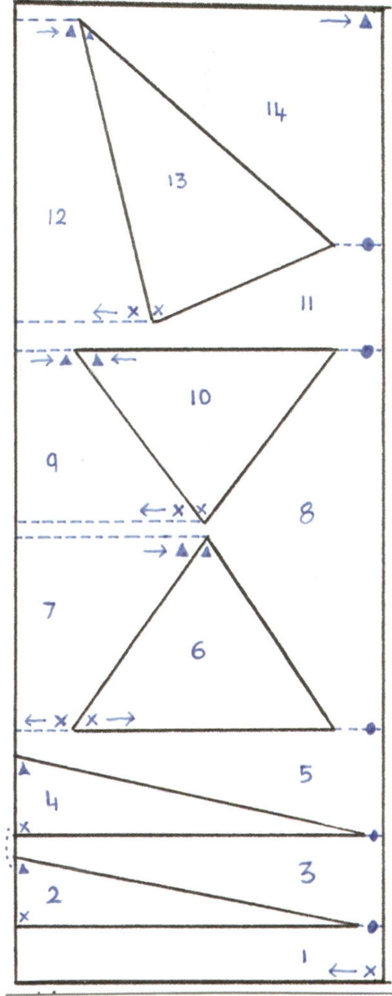

The weaving sequence for triangles sampler.

Turning on a high warp

Here is the first triangle at the bottom of the sample, area 2. You may see that this triangle extends to the third warp from the right and steps back by two warps at each pass, termed -2. Looking closely at the diagram you will note that the turns have been made on warps which were covered in the previous row of weave, passing first under then over the end warp. This is termed a high turn. Although not evident in the drawn diagram, the higher, more pronounced steps show clearly in the woven sample.

Turning on a low warp

Here you will see that the next triangle, area 4, extends one warp further, to the second last warp from the right. By extending by one more warp, the weft now turns on the warp left uncovered on the previous row, thereby making low turns in which the weft passes first over then under the warp. A low turn is lower than a high turn, so although this triangle also steps back by two warps at each pass, forming exactly the same incline, the steps in the slope are much less pronounced in appearance. This is a feature to be conscious of in designing a piece depending on the aesthetic effect desired.

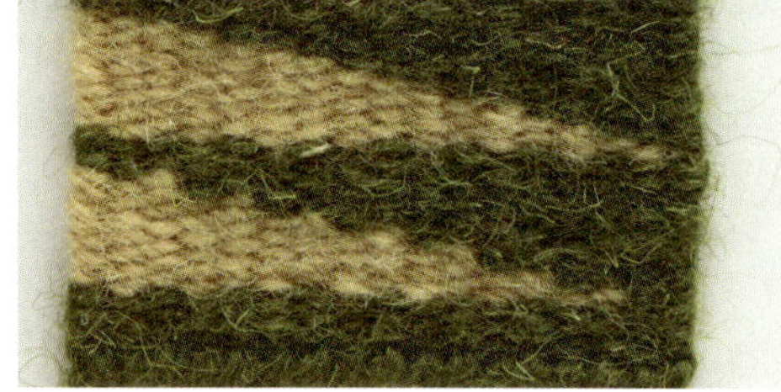

Bottom triangle: turning on a high warp; top triangle: turning on a low warp.

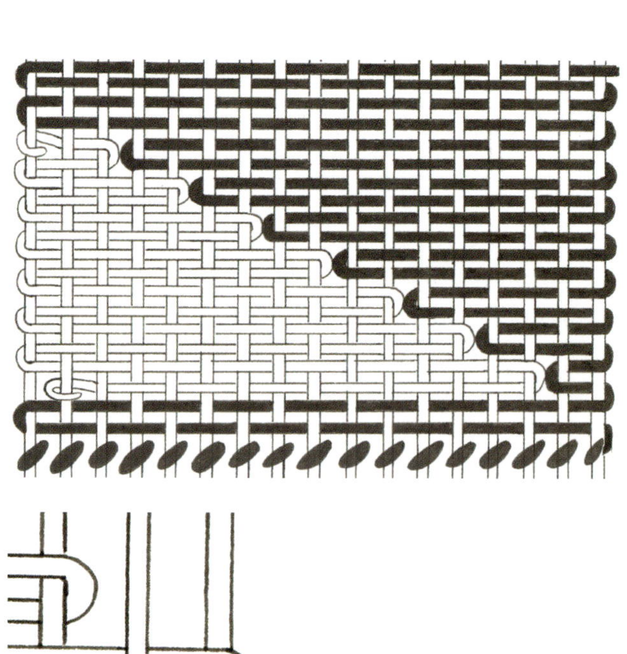

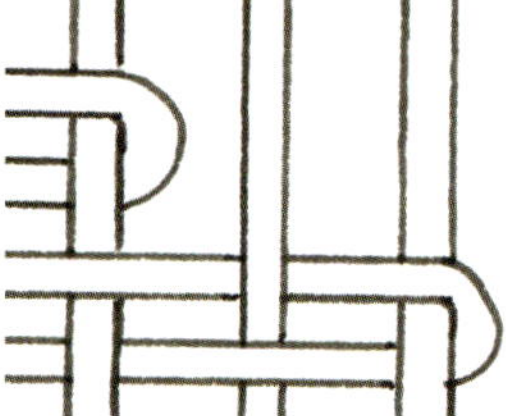

Turning on a high warp.

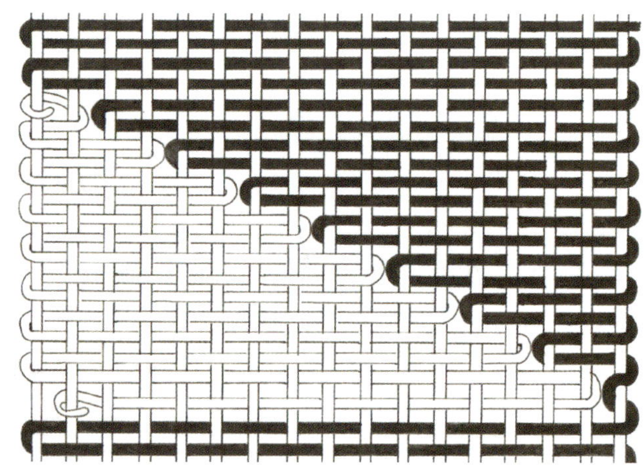

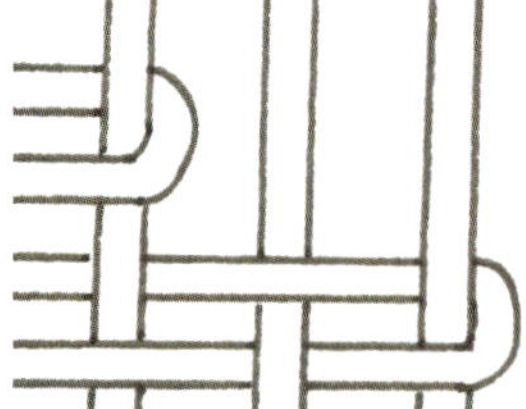

Turning on a low warp.

Triangle area 6

Starting on warp 4 and extending to the fourth from the right, this triangle sits in the centre of the sample. It is advisable to start the weft for area 7 at the same time so that you don't lose track of where the weft for the triangle started (although this can always be checked by looking at the back of the weaving). This triangle makes three passes to each warp before stepping back by one, termed +3.

Note, at the peak, the weft is wound round the final warp three times which could have been secured with a half hitch but since they are soon to be continued at the bottom of another triangle, they will stay secure. The dotted line shows the weft being taken to the back and floated up to start the next triangle.

Once the triangle is complete, the left-hand weft can continue, finishing adjacent to the peak. Finally the right-hand infill can be woven and extended across the whole warp to make a divide from the next triangle.

Triangle area 10

Extending outwards from the point, this inverted triangle has to have the infill woven first so that the background wefts now become the forming wefts and the lighter weft for the triangle is the infill.

Note, there is a warp left between the background areas which will form the peak of the triangle. The right-hand weft which has just completed the dividing pass may continue directly on to weave the remainder of area 8, on which the right-hand slope of the triangle will rest. Next at the left-hand side, either a new weft may be started adjacent to the peak, or the weft floated at the back from where it finished at the corner of the previous triangle. This weft weaves up to the top edge of what is to be the triangle, making three passes to each warp before stepping back (+3, +3 +3), finishing on warp 3.

Finally, the triangle may be infilled. Taking the paused weft from the back three turns are made, right to left around the central warp. The direction is important to establish the direction of weave for the rest of the triangle. Finish to the left adjacent to the left-hand weft on the fifth warp, then weave the right-hand background weft over the top.

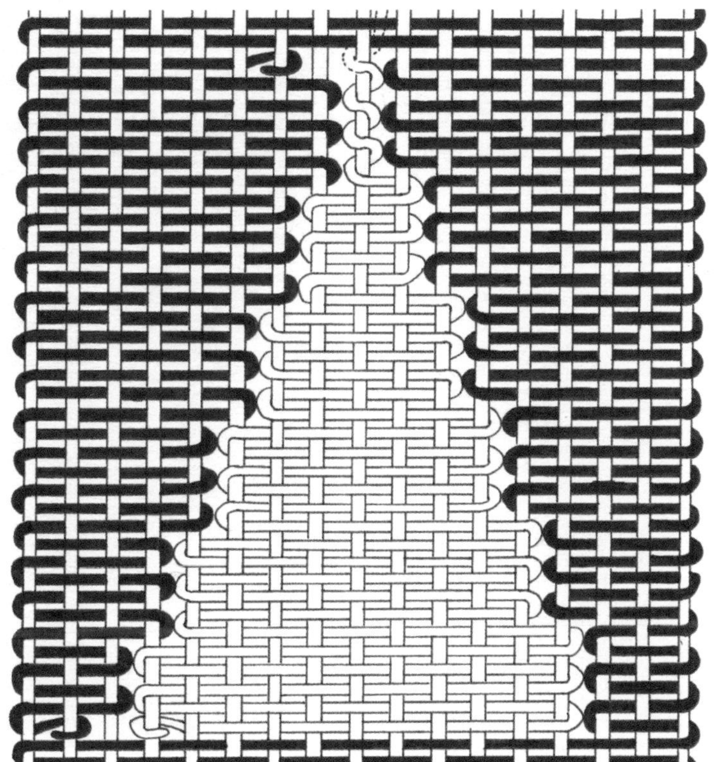

Triangle area 6. Weaving sequence area 6.

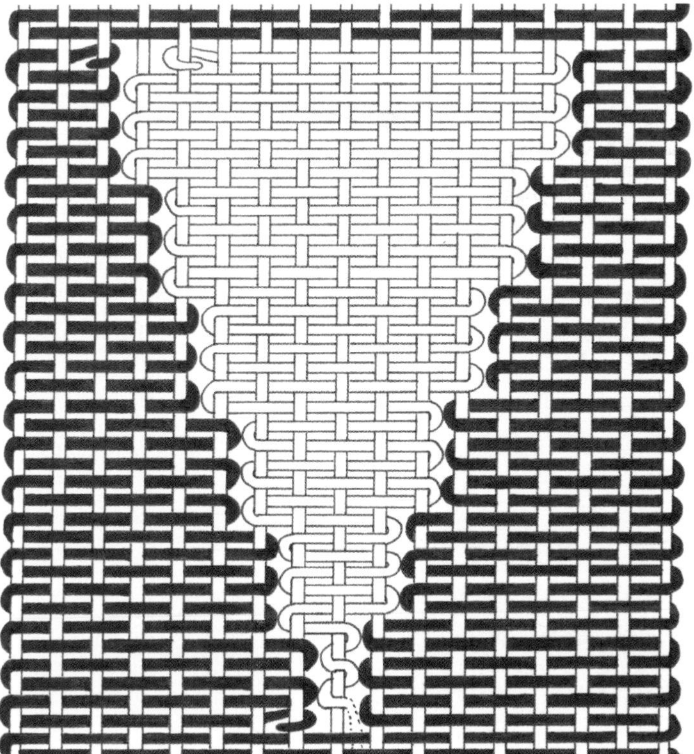

Triangle area 10. Weaving sequence area 10.

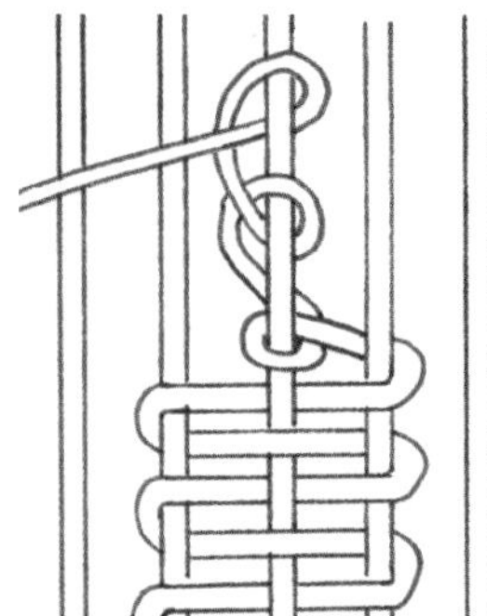

Finishing on one warp. Here the top point of the triangle is shown finished with a turn and two half hitches following the direction of weave from the triangle. As an alternative to just winding round this is more stable, particularly if the weft is finishing at this point instead of being floated up.

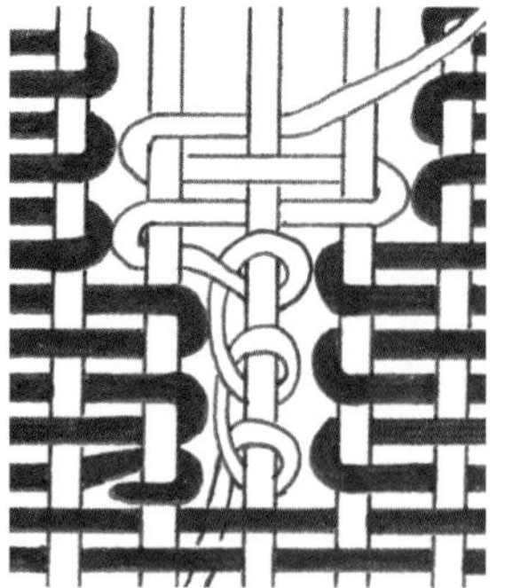

Starting on one warp. Here the weft has been floated up and takes three half hitches around the single warp which will form the point of the triangle. To see what direction the warp needs to turn it is necessary to look further up to the first pass of three warps. This weft will need to cover the warps left uncovered in the previous row, which as the drawing illustrates means it will pass first from left to right.

TRIANGLE WITH THREE DIFFERENT ANGLES

Because the triangle extends outwards from the start, it is the background which needs to be formed first. First the weft which has woven a pass across the sample may form the background area to the right, stepping back -1 up to the point where the triangle turns. This takes a total of nine passes before pausing.

A new weft has been started adjacent to the bottom point of the triangle, leaving one warp to start on. The whole of area 12 is woven up to the top in one go. To weave this extreme angle, an alternating sequence of +7 and +8 has been chosen. Although only stepping back by one warp at a time, the steps are now very marked.

Next the actual triangle can be formed. Starting at the point, the weft turns right to left so that it weaves in the opposing direction to the already formed background areas. Meeting the turns on the left-hand edge it makes two passes to each warp before stepping back by one, termed +2. It finishes on one warp with a turn and two half hitches to secure.

The upper right side of the background (area 14) is now completed with two passes to each warp, +2 finally taking a pass across the piece before securing the sample with a row of double half hitches.

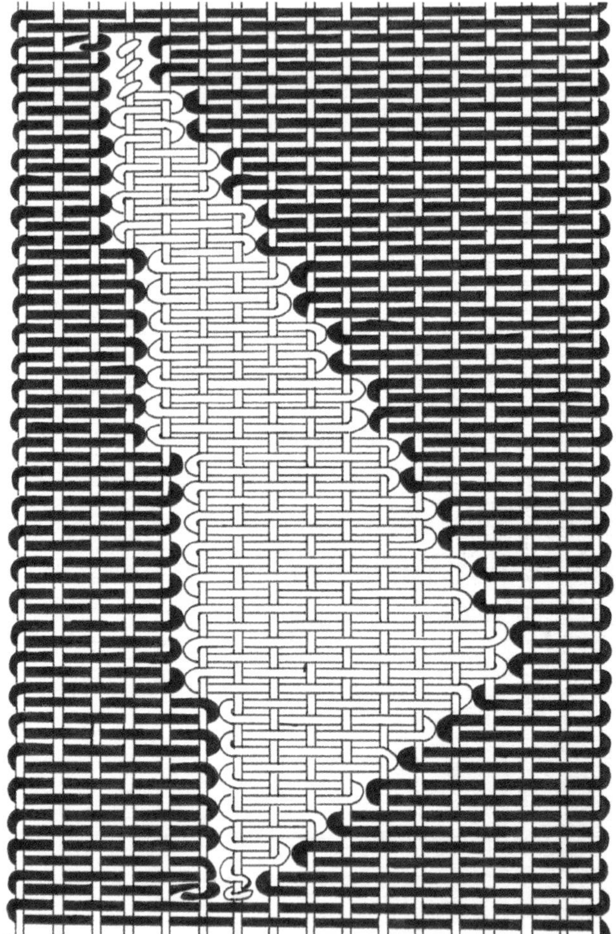

Triangle with three different angles.

TRIANGLES COMING TO A POINT OF TWO WARPS

These two answering triangles have been woven on 16 warps sett at 8 epi. This allows for the triangles to be woven in the centre of the sample, with a minimum of three warps of background on either side. By weaving the triangles with an even number of warps (in this case ten), they will come to a point of two instead of one warp. This avoids the need for finishing on a single warp which can be difficult to do neatly and securely. To weave this sample, you will need to put on a new warp, this time with 16 warps. This will mean that the warp will start and finish at the bottom of your loom. The same warp sett of 8 epi has been used here, with a medium-weight cotton warp. The weft is a single strand of wool rug yarn as before. These have been chosen for ease of learning, being convenient to handle and clear in their woven effect. After the header bands and twining, one of the wefts is used to make a row of double half hitches to secure the weaving, then makes several passes right across the sample. Always insert the weft in a series of mounds rather than straight across to avoid the tension becoming too tight.

Because the background overlays the lower triangle, it is the triangle which must be woven first. Start on the fifth warp with a contrasting weft. You may notice that this is actually one warp in from the corner. This is because the fourth is a high and a weft must always start on a low warp. Choosing the right warp at this stage is vital to establishing a sequence which will work for the whole sample. You may also see that the background weft to the left starts nearby and that the two weave in opposing directions. It is useful to start both wefts at the same time to get their relative positions right. Note, there will always be one warp left in between which will be covered in the next row.

First the triangle is woven, making three turns to each warp and finishing on two warps. Next the background weft which started at the same time weaves the infill to the left, turning at each point it meets the triangle and finishing level with the top. Finally, the original weft can weave up the right-hand side and over the top to finish.

Triangles coming to a point of two warps.

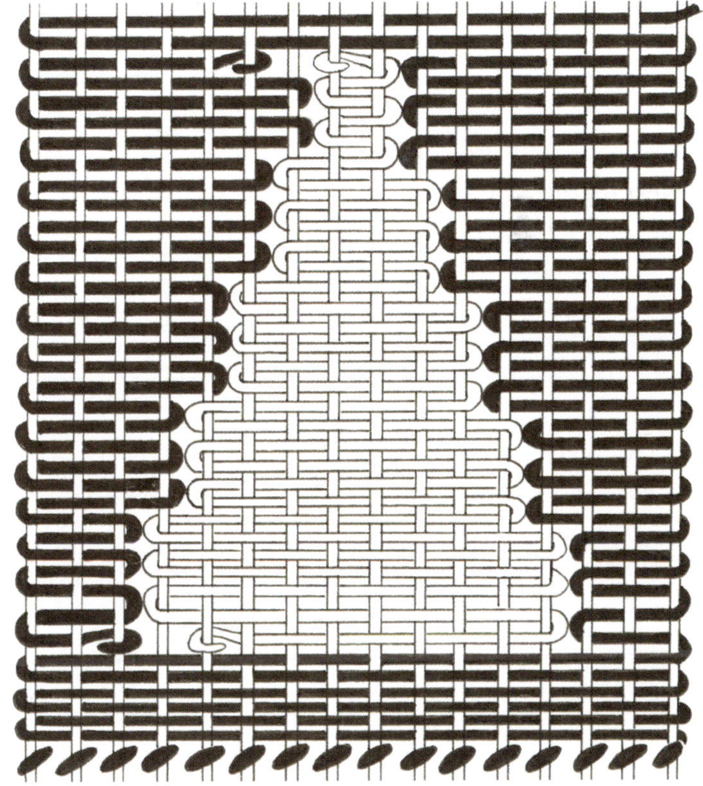

Diagram of a triangle woven with a point of two warps.

Finishing on two warps

Here the finishing of the first triangle in this sample is illustrated. Continuing the sequence of weaving three passes to each warp, the triangle has now reached the final two warps. To finish, the weft has been taken behind both warps in the final row, then back over the second and through to the back of the weaving. The dotted line shows this weft being floated up at the back of the weaving. The next diagram shows how it is used to start the next triangle, coming back through to the front in between the two starting warps, and over and round the right-hand weft before continuing to weave the triangle.

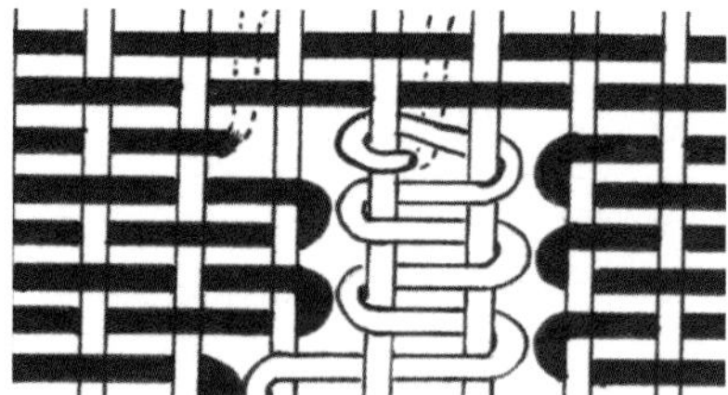

Diagram of finishing on two warps. Wefts are shown floated up at the back.

Weaving the second triangle

After making a couple of passes to divide the two triangles, the right-hand background weft weaves up to where the next triangle will begin. By stepping back by one warp every three passes, +3, it forms the negative shape in which the inverted triangle will sit, then pauses at the level the triangle is to finish. To weave the left-hand negative shape, a new weft has been started alongside what will become the tip of the triangle, leaving a space of two warps. As always, the choice of warp on which to start is the one left uncovered by the previous row of weaving. Using the same +3 stepping sequence as the right side, it forms the infill for this symmetrical triangle. Finishing level with the right-hand side, this weft passes first under two warps, then turns back over one and through to the back below the turn. Next the triangle may be woven in one go, using the weft floated up from the previous triangle. It is finished in the same way, alongside the point where the weft to its left is finished, as ever, with one warp left in between. Finally, the weft paused at the right side may weave a few passes over the top and *knot off* to secure.

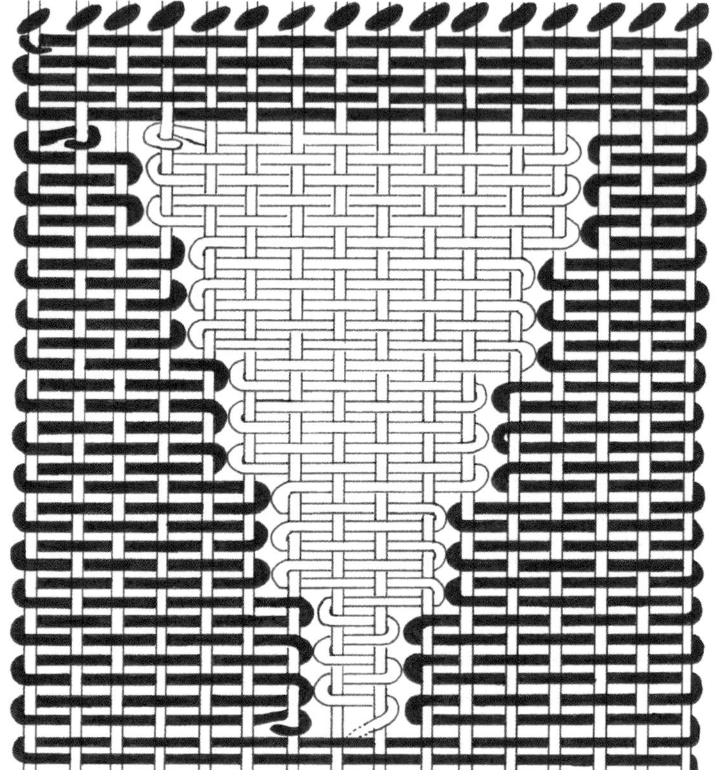

Weaving diagram of the second triangle.

TRIANGLES STEPPING BACK BY TWO WARPS

Here, instead of stepping back on each warp to make the smoothest diagonal line possible, the triangles step back by two warps at a time, with three passes on each level. These block-based geometric patterns are to be found in folk weaves from all over the world and play very much to the strength of tapestry as a grid-based medium.

This sample has a warp of 16 which accommodates this stepped triangular form with a point of two warps width. The warp sett remains at 8 epi with the same rug yarn weft. Note the slightly sloping steps of the lower triangle, where the low turns give a much less definite step. By contrast the upper triangle follows exactly the same weaving sequence, giving very regular right-angled steps formed by high turns.

A design with this kind of stepped line might be one instance where high turns would be chosen in preference to the low turns used to smooth out a diagonal line. As with so many aspects of the aesthetic of woven tapestry, it is the structure of warp and weft which prevails. Whilst this may be seen as a physical constraint, in fact it is the very presence of the warp and the bead formed as the weft passes over it that produces the distinctive surface quality of woven tapestry.

Weaving triangles stepping back by two warps

This sample follows the same order of areas woven as the previous two. The right-hand background weft continues from the start to the finish, albeit being paused at several points. From the bottom upwards, having first woven a pass all the way across, the right-hand weft pauses to the right. The weft for the triangle and for the left-hand infill are started together, adjacent to each other and weave in opposing directions.

First the triangle is woven on a +3, -2 sequence, making three passes to each point before stepping back by two warps, in this case, the same on both sides. Next the paused left-hand weft may weave the infill, finishing level with the top row of the triangle. The right-hand weft may now weave the infill and a few passes right across the piece before continuing to form the right-hand stepped background for the upper, inverted triangle. Again, a new left-hand weft is started, or floated up, allowing a space of two warps for the triangle. With the background complete, the triangle may now be woven, again with three passes to each point before stepping, this time outwards by two warps. Finally, the right-hand weft completes a few passes right across the piece to finish.

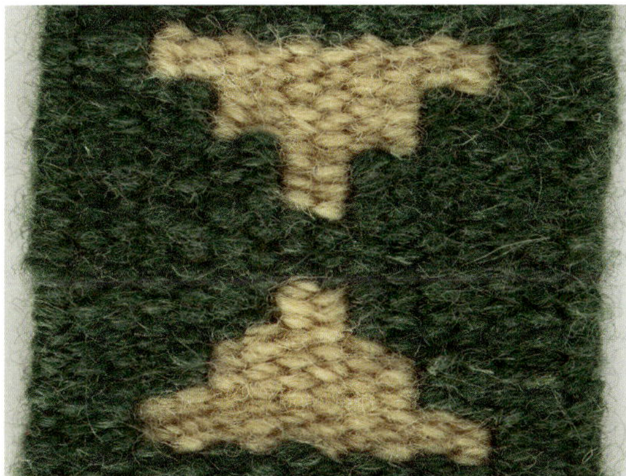

Triangles stepping back by two warps.

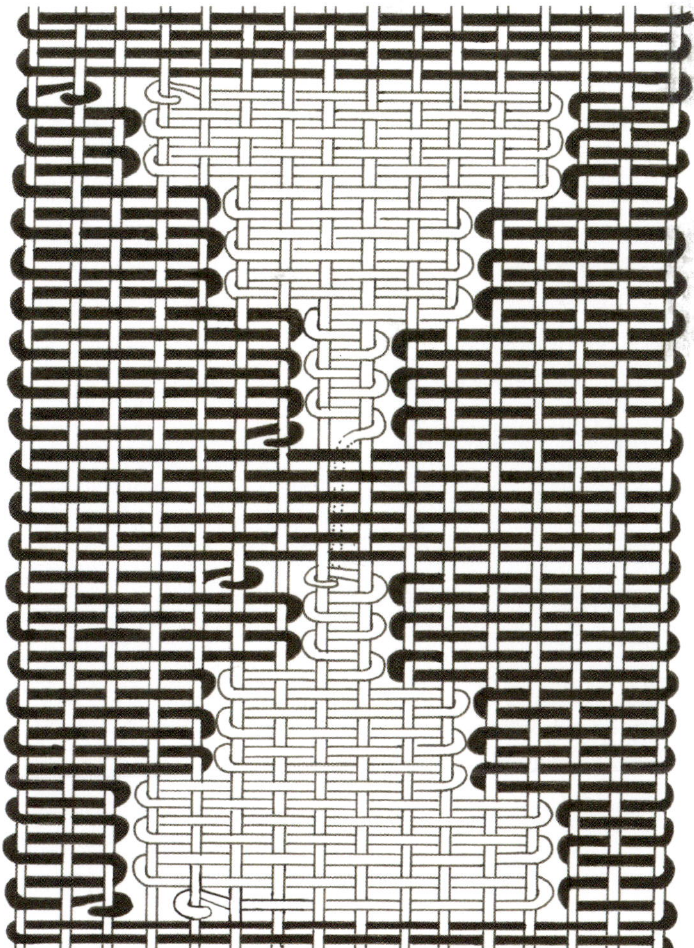

Weaving diagram of triangles stepping back by two warps.

A STRIPED TRIANGLE

Although this sample may appear more complex, the weaving of it is not. There are still only three wefts used, with the striped area made by simply exchanging one colour for another whilst weaving continuously.

This sample uses 18 warps at the slightly closer setting of 9 epi. This allows the triangle to sit centrally with two warps of background to each side at the base. Note, the height of the drawn-out triangle does not represent the reality once woven and packed down. This triangle is woven at +5, so making five passes to each warp before stepping back by one. You may wish to experiment with choosing your own angles for this triangle, in which case choose a stepping sequence and continue with it from bottom to top.

Keep taking care to commence wefts correctly. The left-hand and triangle wefts start adjacent to each other with a warp left in between. When changing from one colour to another in the stripes, take care to start a new colour so that it falls into the next hollow in the previous row. It should weave on from the previous colour as if it were a continuous weft.

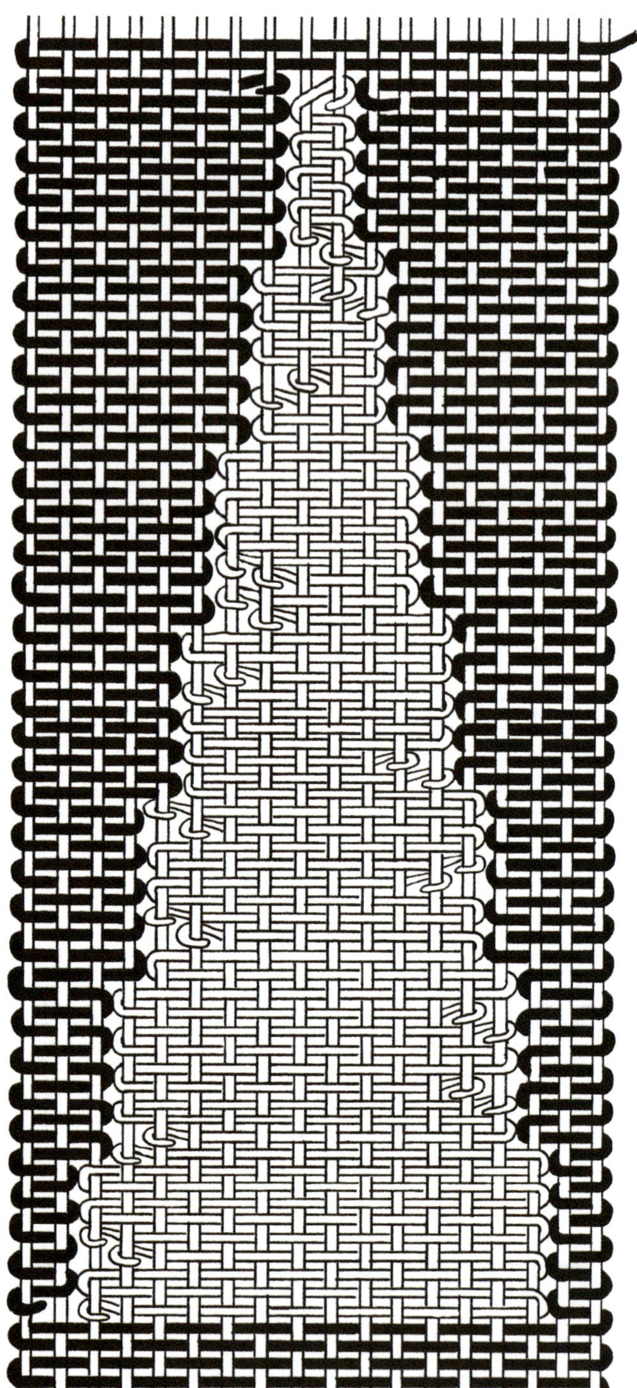

Striped triangle weaving diagram.

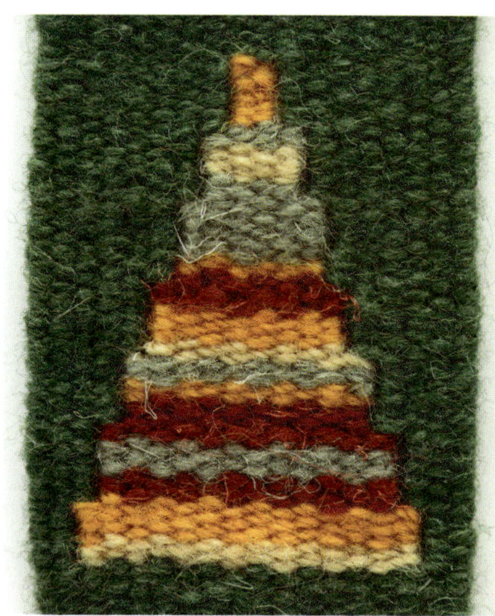

Weaving a striped triangle.

AN EXERCISE COMBINING TRIANGLES AND STRIPES

There are several ways to undertake this exercise in forming different angled triangles with a randomly striped infill. The diagram shows the woven sample graphed out so that the stepping sequence is visible, and the areas of weave are numbered in the order of being woven.

There is a choice to work to a graphed-out design or to work directly onto the loom. Either way, once a stepping sequence for the forming area is decided upon, continue with it till the triangle is complete.

Note, all the wefts here begin at either the left or the right-hand edge. This ensures that in overlaying areas the weft will fall neatly into the hollows left by the previous row as they should.

The infill should always meet the turns of the already formed shape, matching the number of passes. Once the weave is packed down the number of passes may no longer be obvious; if so, the wefts may be pushed up at the turn.

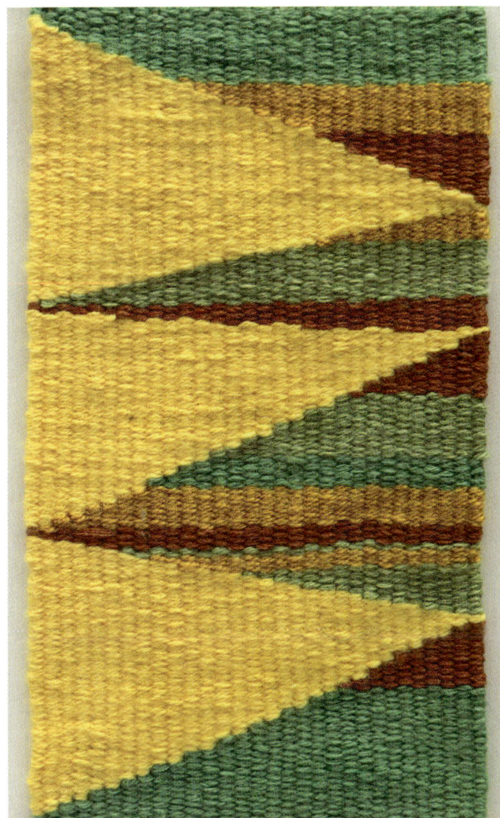

Choosing and forming varied angles. 30 warps, 10 epi.

It is useful to become familiar with what an incline of for example -1 or +2 looks like. A sample including several different inclines can be a helpful reference when making future designs.

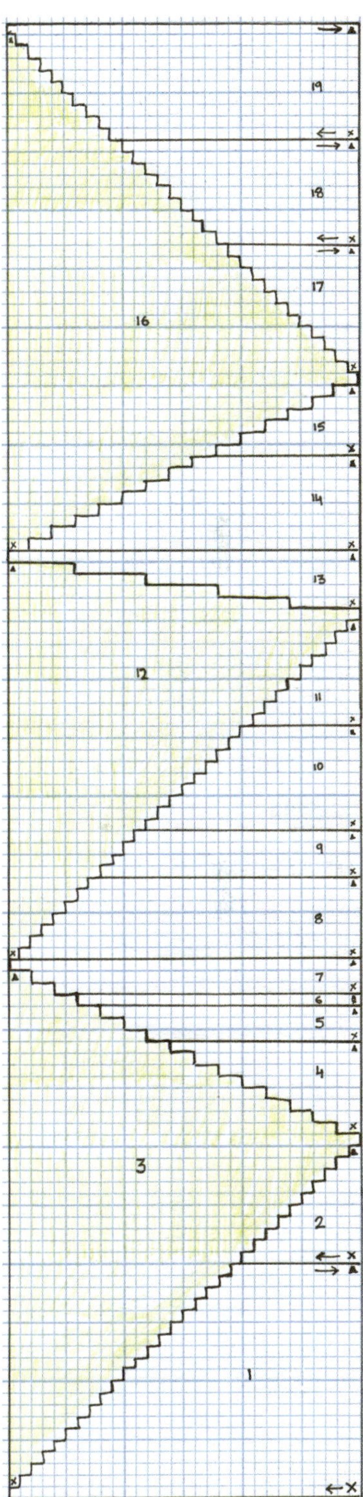

Varied angles sample graphed out.

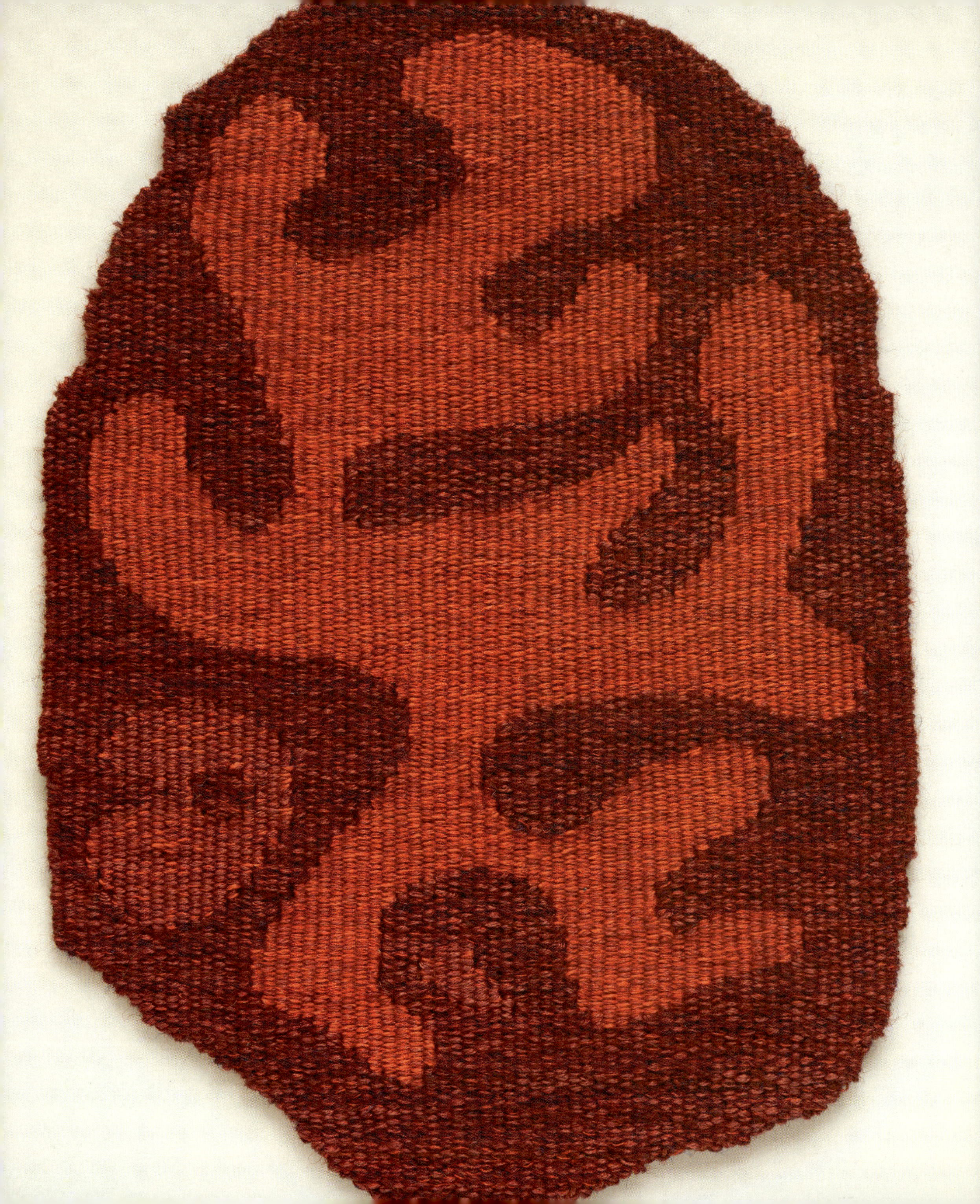

CHAPTER 4

CURVES

This chapter introduces the choices available and techniques needed to weave sweet, visually convincing curves. We aim to demonstrate how concave and convex curves are formed and at variable steepness of incline. As with most marks, a curve in tapestry has a particular aesthetic which offers both expressive possibilities and technical challenges.

Broadly speaking, the forming of curves in tapestry relies on choices about how many passes to make to a given warp, and by how many warps to step. You will see from the samples and diagrams how to translate a drawn curve into weave using both marked warps and by 'graphing out' to work out a stepping sequence.

Having dealt with the more geometric forms of stripes, squares and triangles where warps must be planned and counted, weaving a curve is to some extent a freer, more instinctual process. With experience, it is possible to form curves at the loom without planning. The learning in this chapter is more about making considered choices, and as such represents a transition towards applying tapestry technique by close observation and informed intuition rather than set instruction.

Although the samples in this chapter continue to work with the same warp sett and weft weight, once the principles are learned we hope that you will be able to make different choices of warp and sett, and to begin working with other weft yarns.

Through the exercises, you will see that when weaving curves, areas need to be formed and filled alternately. At times the actual shape being made will be the one to be woven first. At other times the background will have to lead, by forming the negative shape. There are principles for working out the order in which to weave areas which will be explained.

As with triangles, a curved line in weave is in effect a series of steps. Curved forms may be a combination of steps of one or more warp and include straight vertical sections where several passes are made to the same warp. The piece shown opposite is of 15cm (6in) dimension and has been woven at 12 epi. In this chapter we will begin to see more clearly the effect different choices of warp sett have, in this case on the smoothness of a curved line.

A further factor affecting the line of a curve is the choice to turn on either low or high warps.In a line which is actually a series of steps, the visual impact of these steps will be considerably reduced when making low rather than high turns.

If you are working through the sample, we anticipate that at the conclusion of this chapter you will have become familiar with how the weft packs down to form different curves. You will be equipped to decide on the order of weaving for areas in a design. You will know how to manage the wefts to keep in shed throughout a piece. This awareness we hope will be the basis from which you will be able to weave curves in your designs and begin to explore a wider range of weft material and warp settings.

Shaped tapestry. 12 epi. Red cotton 12/6 warp, cotton, stainless steel and linen weft.

WEAVING THREE DIFFERENT CURVES

This sample is woven on a medium 12/9 cotton warp of 24 at 8 epi, with header bands, a row of double half hitches and twining. Starting a sample with a few passes right across helps settle the warp spacing and make sure the back and *front warps* lie level with each other. The weft used is as before, a single strand of wool rug yarn.

Here the weaving sequence is shown, with warps represented by the vertical lines, and weft passes by the horizontal rows of squares. Unlike weaving a straight diagonal line, a curve is formed of rather irregular-looking steps. The bottom curve is a shallow concave line. The next two are of increasing incline and with both concave and convex sections. Each step is marked, so that for example -2 means step back by two warps. The number of passes turning on the same warp is indicted with a +, so that for example +3 means make three passes to this warp.

Note, the height of the forms in this diagram do not correspond to the actual height when woven. Graphed-out diagrams are included as a plan to follow when learning. They are designed to help a developing weaver to see how making steps or building up passes will appear on the loom.

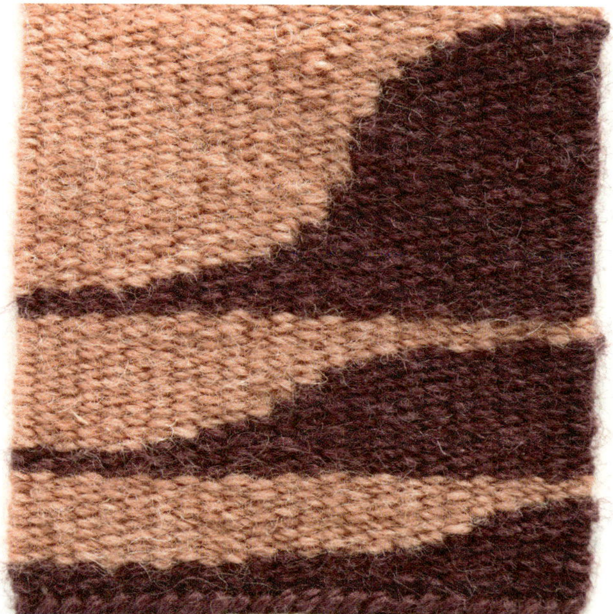

Sample with three curved inclines.

The point at which the wefts have started and ended are marked as previously with an 'x' to start and a triangle to finish. The sequence in which the areas need to be woven is numbered from the bottom upwards.

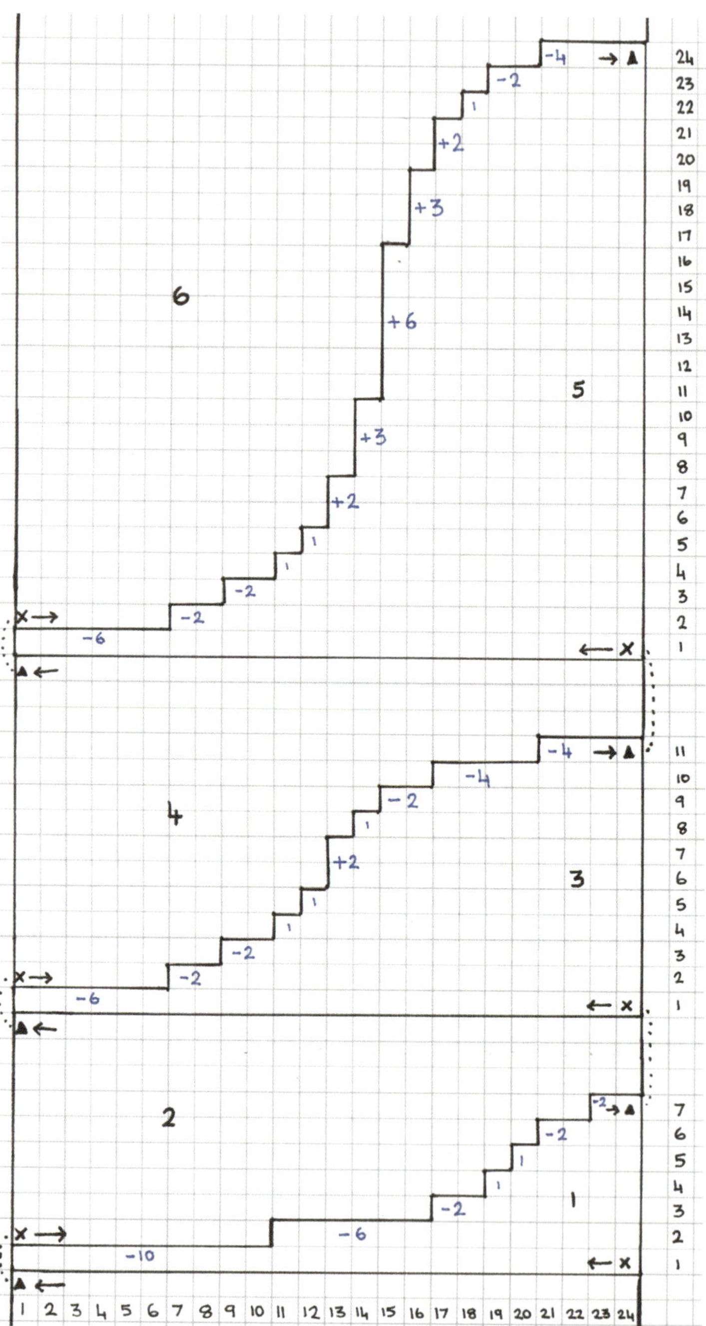

The sample graphed out , with areas numbered 1–6 in order of weave.

Weaving sequence for the first two curves

Here the steps outlined in the previous diagram are translated into actual weave. The weft used for knotting on may then form the first curved shape. Having first woven a couple of passes right across the piece, the first step back is -10 warps, the second -6, then -2, 1, 1, -2 and -2 to finish. Where possible the curve has been drawn so that each pass turns on a low warp, giving a smoother line. Having started with a low turn, subsequent steps back have been made in even numbers so that all the turns will be low. At the top of the curve the weft is taken through to the back and paused.

The next weft is started at the left-hand edge and woven inwards to meet the first turn on the curve. Note, each pass of the infilling area (marked 2 on the previous diagram) meets the turn of the curved form (area 1). After a couple of passes right across, this weft finishes on the left side and the paused right-hand weft is taken through from the back to weave the next curved form. This steeper curve has a different weaving sequence, first making a long step back, -6, then -2, -2 followed by two steps of 1,1, +2, 1, -2, -4, -4 to finish. The weft again finishes at the same side as it began, in this case on the right. Finally, the infill is woven in area 4, including a couple of passes right across to finish.

The third and steepest curved form

Here it becomes clear that a curve in tapestry actually includes straight sections, in this sample up to six passes. In diagram form this may look unlikely, and the step is indeed noticeable in the woven sample. As with diagonals, this stepped quality is simply a characteristic of a curved line in tapestry. As a constructed medium, this is one of many times when the aesthetic effect shows how it has been made. However, you may see from the image at the opening of the chapter, showing dynamic curved lines woven in all directions, that the eye can be persuaded to interpret a series of steps as a curve.

The start and finish points for each weft follow the same sequence as previously illustrated. The curved shape is formed first, taking 24 passes to complete, in steps from single to six passes. As with weaving squares, you will notice a slit forming to the side of this vertical section.

Finally, the infill is woven, increasing to meet the stepping back turns of the already formed curve. A few passes are woven across the whole sample to finish. If there is at least two-thirds of the warp length remaining it may be used for the next example, otherwise make a row of double half hitches and cut off.

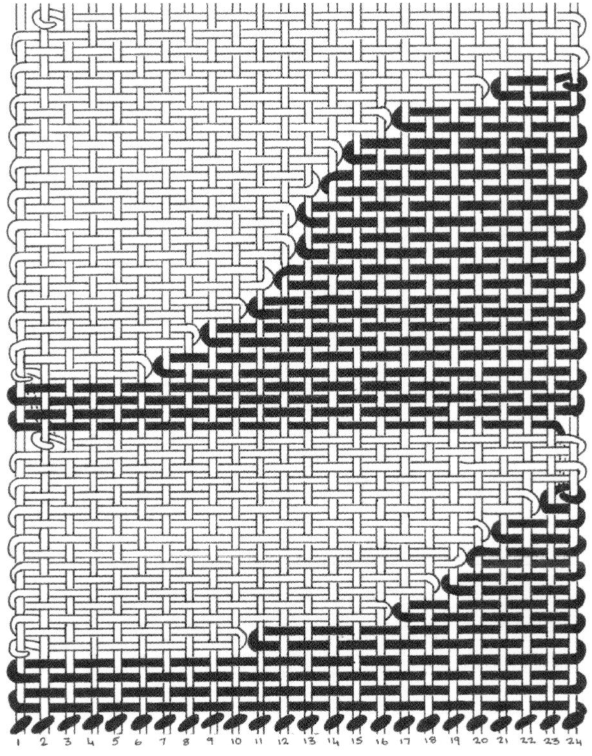

Weaving sequence for the first two curves.

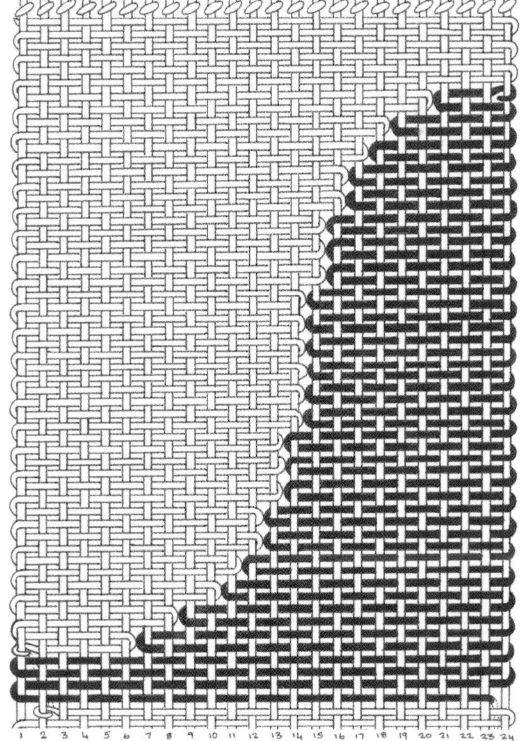

The third curved form.

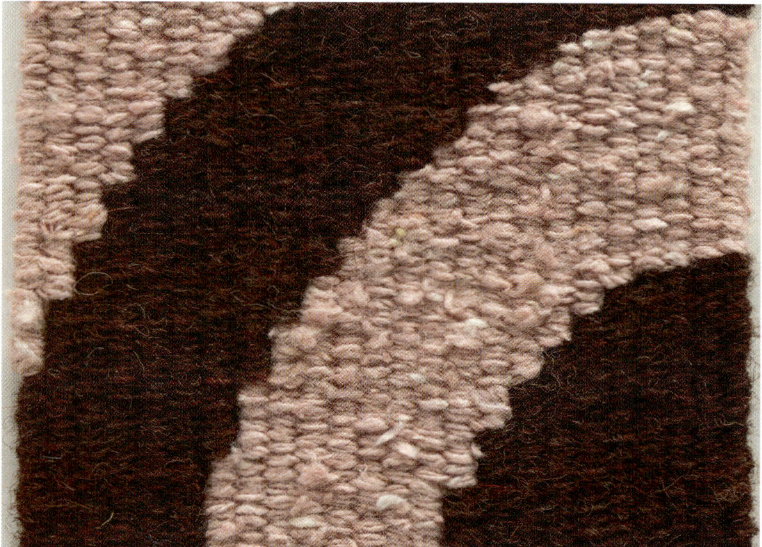

Three curved forms.

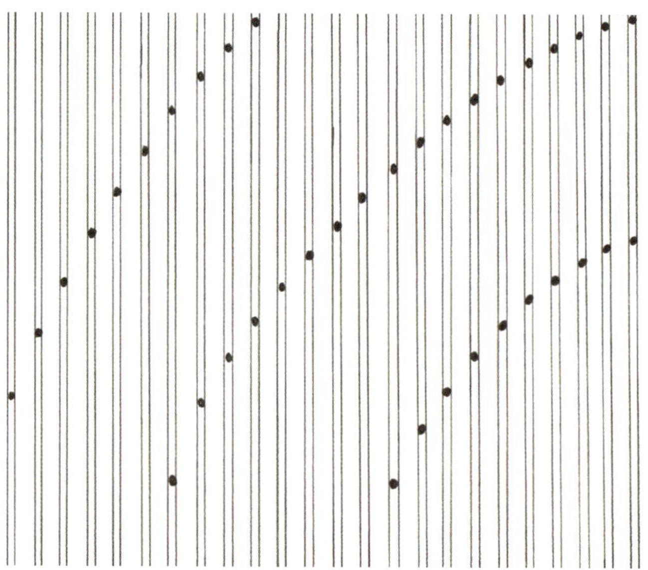

Curves drawn onto the warps.

This sample shows three near-parallel convex curves with a steep start, becoming shallower to the top. It is woven as the previous sample, on 24 medium weight warps at 8 epi and with a silk and wool weft.

Here the curve is drawn directly onto the warp using a permanent marker so that the ink will not smudge during weaving. This may be done by drawing lines freehand or traced from a drawing held behind the warps. Make a small mark on each warp where the line of the curve crosses it. You will find that warps twist whilst being woven so it is helpful before starting to weave to go back over, twisting each warp and extending the mark all the way round. Weave until each mark is just covered. Make sure to pack down firmly, bearing in mind that the most recent pass has a tendency to bounce up. You may also make a choice about turns, making a low turn where possible to minimise the stepped appearance.

The graphed-out sequence shows the steps which may be followed. The areas are labelled 1 to 4 in the order in which they need to be woven. The starting point for each weft is shown by an 'x', and the finish by a triangle. A weft should always start on the first warp due to be covered in the current row of weaving, as detailed in Chapter 2.

Note the steep start to each of these curves, necessitating a vertical section of between 6 and 12 passes. With several curved forms in play, the first and last weft are now forming and infilling at the same time.

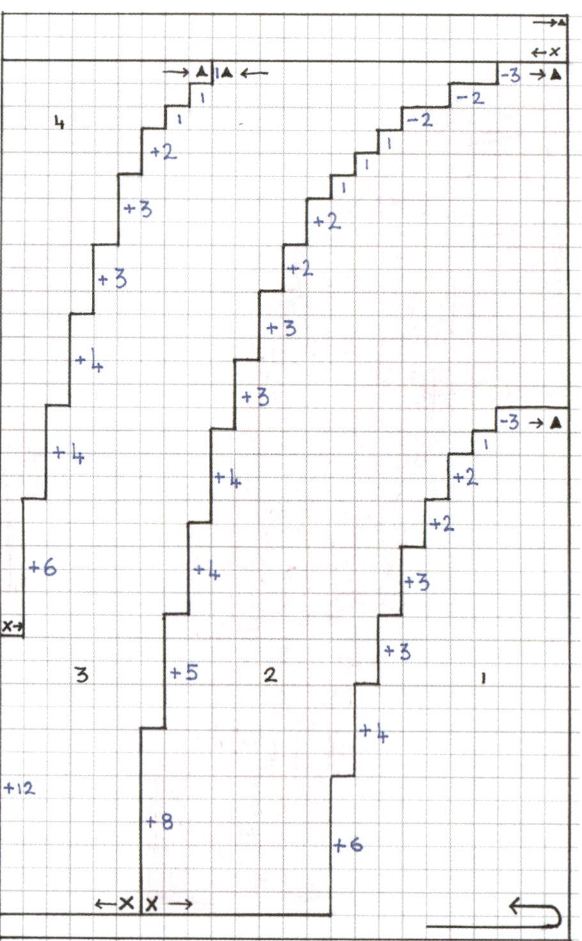

The weaving graphed out.

This sample is woven on 24 warps at 8 epi, with a single strand of rug yarn. The drawn diagrams show the sequence used for the woven sample, following the same pattern and principles as the previous samples in this chapter. Look to see the sequence in which areas need to be woven, depending on which overlays which, and aim to weave the largest area possible in one go. In the case of the lower mound, a couple of initial passes are woven and the weft paused at the right side. The curved 'mound' is the first area to be formed, following the pattern +6, +4, +3, +2, +2, 1, 1, -2, finishing on the central warp. This is followed by the infill to the left with a second weft of the background colour. Finally, the background weft which was paused may infill the right side and extend over the top to finish.

Conversely, in the case of the inverted mound, it is the background which needs to be formed first. The right-hand background yarn can weave up to what will be the top of the inverted mound, followed by a new background weft to form the negative space to the left. Next the mound, starting from the left side of its bottom row and woven in one, finishing back on the left to maintain the same shed. Finally, the right-hand background weft may be picked up and woven across the whole sample to finish. Note the start and finish points for each weft, chosen in order to maintain the shed.

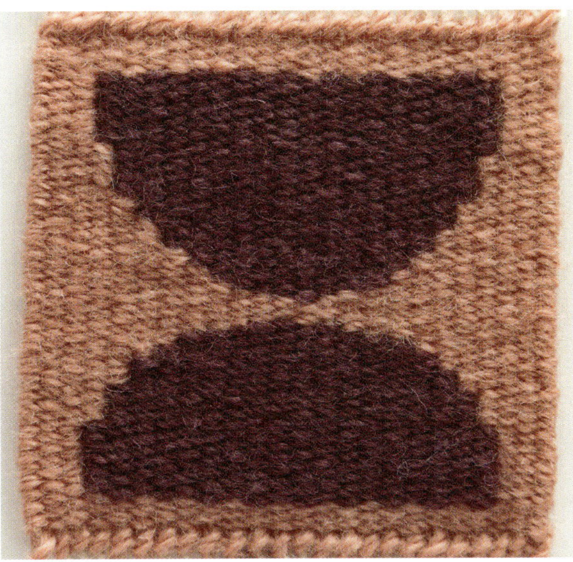

Two embedded curved forms.

Weaving diagram, mound form.

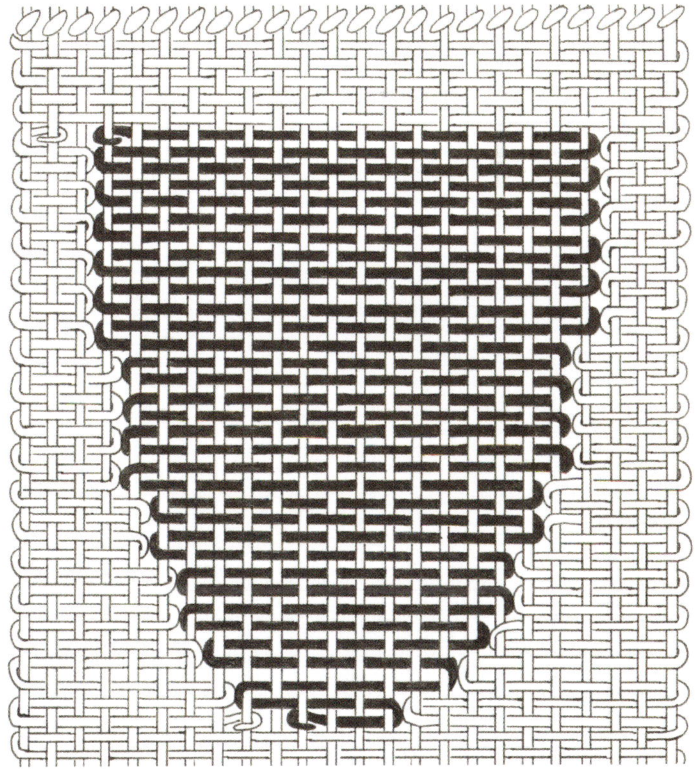

Weaving diagram, mound form inverted.

EMBEDDED OVAL FORMS AT THREE DIFFERENT WARP SETTINGS

These samples vary in the number and spacing of the warps, but all are of the same width when woven. The first has 17 heavy cotton warps at 6 epi, slightly wider spaced than the previous samples in this chapter which were woven at 8 epi with a medium warp. The background weft is worsted wool and the oval woven with silk, with a bundle of seven fine strands woven as one to obtain the right thickness for the sett. The steps at this warp setting are quite pronounced. The drawn diagram shows the stepping sequence. The right-hand background weft first forms the negative shape, pausing at the point where the oval curves back inwards. Next a second weft forms the left-hand background area, pausing likewise at the narrowest section. The oval may then be woven in one go before first one side then the other of the background above is infilled.

The next sample shows the same oval woven on 24 medium cotton warps set at 8 epi, with three strands of weft in a bundle. Note, the form is now more rounded in appearance because with the warps closer together, the steps are smaller. Also the bead made as the weft passes over the warp is finer. The stepping sequence is also slightly altered because of the greater number of warps used.

Finally, a third version of the same oval, woven on a medium cotton warp at 10 epi. Thirty warps are now needed to weave a sample of the same width. The weft is also thinner with only two strands in each bundle. Again, the stepping sequence is slightly altered. The different aesthetic qualities of the outline and the woven surface are now very evident.

When weaving with a bundle of weft yarns, simply cut them all to the same length, gather them together and weave with them in the same way as a single yarn. They will sit best if left free at the ends rather than tied, and there is no need to twist them together.

With experience, most weavers form a definite preference for particular warp settings based partly on the design and scale of a piece or on preferred weft materials. Naturally, the process becomes slower with a finer weft, but a closer sett allows for greater detail and smoothness of line. The whole appearance of the woven surface is also different. It is worth trying out different warp settings to get a feel for how they weave, and the different aesthetic they offer.

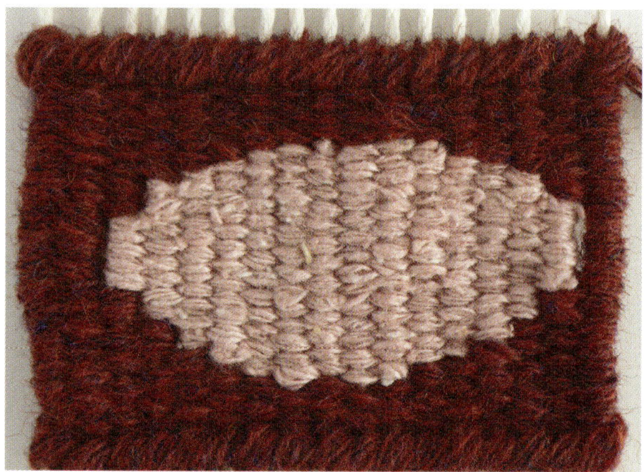

Oval woven at 6 epi.

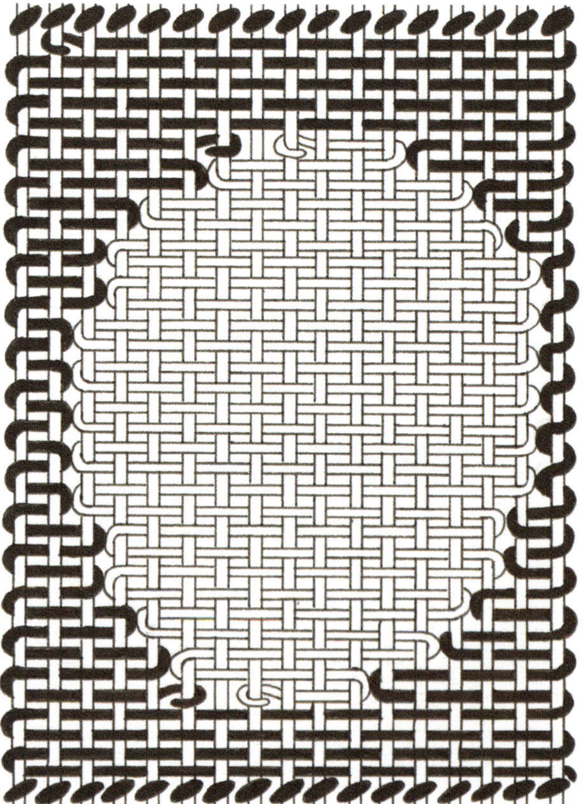

Weaving diagram of oval at 6 epi.

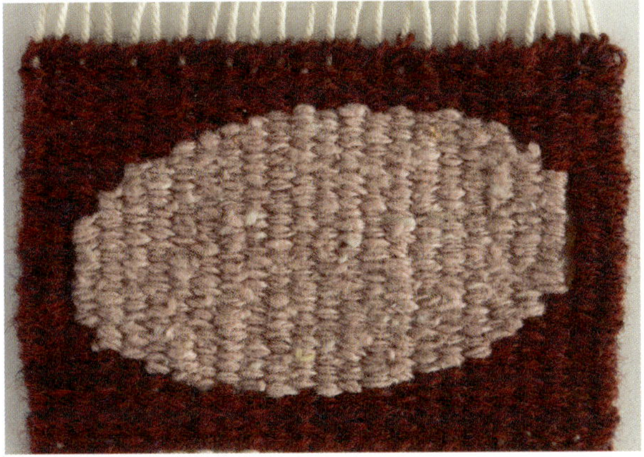

Oval woven at 8 epi.

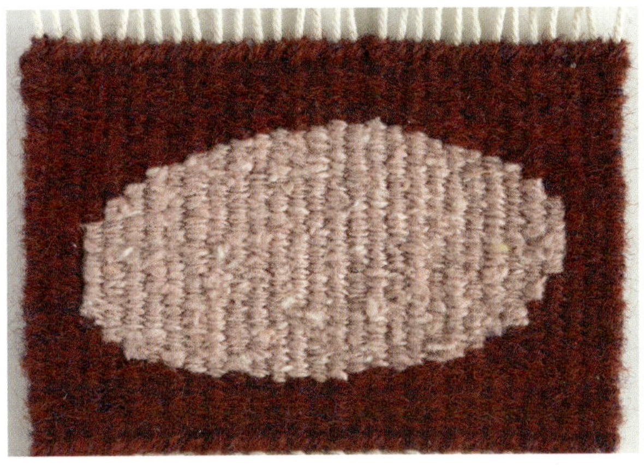

Oval woven at 10 epi.

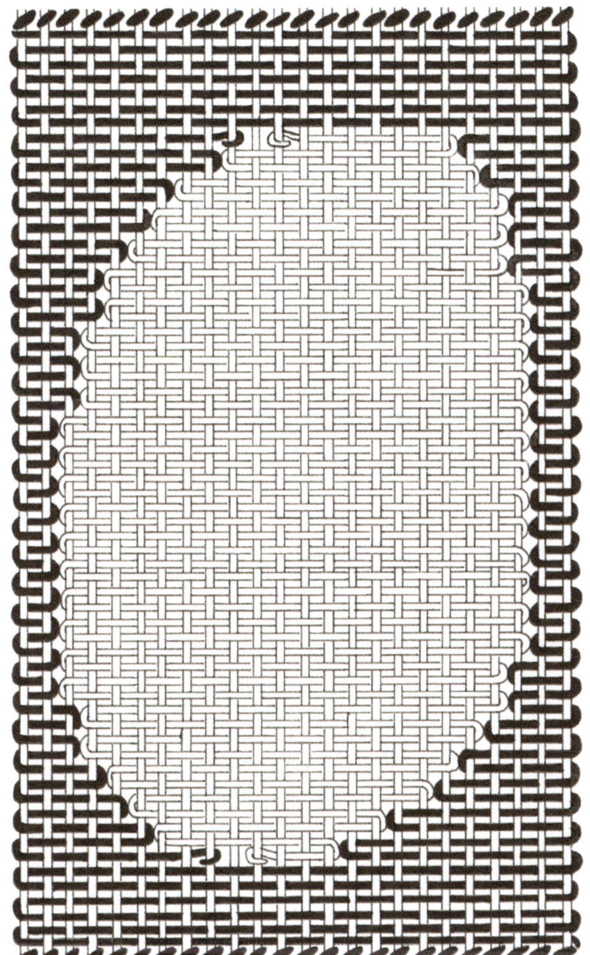

Weaving the oval at 8 epi.

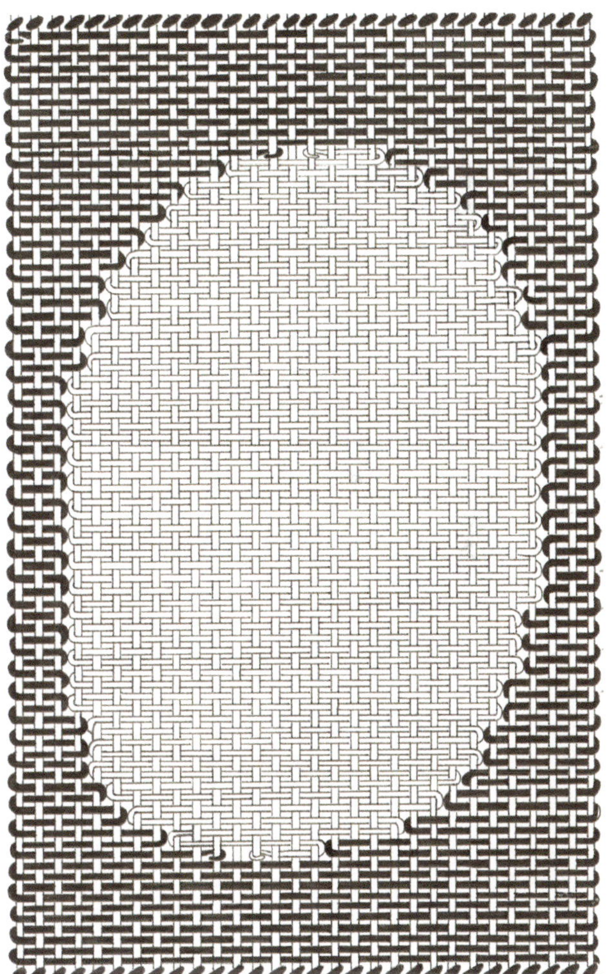

Weaving the oval at 10 epi.

A MEANDERING LINE

Although this design is simply one area overlaying another, the dips in the line mean that consideration needs to be given to which area to weave first, and where to start new wefts to make them all work together.

The numbered drawing shows how the area marked 1 may be woven right across the sample, up to the base of the deeper dip. At this point there is a choice to be made to proceed up one side or the other. The right-hand side has been chosen because in so doing, the whole of the right-hand area including forming the shallower dip may then be woven without changing weft.

To complete the left-hand hump in the dark area 2, another length of weft of the same colour is needed. Next the dip to the right, area 3, has been infilled with a short weft length.

Finally, area 4 starts in the bottom of the deeper dip, adjacent to where the weft for area 2 started and weaves in the opposite direction to it. This should ensure that once the weaving reaches the top of the hill, the weft will continue over the top of area 3, still falling into the hollows left by the last row.

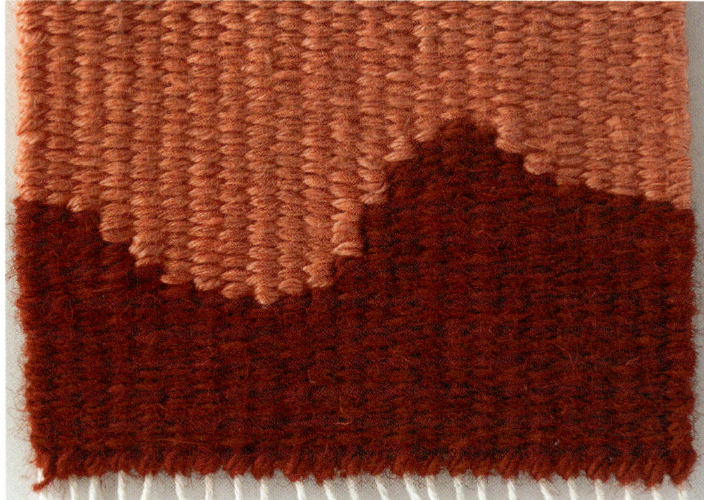

Meandering sample using 24 warps.

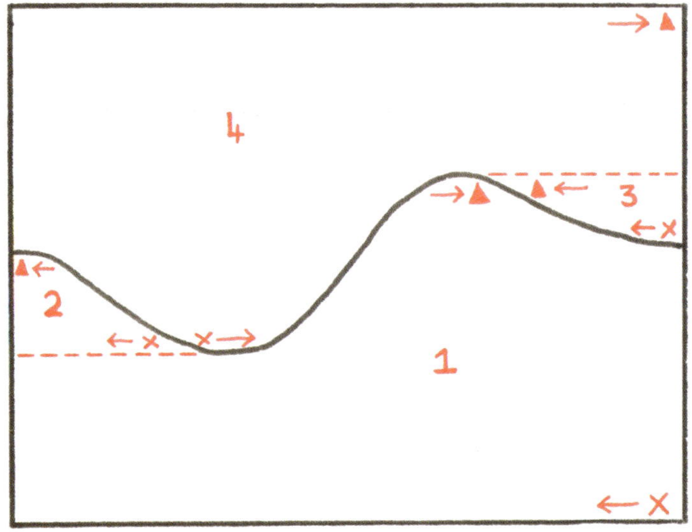

Sequence of wefts.

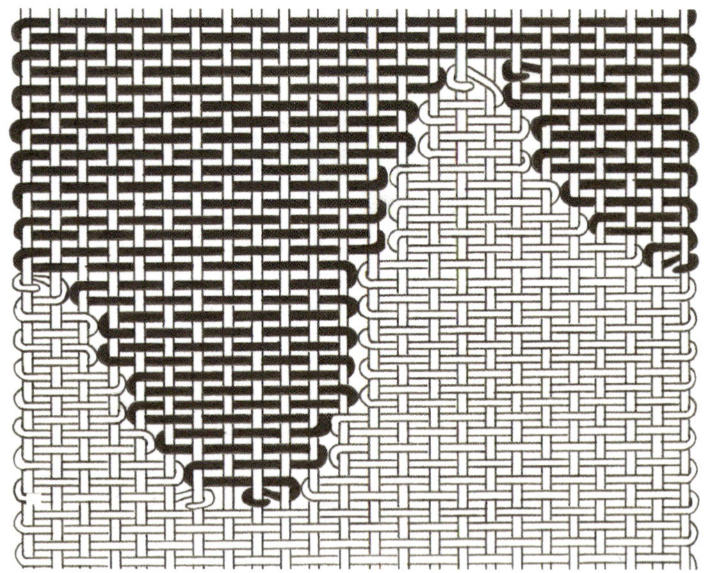

Weaving pattern.

FLOWING FORMS

Here we have five areas of weave using free-flowing curves, formed in nine stages using two coloured wefts. The weaving plan shows that the bottom and top areas may be woven in one weft each. The lighter-coloured bands are woven in two wefts. The central band curving in both directions needs three wefts to complete. Following the principles summarised in Chapter 2, each weft has been marked with an 'x' to start and triangle to finish with arrows showing the direction of weave. By taking care to follow these indications, the wefts will remain in shed, and so be able to weave over the top of each other. Eventually this pattern becomes habitual. Wefts either start and finish in pairs weaving away from each other, or from opposite sides and weave towards each other. The weaving diagram shows weaving direction, starting and finishing points, and the steps and number of passes made to form the curves shown in the woven sample.

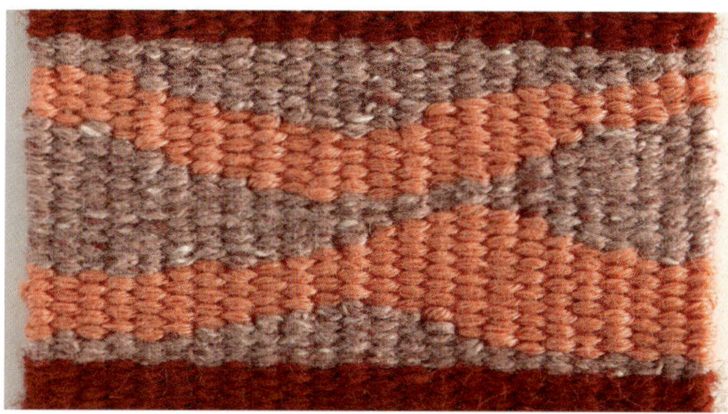

Flowing forms with 24 warps.

Sequence of wefts.

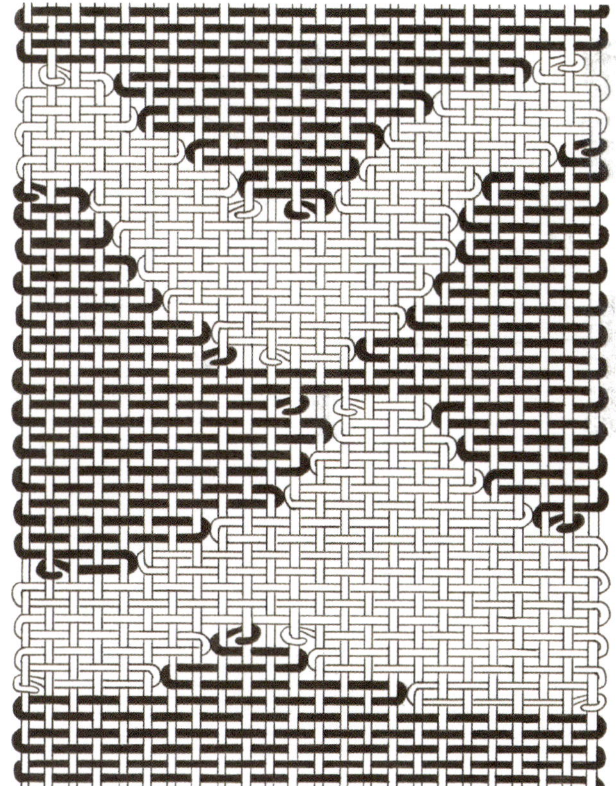

Weaving pattern.

A LINE OF MANY CURVES

Here is an exercise applying the techniques covered in this chapter. Take two sheets of contrasting coloured card. Draw a freehand curving line similar to the illustration on one sheet. Cut along the line and mount one half onto the other sheet of card. Although it is possible to weave a curve which dips down then rises again, this becomes more complex. At this stage it may be best to keep to simple curves like these.

This example is 3in wide and has been woven with 26 warps at 9 epi. You may now have a sense of how different warp settings feel and wish to choose your own.

Starts, pauses and finishes

Next make a line drawing of your design to map out the areas in order of weaving and the number of wefts needed. Starting from the bottom up, look to see how far an area may extend in one go. In this design, the bottom left starts but must pause where the line turns to the right to allow the area beneath to be woven. The areas will weave in an alternating left/right rhythm.

Next consider where wefts need to start, finish and pause, following the principles outlined in Chapter 2. This is worthwhile since when wefts get out of shed, it will show in the weave and isn't easy to put right without reweaving. With care and thought, this will become instinctual, leaving you free to concentrate on the weaving.

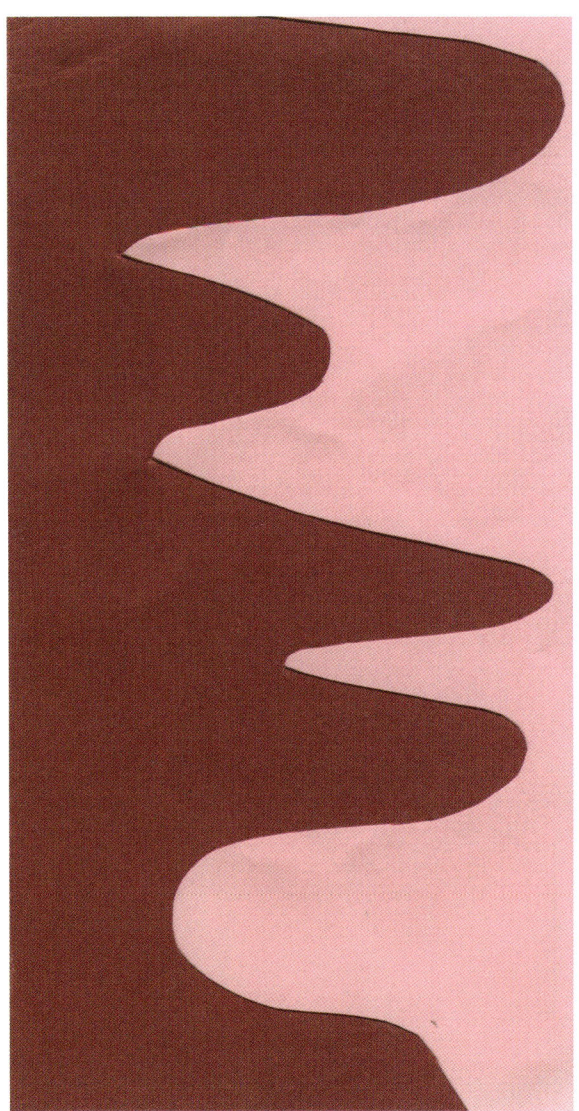

A line of many curves.

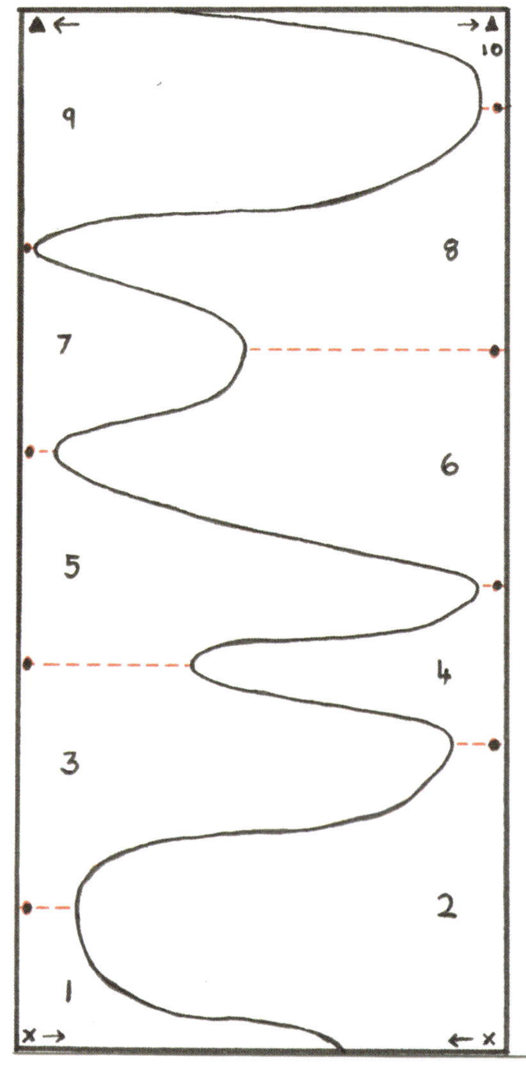

Ten stages showing starts, pauses and finishes.

Marking up the warps

Once you have warped up, hold the design snugly at the back of your warps, above the twining. You may wish to secure the paper in place by taping it to the sides of your weaving frame. With a permanent marker, make a dot on the warp at each point the curving line crosses it. Try to keep the marks small, particularly if working with a white warp and light-coloured wefts. You may find it necessary to touch up the marks if they twist round to the back during weaving. Note, the inner and outer ends of these curves are the most difficult areas to make look smooth, since they inevitably require a straight vertical section.

Weaving your design

Laying in a half pass in a spare length of weft after knotting on can be helpful to make a shed to start working from. This can easily be pulled out afterwards.

As you weave, you will alternately form and infill the shape. Rather than being too worried if the woven curve doesn't exactly follow your drawn line, it is worth opting for low warp turns to make the curves smooth. As you weave, try to get a feel for how many passes are needed to form the shapes. This will not be evident until the weaving is in progress since the warp sett, weft fibre and weight all influence the number of passes needed to make a form.

Having been introduced to stripes, squares, triangles and now curves, this completes the forms which require quite precise counting of warps and weft passes. We will now be moving onto techniques where the choices involved are more fluid and free. Learning through experience and close observation, your choices will become increasingly personal and instinctual.

Marking the warps.

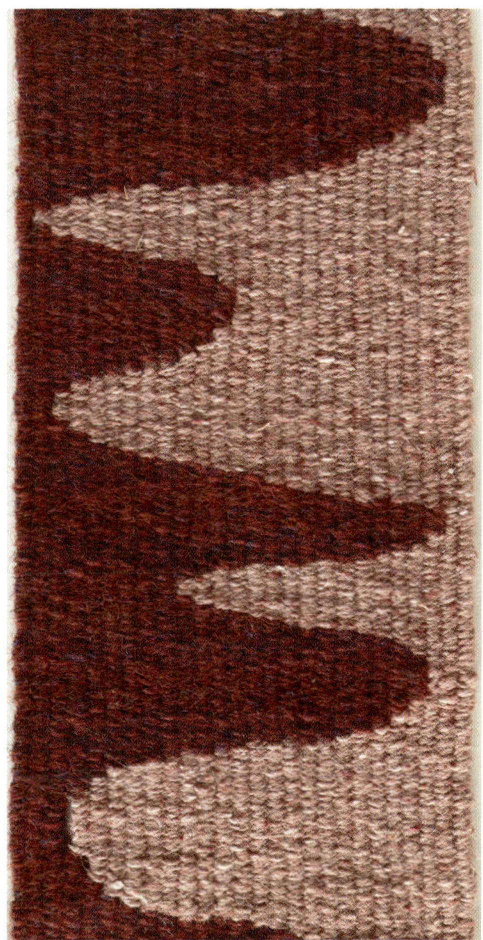

The design woven.

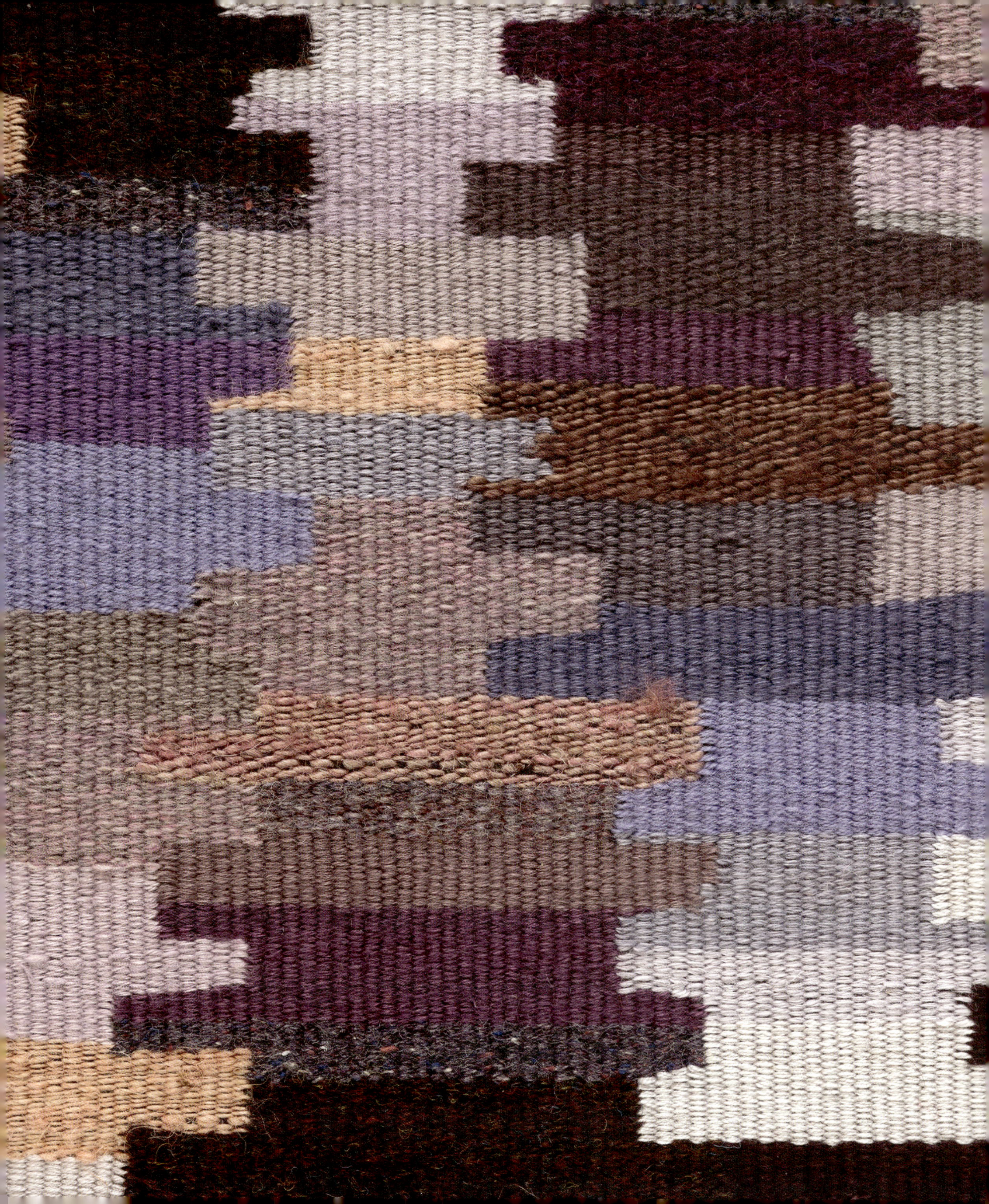

CHAPTER 5

INTERPRETING A DESIGN

This chapter moves on to look at how to make choices when weaving a design of more complex or multiple forms. We will show why and how a design may be planned and woven, and how this might influence your design choices. Although not universally attractive, the major benefit of preplanning is to allow the weaving to flow freely once started. This can mean less time spent fiddling with multiple weft ends and being distracted by working out next moves.

Questions to ask when mapping out a design:

- At what scale do you wish to weave the design, and what is a suitable warp setting?
- Will the piece be woven in the orientation it has been drawn? Might turning the design sideways to weave be a better choice?
- Is your design weave friendly? Anything is possible in weave but there are practical consequences to any choice.

Looking at a design from bottom to top, in the direction it will be woven:

- Look to see if there is a direction to the main lines, and what areas overlay others. This will indicate where the weaving needs to begin. Like stones in a wall, tapestry needs to be built from the bottom up.
- Continuing up the piece, number the areas in the order in which they are to be woven.

The criteria for these choices include:

- Which overlays which?
- What is the largest area which may be woven in one go without changing wefts?
- What positions for starting and finishing wefts will result in adjacent areas remaining in shed with each other?

The number of wefts needed will not necessarily correspond to the areas within the design; some will need to be divided. The principle is to look at how far a weft may proceed within a piece. It is often the case that a simple exchange of colour may be made, and the weft continued.

A simple cartoon will be used to look at six quite different interpretations of the same design made simply by altering the choices of warp and weft. We'll see the contrasting effects of using solid or mixed colour, yarns of differing thickness, of fabric strips and of weaving under and over two warps at a time.

Finally, there is an exercise in making and weaving a design through which you should be able to apply the knowledge of how to plan the weaving. Several different interpretations are illustrated, including turning the design sideways to weave. Also illustrated is how making subtle changes, such as the choice to interlock rather than leaving a slit, may change the aesthetic of a piece quite radically.

By the end of this chapter it is our hope that you will be able to make, plan and interpret designs, understanding how readily they fall within the grid of warp and weft – and how to manage when they do not. You should be able to weave them using multiple wefts at the same time and begin to explore the effects available by the simple means of choosing weft. Understanding the principles underlying the construction of complex imagery will we hope be a passport to making designs which are faithful to the nature of weave.

Tapestry woven with black cotton warp and nettle, linen, cotton, rayon, silk and wool weft. 10 epi.

WEAVING A SHAPE IN DIFFERENT POSITIONS

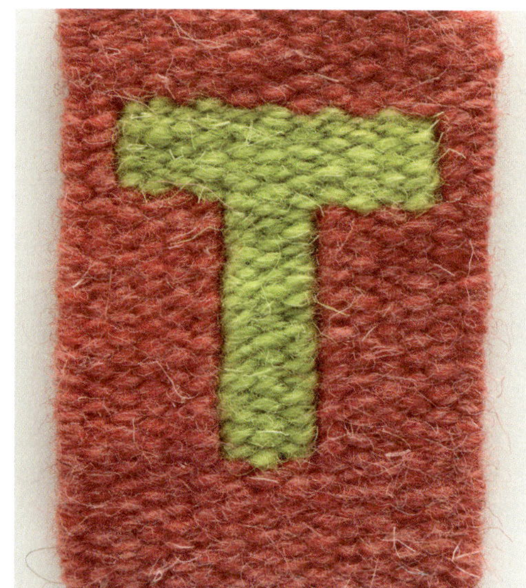

A woven shape with slits. Here is a simple 'T' form woven using 15 warps, at 8 epi. The weft is rug wool, in single strands of pink and green. The vertical stem is three warps wide, and the horizontal bar is woven in six passes, giving both the same width.

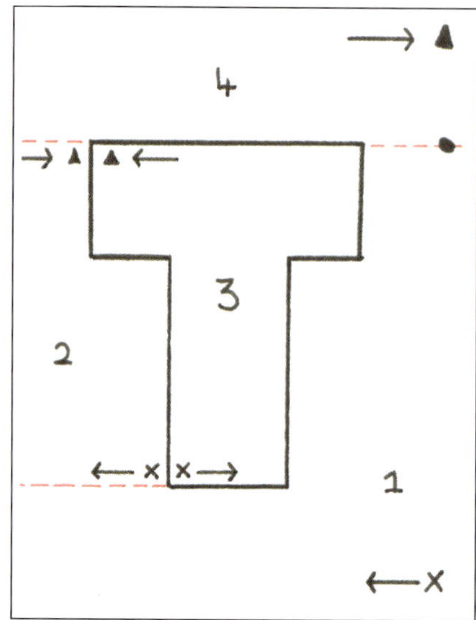

Weaving plan. The starting point for each weft is marked 'x', a triangle for the finish, a dot to indicate a pause, and an arrow for the direction of weave. The sequence of weaving for the different areas is numbered in order, 1 to 4. After area 1 is woven, the warps for areas 2 and 3 are started on adjacent low warps and weave in opposing directions.

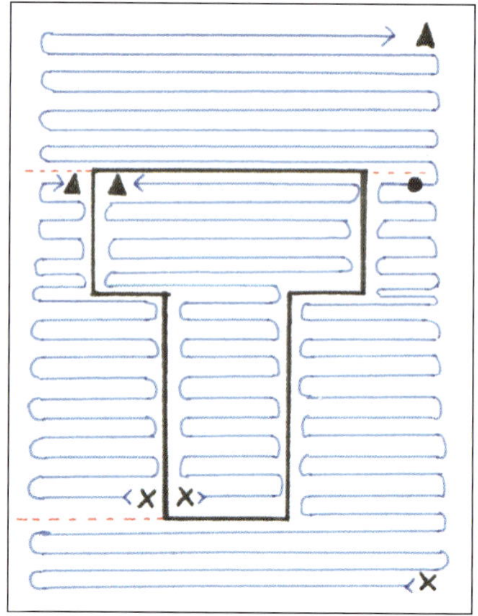

The blue line shows the weaving of each area. Starting at the bottom right, the weft continues till level with the top of the T, where it pauses. Next the left-hand of the two new warps weaves area 2 to the top of the T. The remaining one weaves the T shape itself. The two finish together at the top left corner. The paused first weft then weaves over the top.

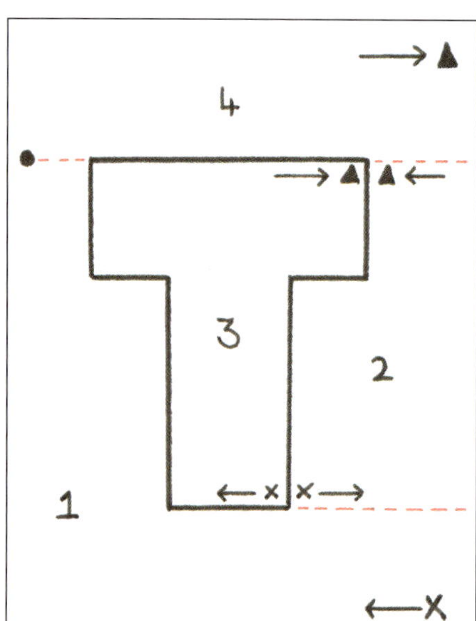

An alternative weaving plan. This time the first weft continues up the left- instead of right-hand side of the T. This means that the two new wefts now start together at the bottom right of the T, and finish at the top right. There is no visual difference, the choice would depend on the context within a piece.

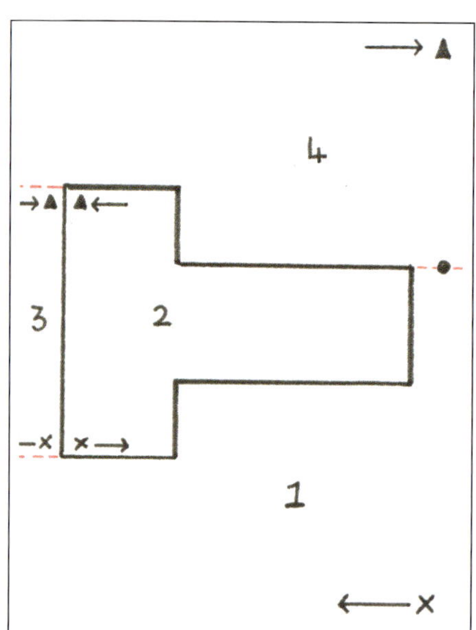

The design turned sideways. The first weft now forms what was the right side of the T shape before the two new wefts start. Either area 2 or area 3 could be woven next, since neither overlays the other. The first weft is then picked up to infill the right side of the T shape and complete the sample.

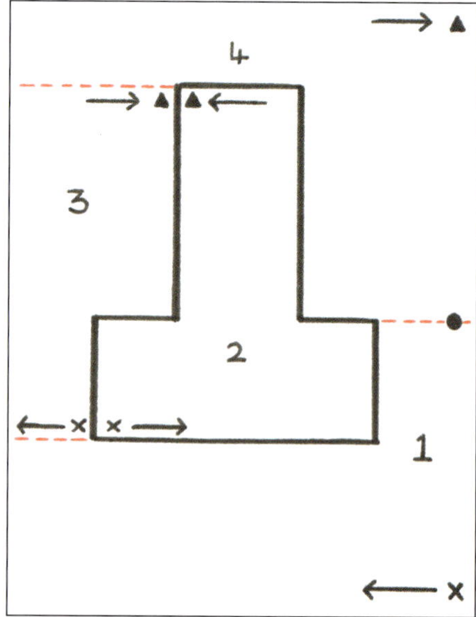

T shape upside down. The first weft can weave to what was the base of the cross bar of the T form on one side. Next two new wefts start together forming first the T form then the infill to the left which overlays it. The paused first weft now infills the right side and is woven across the top to finish.

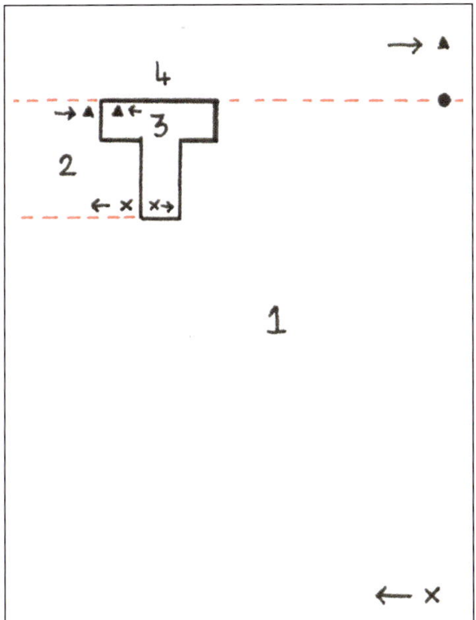

Smaller T form, set to the top left corner. The number of warps taken to weave the T at this scale needs to be decreased. The wefts start and finish in the same way as the first T example, and the numbered areas are woven in the same sequence.

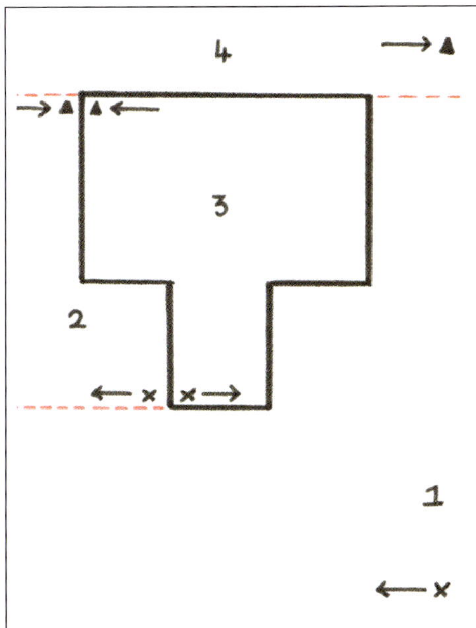

Altered T form. Here the top bar is much deeper in relation to the stem, so that many more passes will be needed to weave it to this depth. Despite this difference, the order in which areas are woven and the starting, finishing and direction of each weft is exactly the same.

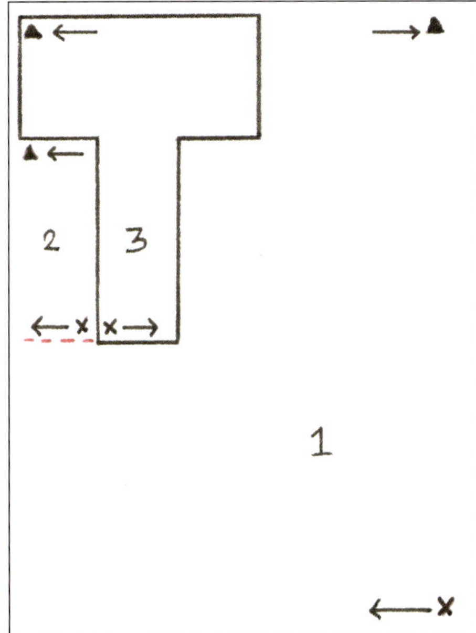

T form set at the top left corner. The slightly different vertical proportions will again be made by adjusting the number of passes woven. The altered position needs a different weaving sequence. Area 1 now extends all the way up the right-hand side. The area marked 2 finishes at the base of the cross bar before the T, section 3 is woven.

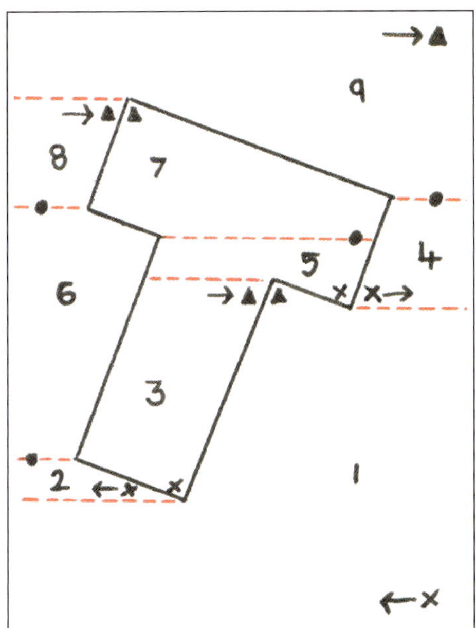

T form leaning to the right. Since the T form no longer follows the line of the warps, the weaving sequence becomes more complex. Area 1 extends up into the join of stem and crossbar. Area 2 stops at the bottom corner to allow area 3 to be woven. Area 4 comes next because 5 and 7 overlay it.

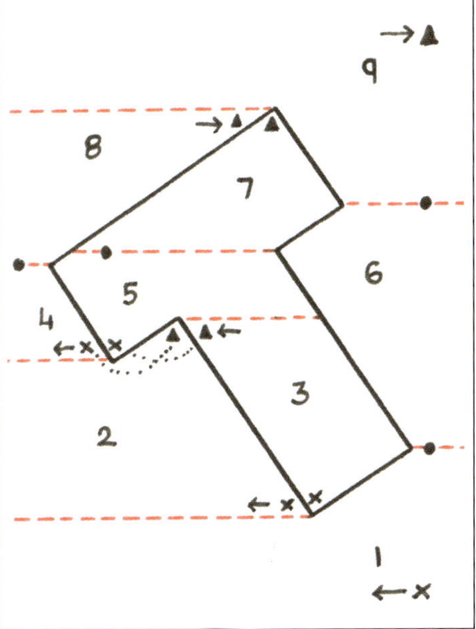

T form leaning to the left. Again, each area is woven up to the point where another area will overlay it. New wefts are started in pairs and woven away from each other so that when one passes over the other, they will still be in shed. There are now nine separate sections of weave in place of the original four.

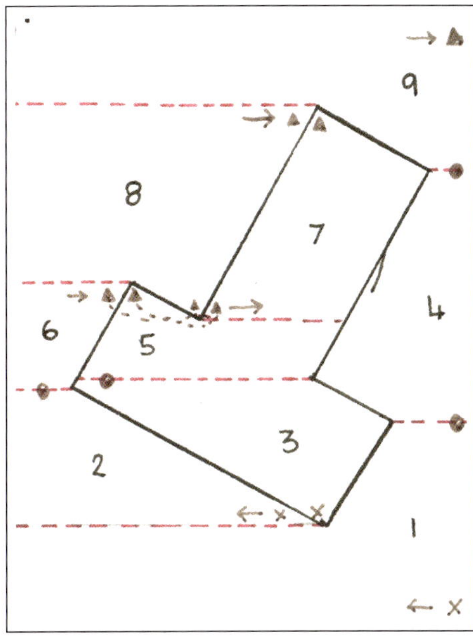

Inverted diagonal T form. Again, with nine areas in total, the order of weaving is now quite different. Though not the only choice possible, this order of weave has been determined by the same principles – weave as far as possible in one go, start and finish wefts so that areas stay in shed.

A DESIGN OF MULTIPLE DIAGONALS

The more complex a design, the more worthwhile it is to plan before weaving. It is much simpler to see the order of areas to be woven and the start and finish positions of wefts on paper than it is to work it out whilst weaving. To weave such a design without planning is likely to lead to wefts getting into the wrong shed and many more starts and finishes being needed.

Looking at the design, it falls broadly into five areas; three background areas in orange and two forms in white, all leaning towards the left. There are many different angles to be formed. Each angle will need a step sequence decided upon following the principles outlined in Chapter 3, Triangles. With experience, you will learn what patterns lend themselves readily to weaving and which do not, but it is always worth making a plan.

Planning how to weave the design

First look at which areas overlay others to decide which should start first and how far it may weave before having to either finish or be paused to allow for another area to be woven. Note, although there are 13 areas, they have been woven with only five actual wefts. The bottom left has been chosen to start because it must be woven before area 8 is able to overlay it. It must pause at the level where area 2 starts to slope to the right otherwise it also would be weaving over an unwoven section of warp. The warp for area 2 needs to be started at the opposite side to the warp for 1 so that they weave towards each other. It is paused at the narrowest point after which the angle turns to the left, overlaying area 3. Blocks 3, 4, 5 and 6 follow, infilling and forming alternately. A new weft is added for area 7, adjacent to where weft 2 started, pausing to allow for 8 to be woven with a new weft started at the bottom right corner. This weft pauses at the point the angle turns to the left. Areas 9/10 and 11/12 are woven and paused alternately using the paused wefts from areas 7 and 8. By finishing together at the top they remain in shed. Finally, to the top right, a final weft fills the overlaying area 13.

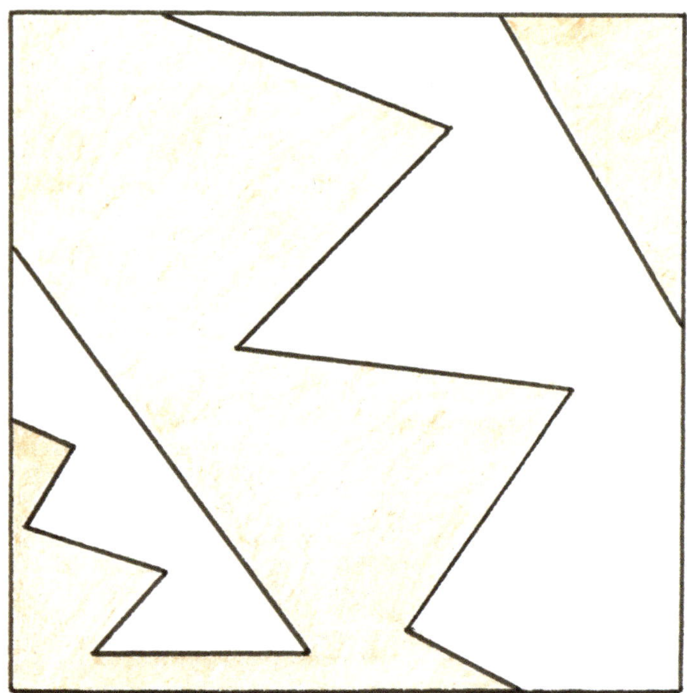

Weaving a design of multiple diagonals.

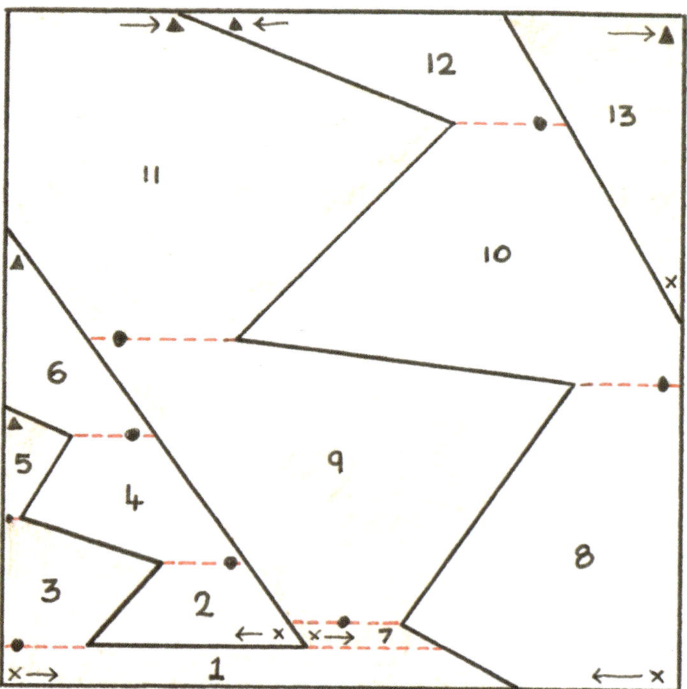

Weaving plan for multiple diagonals design.

A WOVEN SPIRAL

Although the actual form in this design is clearly a spiral, it is impossible to weave as a continuous form since weaving has to be constructed from the bottom up, in layers like stones in a wall. However, there are workable solutions to making virtually any form in tapestry. The simplest way to form the curves would be to mark them onto the warps with a permanent marker, either freehand or by holding a drawing behind the warps as a guide. Now there is the added challenge of making convincing curves on a grid of warp and weft. The more wefts available in which to form a design such as this, the smoother it will be possible to make the curves. As a rough guide, this design needs to be woven on a minimum of about 30 warps. Choices of warp sett and weight, of weft fibre, colours and tone will all affect how the design will work as a finished piece. For example, hard spun fibres and strongly contrasting tones will be less forgiving than a mixed bundle of wool yarns might be.

Weaving the spiral

From this weaving plan, you will see that the form can be woven in 20 areas, and with 13 individual wefts. There are several wefts, mainly on the edges, which weave only one or two areas before finishing. At first sight the weaving order may look random but in fact follows an alternating pattern. Area 1 must be woven first since the next two areas lean onto it. First the lower half of the spiral is formed in areas 2/3, 4/5, 6/7, 8/9, 10/11. Areas 2 to 9 all start with new wefts which are paused halfway up, and which later weave the top half of the spiral. The final two areas, 10 and 11 at the centre are each woven with a weft used for that area alone. The pattern in which areas in the lower half of the spiral was woven is reversed to form the coils of the upper half. The paused wefts are picked up so that first the weft from area 8 weaves area 12. The pattern continues left to right, forming each loop in two halves. The top corners of the piece are formed with one weft each.

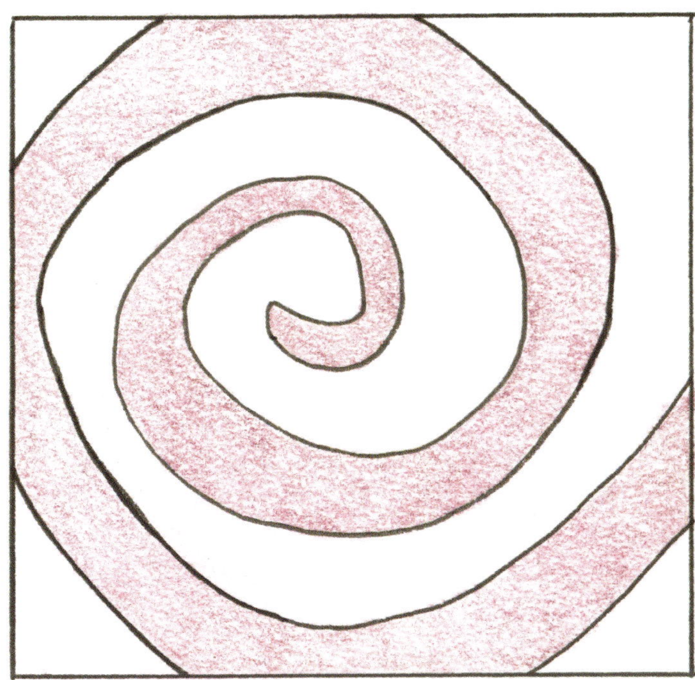

A spiral design.

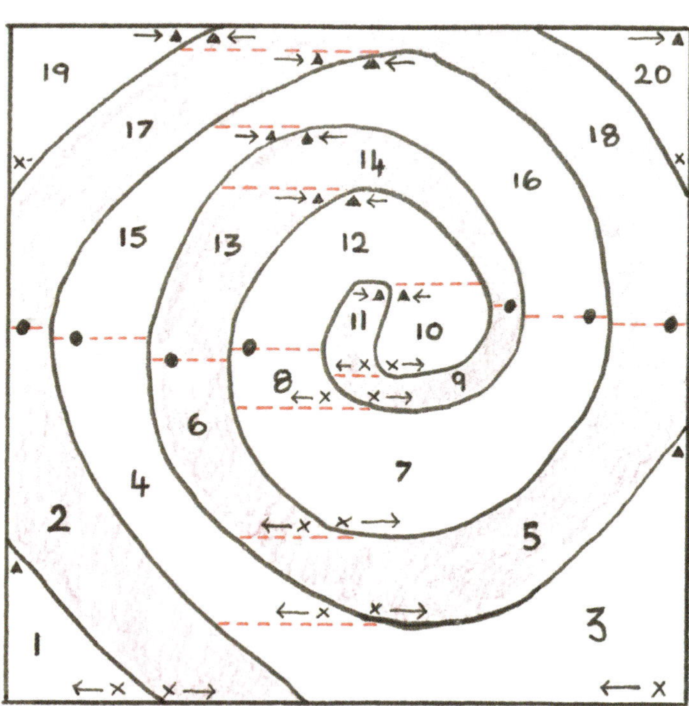

Weaving diagram for the spiral.

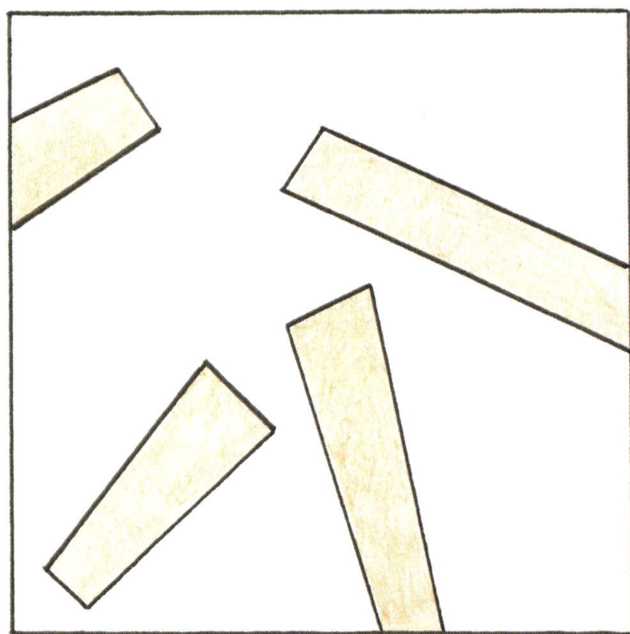

Four angular forms in a background. Although this design may appear to consist of just four shapes and a background, in fact it needs nine separate wefts in order to weave and must be divided into 13 individual areas. Again, because the forms are set diagonally, the complexity of the weaving increases.

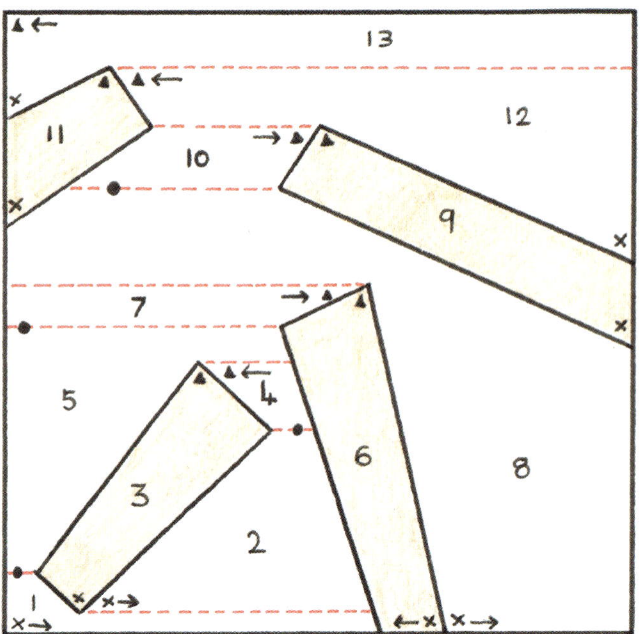

Plan for weaving. The order as ever is determined by which areas overlay which. Looking at area 6 for example, although it starts at the bottom of the piece, because it leans to the left, all the areas to its left must first be woven, in the order in which they lean on each other. The same applies to all four of the leaning shapes.

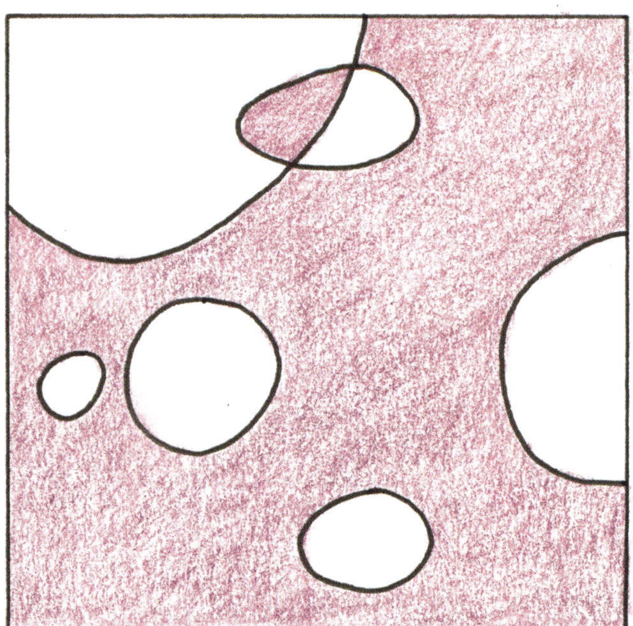

Circular forms embedded and overlapping. At a glance, this drawing shows simply five roughly circular forms of variable size, and a small one overlapping the largest. These are set in a background which it might be tempting to think of as one area of weave. The whole piece needs to be divided into 19 areas.

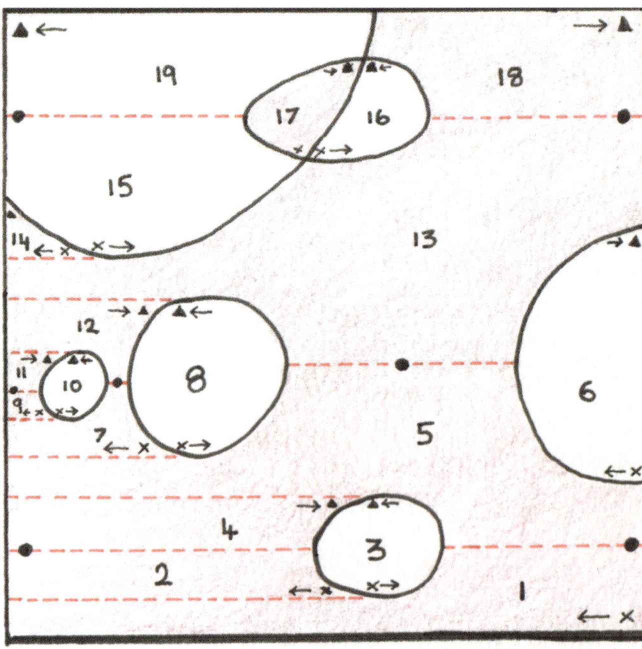

It is clear that each of the small circles will need a weft of their own. By choosing to start at the bottom right, the whole of the right side of the background (areas 1, 5, 13 and 18) may be woven in one continuous weft, paused three times. The background areas to the left of the circles need more changes of weft to infill.

ONE DESIGN, A CARTOON AND SIX INTERPRETATIONS

First the drawn design has been mapped out to show the most convenient and simple division of the design into areas, numbered in the order of weaving. The wefts as before are marked with starting, pause and finishing positions, and their direction of weave.

The loom has been set up with warp, header bands and twining as for all previous samples. Two additional lengths of warp yarn have been tied at the back, between the side bars of the frame and the paper cartoon slid in behind the warps.

Keeping the cartoon in place is important to get an accurate rendition of the design. To assist with this, it has been taped to the upper of the two warp lengths stretched across the frame. When following a cartoon view it at a consistent angle, otherwise the weaving won't be accurate.

In the following pages, six quite different weft choices are used to weave this design.

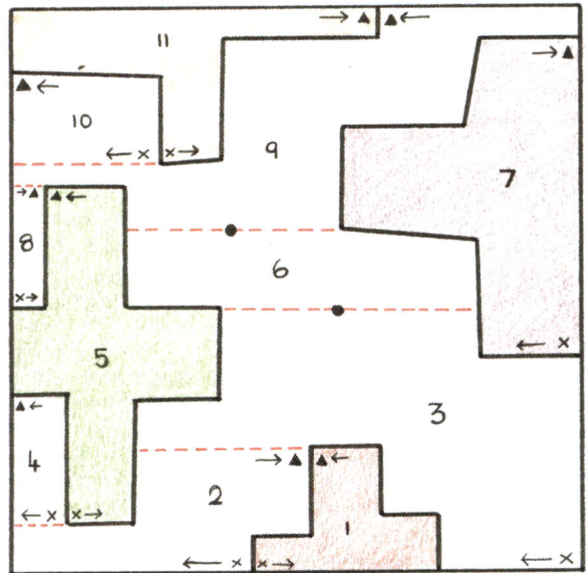

Plan for intersecting rectangular forms.

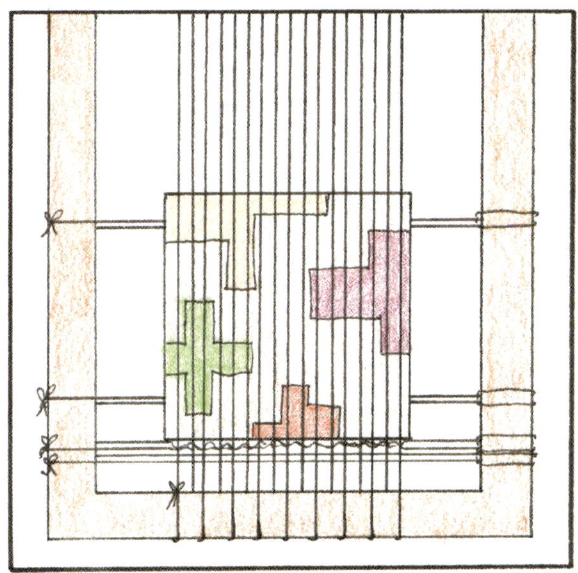

Placing the cartoon behind the warps.

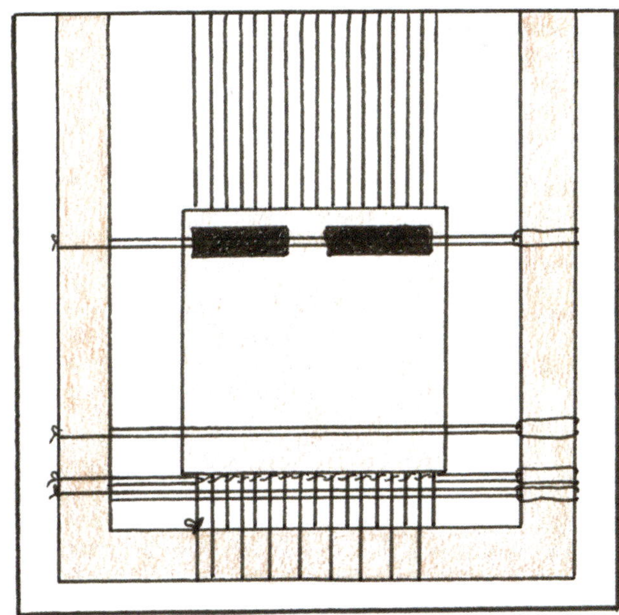

Attaching the cartoon to the additional lengths with tape.

Woven in solid colours with a single strand of wool rug yarn

Perhaps the simplest possible interpretation, the robust wool rug yarn used as weft for all the areas in this interpretation needs only a single strand to fill the warp of 8 epi. Each weft is of solid colour producing bold, simple and clear forms against the light background. This weft yarn is the same as that used for the samples in the first three chapters where it was chosen for ease of handling and to show passes and turns as clearly as possible. The vertical joins have been left as simple slits, giving a clean boundary. Although most weavers would choose to move on from this simple choice, there is nevertheless a no-nonsense quality to solid colour and a single strand of weft that has its place in a repertoire of more sophisticated choices.

Linen in solid colour against a flecked wool background

The contrast between the properties of wool as against a linen yarn are immediately evident in this sample. The background is woven in a variegated wool yarn containing orange, red, purple and green flecks. These small flecks of colour act to link the background to the forms set within it. The cross forms are woven with a bundle of eight fine, quite lustrous linen yarns. Because of the long staple of linen fibre, it tends to produce a hard inelastic and lustrous yarn when spun. Wool by comparison is a crimped shorter staple fibre which spins into a yarn with more loft. The effect here is that the linen cross forms sit back from the surface of the background as if embossed.

You may now begin to see the contrasts in the way a weft *fills* the warp. First, the thickness either of a single strand or the combined thickness of a bundle. Next, the type of fibre the yarn is made of will determine how readily it packs down and fills the warp. No two wefts or combinations of wefts will behave the same, even at the same warp setting; if balanced, a weft should beat down readily and be held snugly in the warp. If a weft slips about it may be underfilled; if it is stiff to beat down or shows the warp through it may be overfilled. The aesthetic qualities of these choices are endless.

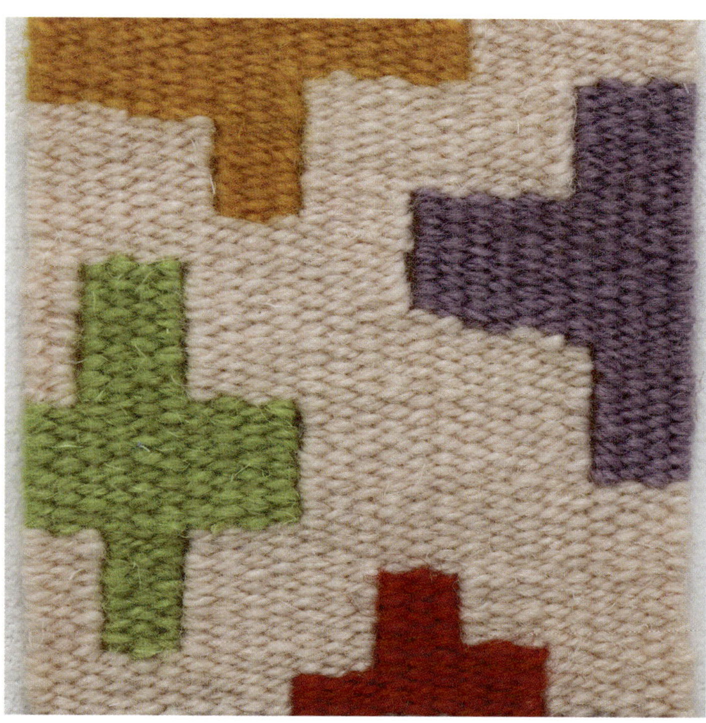

Woven at 8 epi with 25 warps in solid colours.

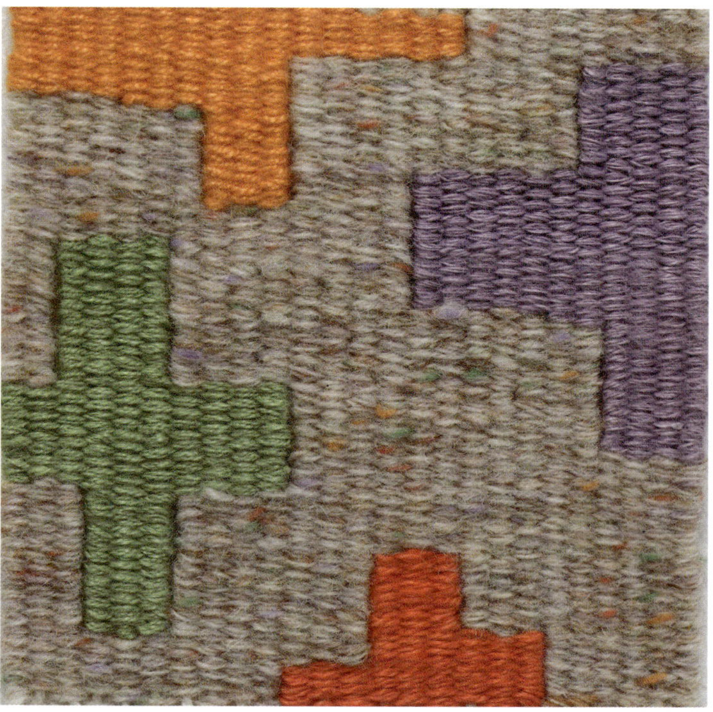

Woven in linen against a wool background.

Woven with a weft bundle of eight strands throughout

Several fine yarns woven in a bundle rather than a single thick one means they tend to lie flatter when beaten down and give a smooth, uniform surface to the weave. These yarns are a mix of linen, cotton and silk. The character of any yarn is influenced by the degree of spin and staple length. Here the yarns are all quite tightly spun, giving a hard yarn which weaves without giving any hairiness to the surface. The green form is woven in linen, showing the fibre's characteristic lustre and hardness and causing the bead to become more pronounced. The weft mixes are all very close tones, giving the effect of solid colour. The background is woven in a mix of 'ecru' or natural undyed colours, which contrast with the quality of colour of the dyed yarns.

Putting on an extra narrow strip of warp to one side of the loom is worthwhile. This means that short lengths of possible mixes can be tried out to see which work best together. The strips can also be useful references for future pieces.

Same yarns woven in different mixes

The coloured cross forms, instead of being woven in a single colour now have at least one strand of the colour from each of the other crosses included in a bundle of eight strands. This adds depth and complexity to the colours. The mixing of colours gives the individual forms more of a connection to each other so that the eye reads them more as a collection and less as separate units. This effect is further increased by the addition of a single strand of each colour to the background mix. Because of the contrast with the undyed ecru, the addition of colour makes a marked visual impact. Now all areas of the sample read together, the colour flowing throughout. From a distance the coloured areas stand out less from the background. Clearly neither is better or worse, just an indication of the degree of subtlety it is possible to achieve by making simple changes.

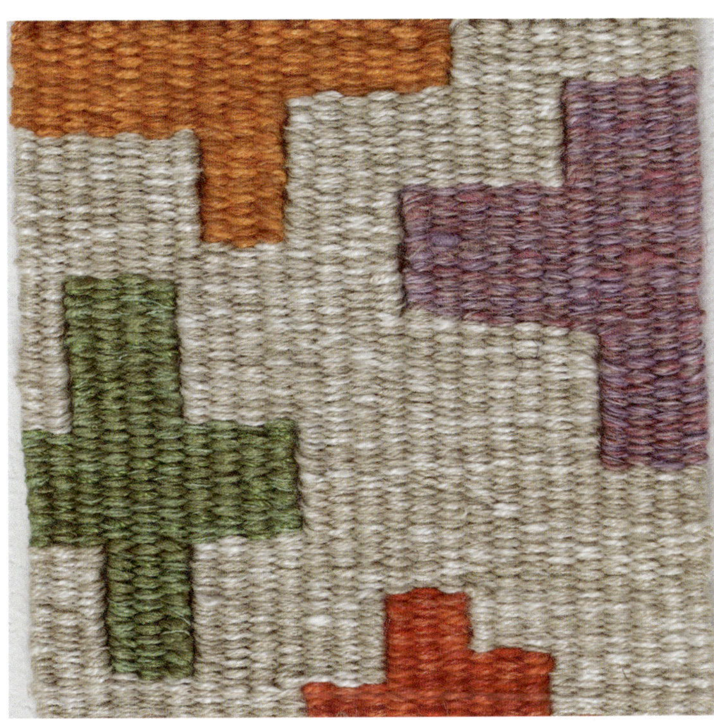

Woven with mixed bundles of cotton, linen and silk.

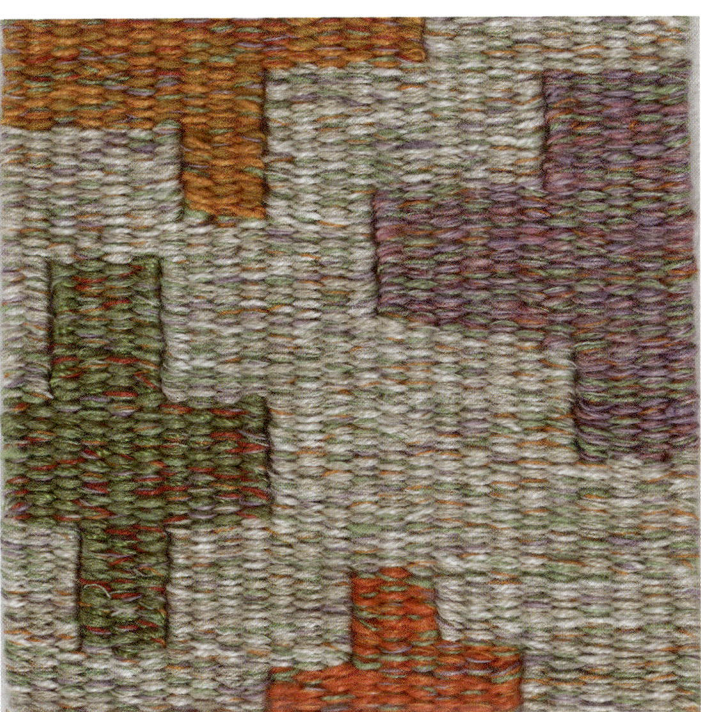

Mixed bundles in each section.

Crosses woven in torn fabric strips

Using the same sett and warp weight, the sample now returns to solid-coloured forms and background. The background is a mix of eight different ecru silks and cottons. The cross forms are woven with 10mm strips of fine cotton fabric. When weaving with fabric strips, care is needed as they tend to break if pulled through the warps in the way a yarn may be. Holding the warps apart and laying in the strip works better. Each pass also needs to be beaten down quite hard to stay in place, as they tend to bounce back up and would otherwise give an unstable weave. The surface texture given by cloth strips can vary enormously depending on the cloth used, and the direction it is cut in. Here, the folds visible where the cloth has crushed down in weaving give a complex texture and the frayed edges have given depth and a soft, hairy surface. The contrast with the flatter, more uniform background makes these areas appear raised.

A doubled warp

In place of 25 medium-weight warps at 8 epi, there are now 50 finer warps at a sett of 16 epi. In place of white, the warps are now coloured red, beige, light and dark green. The finer warp means that the crosses are now woven with only two strands of the same cotton and linen yarns. The background however has been woven over and under two warps at a time. Although this gives 8 epi as before, weaving over two finer warps gives a flatter surface than when weaving over one thicker one. The background weft is a single strand of white nettle yarn, the hardness of which is visible in the pronounced bead, and the way it has packed down. Although it is usual in woven tapestry to pack down a weft so that the warp is no longer visible, there is no reason why this must always be done. There is as much interest and excitement to be found in warp as in weft, which may be lost by regarding warp as simply a structure to support the weft. By not being fully packed down, the nettle yarn is able to show its characterful qualities. Hand spun, this thick single-ply yarn shows the variable touch of a human hand and the soft lustre of nettle fibre.

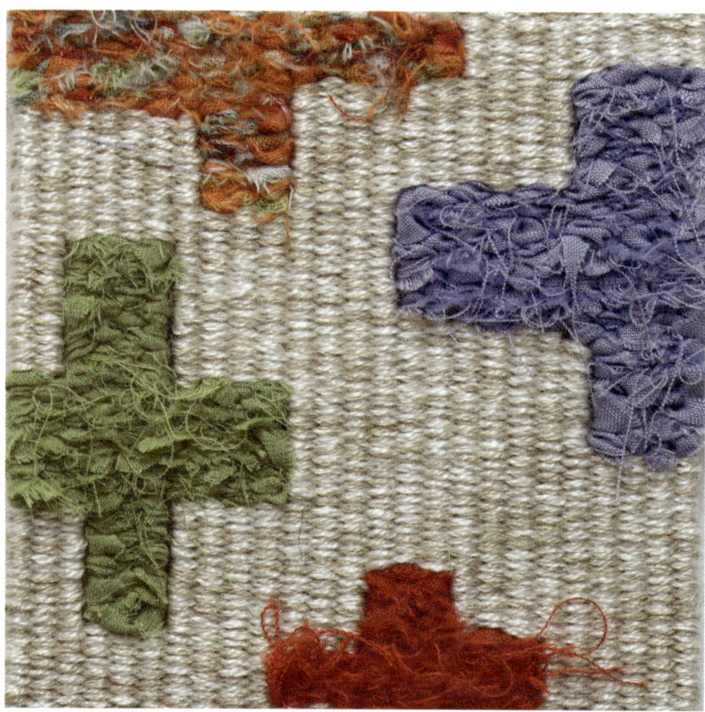

Silk and cotton background, fabric crosses.

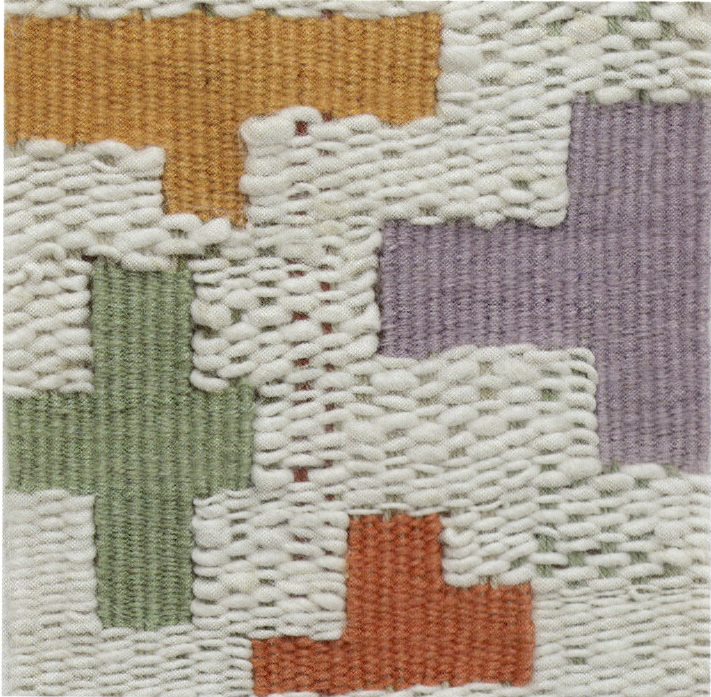

Nettle background, linen and cotton crosses.

A DESIGN OF MULTIPLE RECTANGLES

Ease of weaving – practical considerations

To weave to a pre-drawn design of many areas such as this, it is important to keep the different areas in the same shed. This will mean deciding on what order to weave the areas in. Assuming we are to leave slits between the rectangles, there are choices to be made. The piece starts with five rectangles and a section of the background. Looking at the 'x's marking the start of the wefts, you'll see we have chosen to group the areas into three pairs with their wefts starting together and weaving in opposite directions. Except at the edges, adjacent weft areas must always be started and finished in pairs. Avoiding starts and finishes at the edge can avoid the need to sew in ends afterwards. Areas 9 and 10 have been dealt with as independent units, each finishing at the same side it started so that the direction of weave remains unaltered and the background weft can be woven over the top. In general, it is not possible to start a single weft in the middle of the piece which has been done to form area 9. However, it is possible here because having vertical sides, the surrounding areas do not overlay it.

Note, the weft for area 6 can weave the whole of the background right up to the top edge, with only one pause along the way.

The weave showing starts and finishes to remain in shed

Here the actual wefts have been illustrated, starting and finishing in the positions marked on the plan, and weaving in the directions indicated. In addition, you may note the choice of warp on which each weft starts. The principle is always to start on the next warp in the row which was left uncovered by the weft in the previous row. The warp to start on will therefore always be a low warp (the one which the weft passed under). This means that when two wefts start adjacent to each there is always one warp left in between. The same applies for the finishes which are made in pairs with a high warp left in between. The weft for the rectangle at the bottom right has finished on the opposite side as it started, in this case the right, in order that the background weft may then weave over the top of it and remain in shed. The squares above, areas 10 and 9, each have a weft which finishes at the same side as it started, which again ensures that the background may weave over them.

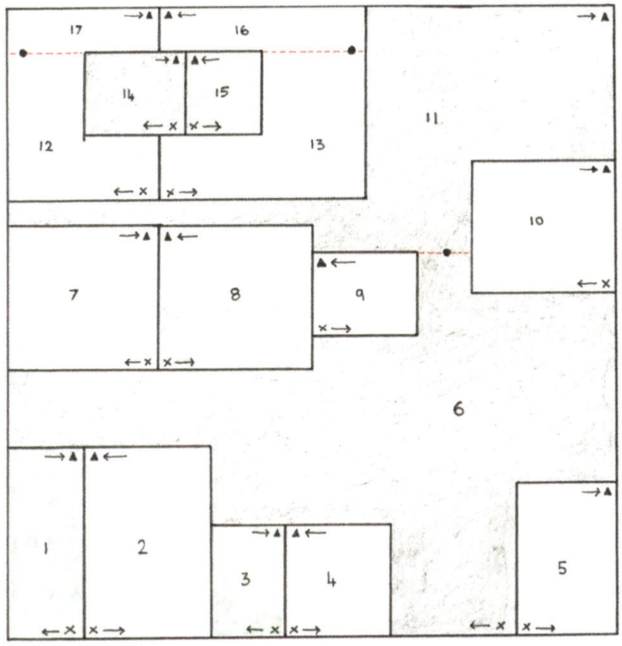

Plan of the multiple rectangles design.

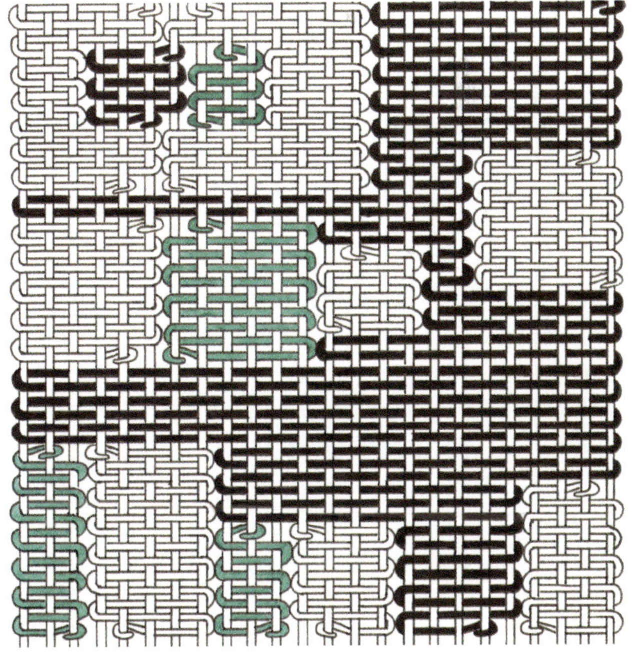

Woven diagram of the plan using 24 warps.

COLLAGE AS A DESIGN TOOL

As with any art medium, the design for a tapestry may have its origin in absolutely anything in the world which catches the attention of the weaver. The journey from initial excitement to finished tapestry can be bewildering. Here we hope to demonstrate how a simple design may be formed and how the language of tapestry is able to bring it to life. A pile of random but simple triangles, rectangles and curved shapes in different sizes have been cut out from several A4 sheets of coloured paper. These will be chosen and arranged freely to form a design which feels balanced and interesting, and for which a plan is given for how best to manage the weaving.

Working quite quickly and if possible freely, throw the pile of paper shapes in the air and let them land. Take up to half a dozen off the top of the pile. Arrange these roughly on a sheet of different coloured paper, either separately or overlapping each other. Keep it simple and try to avoid being too concerned about the outcome.

Looking at the shapes rather than the colour, observe the angles formed and spaces in between, look for any repeated or mirrored forms, contrasting curved and straight lines, run with what interests or pleases you. Take an A4 sheet of card and cut a rectangular window of about 10cm × 10cm (4in × 4in) in the middle of it. Place the window over an area of the arranged shapes. Observe how the forms sit when framed, which are most prominent or interesting. Move the window slightly side to side and view it in different directions, considering how this makes the arrangement more interesting or satisfying.

This quick exercise could be repeated a few times before committing to weaving, looking at each to see what stages would be needed to weave them. Some designs will turn out to be much more weave-able than others. It's also worth sampling weft mixes, and consider using techniques learned in the previous chapters, either within areas or at transitions between them. In settling a design, simplicity is often good to aim for. Question what is essential and leave out anything unnecessary. Once resolved, the simple bones of a design are ideal to start weaving from. This leaves space and freedom to make choices at the loom as the piece develops.

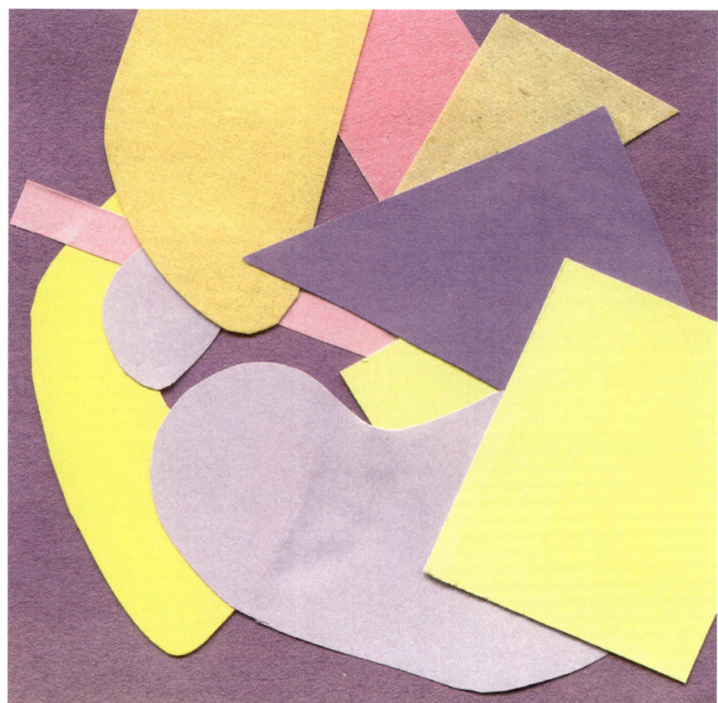

Curved, rectangular and triangular shapes cut to help create designs.

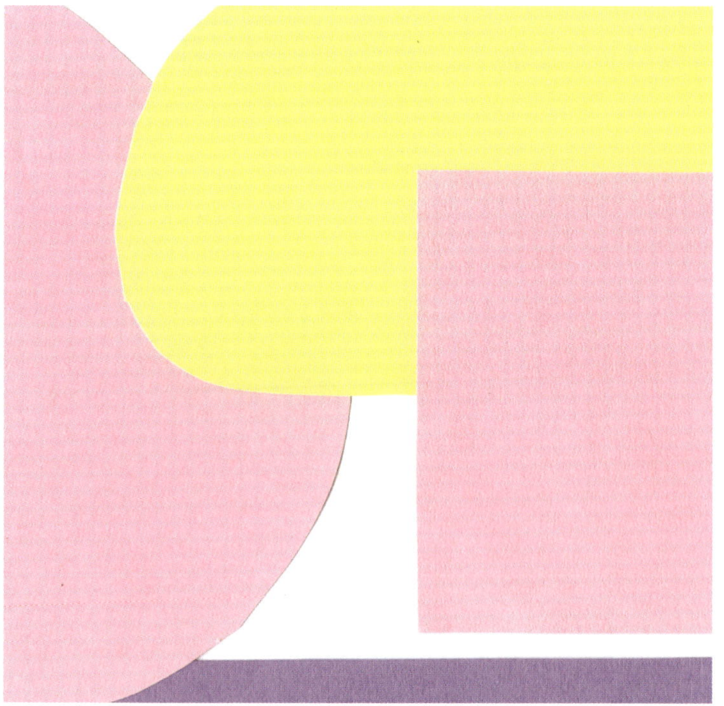

Collaged paper design.

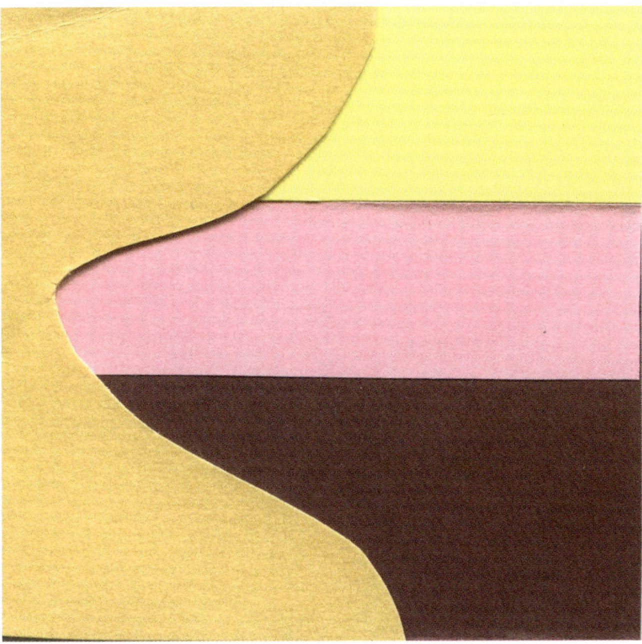

Collaged curved shape on top of three rectangles. This design could be seen to consist of four areas, or two, one of which is in stripes. The curved form appears to come forward adding perspective. The stripes, particularly the darker one, appear to recede. The counterpoint of curve against straight line adds tension.

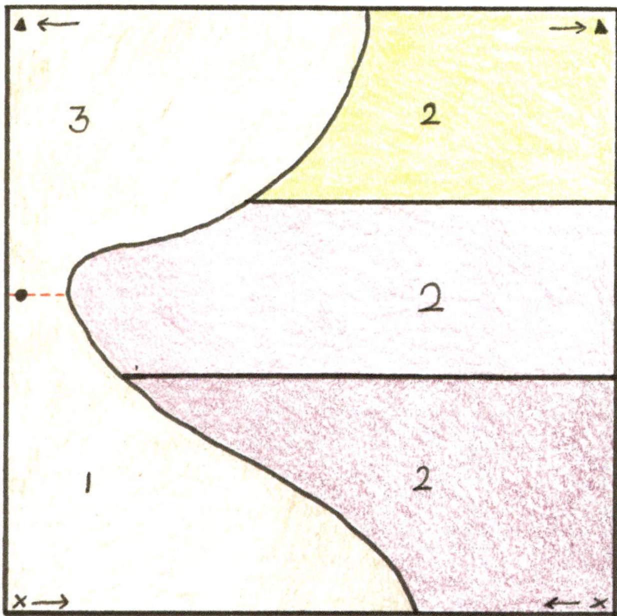

Plan of the collaged design. In this plan there are two wefts needed to weave the three areas. The bottom left area must be woven first. It must pause where the curve turns back towards the right until the infill on the right-hand side has been woven and the striped area continued to the top. The right side, although of three colours, may be seen as one area with changes of weft to form the stripes.

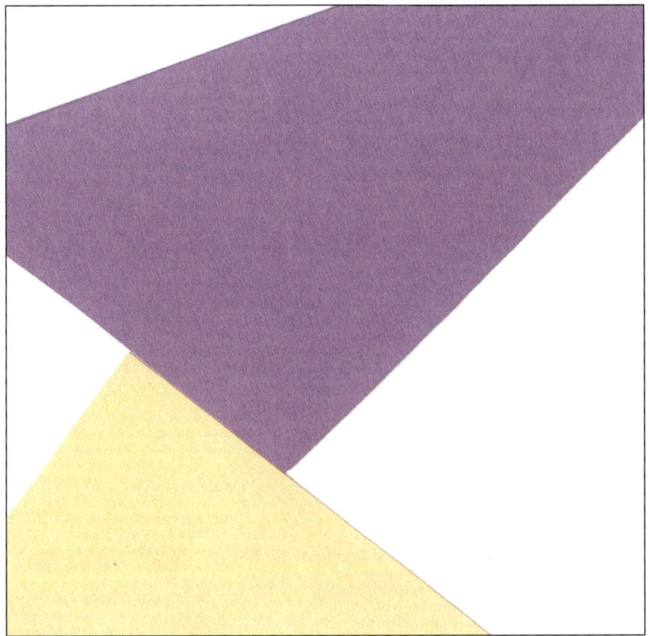

Two triangles and a background. Two differently angled triangles sit alongside but offset from each other. The design has been cropped so that some of the points of the triangles are removed. On first impression it may appear that each of the areas in this design could have been woven in one weft, but they would not then have remained in shed.

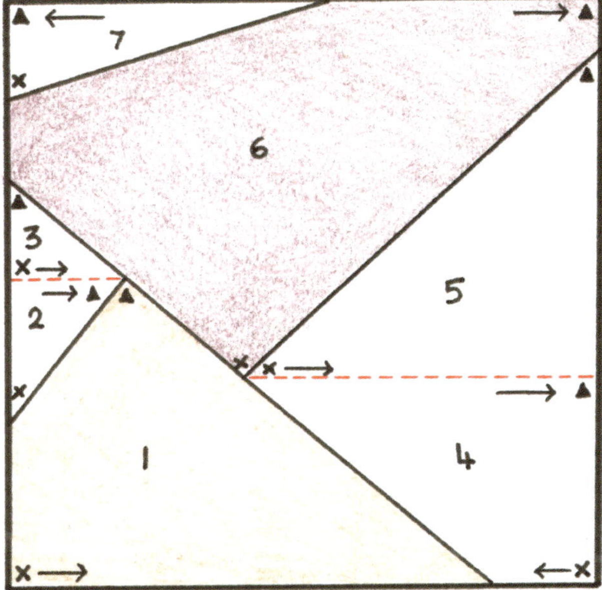

The collaged design planned out. Area 1 is the clear choice to start. This leaves the question of which direction to weave the triangles to either side. The answer is both, so the two areas are divided into 2 and 3, 4 and 5 with the top halves woven in the opposite direction to the bottom. This enables area 6 to remain in shed.

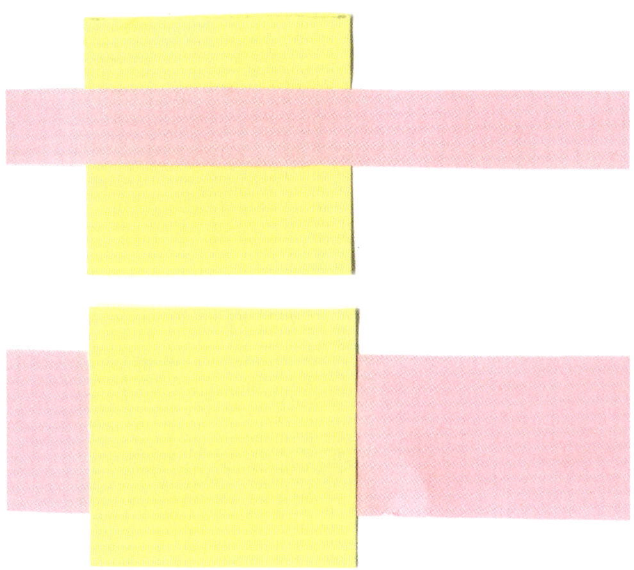

Two stripes and two squares collaged. Set on a background are two horizontal stripes and two squares, one passing under and the other over the stripes. This bold, simple design has been chosen to demonstrate how it may be interpreted using several different technical approaches with contrasting aesthetic effects.

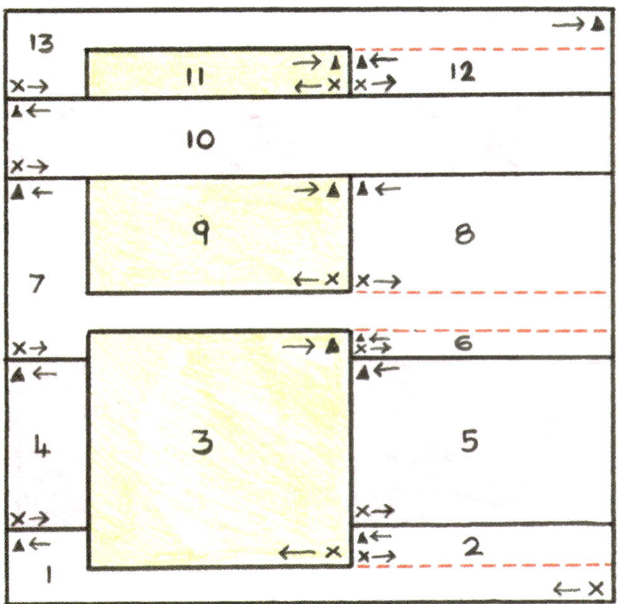

Weaving plan. Despite having 13 areas of weave and 12 changes of weft, there are only three wefts in play at any time. Areas such as 3, 4, and 5 need a weft each. The stripes to the right of the squares need to be divided into two and three sections, the weft starting and finishing each time.

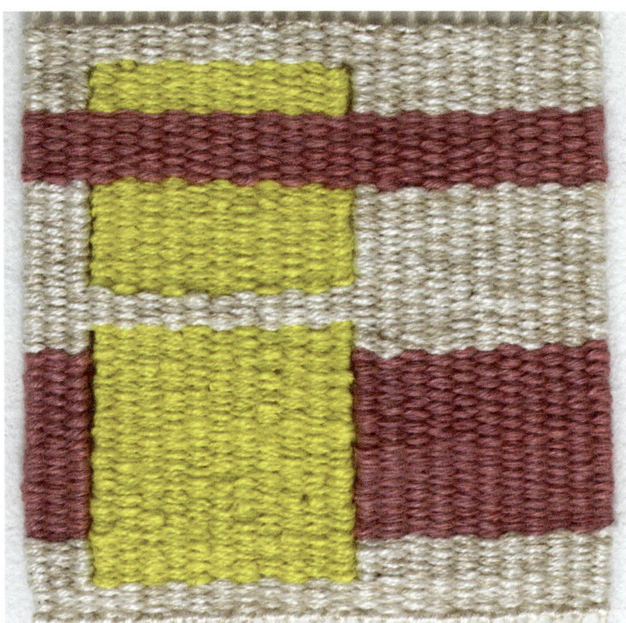

The design woven with slits. This sample uses 25 warps set at 8 epi. The wefts are linen and silk. In order that the two pink stripes sit level on either side of the yellow square, it is important to weave an equal number of weft passes in the areas on both sides.

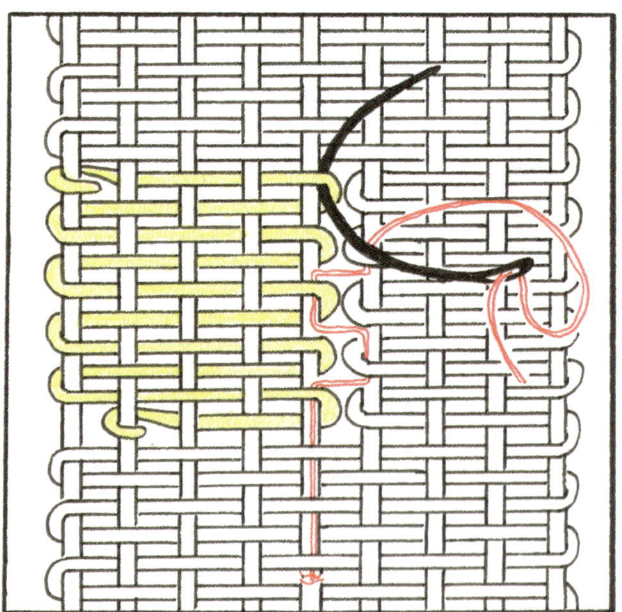

Sewing up slits. This may be done once woven – a curved needle works best. Wrap a double sewing thread round a warp and pass the ends through the loop to secure below the slit. Thread the needle and take the thread up inside the weave as far as the slit, then sew from side to side taking in alternate turns. Run the thread up under the surface, split and tie off, rethread and run further up before cutting off.

Weaving sideways. The same collage of stripes and squares has been now turned on its side, a choice which will mean that it weaves very differently. There will now be long vertical joins to the sides of the pink stripes which present a challenge as to how best to weave.

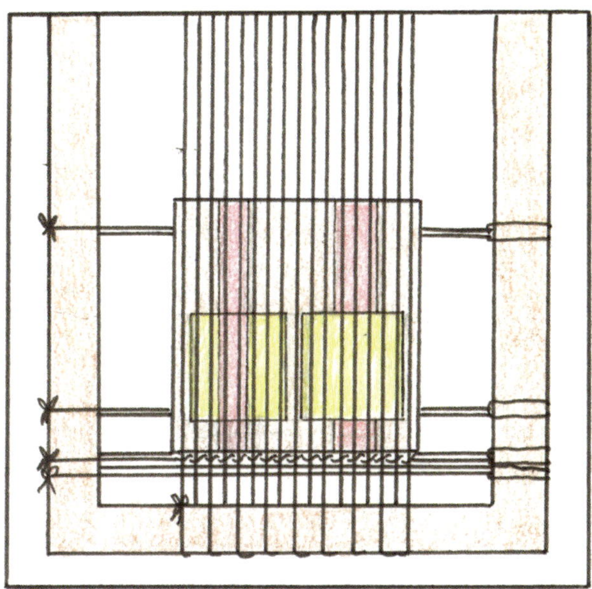

Using the collage as a cartoon. The actual collage is shown being held close to the back of the warps by two warp lengths tied across the loom. The collage is taped to these to secure. An alternative would be to make a line drawing to use as a cartoon keeping the coloured version to the side for reference.

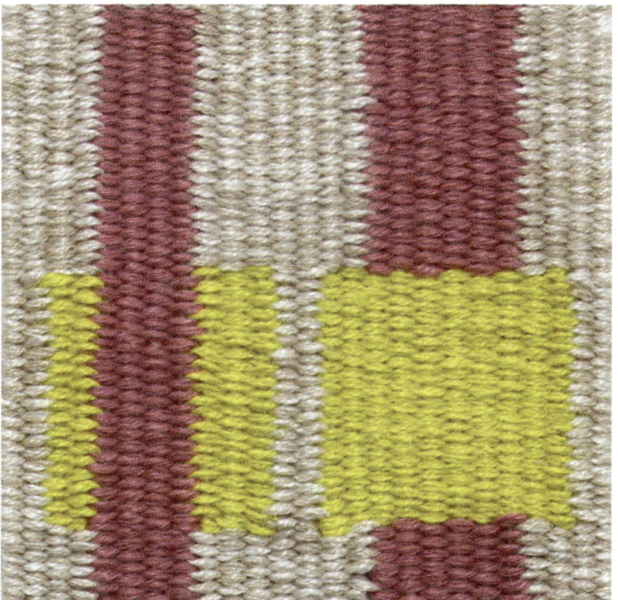

Design of stripes and squares woven on the side. For any design, there is the choice to turn the drawing sideways, either for visual reasons or for ease of weaving. In this case turning the design has resulted in long vertical joins which have been interlocked. Although taking longer to weave, an interlocked join is firm and does not need to be sewn up afterwards.

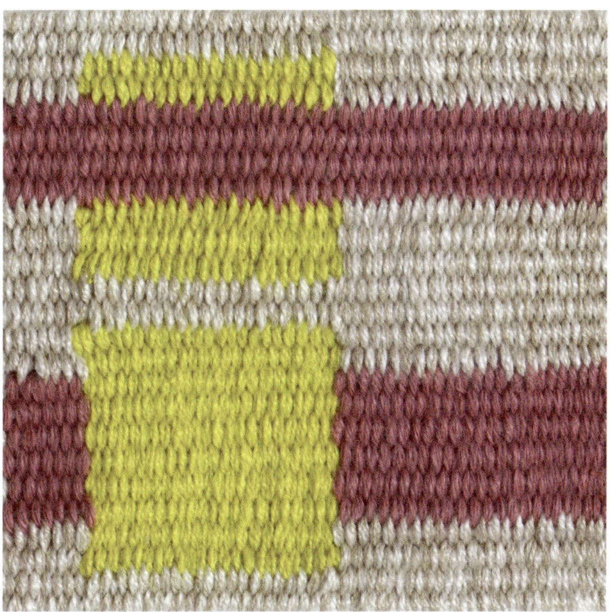

Appearance of the design woven and turned back to the horizontal. Although this is the same image as the previous one, just rotated, the effect of having the warps running sideways across the piece feels very different. The zip-like appearance of the interlocked joins appears more prominent, and certainly very different to the first version of this collage which was woven the other way round.

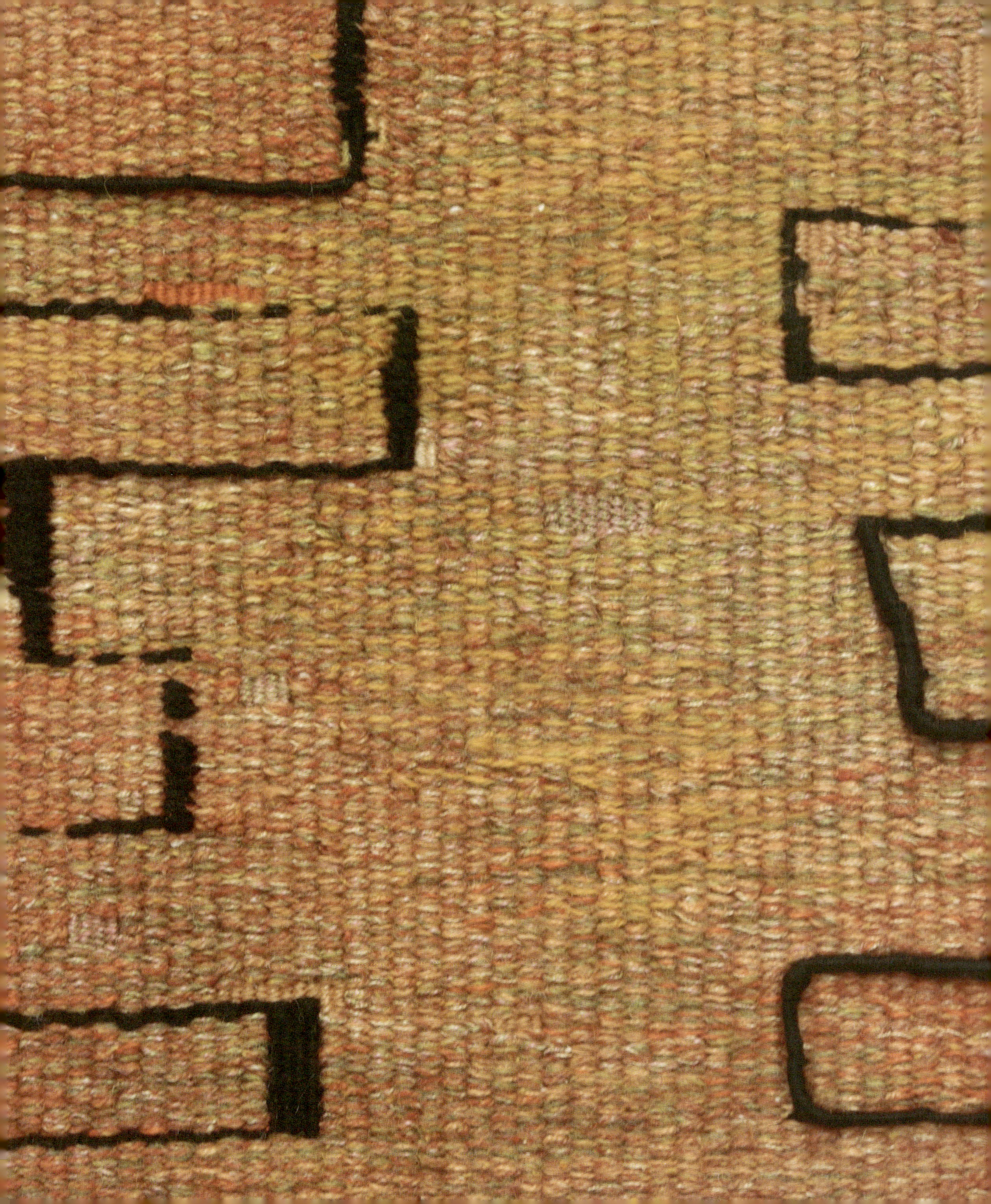

CHAPTER 6

TRANSLATING A CARTOON

Having dealt with the forming of shapes and management of wefts in the previous chapters, this chapter will move on to woven techniques which may bring these forms to life within a simple design. Here we will be making freer, more aesthetically driven choices. A range of subtle interventions will be illustrated. These may be applied in as many ways as can be imagined by the simple means of choosing yarns and by altering the scale and prominence of the marks. Whereas the previous chapters were about mastering the mechanics of weave, this chapter moves on to applying its essential language.

There are many ways in which one area of weave may be demarcated from another, marking both horizontal and vertical intersections and lines. Techniques may be chosen for aesthetic and structural reasons. This simple cartoon of only two lines has been designed to be able to be interpreted and woven in many different ways. These will be illustrated and their techniques explained. Simplicity in a weaving design is generally ideal, since it allows freedom to make more responsive and weaverly choices as the piece develops.

Having worked predominantly with a single strand of weft yarn in the previous chapters, we will now begin to explore further the mixing of yarns in a weft bundle. We will look at how strands of different colour and tone in a mix will alter its woven character, and how to judge how any combination of yarns might interact in a mix. Ways of interpreting a design by dividing it into different colour areas, how to change colour within areas and transition from one area to another will all be introduced.

Having covered the fundamentals of tapestry technique in the preceding chapters, this chapter is more about beginning to appreciate and understand some of the distinctively weaverly marks and qualities available to an artist choosing to work in tapestry.

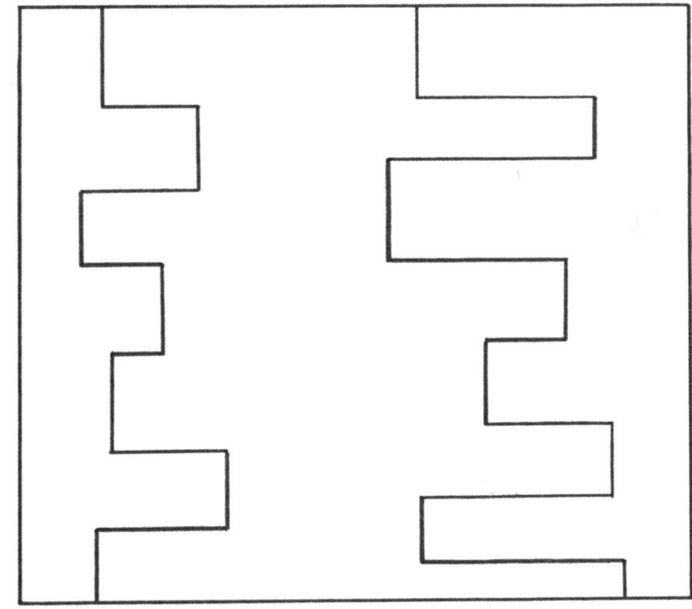

Sample cartoon as a line drawing

8 epi.Coloured double warp. Silk, linen and wool weft.

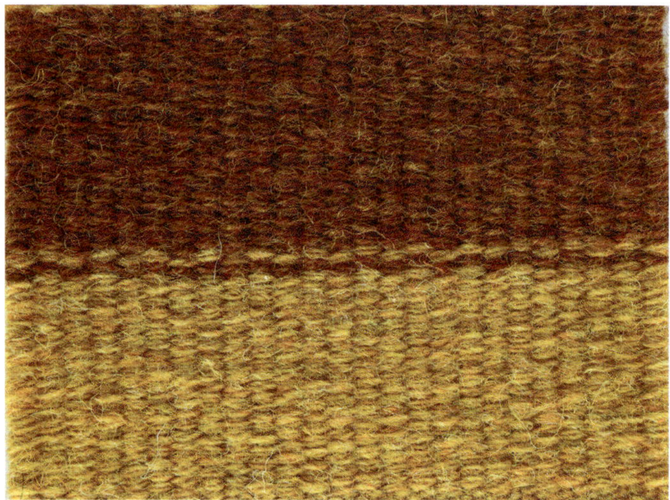

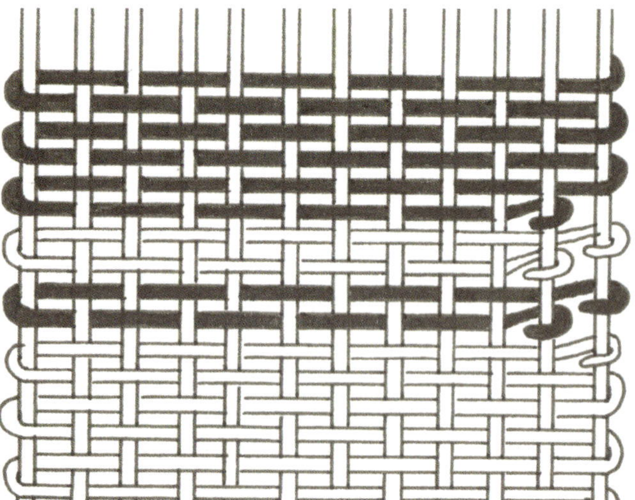

Pass for pass between adjacent areas at the transition. Pass for pass simply means a pass of one weft overlaid by a pass of another alternately. A pass is defined as a row both across and back, just one way being a half pass. Instead of simply changing from one area of weave to the next, one pass of the darker yarn then one of the lighter have been introduced before moving into the upper darker area. By alternating passes of dark and light weft the distinctively wavy nature of the woven line is highlighted. This sample has 25 warps at 8 epi. The weft in this case is a bundle of four strands of a slightly variegated worsted wool yarn.

For simplicity, all the wefts have been started at the right-hand side though this could equally well have been the left. Most important is to start and finish wefts on the correct warp to maintain the over/under sequence as detailed in Chapter 2. Although the wefts have been drawn starting and finishing, they could also have been floated up at the back to begin the next area. The number of warps drawn here doesn't correspond to actual warps, the scale has been increased for clarity.

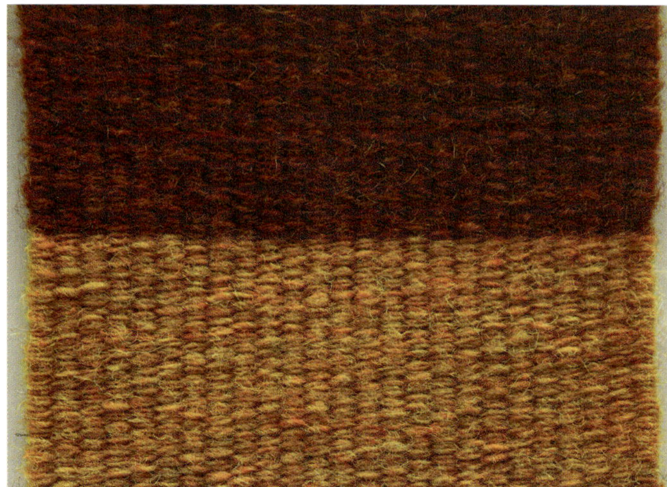

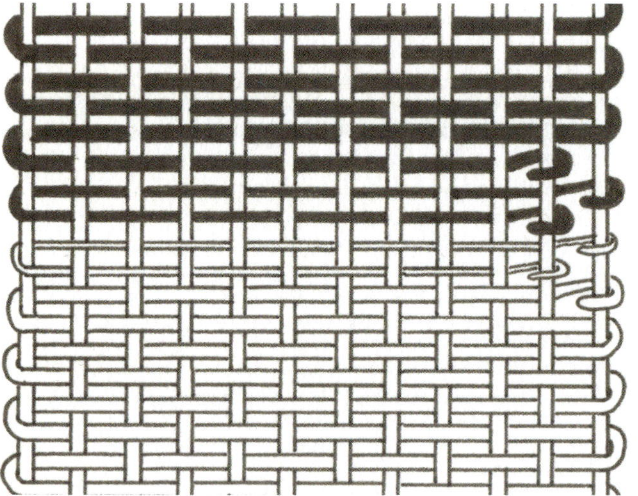

Creating a smooth transition between colours. This transition has been made as smoothly as possible, levelling out the natural waviness that would otherwise mark the change between areas. This technique relies on having two or more weft yarns in the bundle rather than just a single yarn as used in previous chapters. At the change of colour, a pass of only two in place of four strands of first the light then darker colour has been inserted. The effect of using a thinner mix is to make a slimmer bead as it passes over the warp and so reduce the undulating appearance.

Using the same starting and stopping places, one pared-down pass of the lighter weft mix containing only two in place of the previous four strands has been inserted. This is followed by a pass of an equally thinned down mix of the lighter colour. This way of making a transition effectively negates the weaverly nature of the line, but it can be useful where the aesthetic of a piece demands a clean line. Rather than starting a new thinned-down mix it is possible to simply take two strands from the bundle and add them back in at the edge. They would then either be finished with the whole bundle or picked up to continue weaving with as needed.

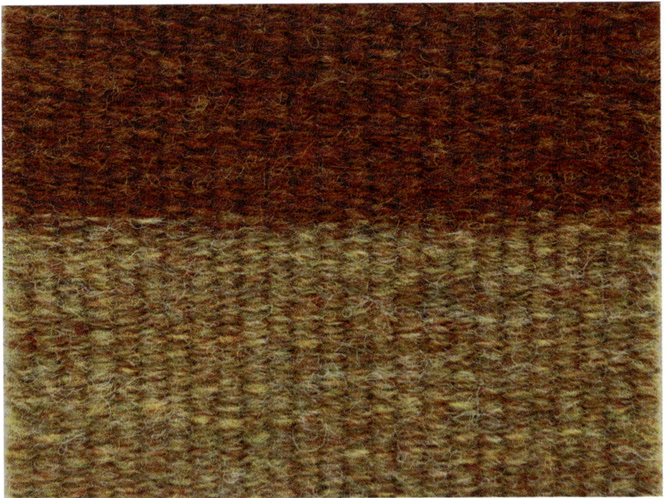

Blended transition. Here the transition has been made diffuse by the introduction of a single pass of a weft mix including both colours. Used here to soften the line, the blending of wefts between adjacent areas can be made simply and in many nuanced ways. Blending could be used to introduce a different colour, tone or texture, either closely related or contrasting. Both the proportion of the two colours in the mix and the number of passes made could be varied to alter the transitional area.

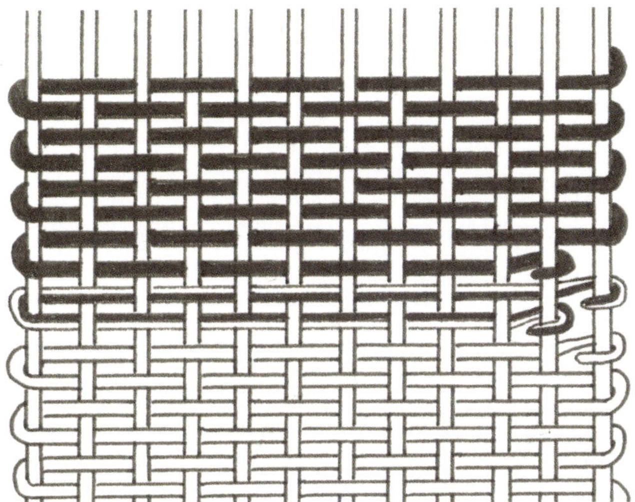

At the change from one colour to the other, a single pass containing two strands of each of the two colours has been woven. It would have been equally possible to put in a broader band of this mix or to have included a pass of 3:1 mixes before and after the 2:2 mix to make the transition more gradual and softer. A bundle of two colours does not need to be twisted together to create a mixed effect when woven. It should work to simply lay in the mixed weft bundle and beat down. Occasionally they will fall into a visible stripe, in which case simply raise that section into a mound and beat it down again.

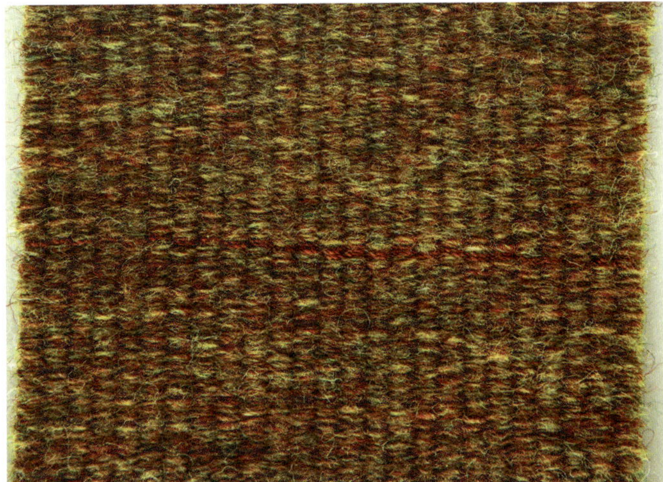

Inserting a pass of another colour. With the same yellow variegated weft used above and below, one pass of a darker brown weft has been introduced, forming a slim line showing the characteristic undulation of a weft passing over and under the warps. Here the line sits back from the surface, having been woven with a single strand of a rayon yarn. Being thinner and more tightly spun has caused it to bed down into the softer surface of the surrounding wool. The lustre of the rayon glints through in contrast to the surrounding woolly texture. Although the fibre is different, the colour is one which is contained in the wool mixes around it.

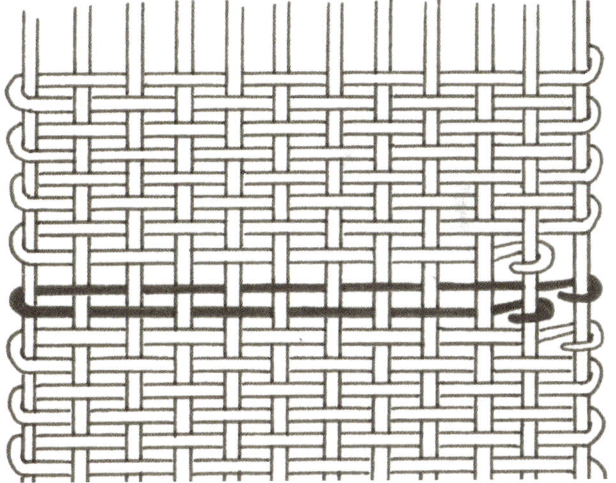

Here the single pass is shown starting and stopping at the right-hand side. Although the pass continues unbroken across the piece and back, because of the thinness and hardness of the mix, it is embedded into the softer wool. At times it is visible as quite a straight line, at others it becomes more wavy and to the right, almost disappears, although there is actually the same volume of weft all the way across. If a more definite line was wished for, then a second pass of the rayon weft would have provided this. This is one example of how yarn being a malleable material is not always predictable in the way it will weave.

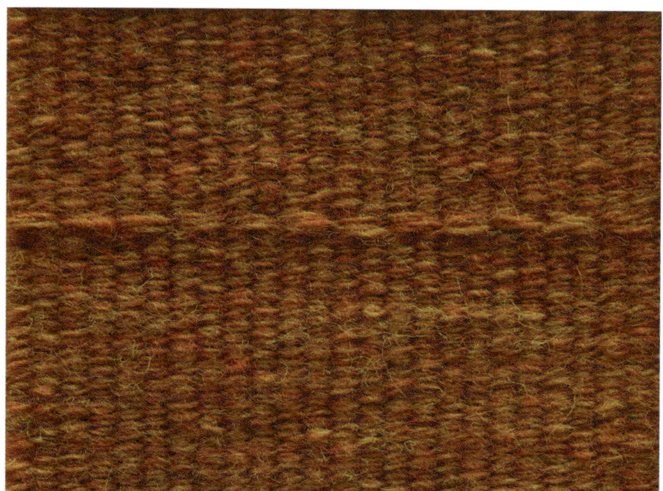

A double weave line. Double weave is simply weave which passes over and under two warps at a time instead of one. Although the mix is no thicker, the longer bead made when passing over two warps stands out from the surrounding single weave casting a shadow. A broader band of double weave would equally have been possible, giving a more marked effect. It could also have been made in any number of contrasting weft mixes in which case the personality of the yarn chosen would be particularly evident. For example, a bundle of many fine silk yarns might have produced a streak of reflective colour accentuating the longer bead.

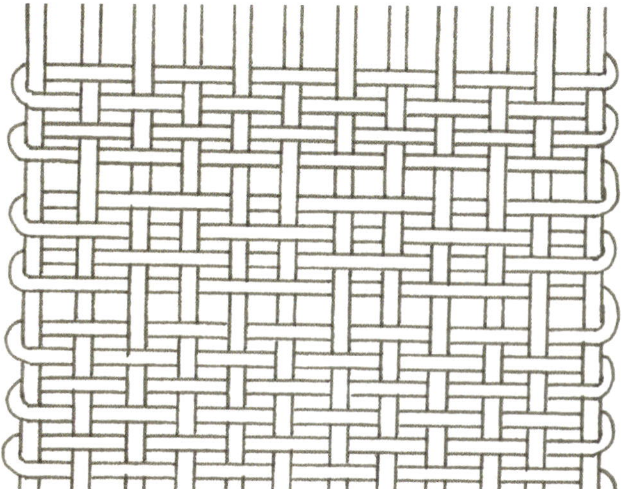

To form this line, the weft mix used to weave the lower area simply continues, changing from weaving under and over each warp it now passes under then over two warps at a time. This double weave continues for two passes before reverting to a single weave. You may note that when changing from single to double and back the weft will pass under and over some of the same warps. Because of the softness of the double weave, it is likely that any warps left showing will be covered once a couple of passes have been packed down. Care is needed to avoid pulling in when weaving double, as drawing the warps together can happen more easily.

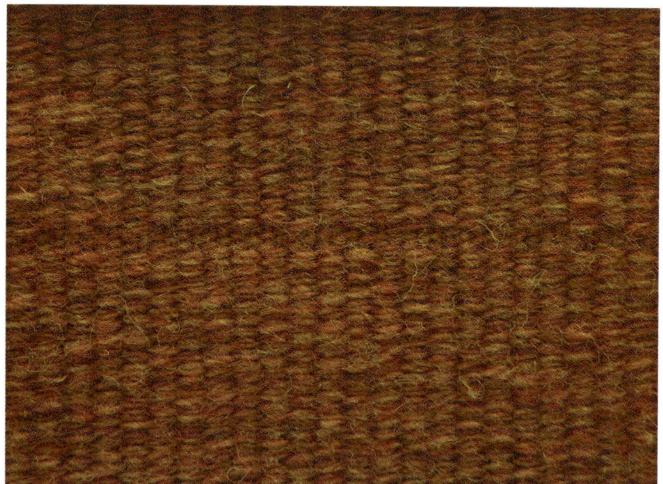

Single weave in a double weave background. In a reversal of the previous sample, here the background is made entirely in double weave, with a line made by weaving two passes of single weave. A thicker bundle of the same wool yarn has been used for the double weave background. This was thinned down by half to make the two passes of single weave. The resulting line has a harder texture set down into the surface of the surrounding area as if embossed. It catches the light rather as if part of an under layer of finer weave.

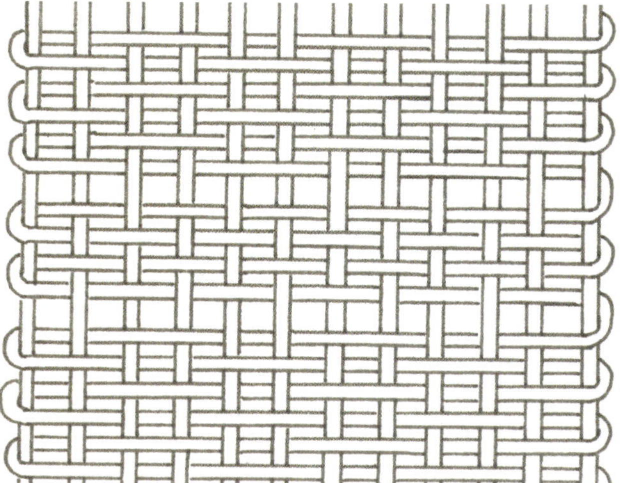

The transition from double to single weave has been made simply by starting to weave under and over each warp in place of two. The warps will group together into pairs because of being woven double. The first pass of single weave will need to be packed down extra hard to force the warps back into an even spacing. Make higher mounds to give extra weft length. Once the pass of single weave is complete, the double weave simply restarts, the first pass again being a little awkward as the warps have yet to settle back into pairs.

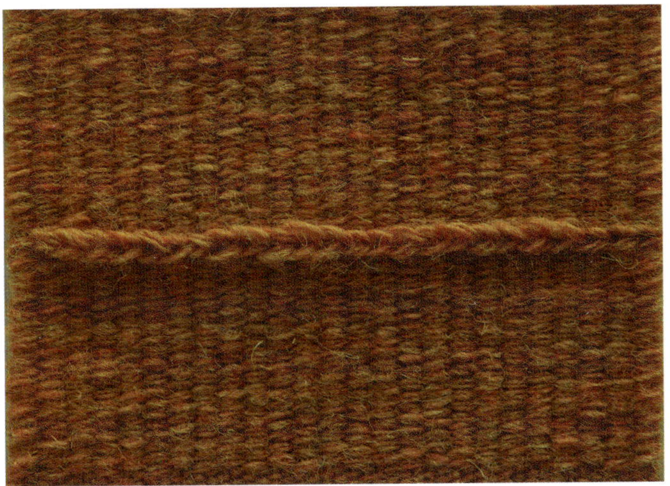

A 'chain stitch' line. Dividing two identical areas of plain single weave is a line with a similar appearance to a row of chain stitch in embroidery. Sitting on the surface, it is more raised than the line of double weave shown previously. Although here the 'chain stitch' line has been made by continuing with the same weft, it would have been possible to make a thicker mark by increasing the weft volume. As ever, there are many more possibilities to be experimented with. Here the 'chain' has been made with quite uniform loops, but this need not have been so.

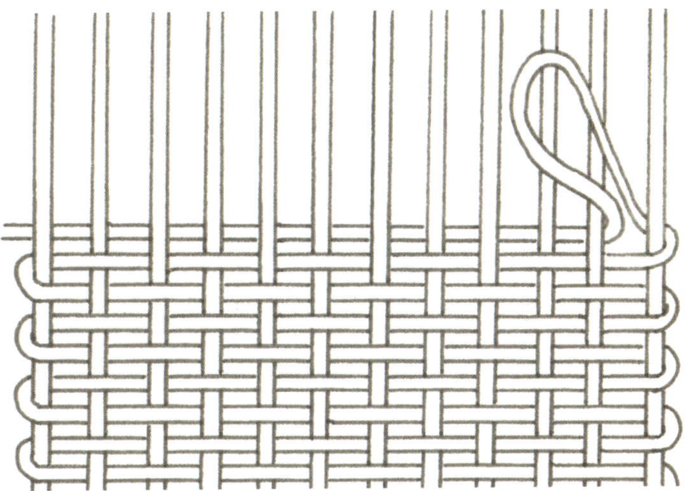

At the level the line is to be made, the weft is laid behind a whole row of warps, and then a loop is pulled forwards between the last two warps, shown here on the right-hand side. The weft will need to be held with one hand at the back of the warps whilst making the loops to create resistance. Note, forming a chain takes a much longer length of weft than plain weave. It is important to have at least double the length of the line to be made remaining before starting a chain since it's fiddly to renew a weft part way and is likely to look clumsy.

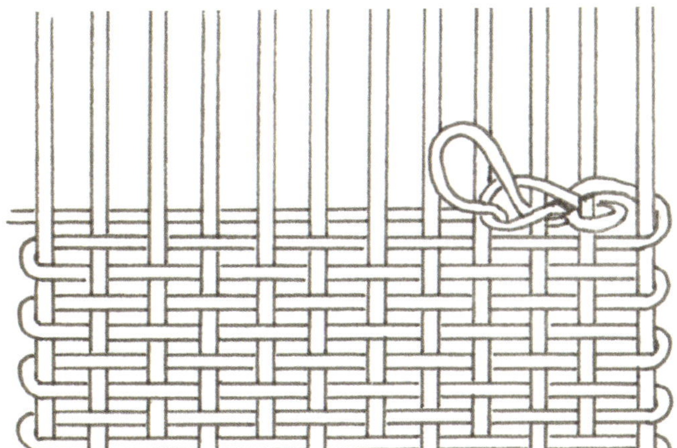

Working right to left, the weft which lies behind the warps is drawn up through the space between the next two warps, up into the loop previously formed and making a further loop between the next two warps. This action is continued working towards the left, drawing the weft from behind up through the loop in the space between each successive pair of warps. A crochet hook may be useful in taking one loop through another. In this sample, a loop is formed in each warp space, but there is also the choice to bring the loop out between every third, fourth or more warps which would form a more raised chain with longer loops.

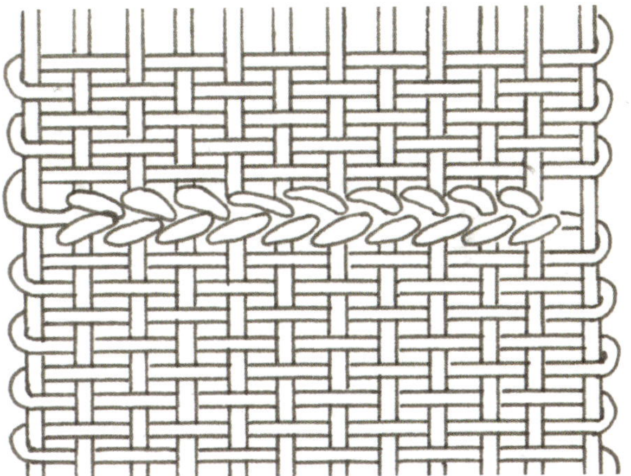

To make the loops even is quite tricky, requiring the open length to be held at the back, and each loop to be pulled through to the same length. If a regular chain is aimed for, it is necessary to make the loops equal as they are formed, as it is not practical to adjust them afterwards. On reaching the last warp, draw the weft right through the last loop, then continue to weave under and over each warp as before. The raised chain will pack down considerably after the first pass of plain weave but remain prominent on the surface.

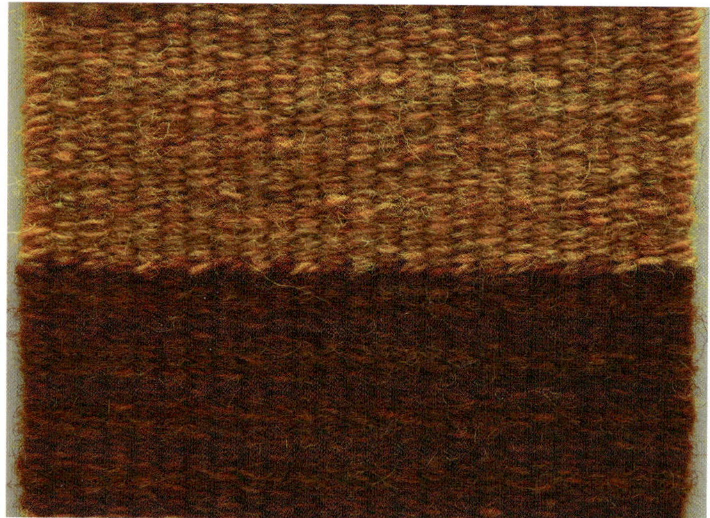

A line made by twining. We now return to transitions between contrasting-coloured areas of plain weave. Here the technique of twining, more familiar from setting up a warp, is used to make a line of slanting beads in alternating colours. The effect is of a softened line with a directional slant. Full instructions for the technique of twining are given in Chapter 1 which may be followed with the exception that here the twining wefts are not tied to the sides of the frame.

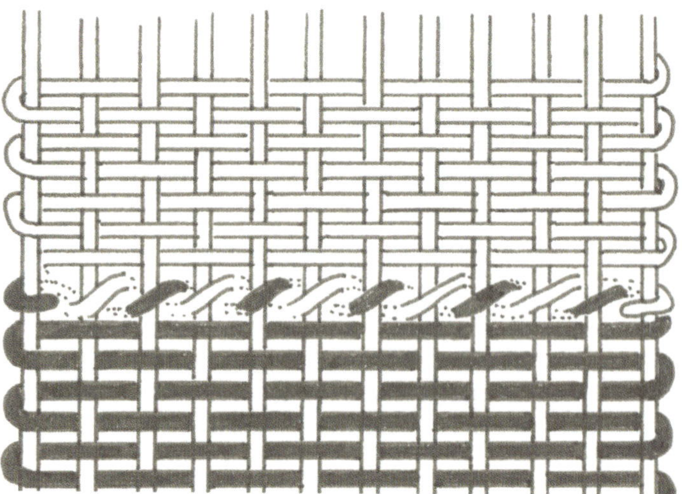

After weaving an area of plain weave, start a length of your contrasting weft mix as shown here at the right-hand side. Holding both wefts in one hand, twist one over the other in each space between warps. Then take alternate wefts over and under the next warp, to meet and twine over each other again in the space between the next two warps. The effect when twining two contrasting colours is of a slanting spiral. At the end of the row, the darker yarn has been finished with a half hitch whilst the other continues in plain weave. If the twining had been started at the left-hand side, the beads would have leaned towards the right.

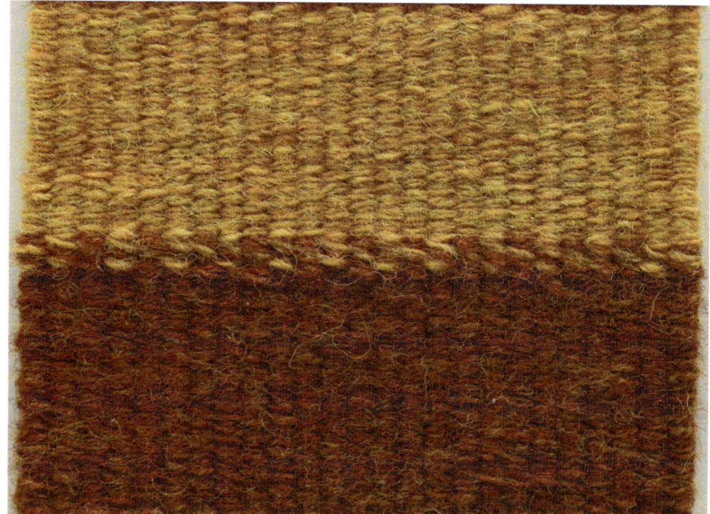

A wedge weave transition. This sample is similar to the previous sample in that the transitional band between the two-colour areas is made with alternating diagonal marks. These are now deeper and more pronounced. The marks now slant upwards from left to right. The technique in use here, termed 'wedge weave' is borrowed from Navajo folk weave and is explained more fully in Chapter 9 as one of several techniques termed 'eccentric', in which the weft passes through the warp at an angle rather than weaving straight across.

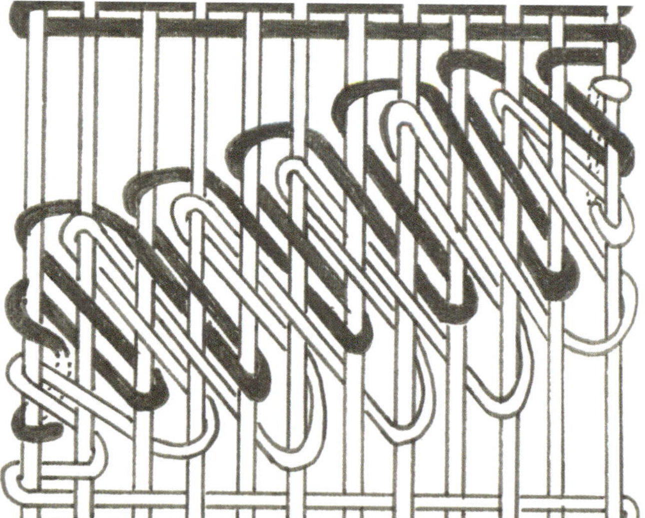

Here the lighter weft is woven two warps along from the left-hand edge before a length of the darker weft is started right to left on the first warp at the left-hand edge. The lighter weft is then woven up diagonally over the turn of darker weft, then back down and along to the fourth warp where it pauses. Next the dark weft is taken through from behind and woven until the third warp. Turning, it now weaves back up diagonally to the left and pauses to allow the light weft to make another diagonal pass, extending back down to the sixth warp before pausing. This sequence of alternating diagonal passes continues in parallel to the end of the row.

WEAVING A PICK AND PICK TRANSITION

This classic woven mark is made by alternate warps being covered by the same one of two contrasting wefts. The crenellated effect of a band of pick and pick is quite graphic and prominent. The bead appears longer with a toothed edge as it meets the contrasting colour. Shown here in a narrow band, pick and pick may be continued indefinitely up the warps and still result in a firm weave, since it does not result in slits in the way that turning on the same warps up a piece would do.

Weaving pick and pick on an even number of warps

In pick and pick, both wefts weave in the same direction. Each weft weaves just a half pass one after the other in the same direction. The lighter weft wraps around the end warp before pausing. The darker weft starts on the right-hand edge warp and weaves a half pass to the left before passing through to the back. The light weft now takes a turn round the left-hand edge warp, then goes under two warps before continuing to weave a half pass to the right, falling into the spaces left by the dark weft. At the second to last warp from the right, the light weft passes through to the back whilst the dark weft comes to the front at the left-hand side to weave another half pass to the right. It then wraps once on the last warp. Each weft continues to make a half pass, followed by one in the same direction by the other. After a few passes a vertical stripe begins to emerge. After three half passes of each colour, the lighter weft has been finished and the darker weft alone reverts to *plain weave.*

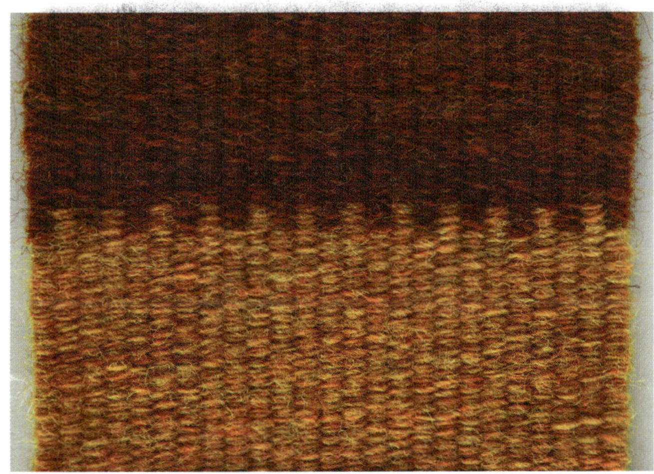

Transition made in pick and pick.

Weaving pick and pick on an odd number of warps

On a warp of an odd number, both edge wefts will be of the same colour. The light weft already in use is taken through to the back before the first warp, then a dark weft is introduced on the last warp to the right and weaves a half pass to the left, wrapping once around the first warp. The light weft then comes through to the front and makes a half pass to the right, going through to the back again before the last warp. Next the darker weft takes another turn round the first warp and back under two to get into sequence before weaving to the right-hand side, where it is wrapped once around the last warp, pausing at the front. After three half passes of each colour, the light weft is finished on the second last warp and the dark weft continues in plain weave.

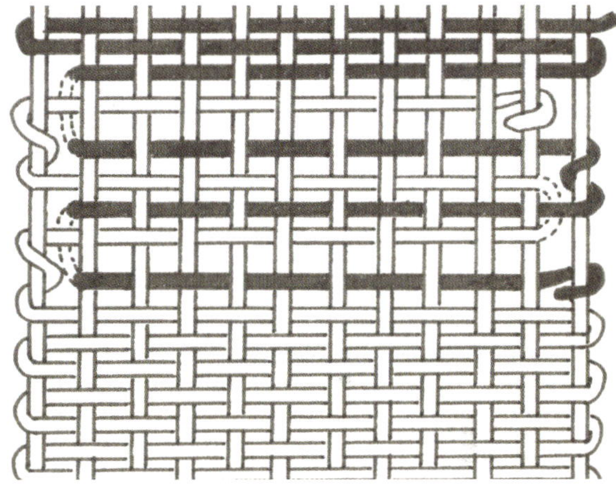

Pick and pick on an even number of warps.

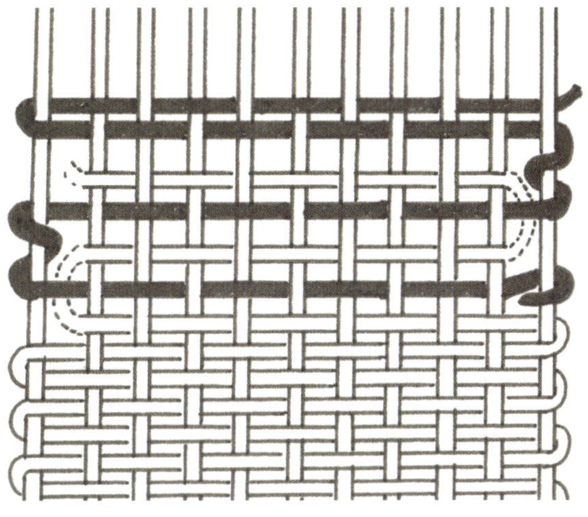

Pick and pick on an odd number of warps.

VERTICAL TRANSITIONS

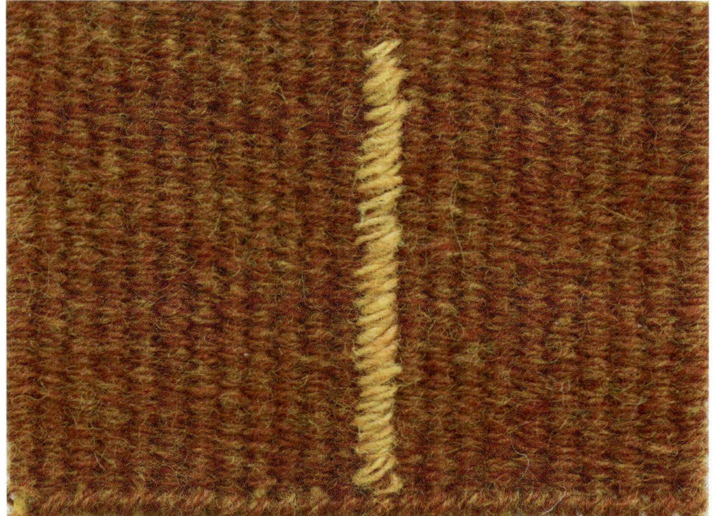

Vertical soumak. Against a plain weave background, one single warp has been wrapped using the lighter weft bundle thus forming a vertical line of turns sloping slightly upwards to the right. The line sits forwards of the woven surface of the background and has a contrastingly toothed appearance. This is a very useful way of creating a vertical line without compromising the strength of the weave by making slits.

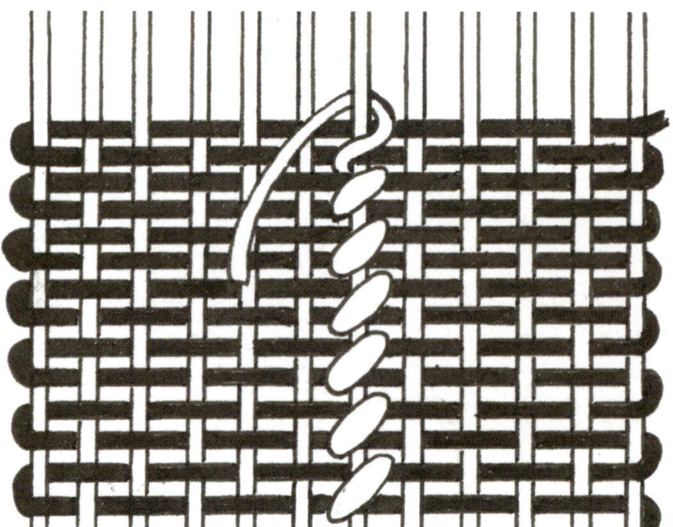

The background area of plain weave continues unbroken throughout, so that the weaving continues behind the wrapped weft. To start the soumak line, either a new weft is laid in or a weft floated up and brought through to the front of the tapestry. After weaving a pass, the background weft pauses anywhere away from the warp which is to be used for the vertical line. The light weft wraps once around the warp to the right after each pass of the background weave. This sequence continues until the line has reached the desired length. The wrapping weft is finished by simply passing the end through to the back of the weaving.

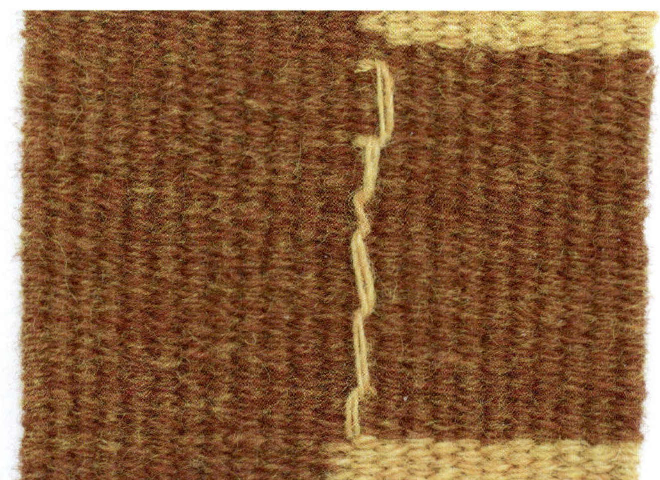

A floated soumak weft. Here this fine irregular vertical line has been formed over a continuous background of darker plain weave. The lighter weft makes a turn after irregular numbers of background passes. This line can move freely across the surface of the piece, a little like a drawn line. Two strands of a wool yarn have been used to wrap. The wrapping bundle could have been much thicker, or a single yarn could also work. The line moves in steps, each leaning slightly to the left or right depending on which way the turn is made.

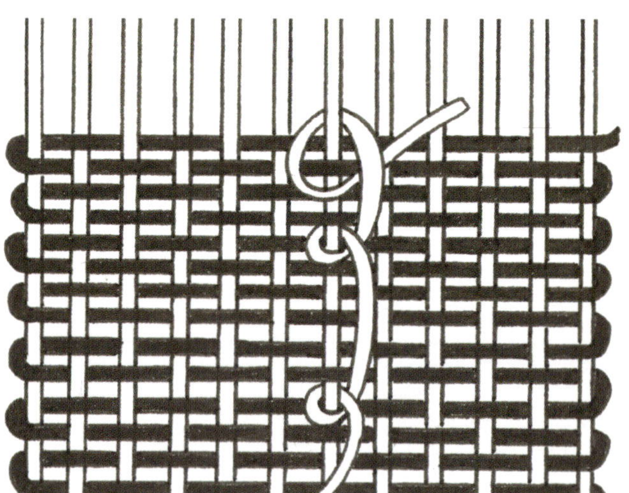

As before the darker plain weave is continuous and the wrap is overlaid. The light weft starts with a turn round any warp and is left hanging at the front. The background is woven up to the desired length of step. The light weft then makes a turn round either the same warp or one to either side just above the level of the background weave. The end is taken down through the turn before pausing again. The background is then built up to the next desired step. This is a useful way of creating a secure vertical line that is finer than a vertical soumak wrap. It is also possible to use a much thicker yarn or bundle to make a heavier line that sits forward of the background surface.

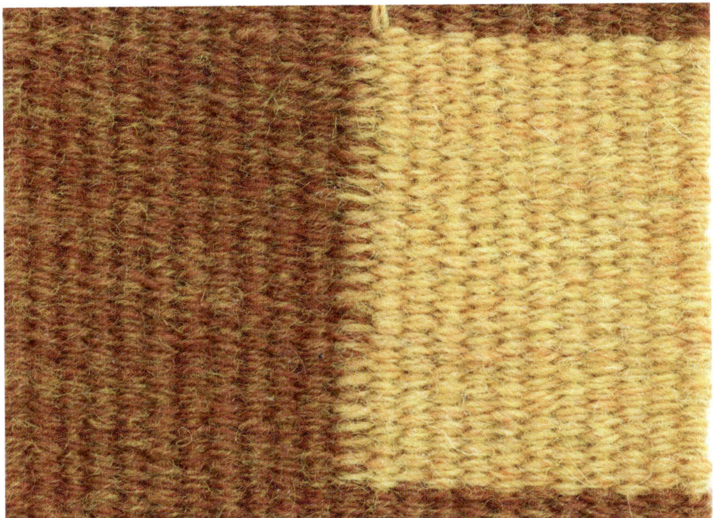

Interlocked transition. Here the vertical transition between the two contrasting colours has been made by an interlocked join. There are many kinds of interlock. In this case there is one warp on which the weft from both sides turns. This means that this warp has twice the number of turns around it. Because of the increased volume, this packs down to form a hard and very robust join. As with the interlocking shown in Chapter 2, the visual effect is slightly toothed, with beads of alternate colours creating a blended, slightly hazy-looking join.

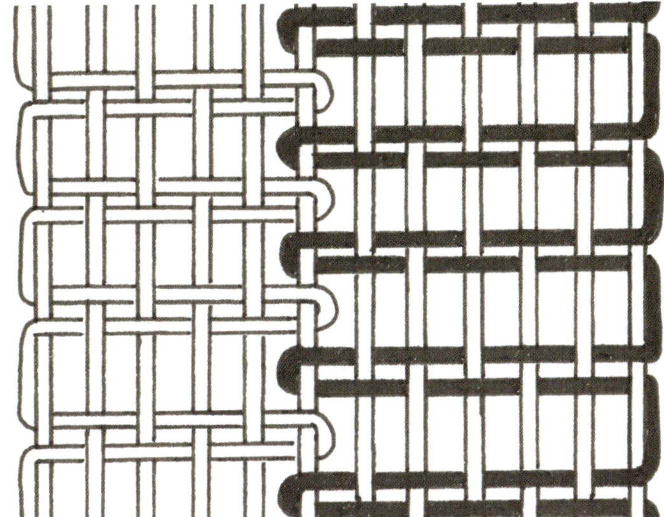

Interlocking may be made in a variety of ways following the same principles. Here, alternate passes of each colour are woven up to and including the warp on which the join is being made. This is different to the example in Chapter 2 when adjacent areas were interlocked in the space between two warps. Now, after making a pass and turning on the joining warp, each weft returns to its own side whilst the other weft does likewise, making a turn over the top of the turn in the other weft. At the point of interlocking, the weft will need to be beaten down very firmly because of the doubled number of turns. This may not work well if the weft is too thick or the warps too closely spaced.

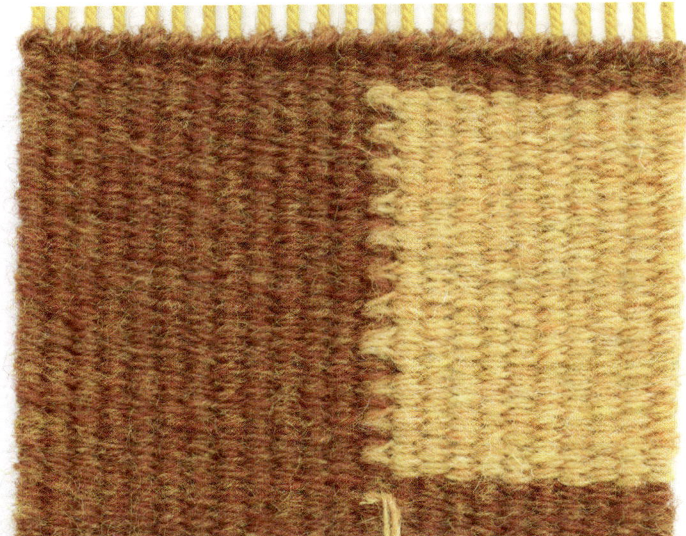

A dovetailed join. This dovetailed join has a more obviously toothed appearance, with intersecting points sloping slightly inwards. Passes from both sides turn on the same warp creating a greater number of weft beads which need beating down firmly. There are different ways to weave a dovetail. An alternative is to weave three passes of one colour, then three passes of another, all turning on the same warp. As with most interlocking techniques, a dovetailed join is very robust and stable.

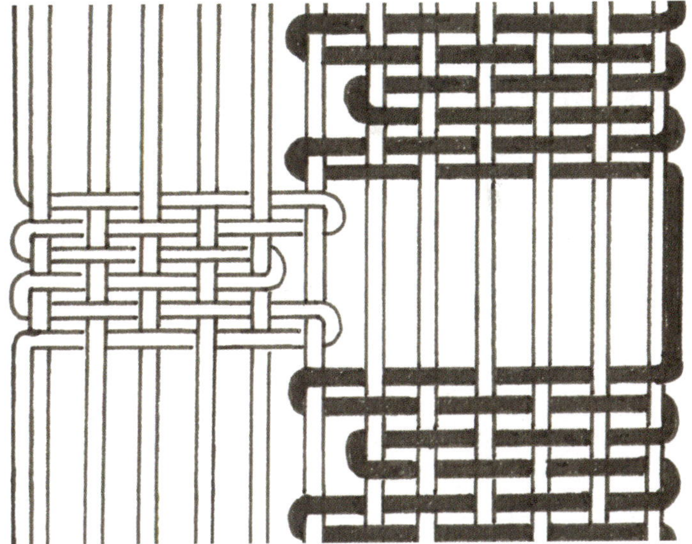

Here there is one joining warp on which both wefts turn. Working from either side of this joining warp, each colour in turn weaves three passes. The first and third pass turn on the joining warp, whereas the middle pass turns on the next warp back from it. This means that when the first and third warps are beaten down, they meet diagonally over the shorter pass in between. This forms the pointed shape of a dovetail. As with any weft which passes at an angle across the warp, care is needed to put in extra weft otherwise the weaving will draw inwards at this point.

TRANSLATING A CARTOON USING BLENDED WEFTS

This design of simple stepped lines has been woven to show several contrasting interpretations, the first being the use of blending. In the preceding chapters, a single thick weft yarn was used for clarity and to simplify learning. However, it is much more the norm in tapestry to work with a weft bundle made up of several strands. These may vary in colour, fibre and weight. Using only five different coloured yarns as in this sample means there are already over 120 possible combinations. Given the range of different fibres that yarns may be spun from, available in all colours and tones and of any thickness, the choice rapidly becomes endless. One could argue that this choice and the way yarns blend whilst retaining their individual characteristics is one of the greatest strengths of tapestry as an art medium. The simple blending of wefts gives the weaver a unique advantage, offering qualities of colour and texture not available in paper or most other media.

It may appear from the many shifts of colour within this sample that the weaving is complex, but this really is not so. The shifts of colour and tone have been made simply by changes in the blending of the weft mix. The sample has been woven with only three individual wefts, one each for the middle, left and right sides. Each weft bundle is made up of three equal weight wool strands chosen from a range of only five colours. They are altered as the weaving progresses vertically by exchanging one strand at a time. In order that the weft changes happen at random and largely unnoticed points, the wefts are cut to different lengths up to 1 metre and so finish at different points. The vertical joins are marked with a simple slit, and the horizontals with a change of weft.

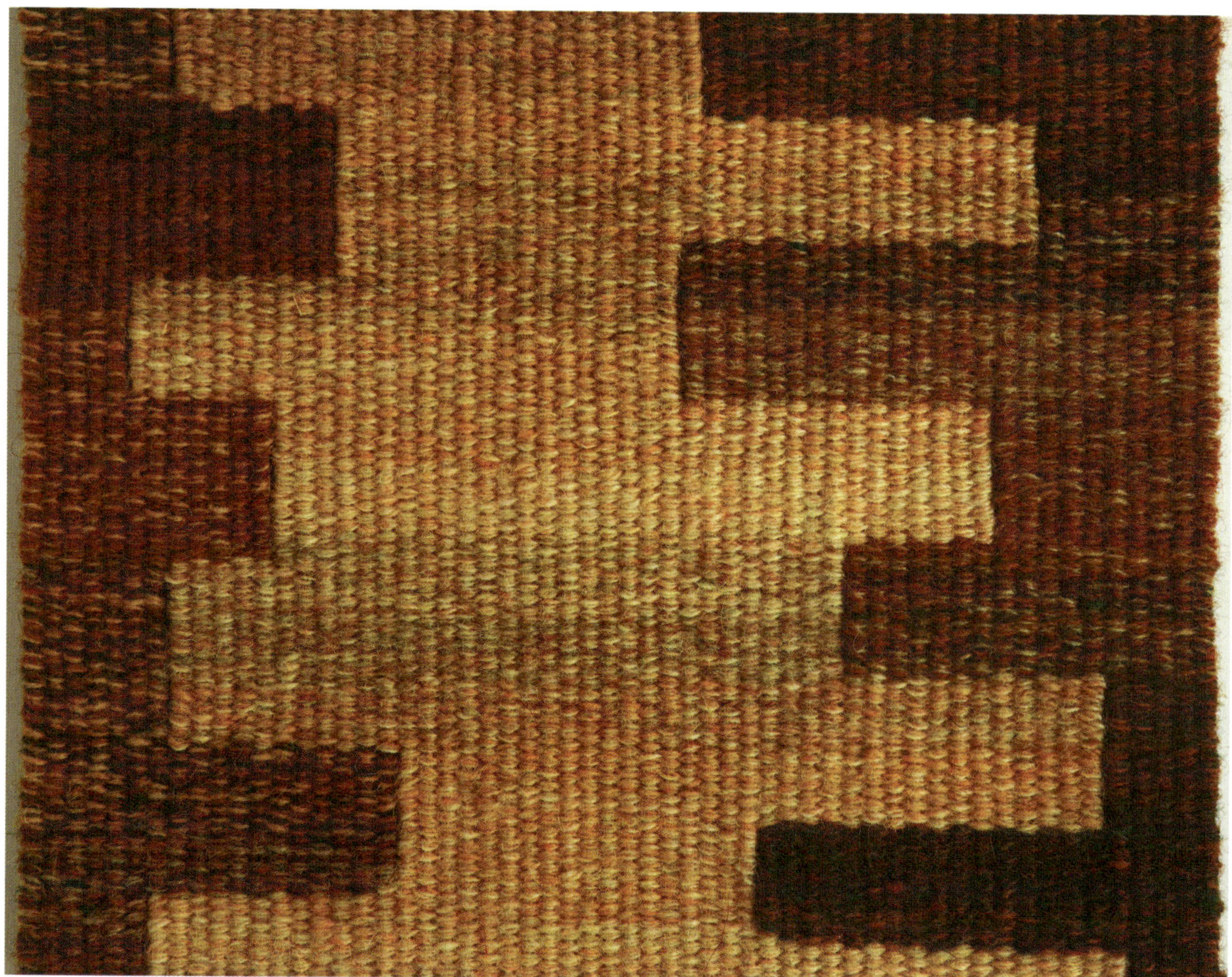

Tapestry woven from the cartoon printed at the beginning of this chapter at 8 epi. Medium cotton coloured warp and wool weft.

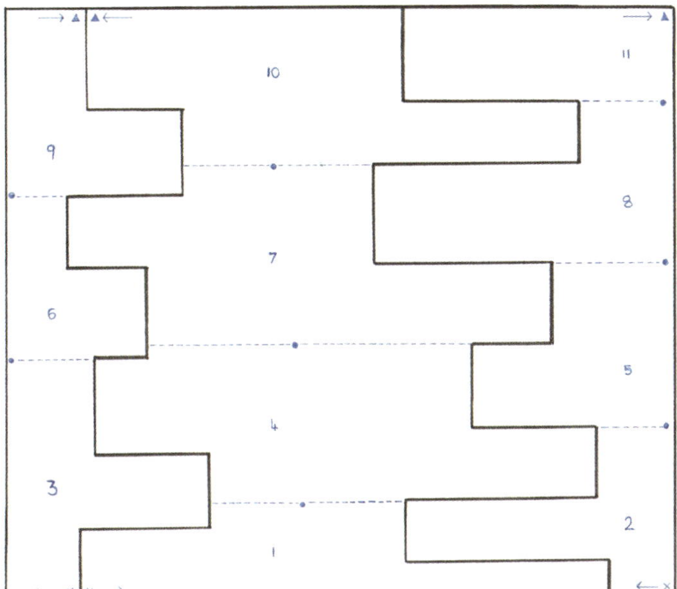

Weaving plan. Area 1 is the largest possible area to begin with. The starting place for each weft is shown with an x, and the finish with a small triangle. The three wefts are woven in turn, left and right across the piece. Note, each weft is woven all the way up, although paused at several points. When each weft bundle runs out it is replaced by another as if weaving continuously, with one of the three strands changed for another colour.

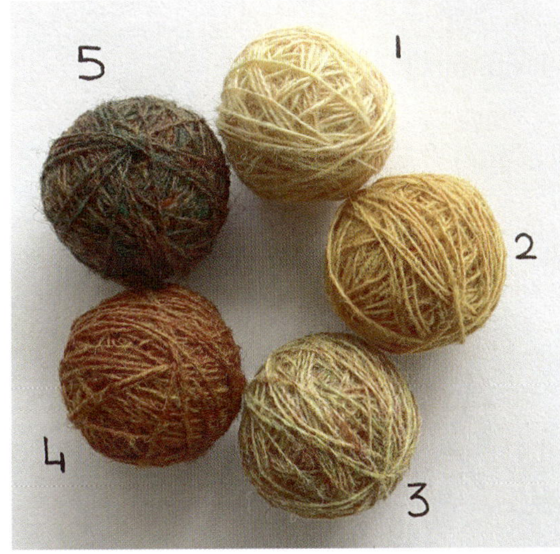

Here are the five weft yarns used in the sample. Each of these is a single ply worsted wool spun from fibres of subtly varied colour (what is termed a tweed yarn). Solid-coloured yarns could equally well have been chosen but variegated yarns can make a particularly fluid transition between mixes. The tonal range within the five yarns selected is quite large, so that the effect of close and disparate tones within a mix can be shown.

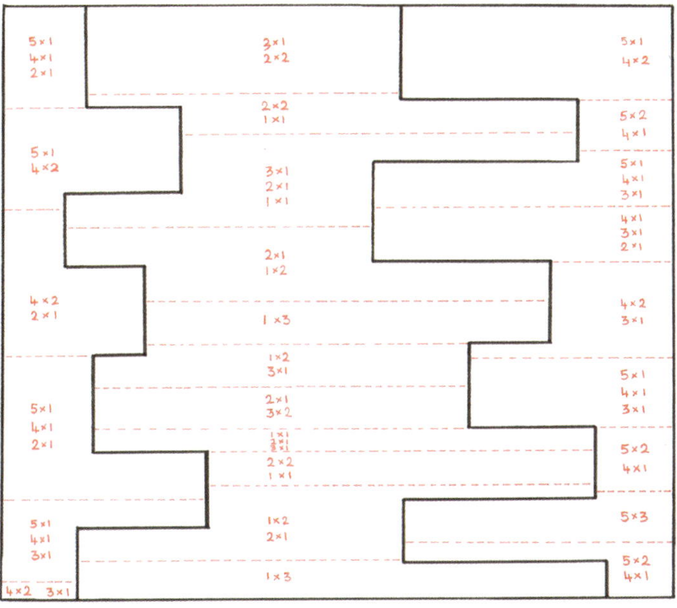

The mixes used. Here, the sequence of changes in the mix throughout the three areas is shown using the numbers with which the illustration of the five yarns is labelled. All the mixes have three strands. Mix 4×2, 2×1 means two strands of colour 4 with one strand of colour 2. The mixes move from three of the same colour in stages, replacing one strand at each change. These changes were not pre-planned and are numbered only for illustration. If weaving this sample, select your own weft mixes as you weave, changing one strand at a time.

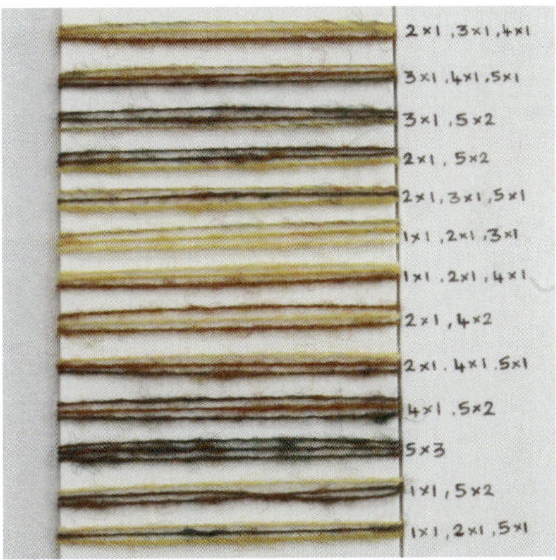

Mixes of three strands from the same weft selection. Three strands have been wrapped together around a card to see how a blend might look when woven. Another way is to twist short lengths of the yarns together, then wind several times around a finger to observe. Weaving a small area gives the best idea, for which a narrow strip of warp at the same sett to one side of the loom is very useful.

TRANSLATING A CARTOON BY WEAVING ON ITS SIDE

Here the cartoon has been rotated to the left so that the wefts now run parallel to the 'side arms', rather than with the broad mid-section. As viewed in this image, the warps run left to right and the weft up and down, contrary to the way the piece was actually woven. It has been rotated back to the original position to demonstrate the difference in appearance when the weft changes work across the piece rather than bottom to top.

Apart from the altered 'feel' of having the warp running vertically, there are various other reasons why the choice to weave a design on its side might be made. Long, narrow or repeated vertical areas for example present difficulties in a way that horizontal ones do not. They necessitate frequent weft changes and mean making the choice to weave with slits or to interlock, which alters the quality of the line. Angled lines which are close to vertical or steep curves are both difficult to make appear smooth. This is because the number of passes needed between each step makes the steps very visible. Both marks become much more weaveable once the design is rotated by making the lines closer to the horizontal.

Historically, large tapestries have generally been woven on the side so that when hung, to avoid the surface buckling as the wefts slide down the warps. The slits then need to be securely sewn up.

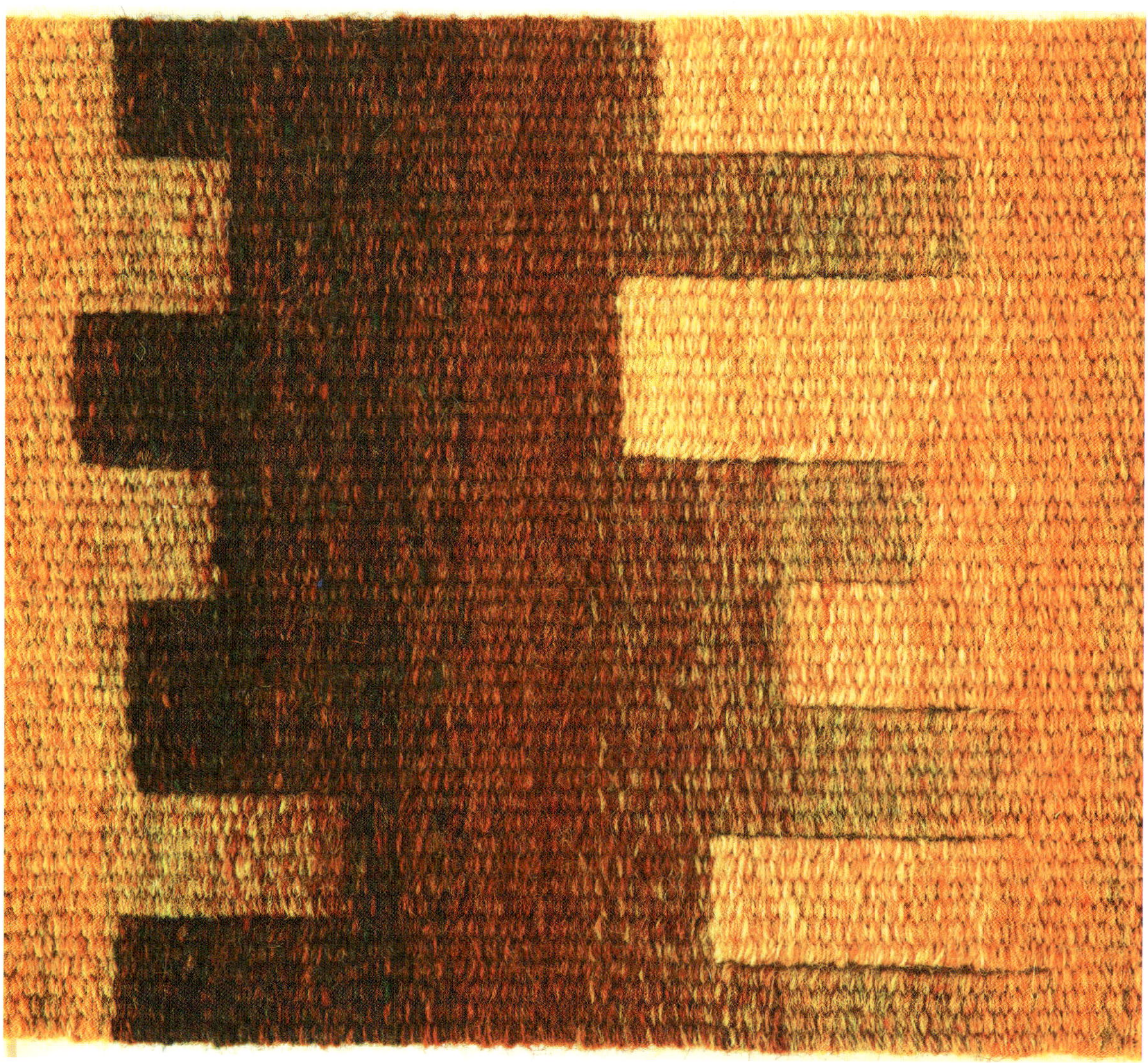

Tapestry woven on its side. 8 epi. Cotton coloured medium warp, wool weft.

Weaving the cartoon

Starting at what is shown as the right-hand side, the wide band of mixes made from colours 2 and 3 becomes increasingly lighter as they rise up between the vertically woven columns. The vertical columns begin softly at an almost imperceptible point, marked more by the forming of slits than the colour change. As the columns extend upwards, beyond the central band, the colour mixes change to include more of colour 3 to 4 to 5.

As the background area re-emerges between the upper columns, the mix initially contains touches of the red/brown yarn 4. These give way to the lighter yarn 3, easing gradually back into the yellow 2.

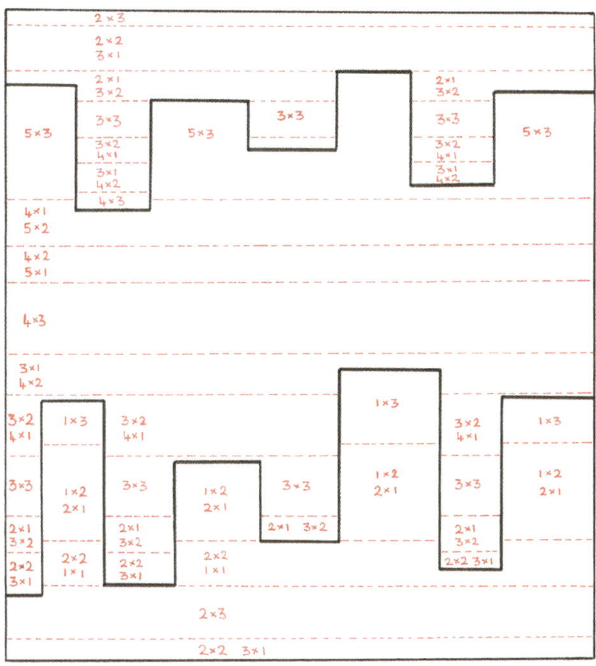

The sequence of mixes. Again, these are for illustration – if weaving the sample you could make your own choices. There are three strands in each weft bundle which are swapped one by one. In this sample the changes have been made incrementally from three strands of the lightest colour to three of the darkest, resulting in a smooth gradation of colour and tone from one to the other.

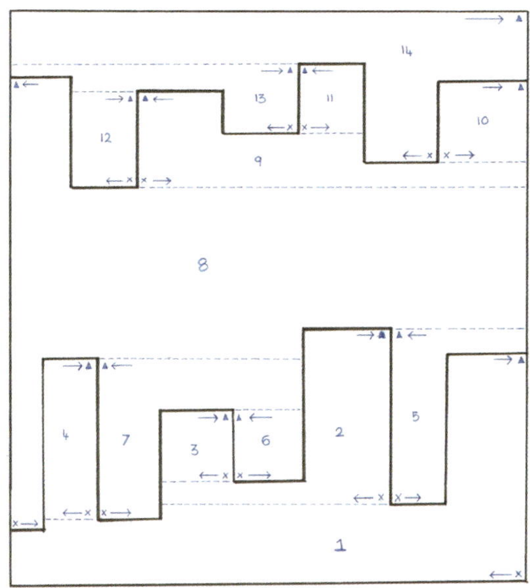

Weaving plan for this design woven on its side. This weaving plan shows how much difference there is in the new order in which areas need to be woven. Because there are more areas to be formed from left to right, this plan now has 14 in place of the previous 11 areas to be woven. Area 1 extends all the way across the piece, forming what will become the right-hand side. The narrow areas are now woven as columns, rather than horizontal arms each needing its own weft. The central area 8 can now be woven right across in a broad band.

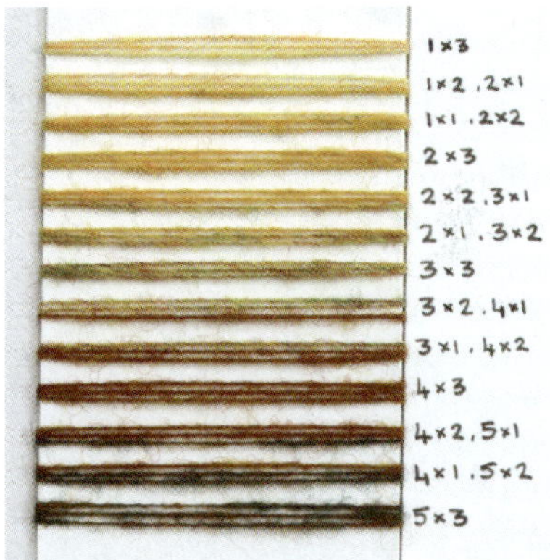

The appearance of the mixes. The 13 different weft mixes used in this sample are wrapped around a card to show their individual appearance and the gradual shift from one to the next. Again, a weft mix of three strands of wool yarn from the same range of five colours has been used throughout. In place of randomly selected mixes, the colours now shift incrementally from a solid mix of one colour to another. In order to focus on achieving a smooth colour transition, the yarns chosen differ only in colour, not in texture or lustre. Here, they are all the same single ply worsted wool tweed.

Same design interpreted with outlining

The intersections made between areas in this version would be unlikely to have been made in any other medium but weave.

The design is now returned to its original orientation as shown, with the warps running vertically and the design sitting with the narrow 'arms' extending sideways. In place of frequently changing colour mixes, this sample has been woven using only two mixed bundles of wool yarns. The weft bundles for each side and for the central area remain the same from bottom to top.

Instead of areas simply meeting in the form of a slit or being marked by a change of colour, the actual outline has now been marked. The horizontals are marked by using alternate passes of light and dark. The verticals have been outlined by making a hatched join on one warp. The effect of these techniques when used between two very contrasting wefts is bold, dynamic and very weaverly. As is often the case, the actual weaving of this outlining is simpler than the appearance might suggest.

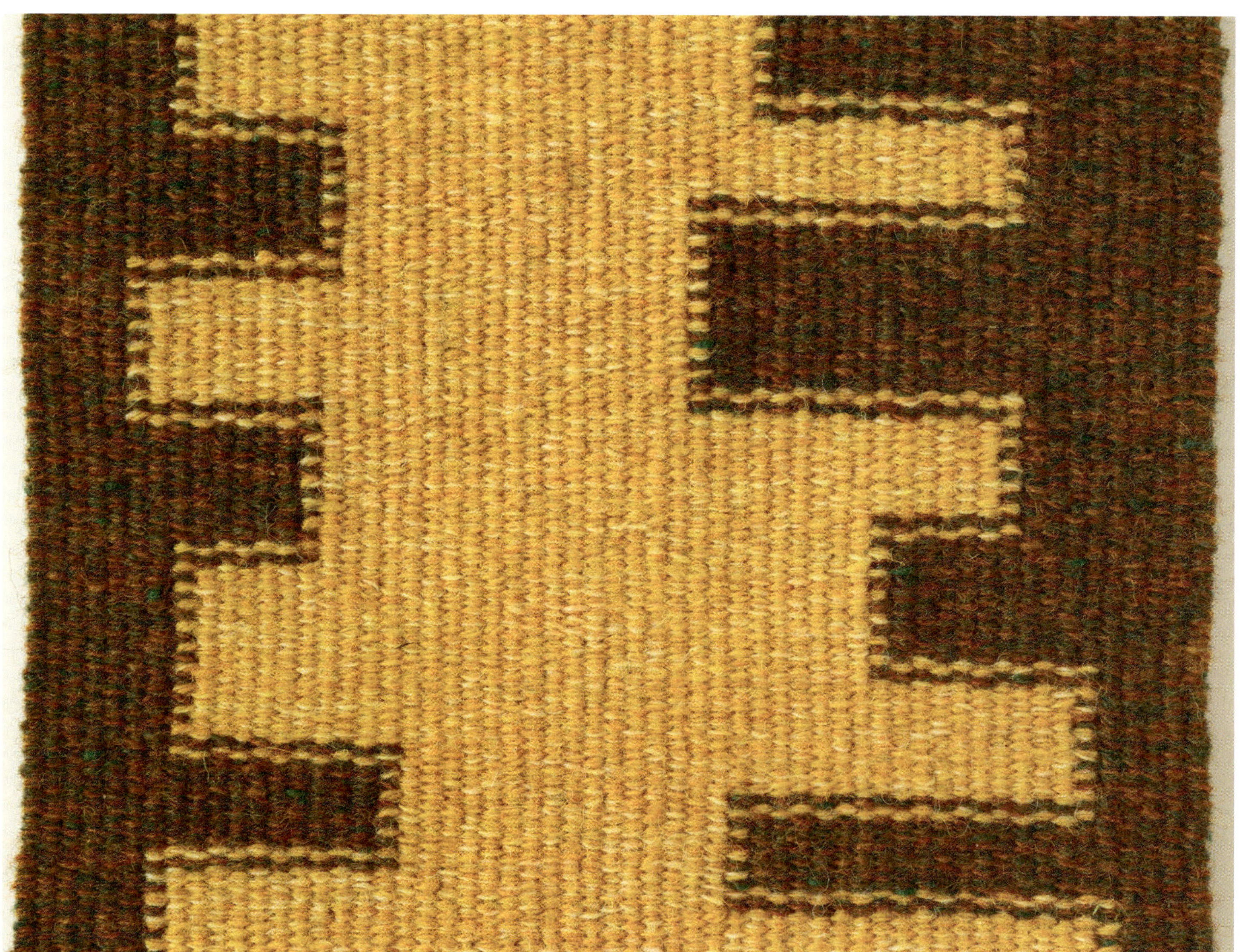

Hatched tapestry sample. 8 epi. Coloured cotton medium warp, worsted wool weft.

This sample is included as an example of how a simple premise can work well as the basis for a piece. The whole design being based on a simple form, here it is interpreted with striking outlining. Although the outlining technique and basic design were preplanned, a simple framework can give freedom to experiment with subtle shifts and changes within it. The choice of working freely or to a drawn design is very much a personal one. Making considered choices before starting often means being able to think about what is really wished for. Avoiding unnecessary complexity is always worthwhile in weave, and often results in greater impact. It also frees mental energy, allowing the weaver to observe and respond instinctually to the weaving as it develops.

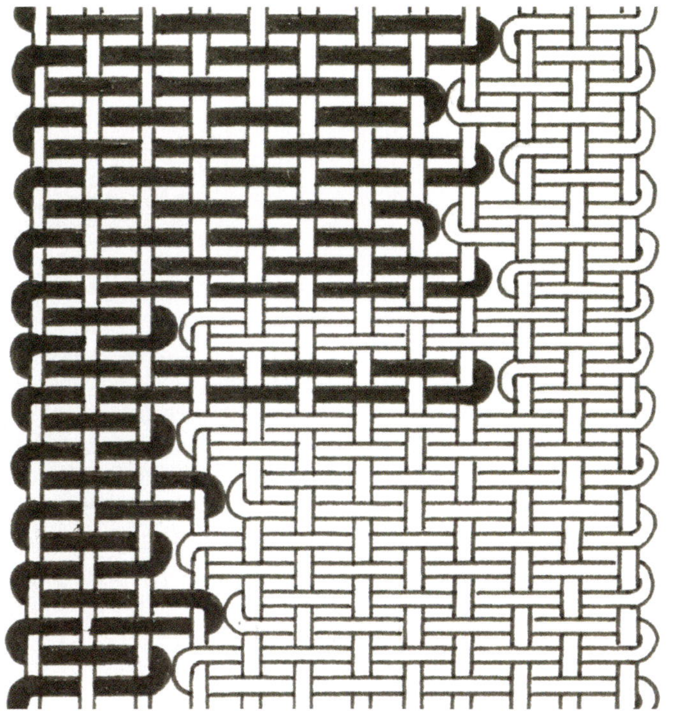

The illustration here of a small section of the woven sample shows how the vertical and horizontal outlines are made. Despite the difference in appearance, these two employ the same technique of hatching which will be dealt with more fully in Chapter 7. To make the vertical joins the two wefts each weave two passes at a time – one pass to the joining warp and one to one warp back from it. This means that the two colours alternate on the joining warp. At the horizontal outlines, each weft again weaves two passes at a time. One pass extends to the full length of the horizontal 'arm', the other turns on one warp back from the vertical joining warp.

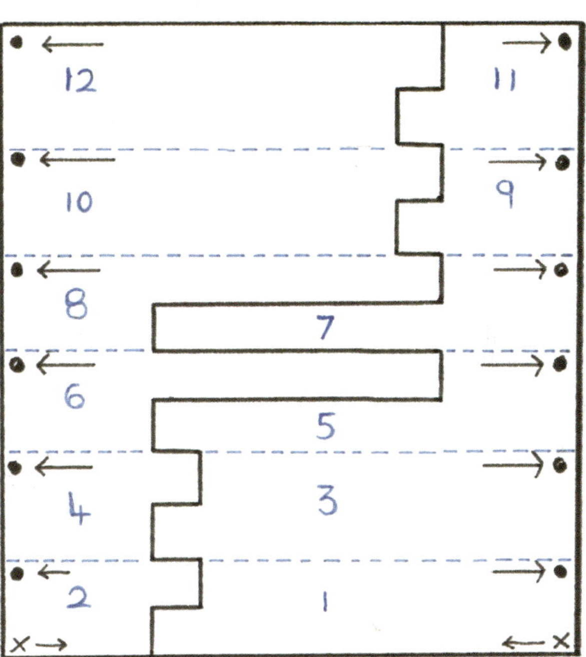

This section illustrates how each of the contrasting weft colours can weave from bottom to top without changing, except when needing to replace a finished length. All the wefts are in play concurrently, pausing in turn every two passes to allow the other space to weave. One weft forms the shape, the other infills. In this case the light weft begins with its longest pass first, then a shorter one (a pattern repeated in areas 3, 5, 7, 9 and 11). The darker weft infills with a shorter pass first, then a longer one. This repeats all the way up the sample. Only the length of the pass changes.

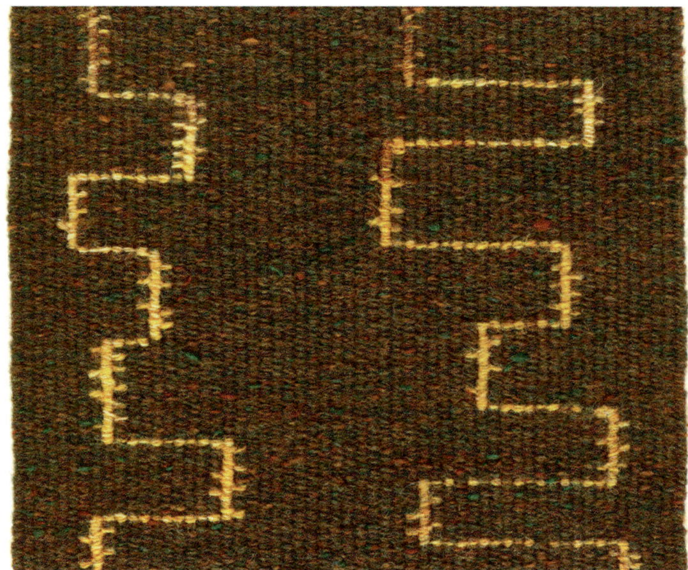

Tapestry woven with soumak and interlocked wefts. 8 epi.
Coloured medium warp, wool weft.

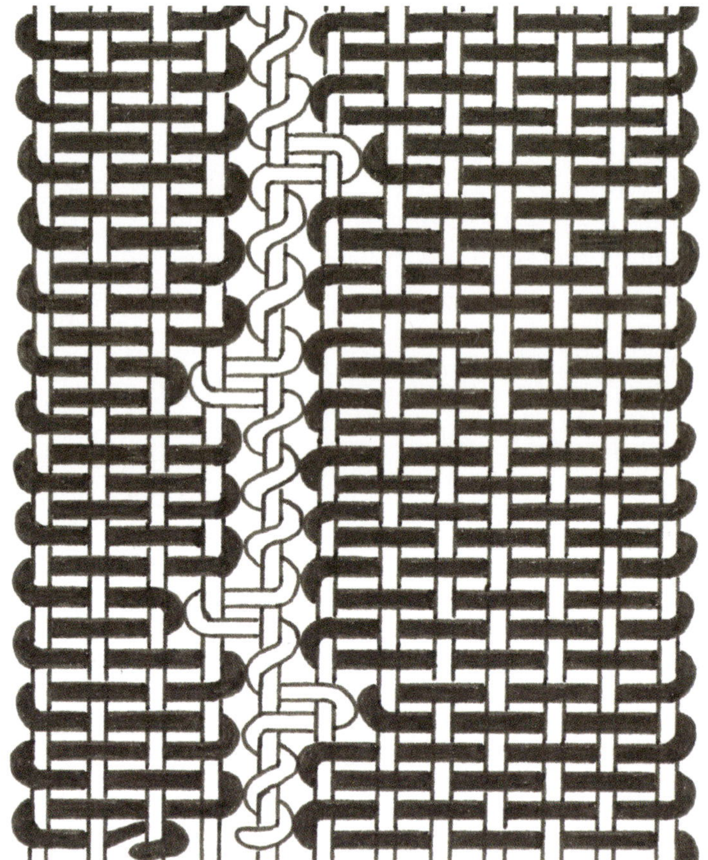

The vertical interlocked line.

Although designs in tapestry are very often based on areas rather than lines, this is another example where a distinctively woven line can make a graphic and dynamic effect. The background mix remains constant throughout but has actually been woven as with the previous sample in three sections; the middle, left and right-hand sides. The vertical outline has been made by wrapping a single warp in between adjacent areas of background, taking in an extra warp to right or left at random intervals. These extra steps to one side or the other serve the double purpose of stabilising the wrapped warp and closing up the slit, making another kind of interlocked join. This means that the three background areas and both outlining wefts must all be woven concurrently pass by pass. The horizontal lines have been made using a soumak wrapping technique.

The vertical line

Here the two adjacent areas of dark plain weave are joined by a single wrapped warp in a contrasting light-coloured weft mix. Instead of meeting to form a slit at the join, the two dark areas have been woven with one warp left in between. A length of the lighter weft has started on the warp left between and is wrapped round a random number of turns corresponding to passes in the background weave. After the background has been built up by anything from three to six passes, this wrapping weft weaves over the next warp either to the right or left. Correspondingly, in that pass, the background weft has stepped back by one warp to accommodate the wrapping weft.

The horizontal line to the right

This has been made using a technique called *reverse soumak*, which will be explored more fully in Chapter 8. At the change from a vertical to a horizontal line, the wrapping weft passes across the warp by making a turn around each warp. In effect the weft passes under two warps then back over one. Once complete, this weft reverts to making a vertical line by wrapping round one warp. Once beaten down, the line produced by a row of reverse soumak appears straight. It is formed of a level row of beads and does not have the natural undulations made by a row of plain weave.

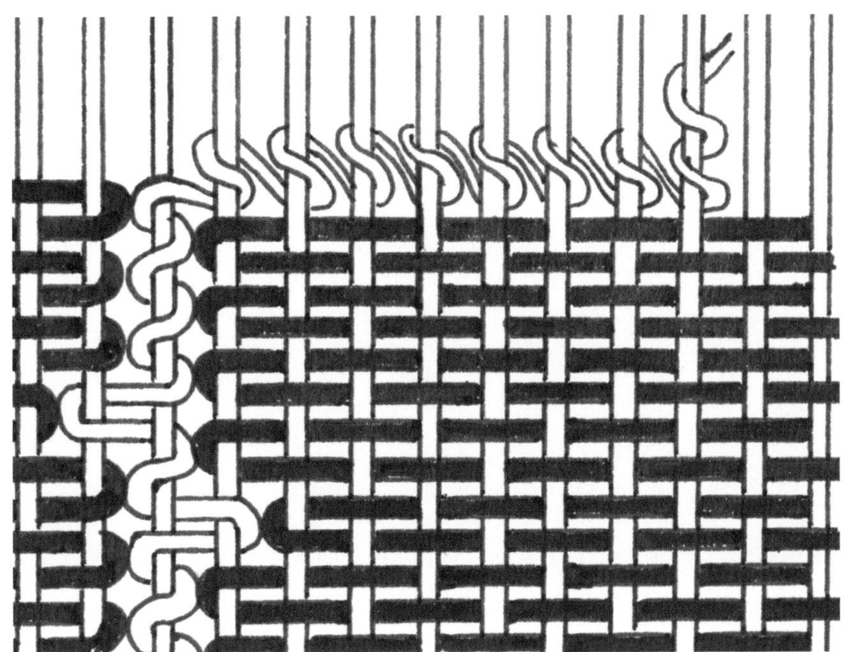
The horizontal soumak line to the right.

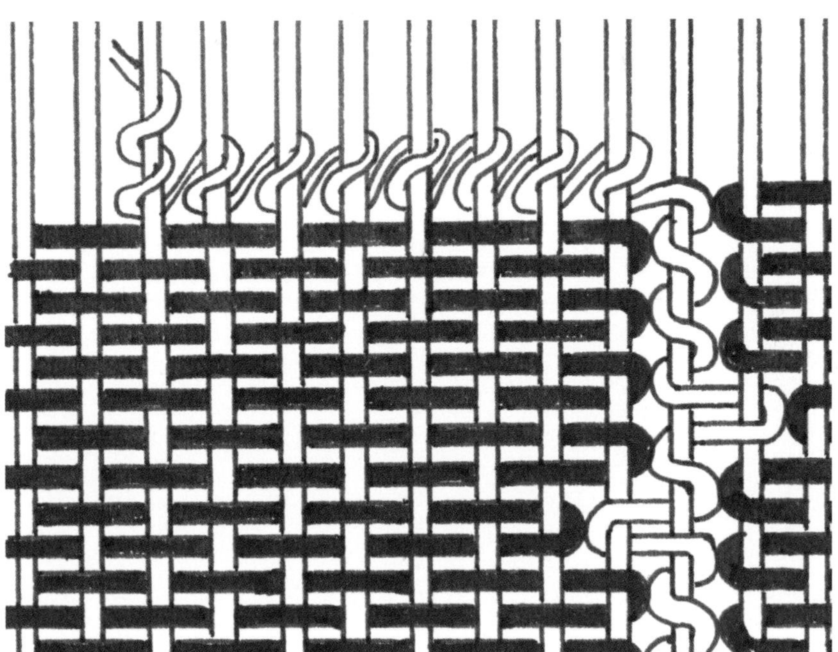
The horizontal soumak line to the left.

Horizontal line to the left

Here the corresponding technique for making a reverse soumak line from right to left is illustrated. Again, the light-coloured weft making the vertical line begins the horizontal line by passing under the next warp, this time to the left. Next it passes back over the same warp, then under both it and the next warp. Moving on to the next warp, it again passes backwards over the warp to continue the sequence. Essentially the wrapping weft passes under two warps, then back over across the warp from left to right. Note the bead of a soumak looks slightly different to the plain weave. It hugs the warps as it wraps so is a little shorter and rounder and casts more of a shadow.

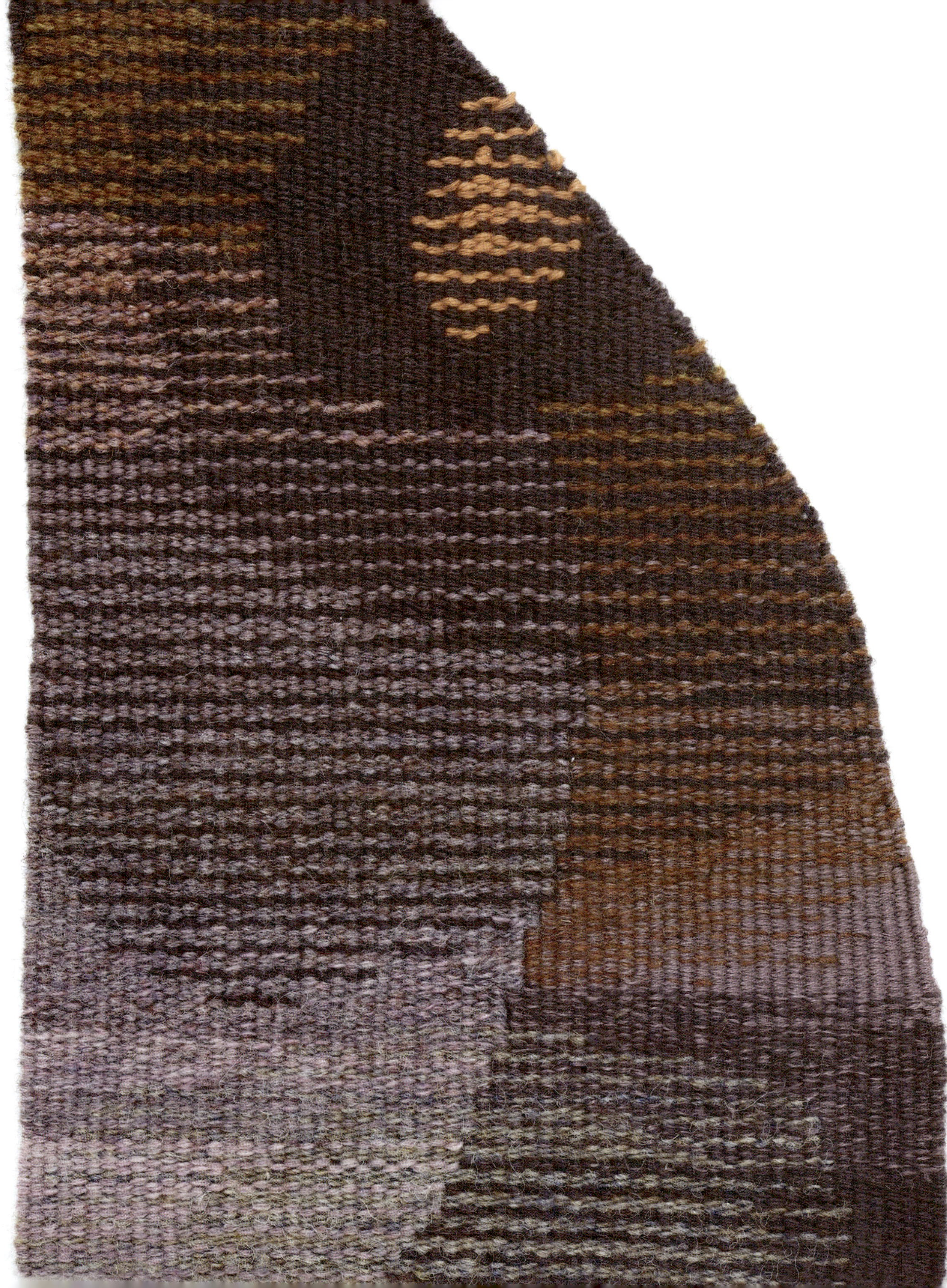

CHAPTER 7

HATCHING

Hatching is a technique used between adjacent areas within a tapestry. The two adjacent wefts alternate in making long or short passes, meeting at different points either at random or to a planned design. This technique is one of many made possible by the structure of warp and weft and offers the weaver the ability to make lively, free, subtle or graphic effects.

We will illustrate four main ways in which hatching may be used. These are

- To control tension, either at the edges of a piece, or in the centre within long weft runt
- To make colour shifts and shading within a piece, between areas of either close or contrasting colour, tone or texture.
- To form interim colours between contrasting areas where the eye will see another colour which is actually a mix of the two. This technique was used masterfully by medieval weavers who worked exclusively in solid colour and with a limited range of colours. By hatching, and the use of hachures (the difference between which will be demonstrated) they were able to create intermediate colours, shade and perspective.
- To delineate forms, by hatching to a planned outline using contrasting wefts. Hatching may be used to create the illusion of multiple forms overlaying each as you may observe in the chapter heading piece.

If long weft runs are woven, either extending most of the way across a piece or a significant area within it, the tension tends to increase. Even for experienced weavers, this may cause the piece to draw inwards. Rather than correcting this, it is good practice to divide wide areas into two or more pairs of wefts. By doing this a degree of elasticity is introduced which will help in keeping the warps parallel and evenly spaced.

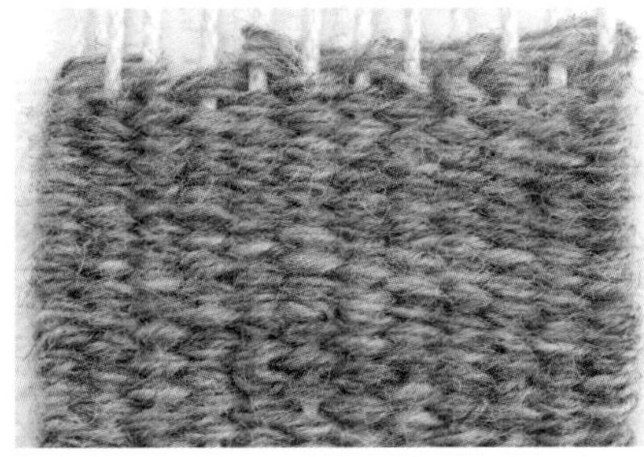

Here is a small area of plain weave which has been woven with two identical mixes so that the joins are not visible. There would be no way to tell by looking at the surface of the weave that it had been woven with two wefts. Only by looking behind the weaving could you see the two wefts where they started.

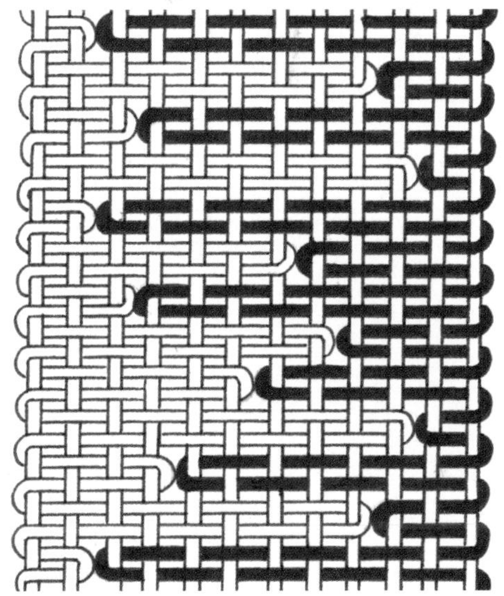

When weaving an area of hatching it is usual to set up an alternating rhythm – one weft makes a long and a short pass, the other a short then long pass to infill. This sequence is generally best maintained throughout an area in order to give an equal mixing of the two wefts. Any change to the weaving sequence tends to be very visible.

Shaped, hatched tapestry with fine (12/6) coloured cotton warp, linen and wool weft. 10 epi.

WEAVING MEASURED HATCHING

Here, the hatched area makes the transition between two solid colours; a dark purple to the right and lighter purple to the left. On alternate passes, the two wefts meet between the second and third warps (turning on warps 2 and 3), or between the third and second warps from the right-hand edge. The high tonal contrast highlights the characteristic waviness of a pass. Alternate wefts can weave both a long and a short pass before pausing and infilling with two passes of the other weft.

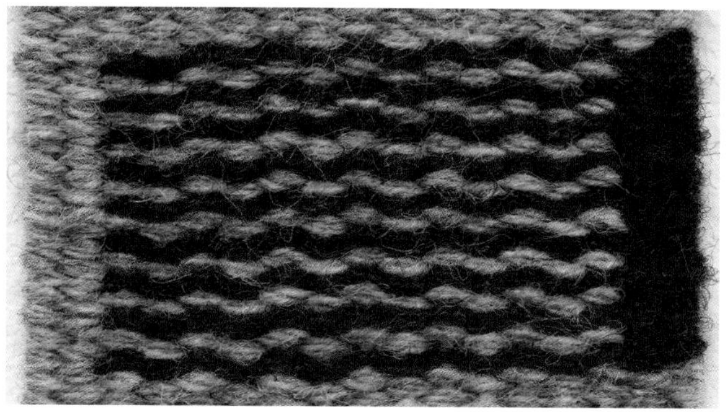

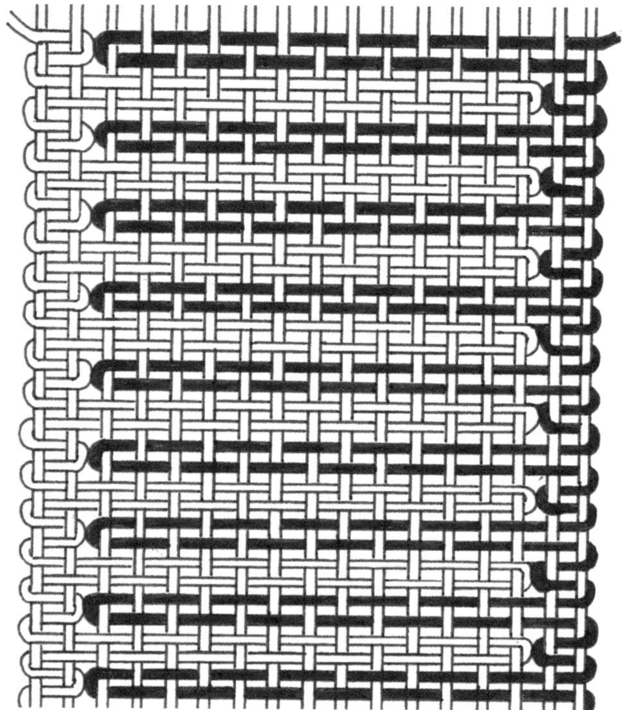

Measured hatching.

WEAVING RANDOM HATCHING

Here, the same two areas of solid colour are joined by an area of random hatching. At each pass, the dark and light wefts meet and turn at different points chosen at random anywhere between the third warp and the third from the right-hand edge. On the drawing, the green arrows marked between the dotted lines show the sections of warp in which the two wefts meet and turn. As with the previous sample, each weft makes a long and a short pass before pausing to allow the weft from the opposite side to infill.

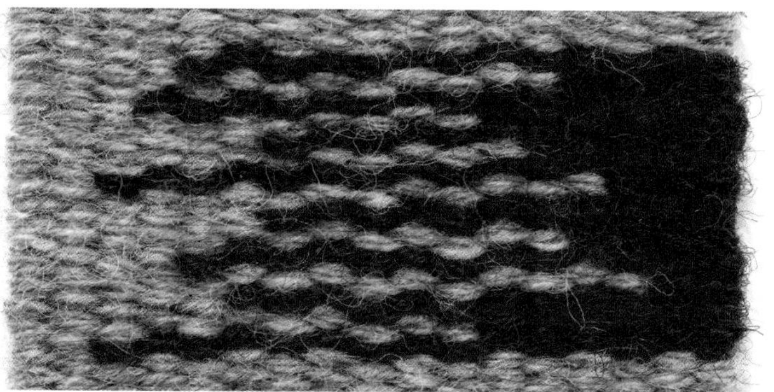

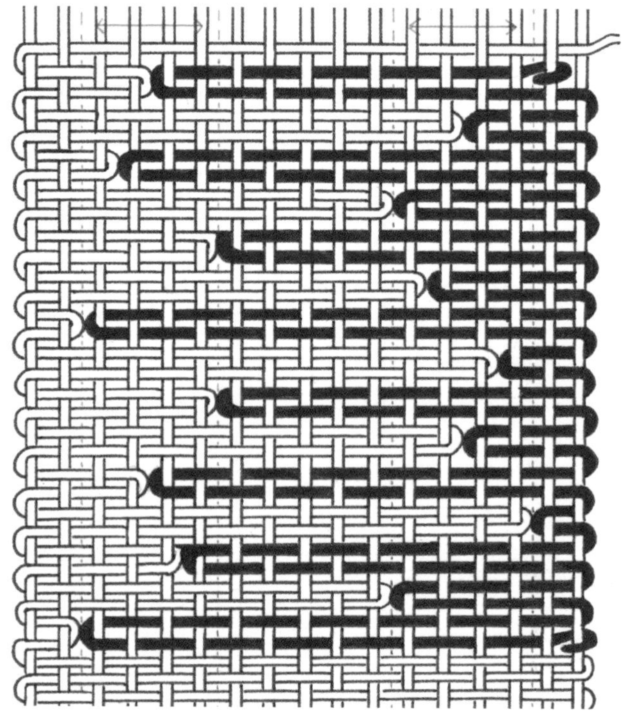

Random hatching.

THREE FORMS MADE BY HATCHING

Here are three examples of hatching being used to form shaped areas set between adjacent areas of solid colour. The contrast between the two colours gives a bold striped effect to the hatched shapes. In each case the drawing shows the pattern of the turns used.

The rectangular form extends over eight warps and is woven in four passes each of the light and dark weft, woven in alternate passes. Each weft turns between warps 2 and 3, and 10 and 11 on alternate passes.

The oval form increases from four to eight warps wide on alternate passes and decreases likewise. It also takes ten passes to complete.

The triangle has been formed by stepping in by one warp at each side on alternate passes, starting on ten warps and decreasing to two warps wide at the top, over ten passes.

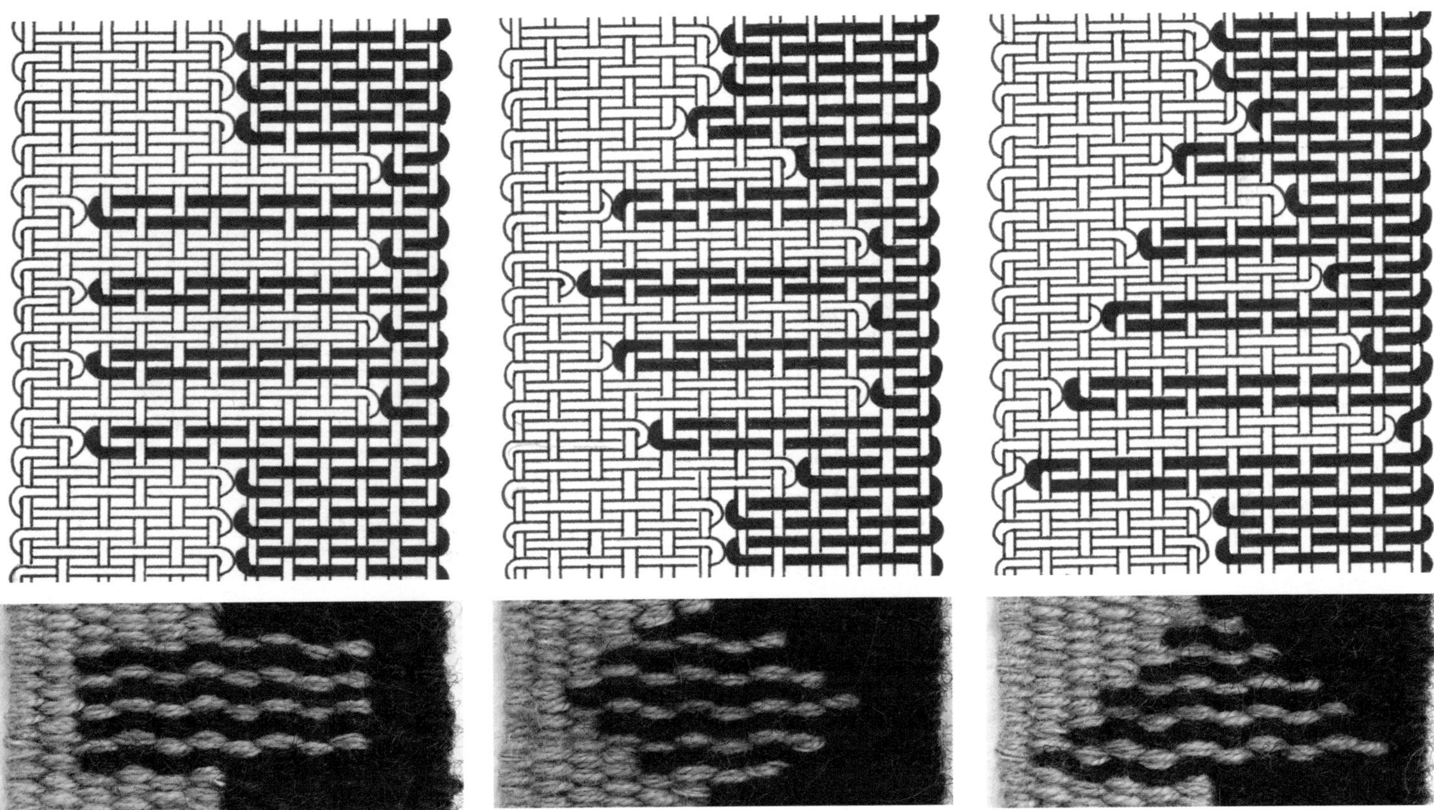

Hatched rectangle with 12 warps.

Hatched oval with 12 warps.

Hatched triangle with 12 warps.

STEPPED HATCHING

Here, instead of the wefts alternating on each pass, the hatching has been made over three passes, giving a bolder mark. First the dark weft makes three passes, tuning on warps 3, 10 and 16. It then pauses to allow the lighter weft to infill before repeating to form the next identical mark. The dark weft has been floated up at the back of the piece between marks. Note, on the longest pass, the dark weft makes a low turn (passing first over then under the third warp) but the two shorter passes finish on high turns (passing first under then over warps 10 then 16). The visual effect is to produce a pronounced step which is noticeable, especially as the shape is repeated several times.

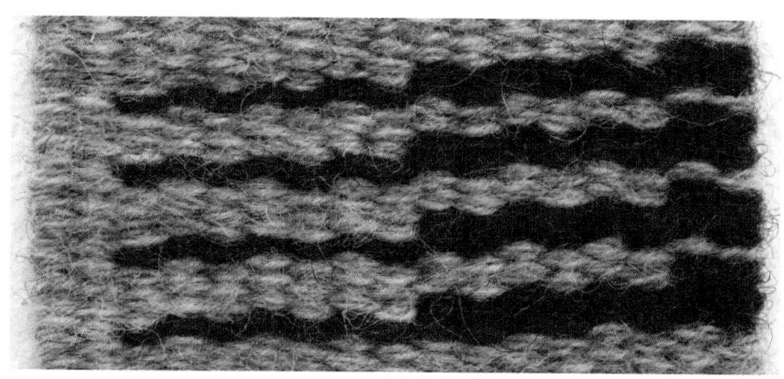

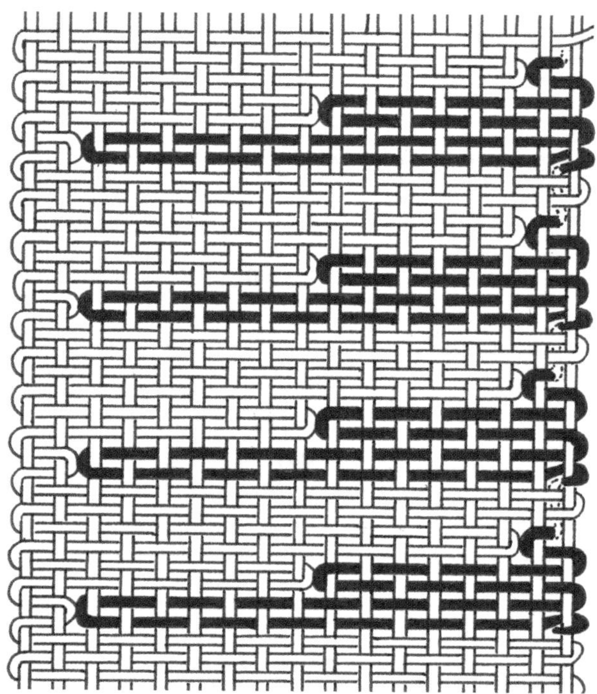

Stepped hatching with 17 warps.

SMOOTH HATCHING

Using the same two weft bundles, the middle and right-hand turns have been moved by one warp so that the dominant dark weft now makes low turns on warps 3, 9 and 15. By passing first over then under the warp, it now makes a low turn. Visually this gives a less pronounced step, and therefore a smoother line.

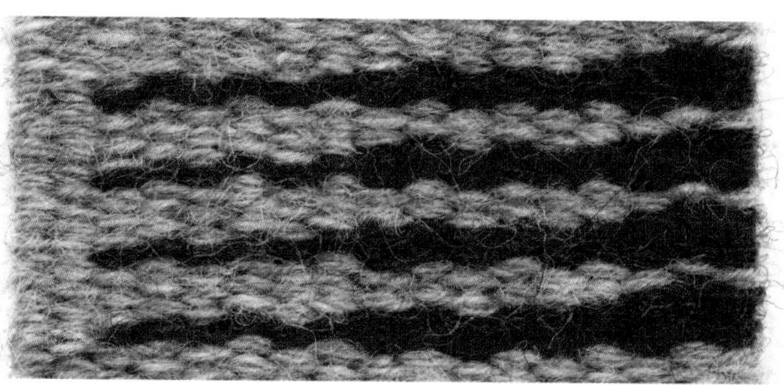

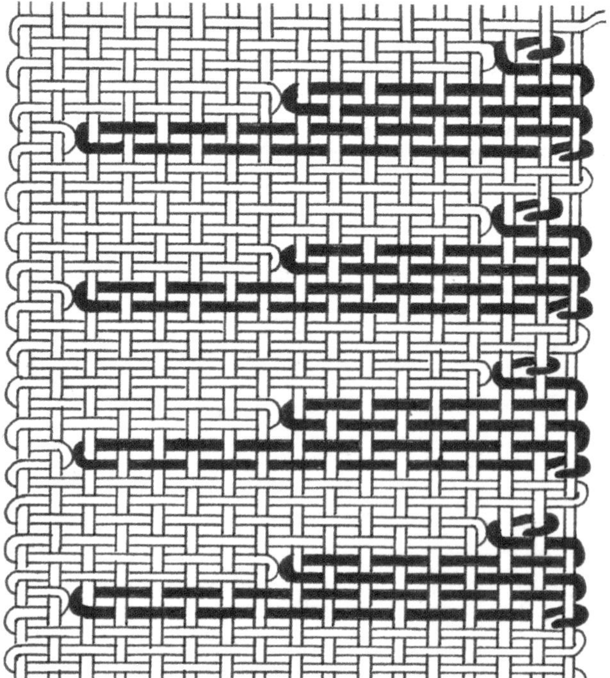

Smooth hatching with 17 warps.

HACHURES

Here, a similar pattern of marks has been made with the same two contrasting wefts, turning on warps 9 and 15. However the technique used is very different, in that these marks are hachures rather than being formed by hatching. These two techniques are commonly confused, and although there are visual similarities, both the technique for construction and their practical and aesthetic characters are quite different.

Unlike hatching which involved two or more wefts weaving alternately, each hachure is formed as a separate unit. Each is woven in one go, independently of the background in which it is set, even when there are repeated hachures in an area. This means that they may be introduced either singly or in groups, more or less anywhere within a piece. Ideally the point (or points as hachures are often double ended) would not land at the edge of a piece, as this means leaving weft ends which are vulnerable and need sewing in afterwards.

As illustrated, the hachure starts at its farthest point. Here, three passes of decreasing length are woven in one go before the weft slides back down over the three layers to finish. Because the weft finishes on the warp adjacent to the one on which it started, the shed is maintained. The background weft will be able to weave over the top of the hachure and remain in shed. To achieve a smooth line, hachures are made with high turns, so that when the weft is taken back down the steps it will fall on the *low warps*. By passing *eccentrically* over the turns, the returning weft smooths out the steps.

The use of hachures was very much the norm in medieval tapestry, where they were used in preference to the hatching which is more prevalent in contemporary tapestry. With only a limited number of colours used as solid colour rather than in mixed-weft bundles, the medieval weavers were able to create the illusion of interim colours and shading. Making use of hachures in contrasting colours, they were able to give depth and dynamism to the forms of figures, animals and plants.

The use of hachures produces a very firm fabric which is important in a large-scale tapestry and remains common in traditional Gobelin studios.

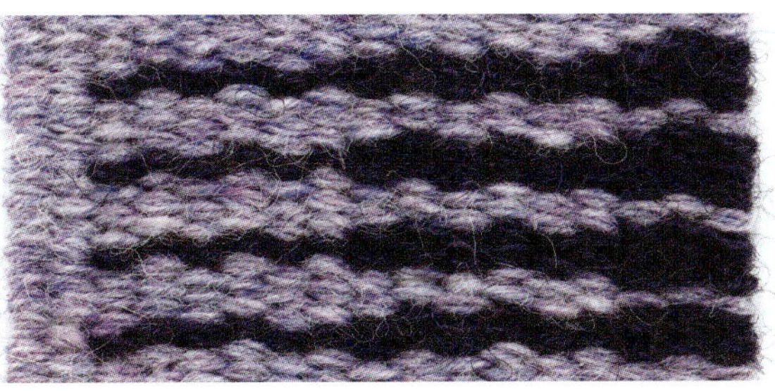

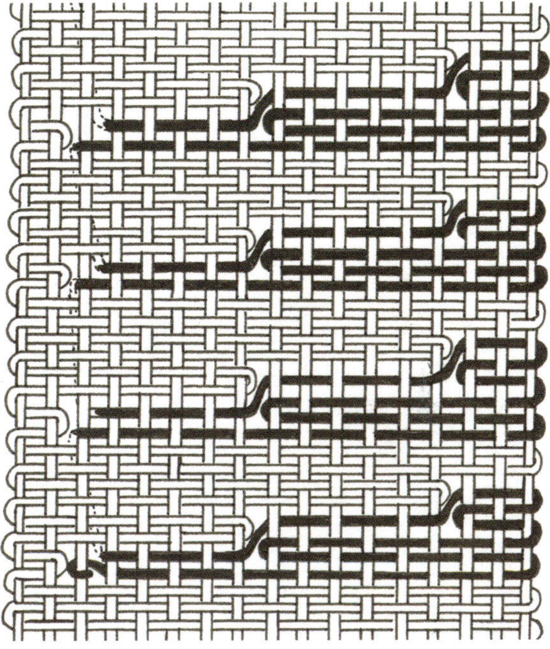

Four hachures.

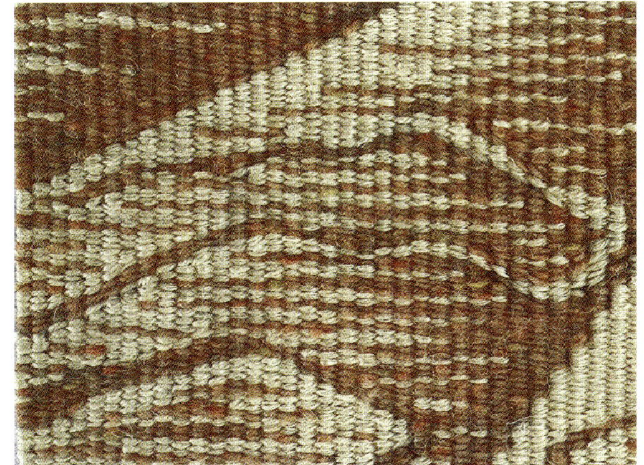

Medieval Costume series detail, woven with hachures.

HATCHED CURVES

You may observe that on the full image of this sample, the beads lie vertically and the ribs where the weft passes over the warp lie horizontally, showing that the piece has been turned on its side after weaving. The weaving of a piece on its side is frequently needed for technical reasons, this being one – hatching vertically is not possible.

Here we have a dark and a light area of solid plain weave, each using a bundle of closely matched weft strands, with a hatched area delineating the curved forms in between. As with the previous samples, the drawing illustrates how the wefts from the light and dark areas extend to overlay each other in alternating passes. At both sides of this hatched area, the turns are made at warps chosen to form the curved outlines. This is very similar to the way curves were formed as solid shapes in Chapter 4. The difference is that being hatched, each of the two outlines have been formed by alternate passes turning at the points which outline the undulating forms. The lines may either have been formed freehand, marked onto the warps or by following a cartoon set behind the warps.

The drawing and smaller image illustrate a section of the weaving sequence for a curved section of hatching, stepping in a pattern of +3, 1, 1, -2. In the last three passes, the solid dark area has finished and the hatching extends to the edge of the sample. The dark weft has been floated up at the back between passes.

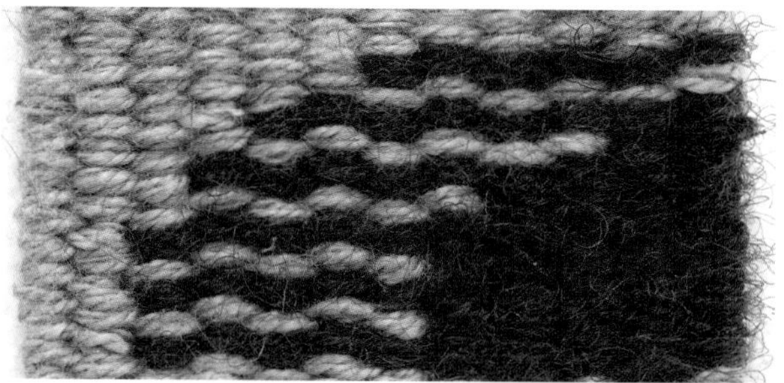

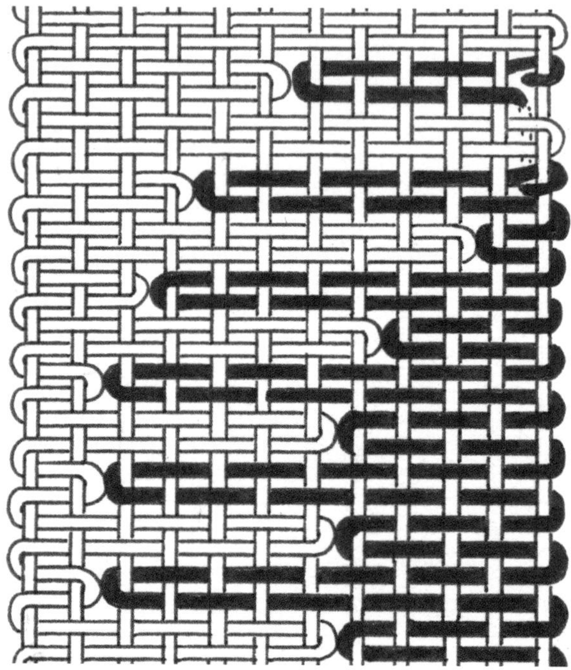

Diagram and weaving of a hatched gentle curve.

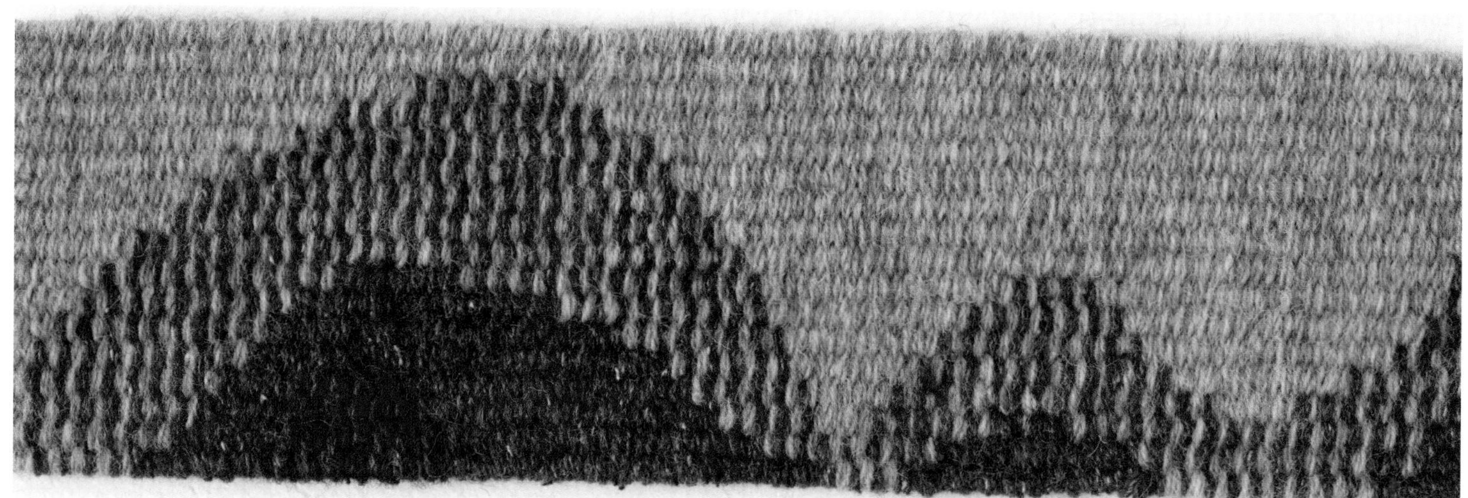

Hatched curves sample with 17 warps, woven on its side. Three coloured wefts.

HATCHING TO CREATE THREE CURVES

This sample has also been woven on its side. Designed to be viewed as shown, the drawing illustrates the way it was woven. Between the light and dark areas there are two parallel curved areas of hatching, one lighter in shade than the other. Because of the high tonal contrast, the effect is quite graphic with the turning points of each pass being clearly visible. Viewed from a distance, the effect of these parallel curved bands becomes more like shading.

On the drawing, the dark weft starts from the right and makes three passes of decreasing length. It then pauses, allowing the light weft to weave the infill. This sequence of three passes is repeated, the turns stepping back and forward to create smooth curves.

The effect as shown here is distinctly striped. Once viewed from a greater distance as part of a larger piece, the effect would be much more one of gradual shading. The alternating passes and their finishing points would be less visible. The two colours would then blend into one as if forming a transitional colour.

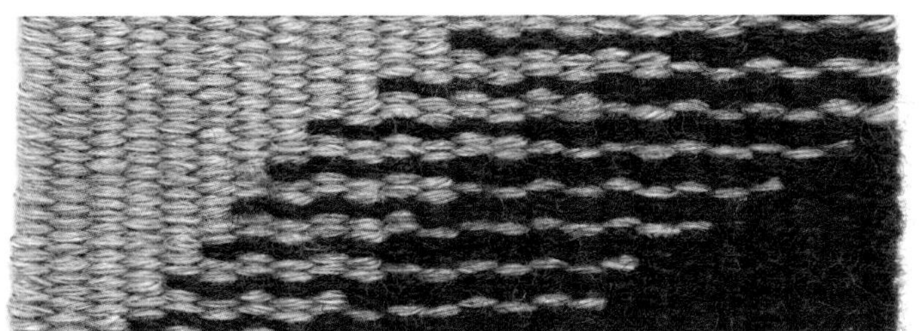

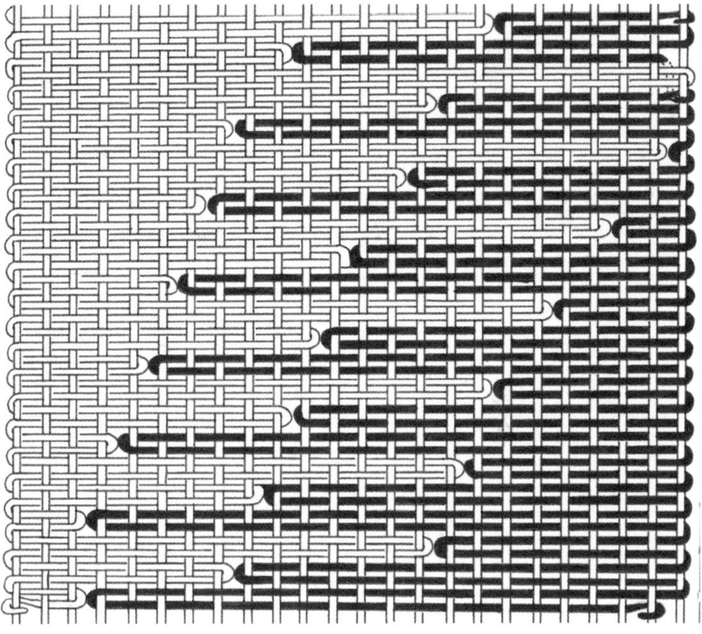

Hatching to create more layers.

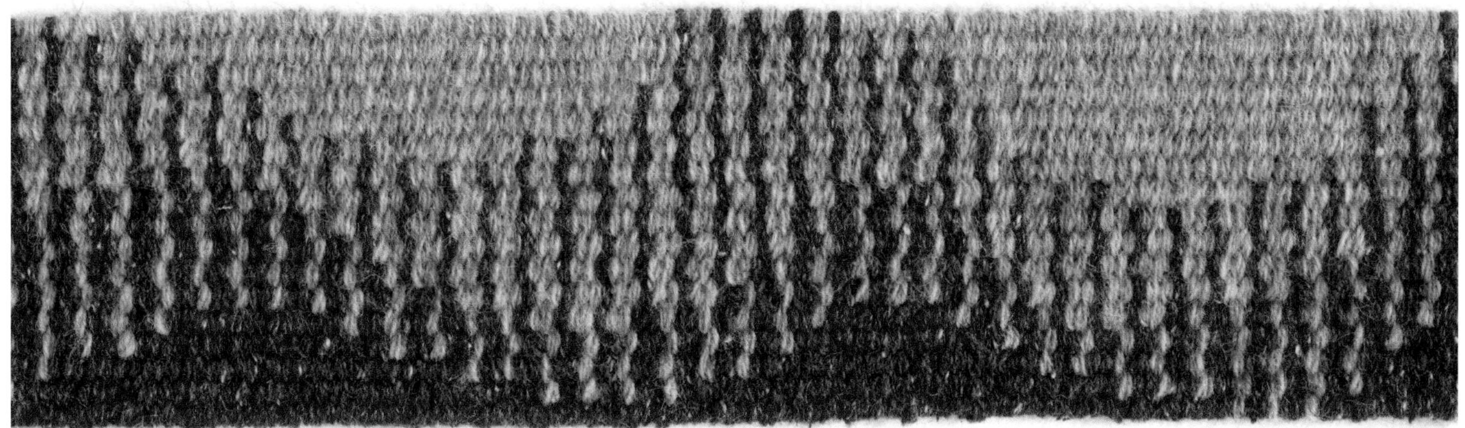

Three curves with two coloured wefts using 17 warps.

HATCHING WITH THREE WEFTS

Here the central S shape has been bordered on both sides by an area of hatching. There are now three wefts in play – a darker weft to either side with one central lighter weft. The weaving sequence now alternates between all three wefts, each weaving a combination of short and long passes in turn. The dark wefts pause to either side and the light weft mid row. To start, dark areas to either side each weave first a long then short pass. Next the light weft infills. As ever, the order in which the wefts are able to weave depends on which overlays the other. For example the first six passes are woven left, right, middle, left, right, middle. This sequence is maintained throughout the sample. It would have been equally possible to start the lighter weft first with a long, then a short pass, infilling with the dark wefts. The sequence middle, left, right, repeat or middle, right, left, repeat.

The curves of the S form have been outlined by the choice of tuning points between the two darker wefts and the lighter one in the middle. Areas are formed and infilled in the same way as a curved area in solid weave except that it is now only every second weft that forms the line.

The hatching outlines transitional areas between the areas of light and dark solid colour in much the same way as the previous exercise in measured hatching except that the form is now curved instead of straight sided.

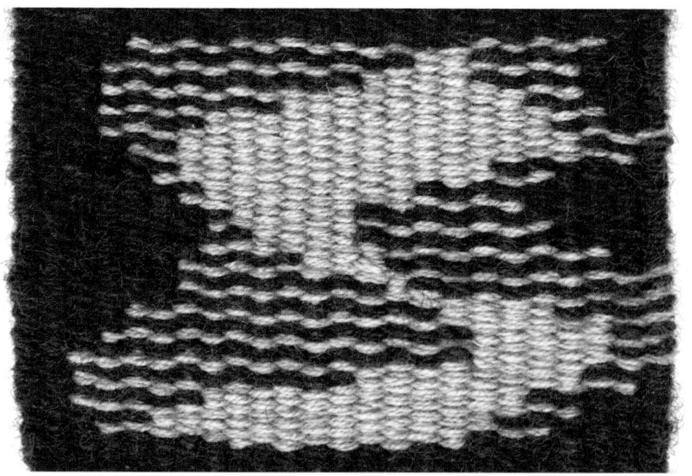

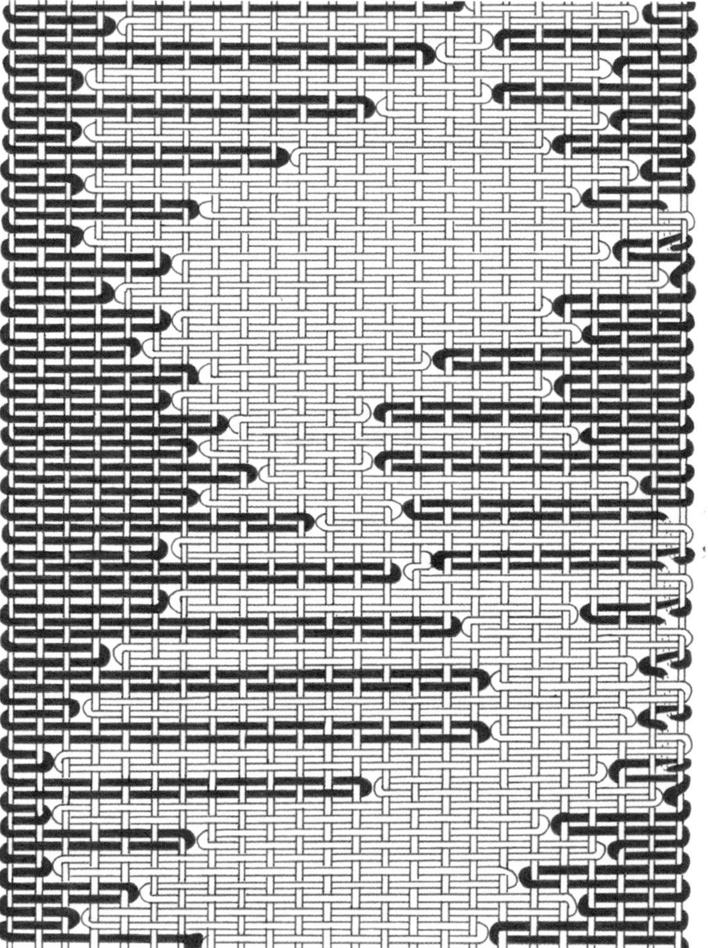

Hatching on both sides of an 'S' shape.

HATCHED AREA IN THREE WEFTS

Again, this sample has been woven on its side – the drawn diagram showing the actual sequence of the start of the weaving. There are three wefts set up along the bottom row; light on the left (or bottom when the piece is rotated), then dark to the middle and mid tone to the right (or top when rotated). When hatched together, the light and dark wefts form an area of strongly contrasted hatching. The dark and mid tones form a less clearly striped and overall darker effect when hatched together.

Following the same principles as outlined in Chapter 2, the dark and mid tone wefts are shown starting alongside each other, on the low warps, with a warp left in between. The light weft is started at the left-hand edge, at the opposing side to its neighbouring dark weft. Weave a pass with the left weft. The right-hand weft makes a half pass and pauses out of the way to the right. The middle weft infills first to the left for two passes. Continue forming two passes each side then infilling two passes in the middle. Repeat. The undulating lines have been formed freehand during the weaving, outlined by the points at which alternate wefts turn. The lines could also have been marked onto the warps or a cartoon fastened behind as a guide.

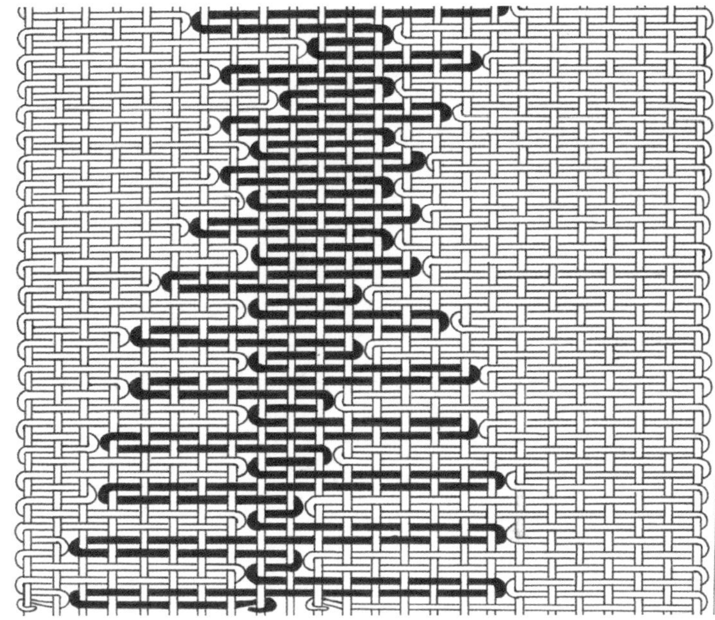

The weaving sequence for hatching both sides of a solid area.

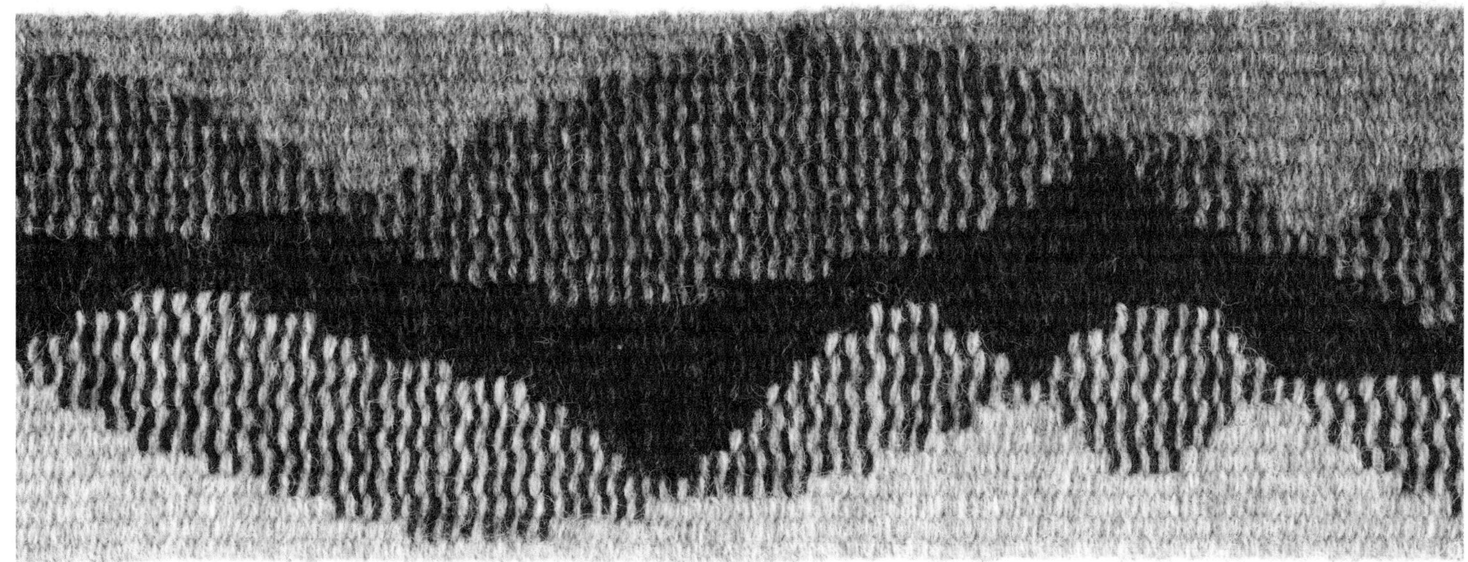

Measured hatching both sides of a solid area with 24 warps.

HATCHING INVISIBLY TO HELP CONTROL THE EDGES

Besides being a technique with varied expressive possibilities, hatching may also be used to manage the tension, either at the edges or throughout a piece. As the weft passes over and under a warp there are many factors which will affect how they interact. Some of these affect the tension, which always needs to be managed. The number of strands in a weft bundle, their fibre, thickness and how they are spun will all influence how they sit in the spaces between warps. The need to balance the relationship between weft bundle and warp setting is crucial and ever changing. The weaving process is neither static not entirely predictable, which is part of its strength as an expressive medium. However, it does mean that managing tension is an ongoing need even for the most experienced of weavers.

The most common tendency is for the edges of a piece to draw inwards with the warps being drawn together, or pulling in. This is usually due to the tension being too great in the middle part of a weaving. This may be particularly so when the main lines of a design lean towards one side or another. Hatching is one way to prevent warps pulling in or to ease warps back out to where they began.

Here, the woven sample is made in contrasting colours for clarity, but in practice the same weft mix would be used. The drawing shows hatching used at a left-hand edge; clearly the same would apply at either edge.

To introduce hatching at the edge, first weave as long a pass as the design allows for. This is followed by two to four more passes of decreasing length, depending on the size of an area you are working. It is important to make the hatching in passes of decreasing not increasing length since this would cause the edge to pull in instead of easing it outwards. If the design and scale of a piece allows, it is good practice to have extra hatching wefts at the sides throughout, unless you naturally tend towards slack tension. It is advisable to use slightly different length passes in each hatching, otherwise the repeated pattern may become visible. The example shown here would be reversed for managing a right-hand edge, again starting with the longest pass first.

It is best to react as soon as you notice the warps pulling in. Despite the slowness of the weaving process, changes in tension can still pass the weaver by unless they are looking out for it.

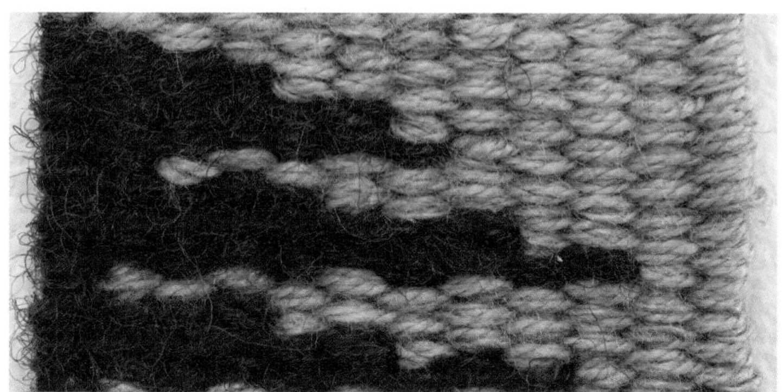

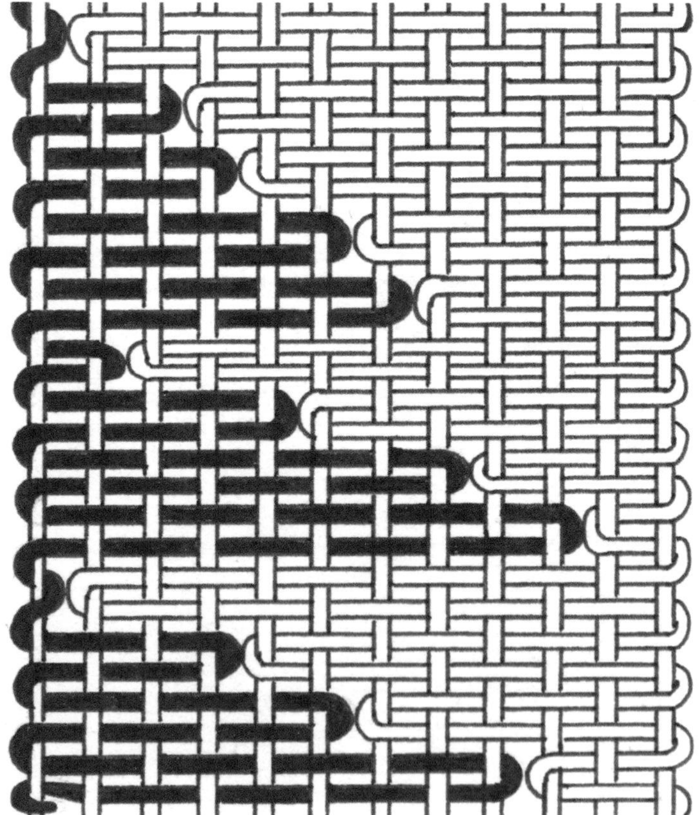

Hatching invisibly to help control the edges.

INVISIBLE HATCHING WITHIN AN AREA

This half-circular form has been woven with two weft bundles in place of one. Because the wefts are identical, the turns and overlaying passes are invisible. One might question why this might be done when there is no visible difference. There are two reasons.

Firstly to manage the tension. If this form we're to be more than about 20cm wide in the context of a larger piece, or if it extended across most of the width of a small piece as illustrated, there would be a risk that the tension would increase. This would cause the warps to draw together and one or both edges of the weaving to pull in. The effect of breaking up an area by hatching is that the weave can move more freely from side to side. Also, the extra turns take up space between warps and so help to keep them from being drawn together.

Another reason for weaving the area in two wefts rather than one is that it allows for a simple change of weft colour when wishing to form an new area. Introducing a new area or colour mid-weave may only be done by exchanging an existing weft or by introducing two new ones. To introduce a single new weft mid-weave would interrupt the shed, meaning that adjacent wefts will no longer weave under and over each other in sequence.

Looking closely at the drawing, you will see that there are no actual starting ends at the base of the bowl form. Instead of starting two individual wefts, both ends of one length have been used. The wefts length was woven over and under the 5 warps at the base of the bowl, then pulled through to its mid point. The two ends then weave in opposite directions in the same way as a pair of separate wefts would. The two ends come together to finish in the middle of the top row.

The added advantage – besides not having to start two new wefts – is that the turns on either side will now fall exactly opposite each other on each pass, making a fully symmetrical shape. If weaving the same form with a single weft, one side would inevitably be a half pass ahead of the other.

Note, by starting the bowl form with two ends of the weft length they form a pair so that the weft forming the left hand side needs to start and finish at the edge in order that its working end meets the working end of the adjacent weft in the bowl form. It will thereby weave in the opposite direction and so maintain the weaving sequence.

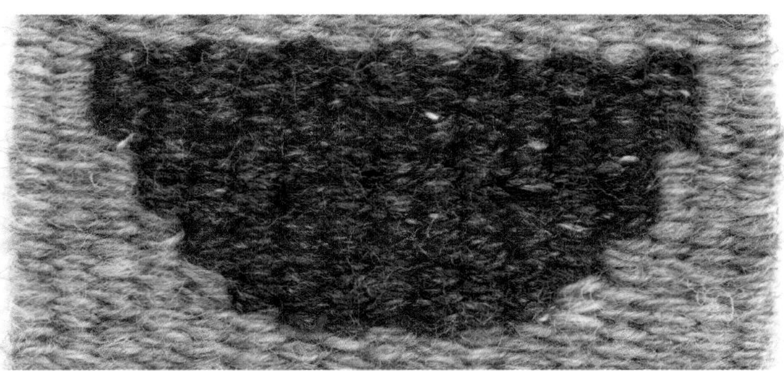

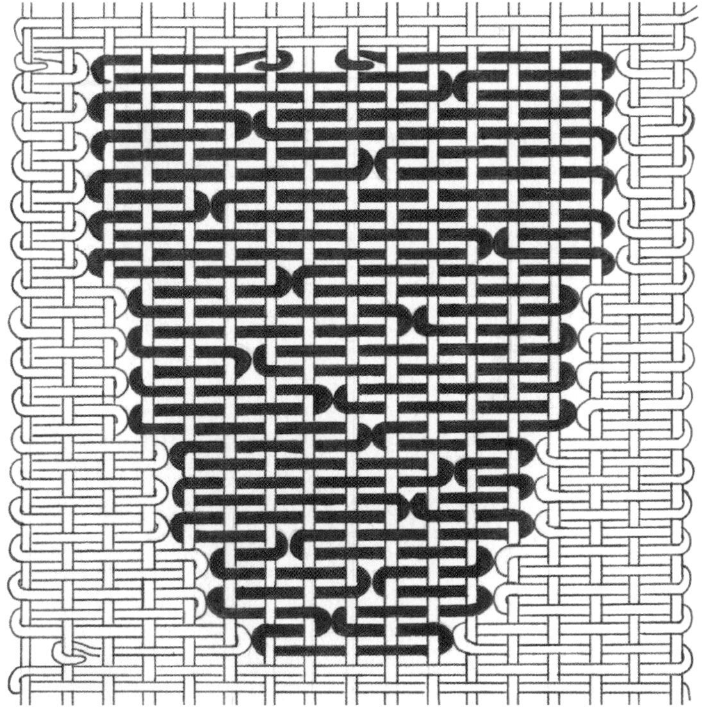

Hatching invisibly within an area.

WEAVING HATCHING WITH CHANGING WEFTS

This sample has been woven to show something of the great range of effects possible when hatching, and the subtle shifts of colour which may be made.

Looking from the bottom upwards, this sample shows first two highly contrasting wefts hatched together, in alternating passes. The tonal contrast here makes the alternating pattern quite visible. Moving up, the next section, the left-hand mix remains unaltered whilst the right-hand mix gradually has more lighter strands introduced. The effect is that with less tonal contrast, the striped effect becomes less pronounced.

By halfway up the sample, the individual passes are no longer visible without looking very closely. There are still just two weft mixes being used, of different colours but similar tone and in this case the same wool fibre. Changing mixes is possible by replacing the whole bundle or by just exchanging single strands within the bundle. By this means it is possible to make the most nuanced of colour changes, to darken, lighten, warm or cool a colour or move towards another. There is also the possibility of changing the weft fibres used. This can give either marked or very subtle variation of surface texture, bead shape and lustre, amongst other qualities.

The appearance of hatching can be quite free flowing and yet it is infinitely controllable. In the weaving of an area of hatching, changes may be made at will without need for preplanning, so the weaver can respond and react freely as the weaving progresses.

The hatching in this sample extends to random lengths, with the two wefts making several changes of mix. What does remain constant is the alternating rhythm in which the two wefts weave. First one weft weaves a long then a short pass, then the other responds with a short then a long pass to meet the turns and infill before the first weft again makes a long then short pass, this time extending to different points.

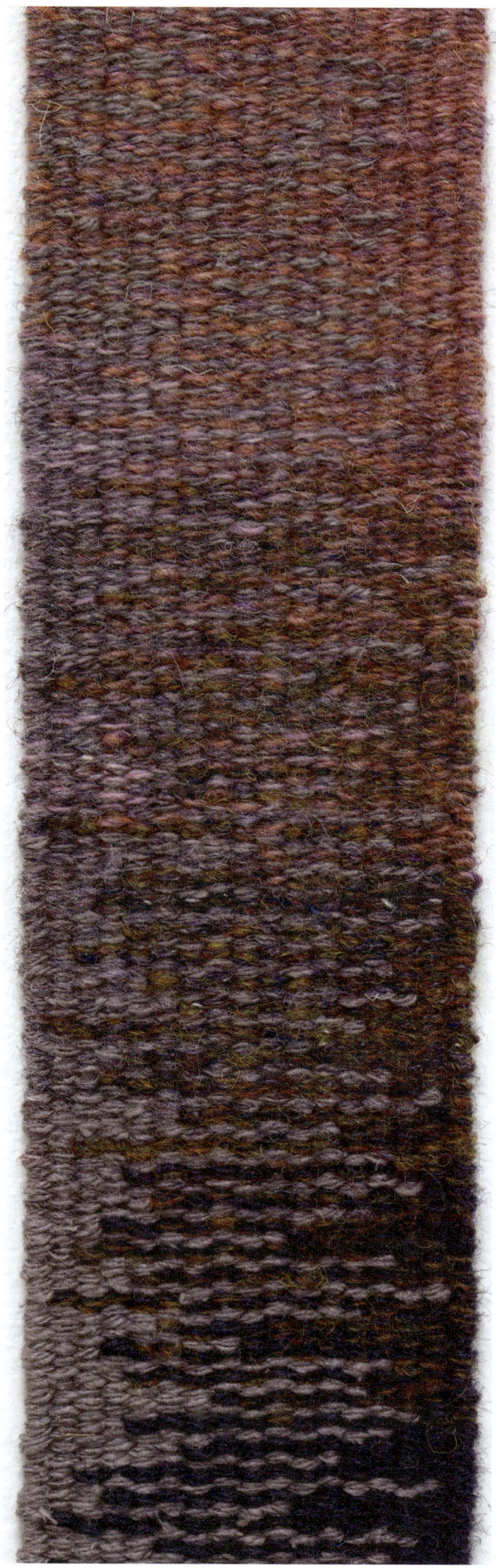

Hatching with changing wefts.

HATCHING TO SOFTEN THE EDGES OF A FORM

Here, several roughly circular forms have been woven in a darker background. The wefts forming the circles and the background are hatched to random points creating a surrounding area which varies slightly in width. At the outer edge, measured hatching has followed a definite line which defines the circular form. At the inner edge, random hatching is made to give the circular area a diffuse edge. The background and right-hand circle are woven in solid weft mixes, the left-hand in a bundle of variegated wefts.

The drawing shows the weaving sequence for the first third of the sample. The light and dark wefts have been started at opposing edges. The light weft starts by making a long pass, then a shorter one before the dark weft infills.

Initially the darker weft makes regular steps on the shorter passes, which gives a quite definite line to the inner edge of the hatched areas. By contrast, the points of turning to the outer edge of the hatching are more varied so that the boundary between hatching and solid darker area is less definite.

Further up the sample, the weft for the second circle is introduced from the right so that now the dark weft is hatching both on its left- and right-hand sides.

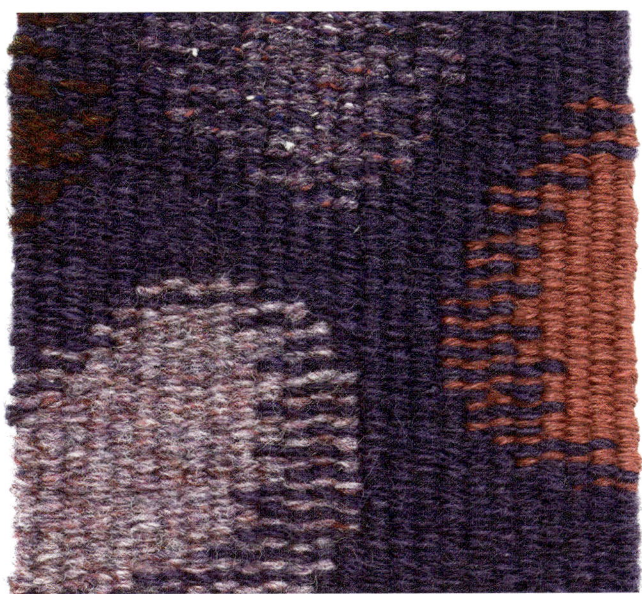

Hatched forms using 25 warps.

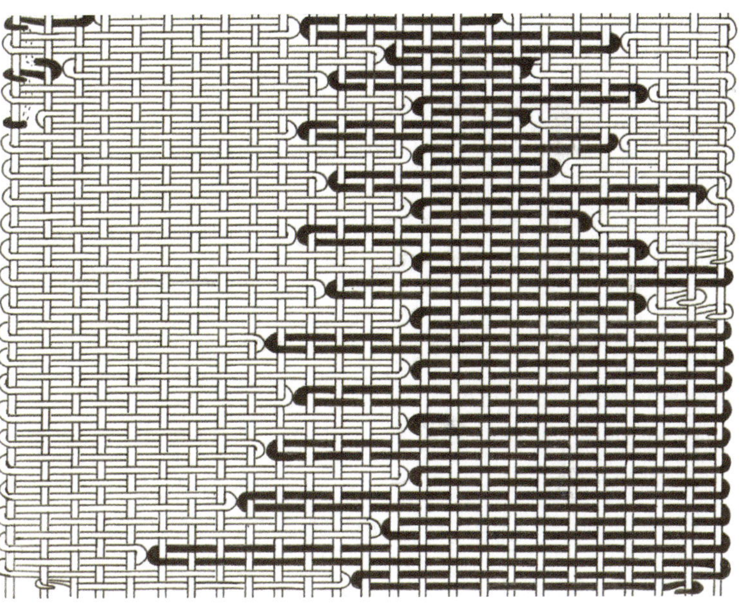

Diagram showing part of the hatched form.

HATCHING TO UNITE TWO AREAS OF SOLID COLOUR

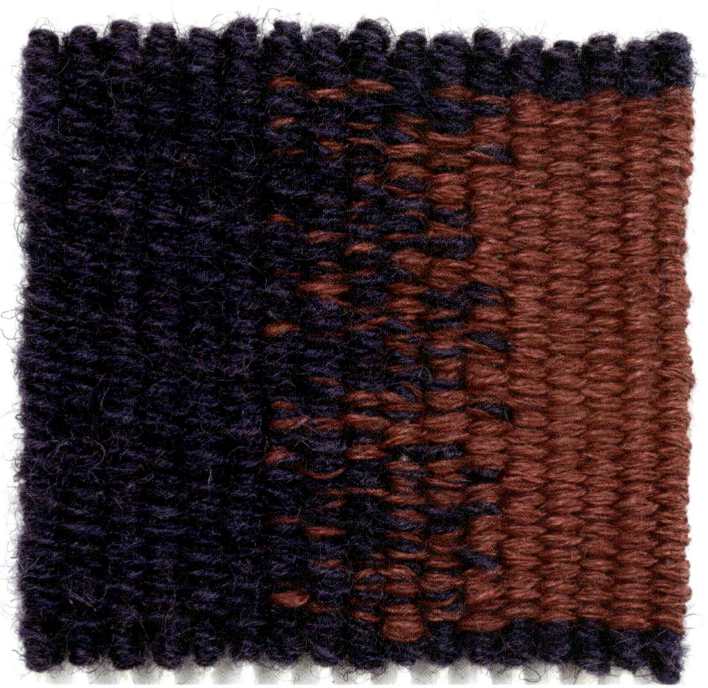

Instead of simply hatching the two solid colour areas with each other, there are now three wefts in play – one for each of the main areas and a third which is a mix of the two. This joining weft combines the colours from either side. It creates a halfway colour and softens the shift from one colour to the other. A band of six warps' width remains constant throughout the sample. Within those six warps, the three wefts are hatched randomly, making a diffuse area between the two solid colour areas.

From the drawing you will see that this joining weft makes only very short passes in either direction, between one and six warps, meaning that there are many turns to be accommodated in this narrow area. To avoid the surface bulging, the turns are made marginally more snugly, but without pulling the warps sideways.

When introducing areas of hatching it is good to consider the boundaries of the area. Hatching is a technique with which it is possible to wander, to extend farther than intended. Its effect can become ill defined and fail to speak. Here, although the hatching is made randomly, the whole area of hatching falls between six warps. This means that the shift between colours happens entirely in this area, with solid colour remaining on either side. It would have been equally possible to extend the hatching randomly to a greater depth, giving a different effect. Here we have two contrasting colour areas with a diffuse transition in the middle third of the sample. It is worth repeating this exercise and altering the zone within which the hatching occurs to create different effects.

In this sample the left and middle wefts have been started together part way along the weaving. Weave one and a half passes of the left hand weft first, pausing on the left. Next weave a pass with the right hand weft and pause on the right. The darker central weft now follows infilling, pausing in the middle. Continue by forming two passes on the left, one longer, then a shorter one. One long pass followed by one short pass on the right, then infill with the middle weft. Repeat the last three steps. This sequence continues throughout the sample with only the turning points for each weft altering.

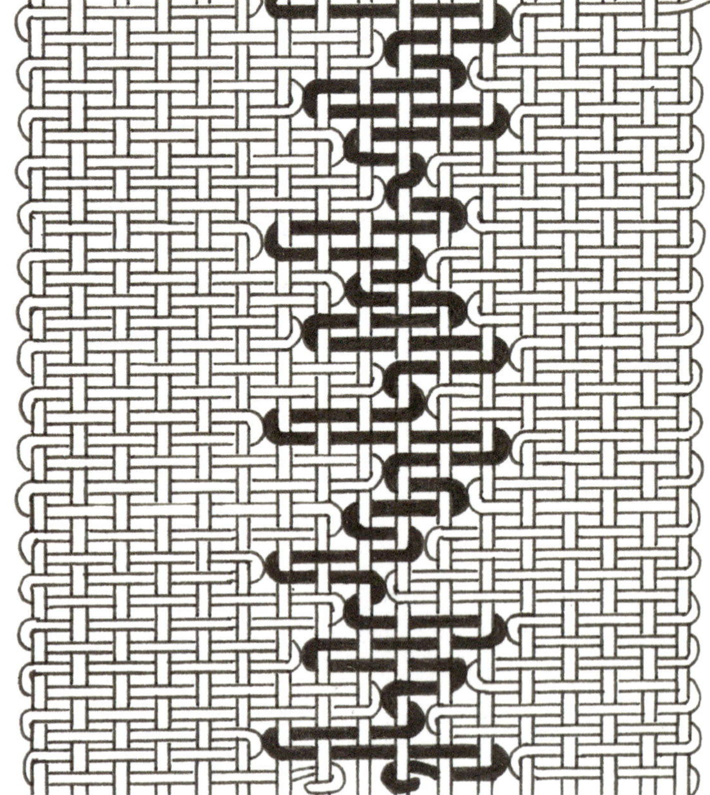

Random hatching to unite two areas.

COMBINING SOLID AND HATCHED AREAS

Here the circular form in the middle is woven as a solid shape without the background wefts being hatched with it, giving a clear, hard edge. Visually it stands out from the background for several reasons. One is because of the contrasting colour. Another is because of a change to a harder fibre, in this case linen against the mixed wool wefts of the background. The background uses four wefts hatched together in colours shifting from magenta/purple in the bottom left through purple, to lighter and variegated yellow to purple/pink mixes in the top. All four are variegated (or tweed) yarns containing fibres of many colours spun together, which further softens the transition between colours.

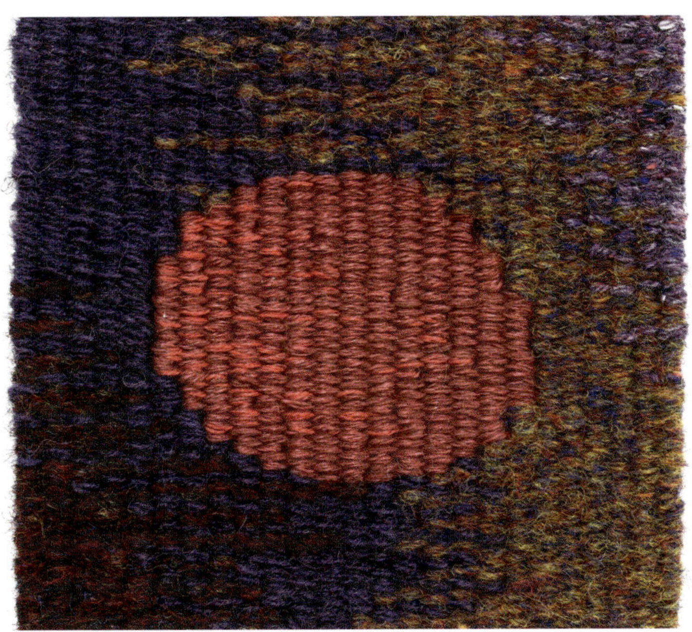

Sample combining solid and hatched areas.

WEAVING ADDITIONAL HATCHED WEFTS WITHIN A TAPESTRY

This sample shows some of the possibilities offered by hatching, both organic and structured. The dark area in the middle begins with a solid mix which produces clearly visible hatching in combination with the mixed background wefts to either side. About a third of the way up, four additional wefts have been introduced, one from each edge, and two in the middle. At the same time the dark weft mix is altered by the substitution of one strand for one of a bronze variegated yarn. This mix continues to change every few passes to include more bronze and less of the dark so that, although still visible as an under layer, the dark area is no longer well defined. This area extends laterally, with the hatching extending into the background area to either side, merging into a many-layered and subtly varied area of colour and tone.

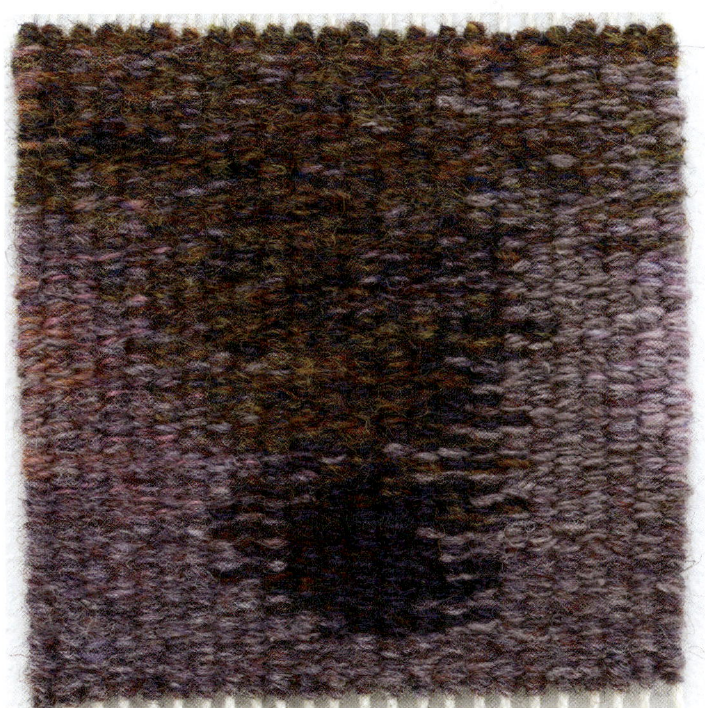

Introducing additional hatched wefts within a tapestry.

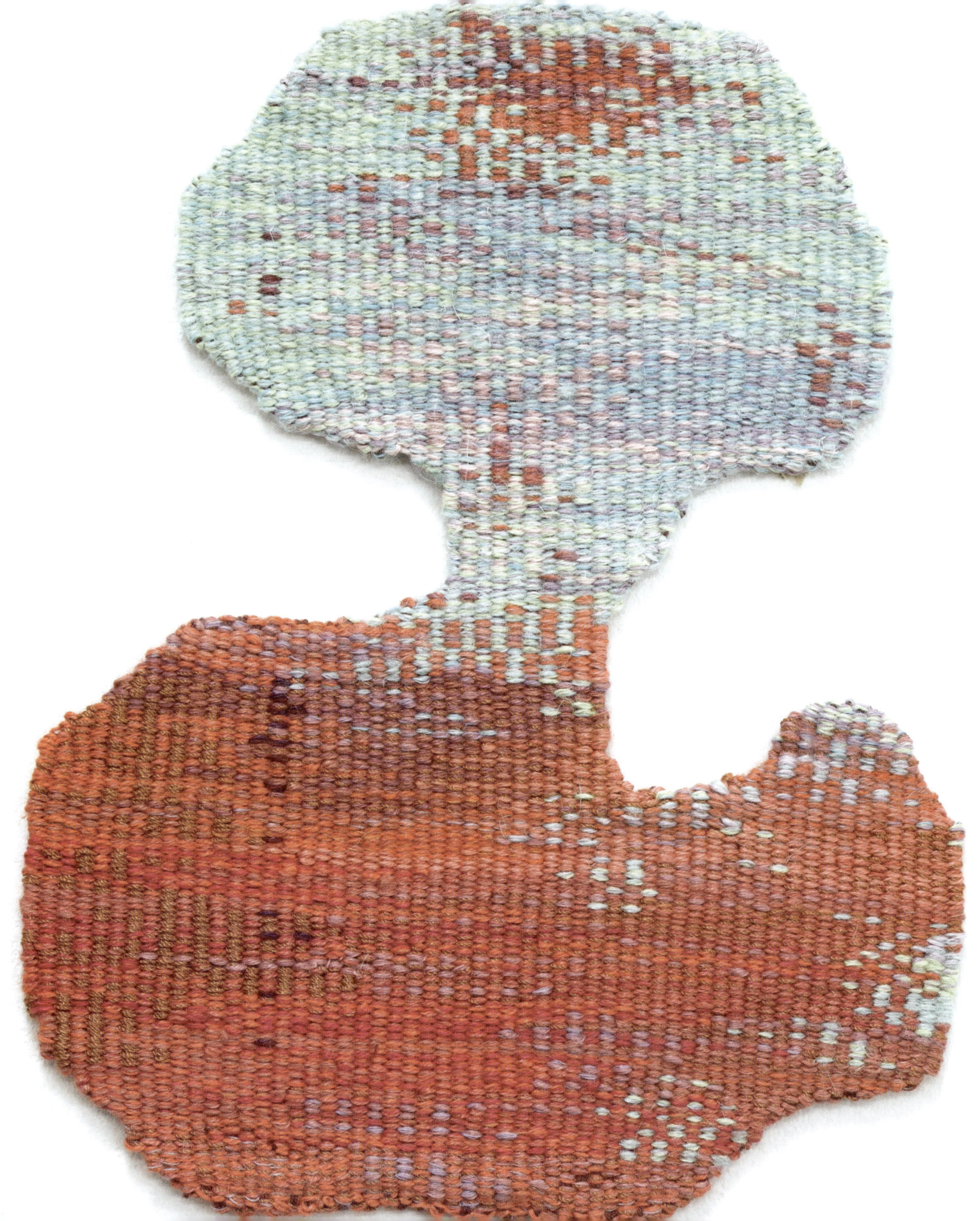

CHAPTER 8

ADDING TO PLAIN WEAVE

In this chapter, we introduce many woven marks and effects which may simply be introduced and withdrawn while weaving without worrying about maintaining the shed. This may come as a relief since most of the techniques demonstrated have relied on careful attention to how and where to start wefts so that they remain in shed and able to weave over one another. This is possibly one of the most difficult aspects of woven tapestry to become fluent with.

Many of the techniques in this chapter are purely woven in that they are made without need to change the weft. Some borrow from rug making or other textile techniques. They are all very versatile – the positions, frequency, scale and intensity can be varied without preplanning. Choices of yarn type and weight may make for a subtle or dramatic effect.

All the techniques explained can be introduced into areas of plain weave to change the surface texture, rhythm or pattern. Some are made freely on the surface regardless of direction and independent of the weave beneath. Others recede into the surface of the weave as if embossed. Although most of the marks are made with the weft, there are some which rely on exposing or manipulating the warp.

Once familiar with this range of effects, they may be introduced whenever you wish. Working more freely at the loom and responding with the weave as it grows should then be more possible. It may also mean that a simpler overall design may work well, since there is freedom to add detail within larger areas of weave. There is also the possibility of completely unplanned weaving, forming a piece entirely at the loom by reacting to what has been woven.

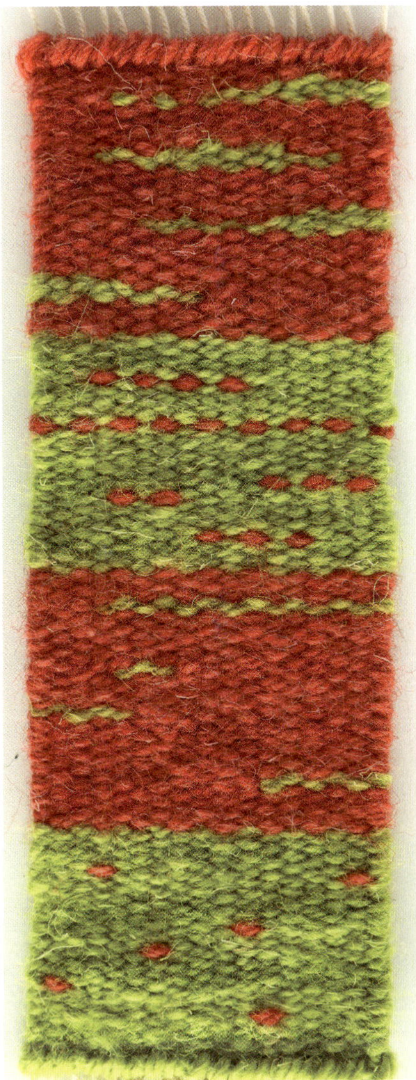

This sample shows marks made by substituting the green weft for pink or vice versa using full and half passes, single beads and hachures within a background of plain weave. In all these cases the weft is simply exchanged one colour for the other, without interrupting the shed. Each is explained in the following pages.

Shaped tapestry with pick and pick. Double warp with red 12/6 cotton. Linen and rayon weft.

INTRODUCING A SINGLE BEAD

The sample has been knotted on as previously, and several passes of the green background woven before pausing to one side. The pink weft starts by making a half hitch around any warp left uncovered in the previous row. It is then taken through to the back and the background weave continues. At the place where the pink weft sits, the background green weft will need to pass under three warps in order to stay in shed. The background is continued till the point at which the next bead of pink is to be made. The pink weft is then floated up at the back of the weaving, so there should be no need to make a half hitch to secure it. When floating wefts up, take care not to pull them; they should sit snug but not tight and remain uncut. Because the warp is under tension during weaving, problems with tension in the weave may be masked, only becoming apparent once the piece is cut off the loom. It is advisable to keep floats as short as possible, no longer than about 5cm (2in) otherwise there is more chance of them pulling and distorting the front surface of the tapestry. Longer floats can also build up bulk at the back, which may look clumsy when a piece is mounted or hung. If a greater distance between marks is desired, it is worth finishing the weft and restarting.

INTRODUCING PASSES

As with a single bead, a section of a full pass may be introduced and finished anywhere for any part or whole of a row. This is shown in green against a pink background on the next section of the sample shown at the start of the chapter. The background weft simply pauses to the front of the weaving at the point an insert is to be made. To stay in shed, the inserted weft must return to finish on the warp immediately before the one it started on. In the case of part passes woven to the edge, the background makes a corresponding pass to even up the level before weaving over the top to continue the background weave.

In the case of an insert mid row, both sides will need to be built up. The background weft will pause at the point the insert is to begin. The inserted weft makes a full pass for however many warps as desired, finishing one warp back from the one it started on. The paused background weft completes the row to one side then weaves over the top of the inserted pass, sliding down the far side it continues to weave in the remainder of the row to level up. The small diagonal mark made when sliding down over just one pass will not be visible once the weaving has been packed down.

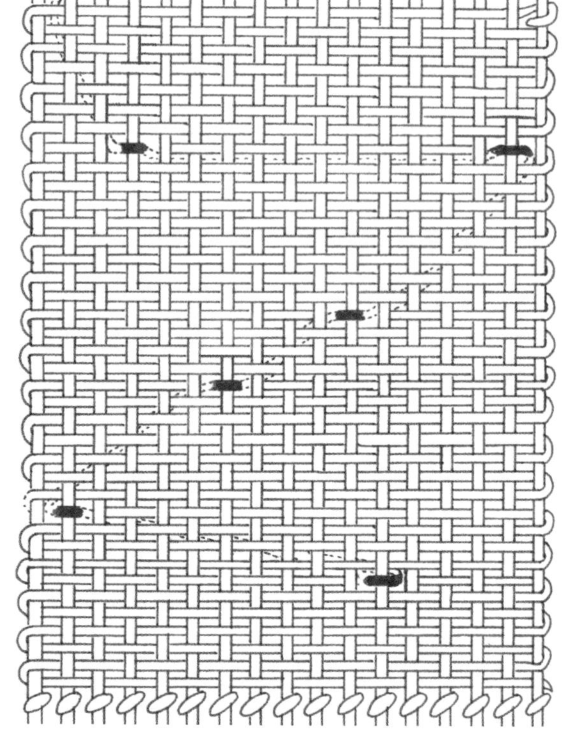

Introducing single beads within a plain weave.

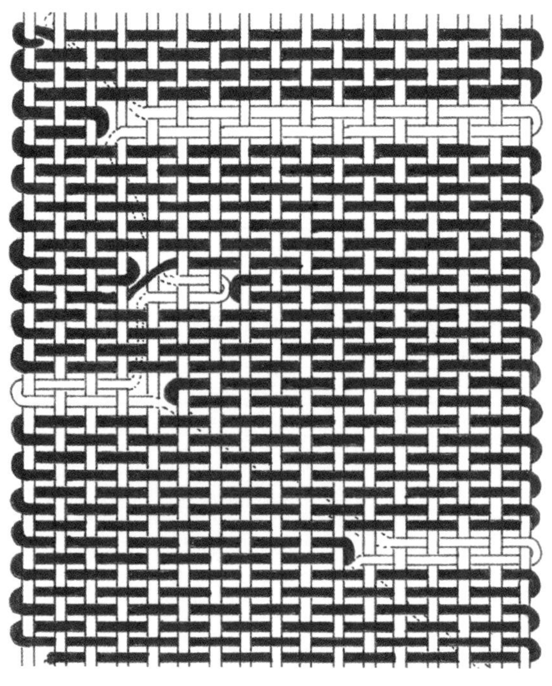

Introducing passes within a plain weave.

INTRODUCING HALF PASSES

These are shown in pink against a green background on the next section of the sample shown at the start of the chapter. Again, the background weft pauses at the front of the weave. The pink weft is inserted either by starting or floating up from the back. It continues the weave by filling the hollows left by the previous row of background. At the end of the desired section, the inserted weft is simply taken through to the back, ready to be floated up later. To continue weaving and remain in shed, the background weft must skip the length occupied by the inserted weft. Taken through to the back at the point the inserted weft began, it is floated along to come out to the front again where the inserted length finished and continues to weave in sequence. In effect, the wefts take turns to come through from the back and return there. Inserting a half pass is just a simple substitution of one weft for another.

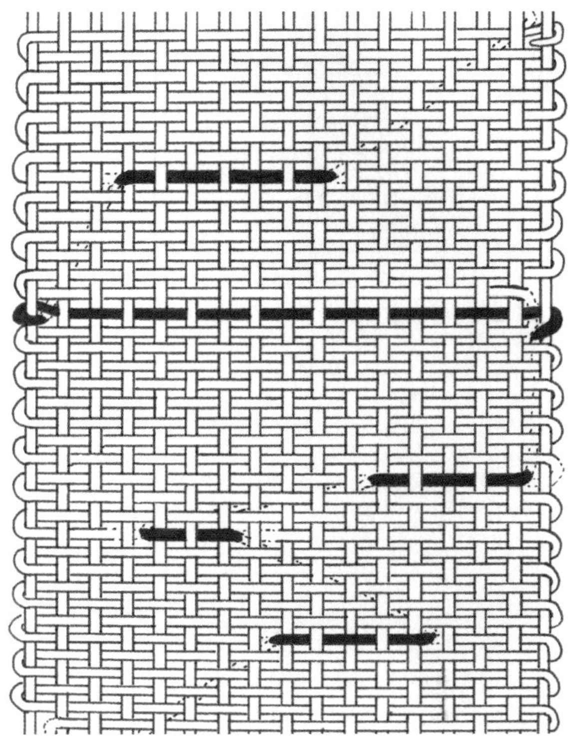

Random half passes within a plain weave.

INTRODUCING HACHURES

These are shown in green on a pink background in the top section of the sample at the beginning of the chapter. As with all the marks on this sample, hachures may be inserted wherever you wish. Hachures may be single ended if woven from one side or double ended if woven in the middle. Their shape and height may vary, from two or more passes.

The background weft pauses where the hachure is to begin and is left hanging at the front. The hachure starts on the next warp along the row needing to be covered. It is woven all in one go, building up as many passes as required before sliding diagonally back from the top to the last warp before the point from which it began. This has the effect of smoothing off the otherwise stepped outline. The background weft then builds up, matching the turns made by the hachure till level with the top. In the case of a double-ended hachure, the background weft then weaves diagonally down the far side to infill before continuing to weave over the top.

You will see that a single weft forms the hachure in one go, as an entire unit. Single- or double-ended hachures may be formed throughout a tapestry, in groups or singly.

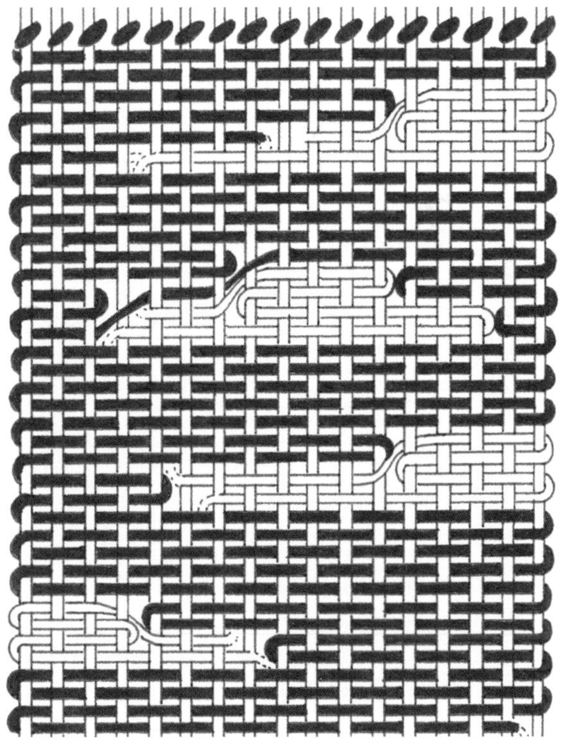

Introducing hachures within a plain weave.

AN ALTERNATIVE WAY TO INTRODUCE PASSES FROM AN EDGE

As with all the other marks included in the opening sample, the marks drawn here may be introduced at any point by simply replacing the background weft with a contrasting insert. The introduced area may be woven in one go with as many passes as are desired. By finishing at the same side as it started, this area will remain compatible with the background in the weaving sequence.

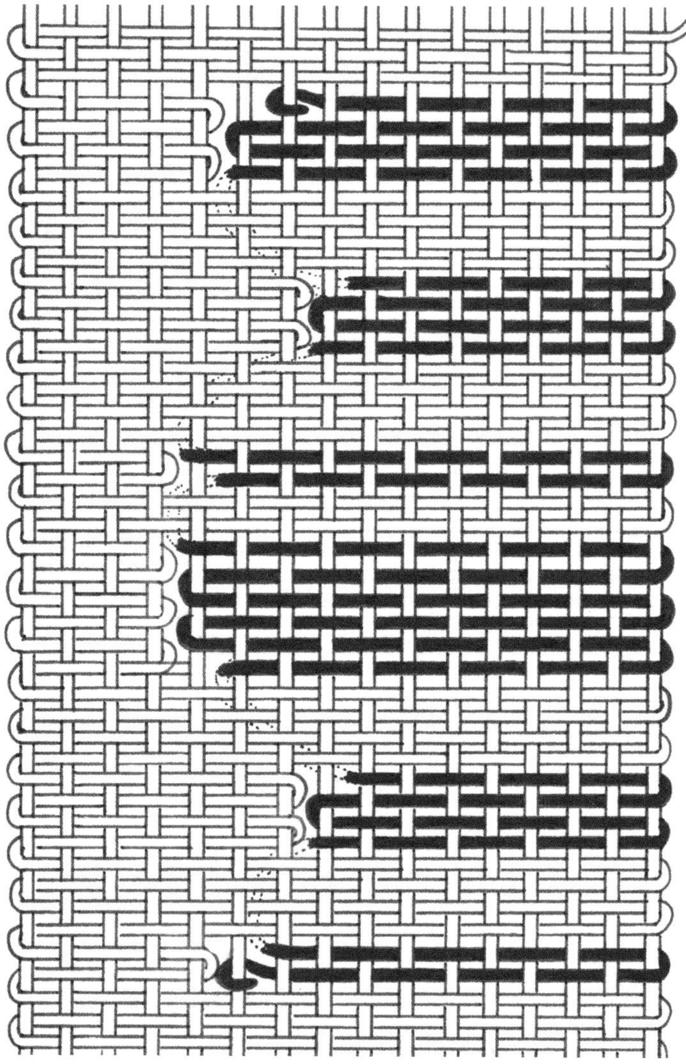

Another way to introduce passes.

The preferred choice is to start and stop in the middle. There is then no need to sew in ends afterwards, as with finishes at the edge. The inserts shown here range only from a single to three passes and are rectangular. Since a weft may always be introduced singly from either edge of a piece, the form it takes is unaffected. The background weft paused where the insert began. Once the insert is complete the background weft is picked up again and weaves the infill, before continuing to weave over the top.

Making creative choices

The marks in these examples were all made by simple substitution of one weft colour for another within the weave. What follows in the remainder of this chapter are 31 other possible ways of making marks or altering the woven texture by other means. They are illustrated as ever on the basis that tapestry technique should inspire and accommodate creative choices. We will look at how they may be used to bring life to even the simplest of designs in ways that respect the integrity and personality of woven tapestry. It is our view that the way a tapestry is constructed is vital to its language as an art form and offers unique aesthetic choices.

So for example forming loops, making knots, wrapping, weaving over multiple warps and at varied angles may all be done at random using the weft in play at the same time. Other techniques involve an added weft which works on the surface with the plain weave continuing beneath. These include tufting and brocade. It is our view that there is much interest to be explored in deliberately exposing the warp, a practice which for some falls beyond the definition of woven tapestry. A few possibilities are illustrated here but there are many more. They may be applied as ways to alter texture, make definite marks or form shaped and sculpted pieces.

Any of these effects may be used as single or scattered marks, or even throughout a piece, either at random or to a pattern, in combinations or one at a time. The resulting effects or textures could only be made by the use of weave, and so have a very legitimate place in the creative vocabulary of a tapestry weaver.

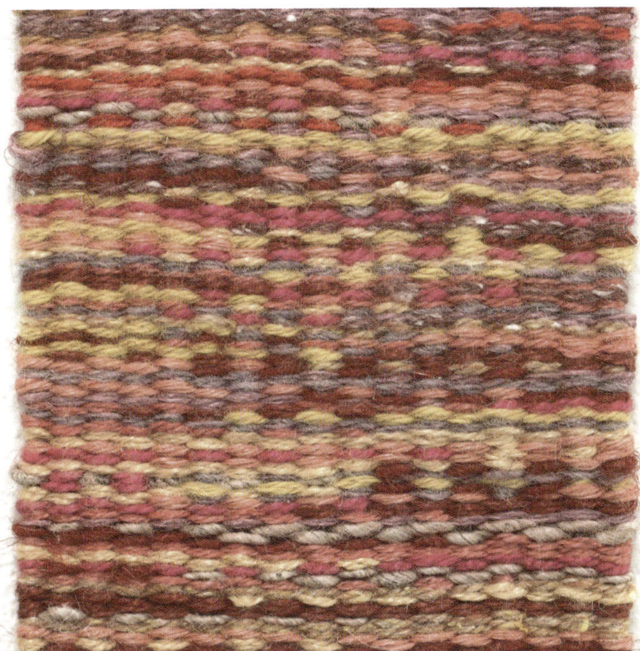

Plain weave with many changing wefts. This mixture of colour and tone within a plain weave has been made by introducing multiple wefts, which when taken through from the back and exchanged for another at random form a complex but unplanned colour mix including fine stripes, dotted lines, contrasting and close colour and tone.

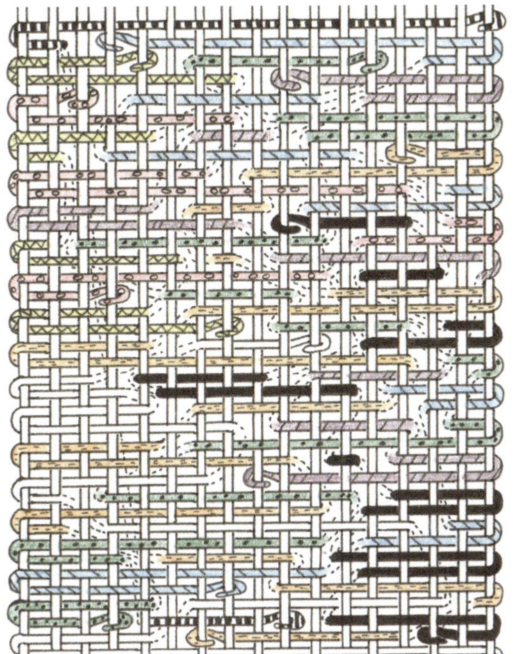

Once the plain weave is established, multiple other wefts start with a half hitch, weave a short length then pass through to the back. The plain weave continues throughout as if woven with one continuous weft except that weft colours are changed frequently for one of several left hanging at the back.

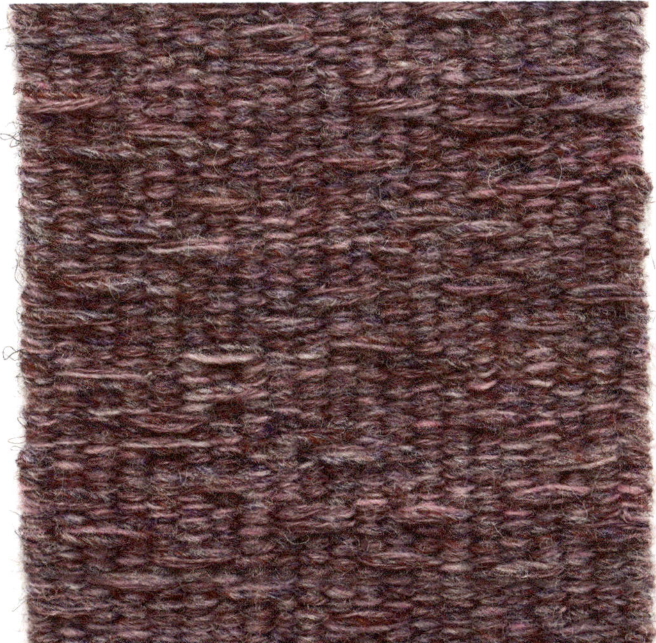

Plain weave with multiple floats. These floats are made at random but might equally have followed a pattern. With the same weft used throughout, this mark is purely textural. The plain weave has continued throughout with floats over three warps being made every couple of passes or so on the front of the weaving. The frequency and length of the floats could vary or be repeated over several passes to form a block.

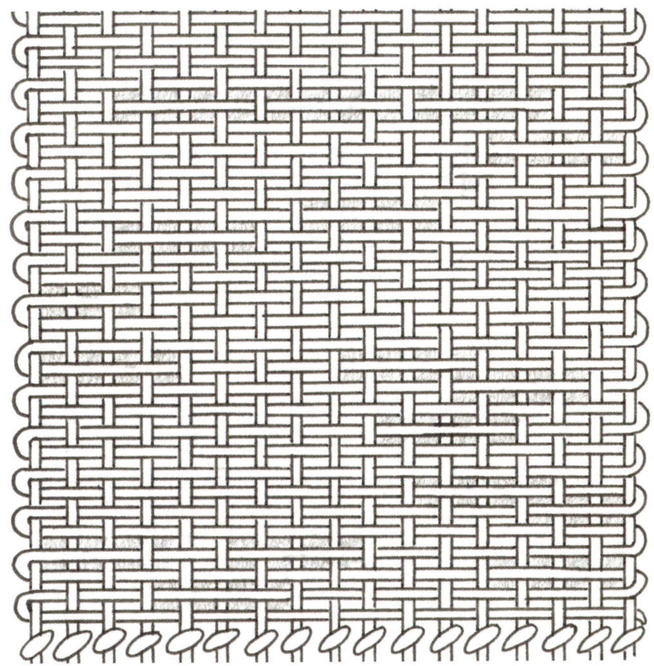

To stay in shed, floats need to be made over an odd number of warps. If making the same float for four or five subsequent passes they should pack down without affecting the level. For greater numbers it would be advisable to make a pass of plain weave midway to stabilise the weave. This pass would pack down and be concealed by the floats.

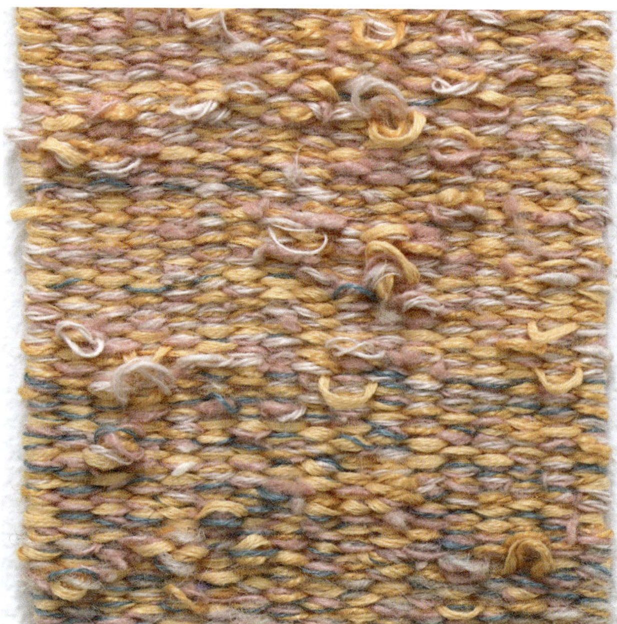

Pulled loops in a plain weave. This background uses a mixed bundle that slightly changes colour throughout the sample. The weft was left free rather than being wound onto a bobbin or making a butterfly which enables one or more of the strands to be pulled making a loop on the surface of the weave and creating a softened texture.

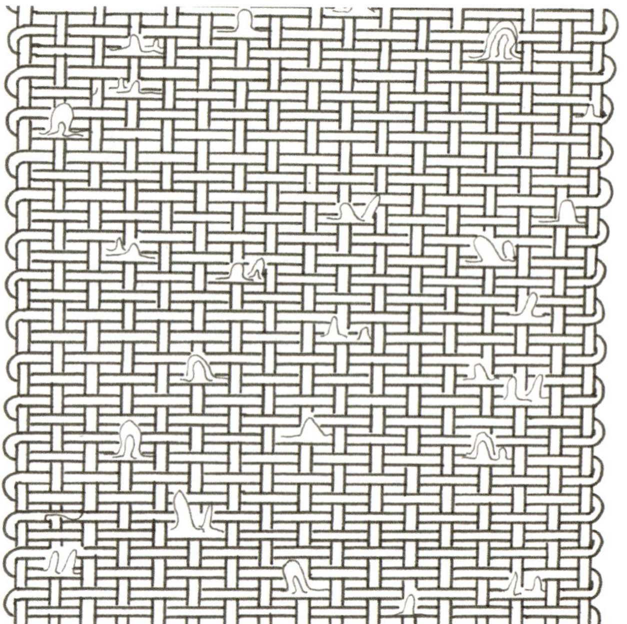

The plain weave is paused at random points to pull one or more strand forwards in a loop of random length. This gives small flashes of contrasting colour or tone from within the background mix. The choice of which strand is pulled, the frequency, length and placing of the loops is all a matter of choice.

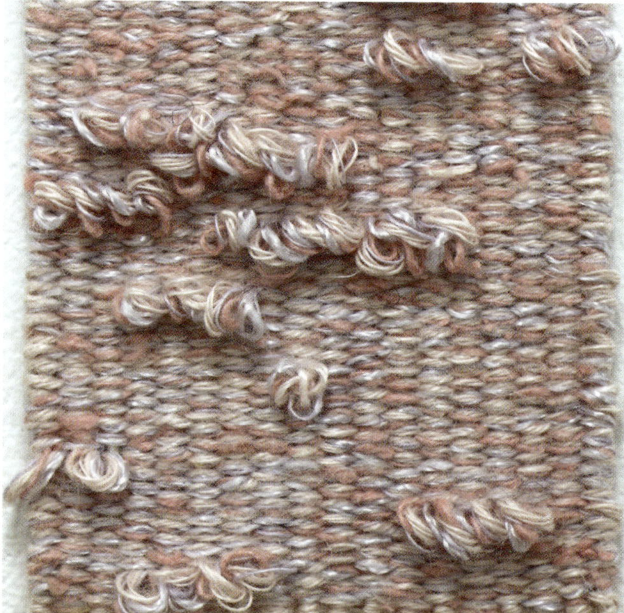

Rows of loops using the whole weft bundle. Instead of pulling forward single strands, the whole weft bundle now makes a loop between warps for varied short, random lengths across a background of plain weave. This gives a more pronounced effect, casting a shadow and adding depth. Multiple loops are most easily formed round a gauge, from the diameter of a knitting needle upwards.

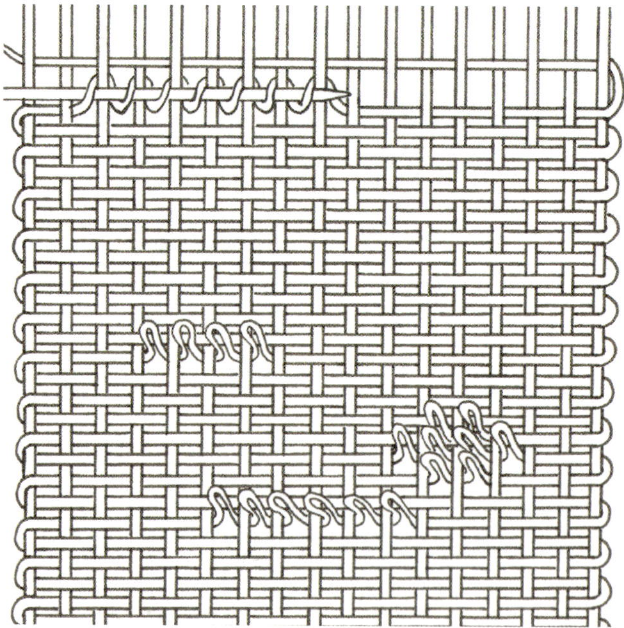

The gauge is laid across the front of the warp as shown. The weft now passes under each warp then over the gauge in the space between warps for as far as the loops are wished for. Reverting to plain weave, a full pass is made over the top before the gauge is pulled out and the weave packed down firmly to secure. If weaving several rows of loops, it is best to secure them with a pass of plain weave.

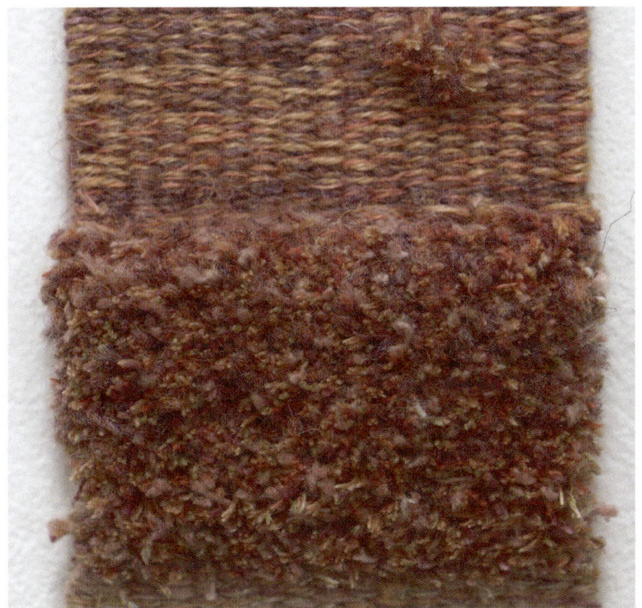

Tufting. This band of tufts has been made in a background of plain weave using the same mix and trimmed so that they are longer towards the top. Plain weave is required between rows of tufts to secure them. Here with just one pass between rows the area of tufting is quite dense. More background passes would have made sparser tufting.

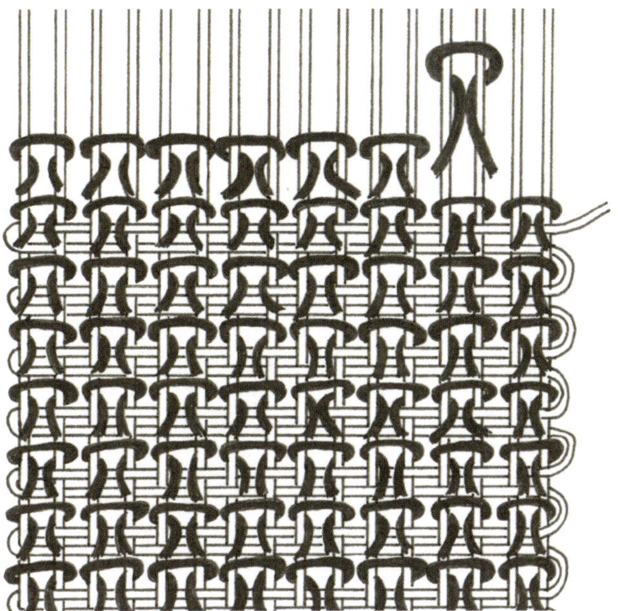

A length of weft is wrapped around a flat gauge of about 5cm (2in) width then cut to make lengths which should be long enough to handle. Lay a length midway across two warps. Take the two ends around a warp each and up into the space between. Trim to the length required.

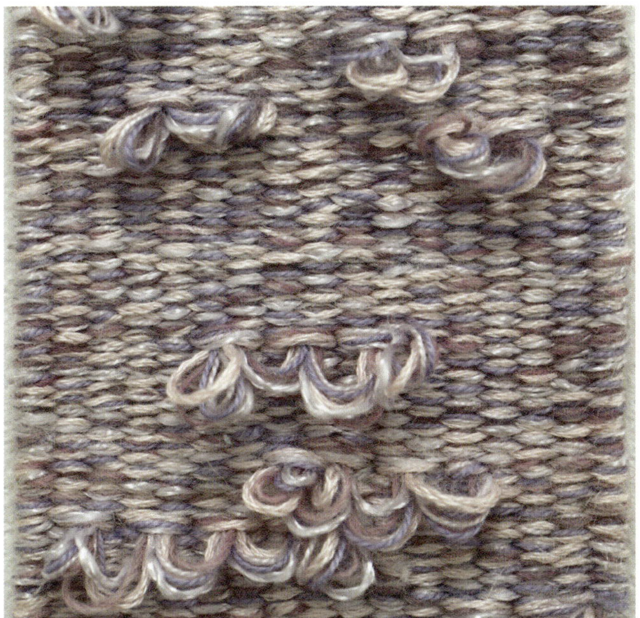

Tufts/loops formed with the continuing weft. Here part rows of uncut loops have been made in an area of plain weave by using the same continuous weft. This method is quicker than making tufts singly. The loops may simply be cut once secured within the weave.

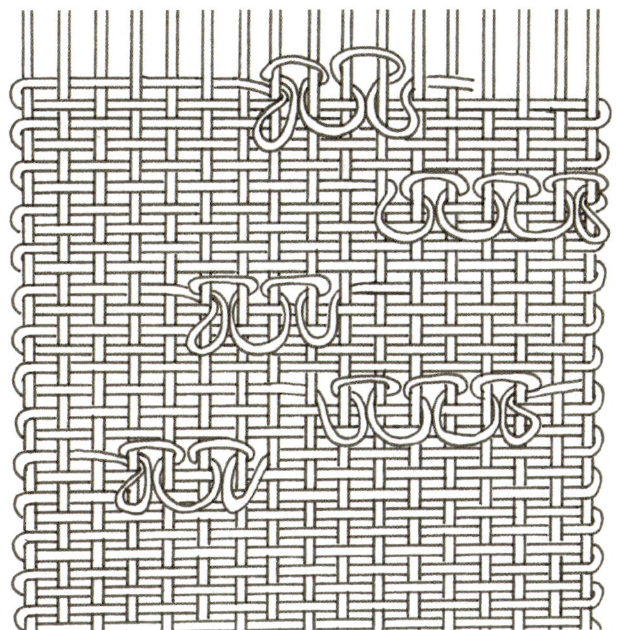

To start, instead of continuing to weave under and over, stop and pull a loop forward between two wefts. Next take the weft backwards under one warp, forwards over two, backwards under one, then over the next two leaving a loop of weft, repeat. Continue at will, reverting to plain weave by making a final loop either over a warp or between two to get back into shed.

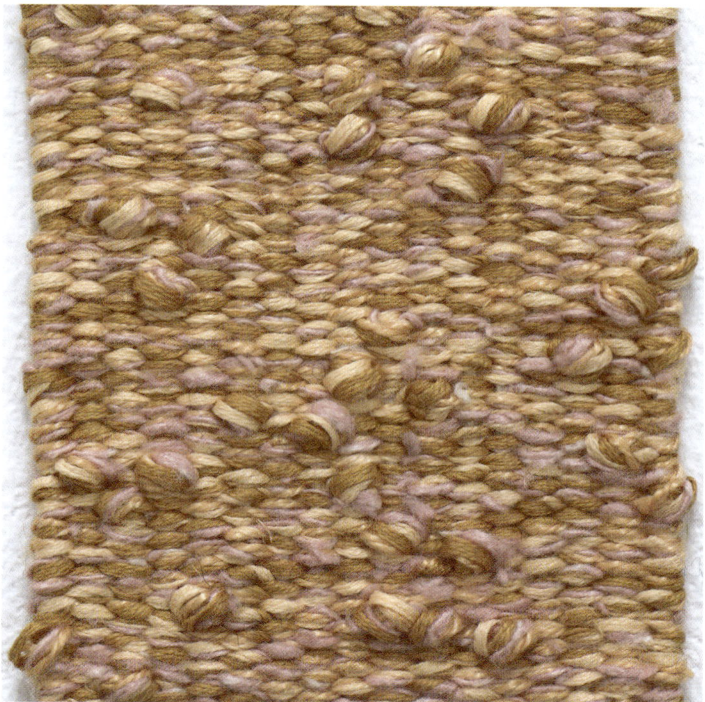

Double half hitches used as a raised mark. Random rounded marks have been made on a surface of plain weave using the same knot as for securing at the start and finish of a piece. They are made with the background weft and lean in the same direction as the row of weaving.

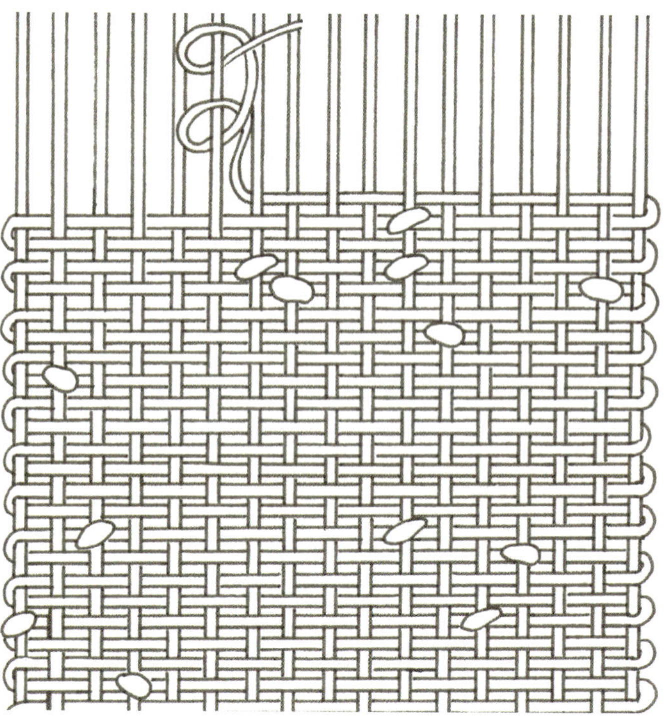

The plain weave has been established and continues throughout. At random points, instead of simply passing over the warps, the weft makes two half hitches by passing over the warp then back under it, twice on the same warp before continuing with plain weave as before.

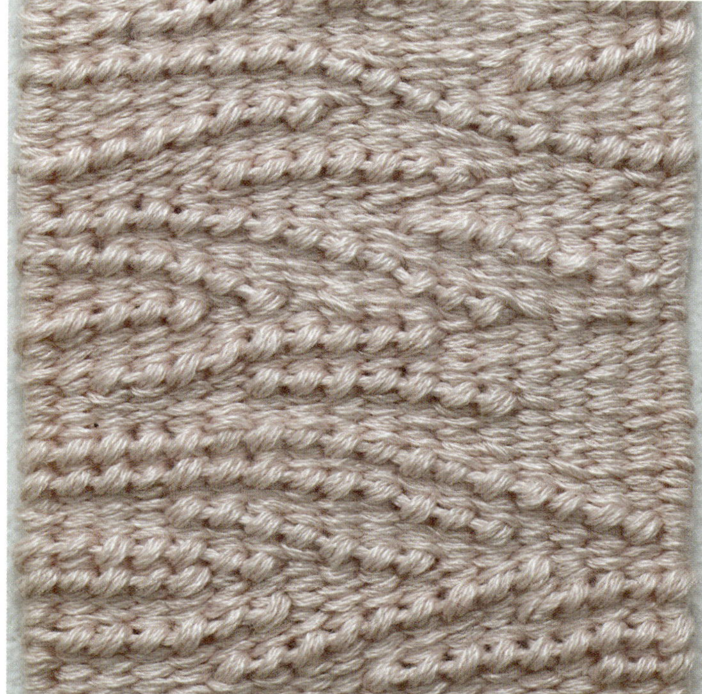

Double half hitch knots used to make a line. Double half hitches have been made on each one of several successive warps to outline curved areas of plain weave. They have all been introduced on rows passing from left to right so that all the marks slope upwards to the right.

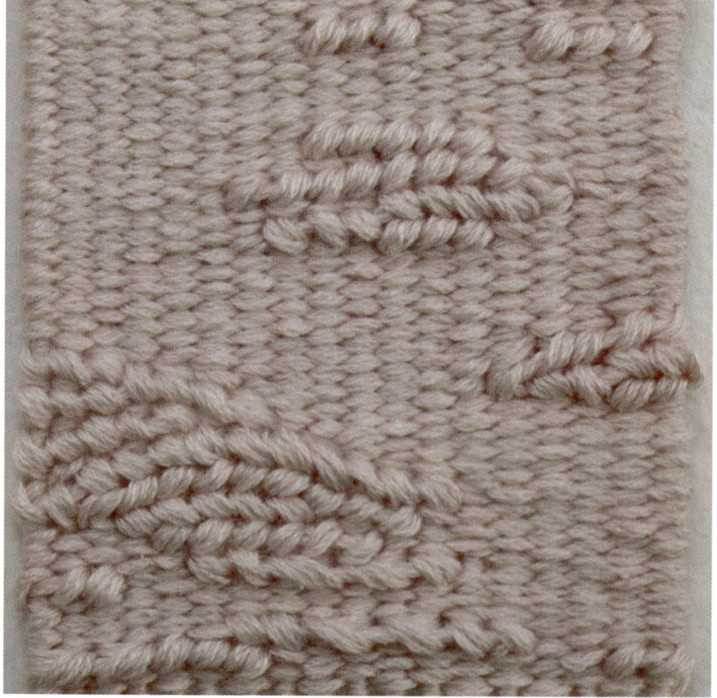

Double half hitches in alternating directions. Runs of double half hitch knots have been made on two or more successive rows. Alternate rows lean upwards to either the left or right. Making half hitches over two or more warps is also possible, giving a thicker, more raised line. A very elastic weave may be made entirely in knotting.

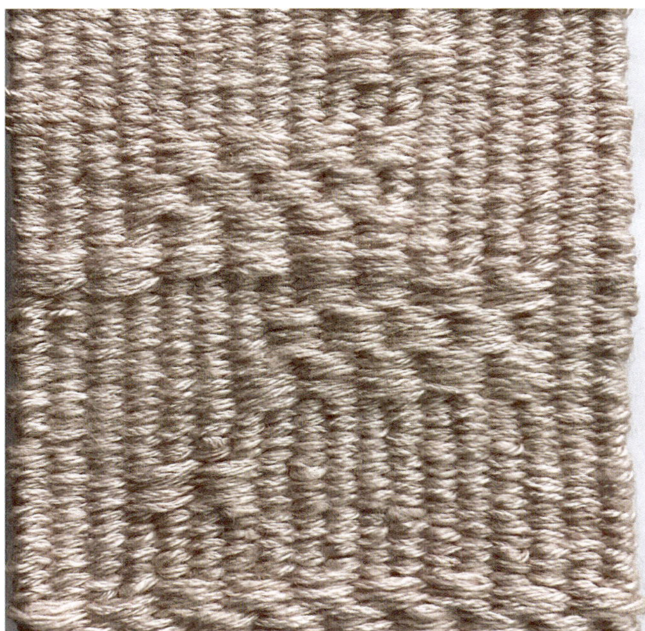

Double/single weave. Here one continuous weft is woven either singly or over and under two warps at a time for three or more successive rows. When weaving part rows the double weave must pass under two over two in pairs to remain in shed. When weaving a whole row in double weave, this does not apply.

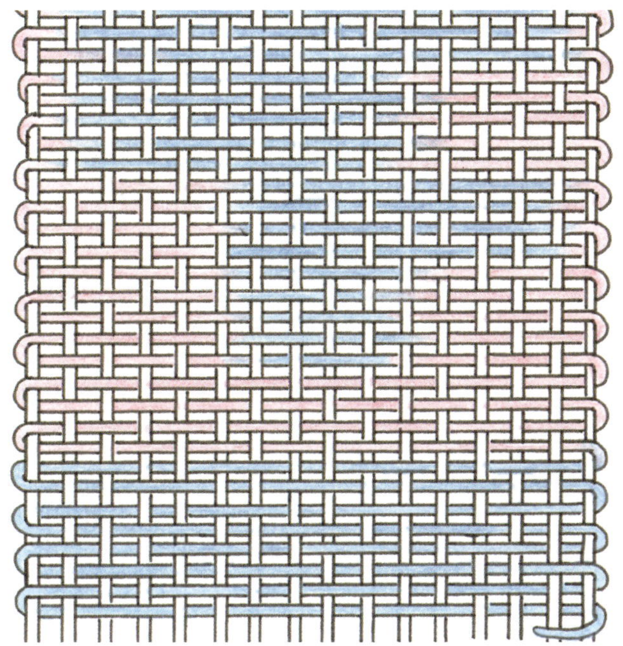

Although the weft is continuous with no colour change, the double weave is marked in blue, and the single in pink. Note, because the sampler has started in double weave, the weft started by passing under four warps, then back over two to secure, in place of the usual one. Occasional passes of single weave are needed to secure when weaving larger areas of double weave.

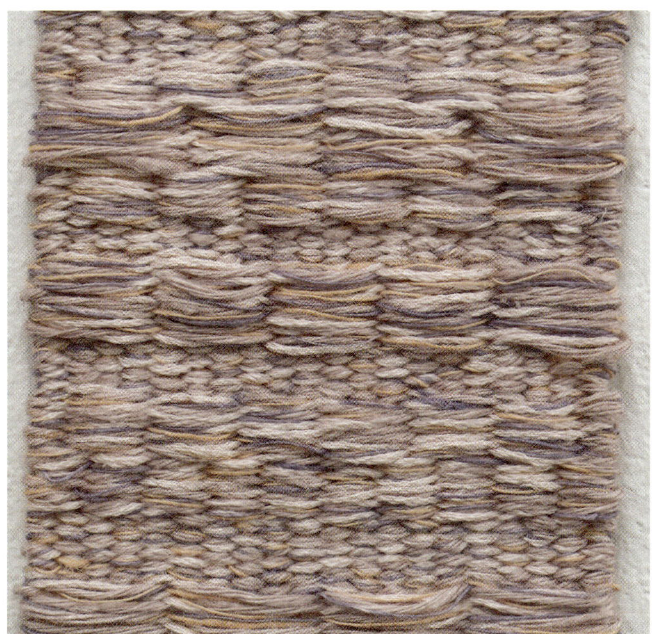

Passing over two to five warps. Raised bands have been formed by passing the weft over and under anything from two to five warps at a time in areas which are separated and secured by plain weave. Note, when passing over/under more warps, the bead becomes looser, elongated and more raised.

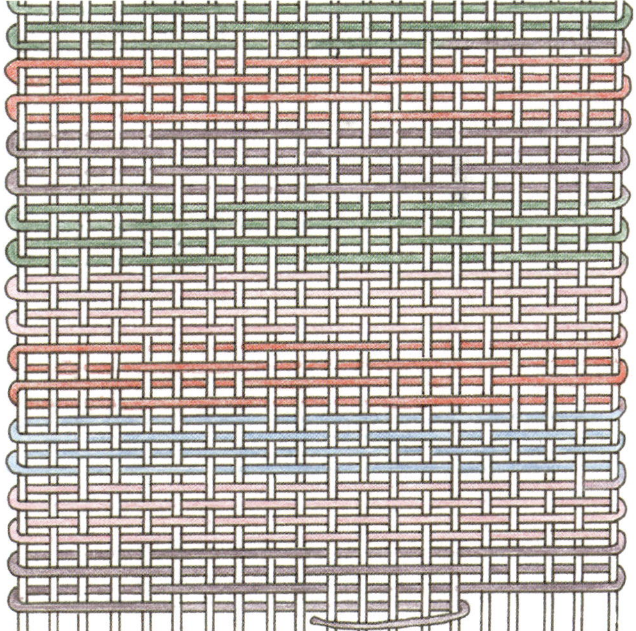

Colours have been used on the drawing to show the number of warps passed over and under on the sample. Because whole not part rows are being woven, the conflict of sheds does not arise. Passing over several warps at a time may cause the warps to pull, so make sure to put in plenty of weft to prevent this.

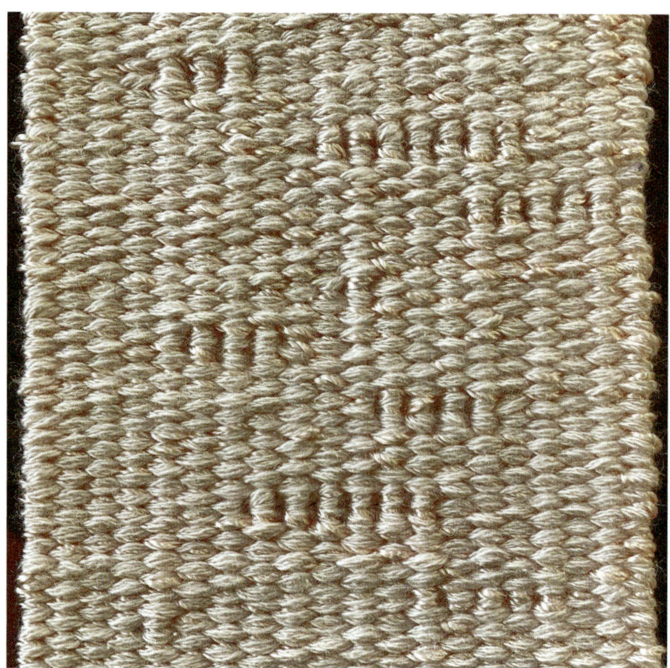

Reverse soumak in single part rows. Part rows of reverse soumak are shown here in a background of plain weave, showing a characteristic shadow where the weft has wrapped around each warp instead of passing over and under. Over larger areas, soumak produces a very elastic weave.

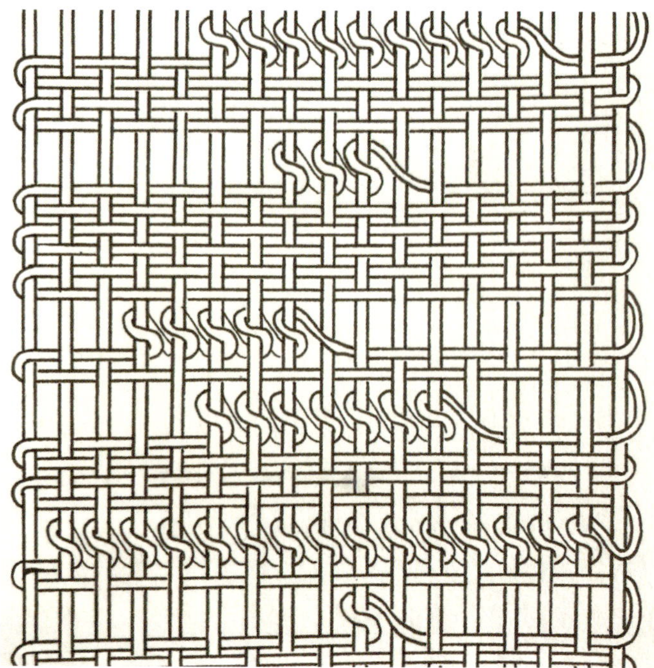

To change from plain weave to reverse soumak, pass the weft under a warp, backwards over it, then forwards under both it and the next warp, repeat – backwards over one warp, forwards under two. The plain weave simply continues afterwards first passing over the next uncovered warp. The diagram shows the reverse soumak running from the left to the right only.

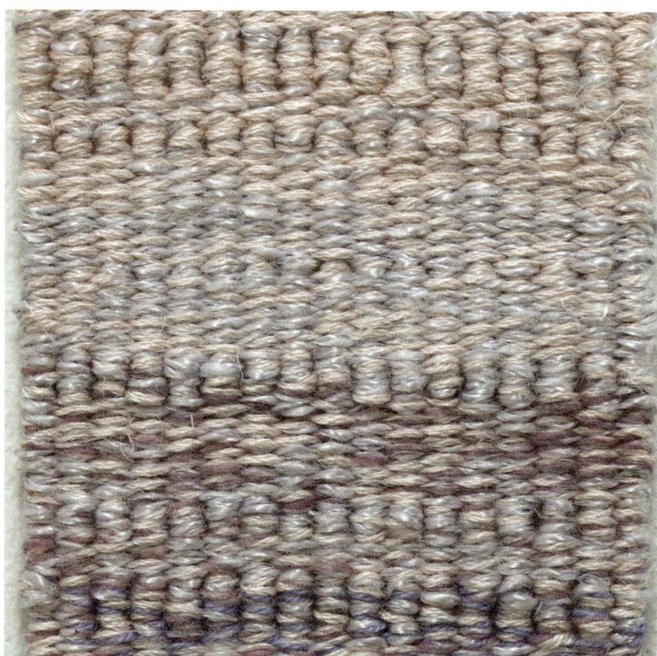

Reverse soumak, in both directions. Here, several successive rows of reverse soumak alternate with sections of plain single weave. The deeply ribbed appearance is now very marked. The weft colour shifts slightly as single strands are added or taken out, but the whole sample is woven in one continuous weft**.**

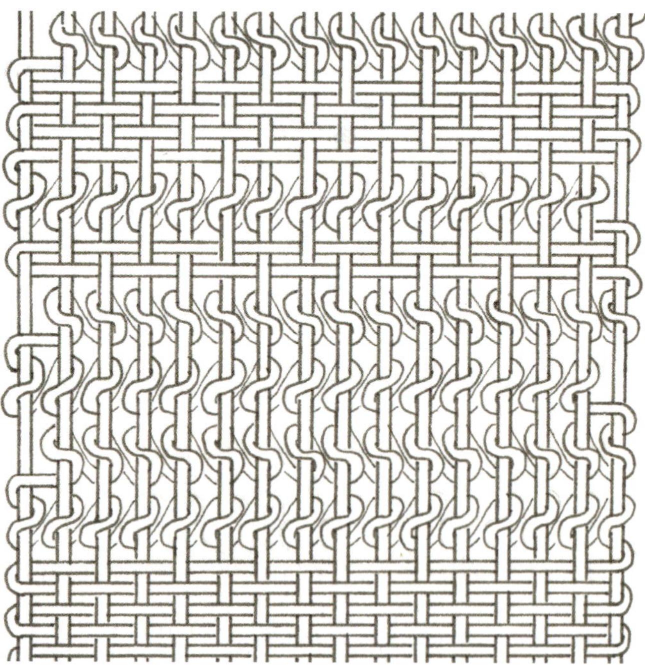

Here, whole rows have been woven in reverse soumak – passing first under the warp, then back over and under the next two. The weft wraps diagonally over the warp in alternating directions but beats down to level. The edge warps are wrapped around twice to equalise the level with the next row.

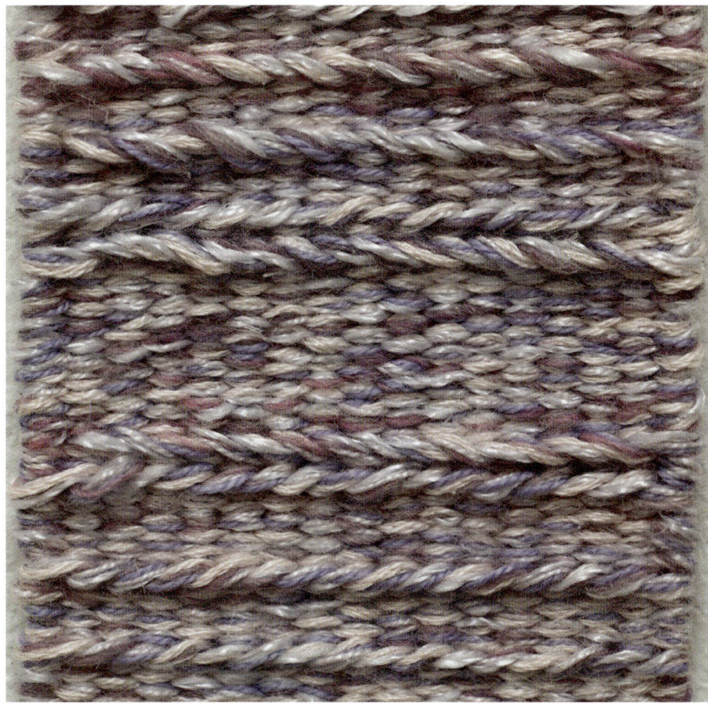

Soumak wrapping over two warps. The resulting rows now stand out from the plain weave background in beads with a clear diagonal direction. When wound from left to right, the wrap leans to the left, conversely when wound right to left they lean to the right.

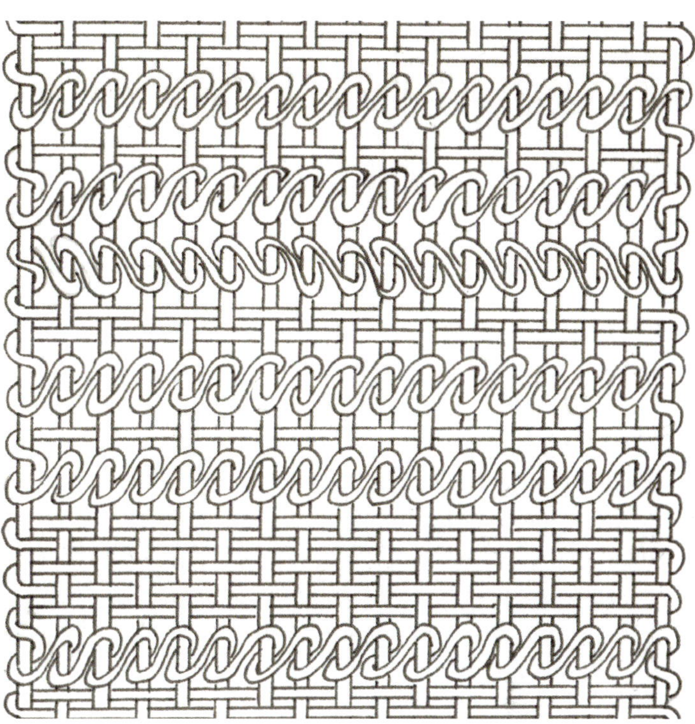

Soumak is a versatile technique, seen in a number of different forms. In this example the weft passes over two warps and then back under one warp. The weft makes an extra wrap around the end warp to level up. The bead slopes up to the right from the direction it has come.

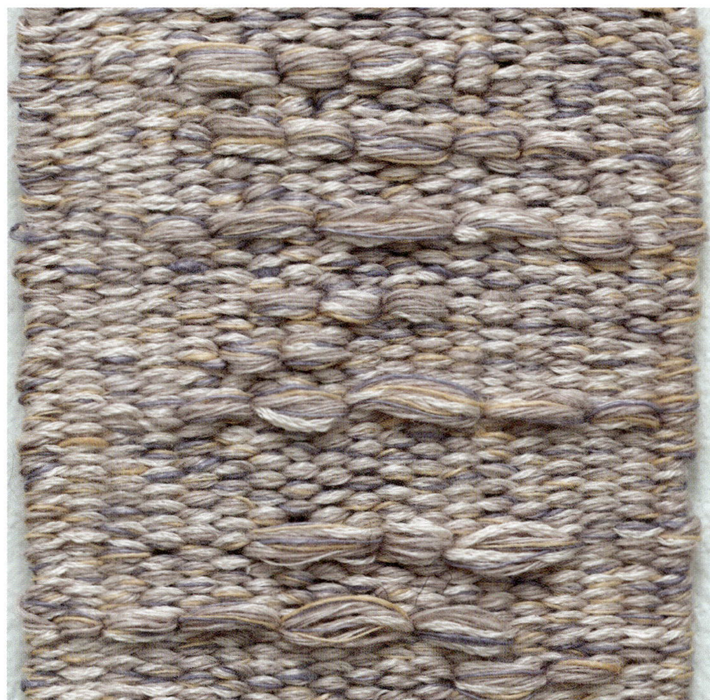

Soumak passing over two to four warps. Soumak can be introduced at any point and also pass over greater numbers of warps. These longer wraps beat down to sit horizontally, standing forward of the surface, casting shadow and allowing the weft bundle to open up, showing the individual strands.

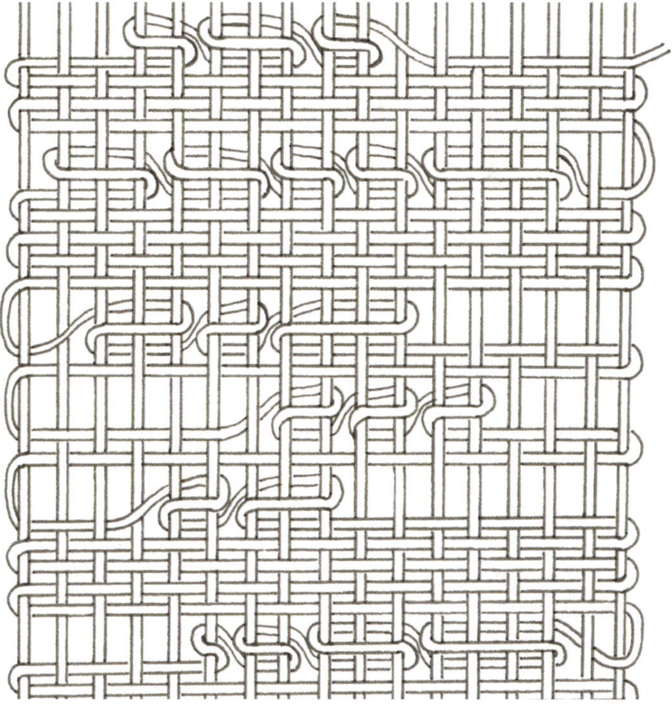

When passing over two or more warps, it is necessary to anticipate how many warps you wish to wrap around. For example, if increasing from two to three warps, first pass over two warps, back under five, then forwards over three. Care is needed to avoid pulling the warps together when wrapping over several at once.

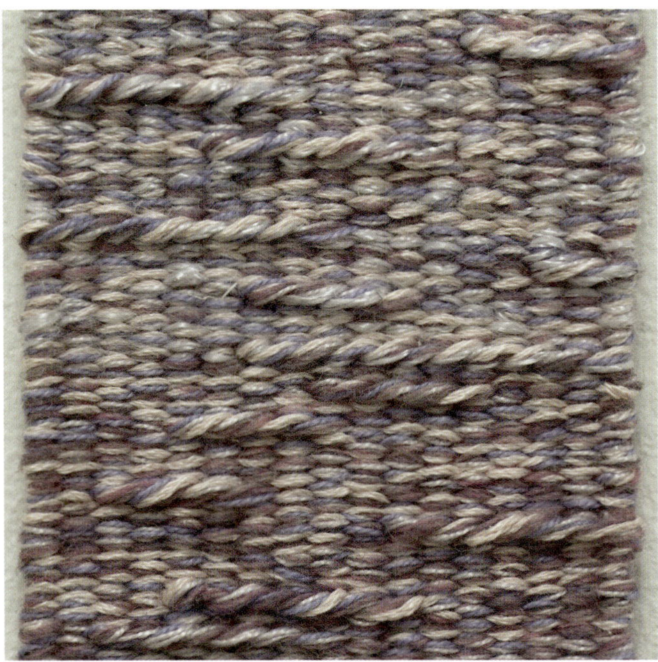

Soumak passing back over below. The weft has passed over two warps then back under one below the point of wrapping. The raised line of diagonally sloping beads is identical in appearance to when passing back under above. The difference is that now the bead will slope in the same direction as the weave instead of contrary as before.

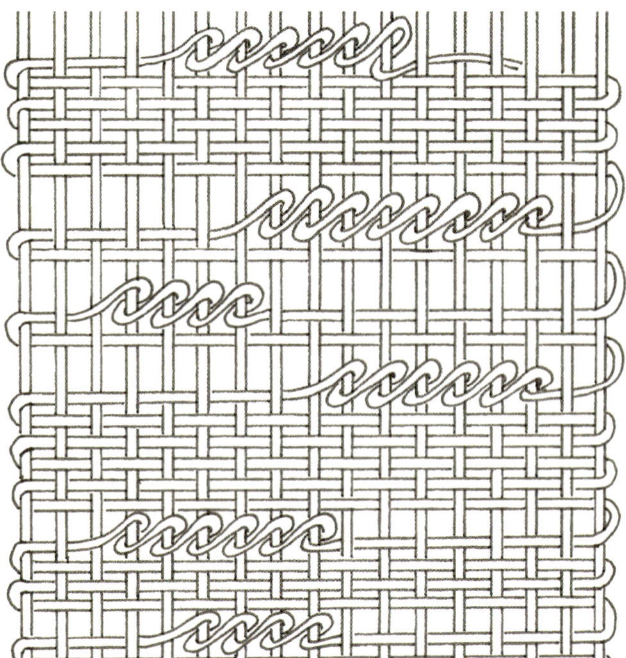

To start the soumak, the weft passed over two warps, then backwards under the second warp below the wrap. The weft length is pulled right through before passing over the warp just wrapped and the next warp to continue. All the lines in this sample are woven left to right and slope the same way – the same pattern would apply in reverse.

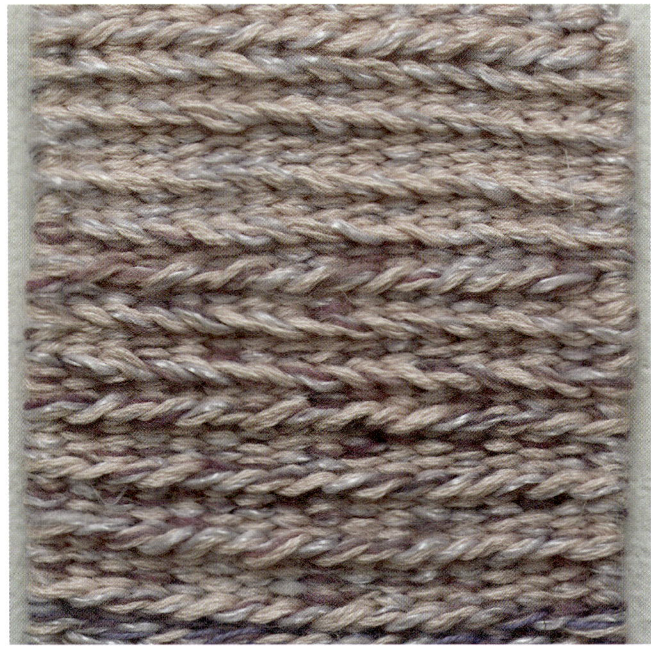

Soumak, turning under, alternating lines. Interspersed with bands of plain weave here we have several full passes of soumak, woven by passing over two, back under one below. The effect varies from single narrow lines to wider bands, sloping in alternating directions giving an appearance a little like plain knitting.

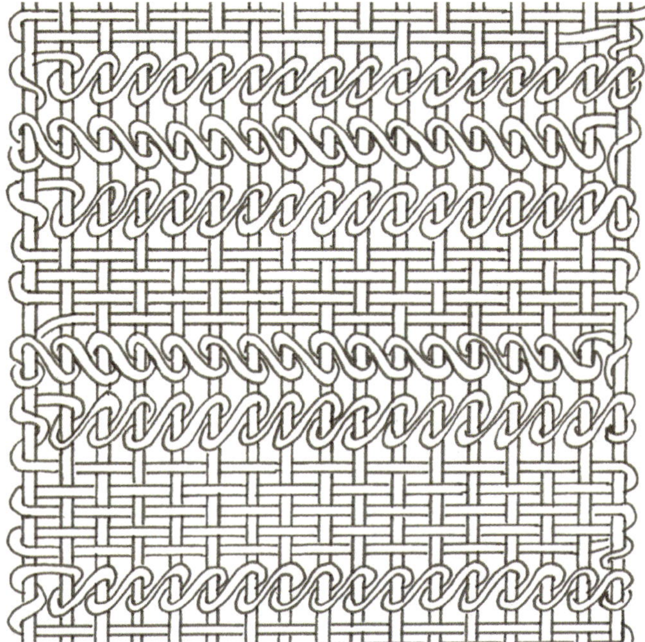

At the edge the weft comes up between the first and second warp, wrapping around the first and over the second to get it into sequence. It becomes evident now that when passing back under the warp below, the bead will always slope the same way as the direction of weave.

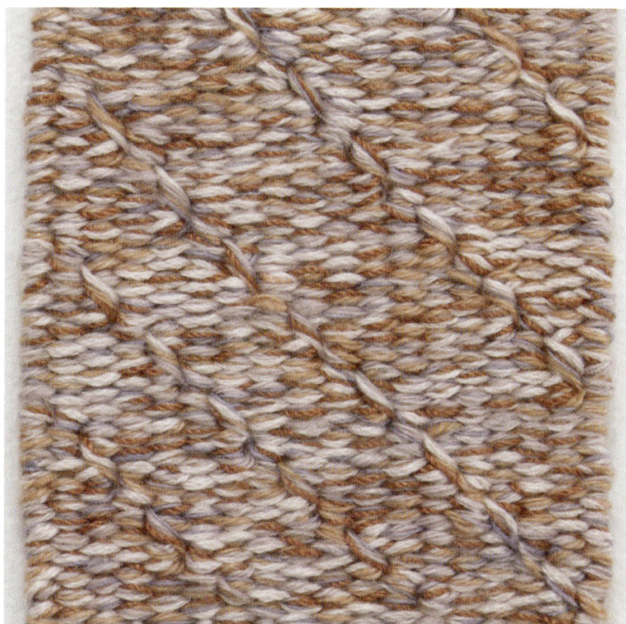

Diagonal half pass to create pattern. A half pass is woven diagonally down an area of plain weave, then the same weft builds the next sloping section. The effect is to outline the area and smooth off the steps made by the steep incline.

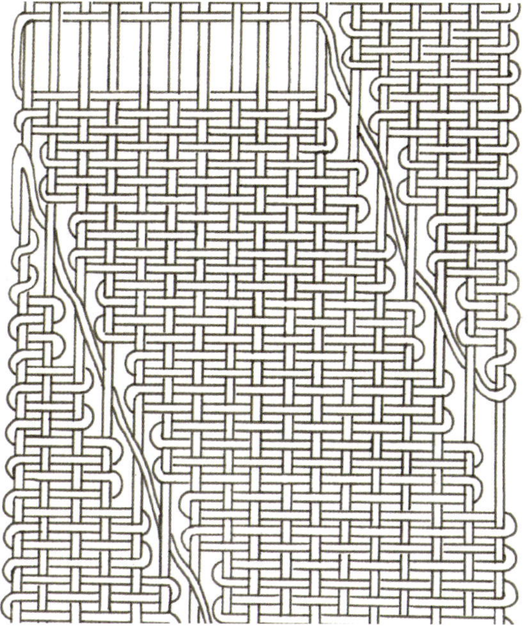

The area of plain weave to the bottom left is woven first then the weft taken diagonally down to the bottom and to the right, ready to weave the next sloping section. The slope is reasonably steep, with two passes to each warp. The steeper the slope, the more visible the diagonal line will be.

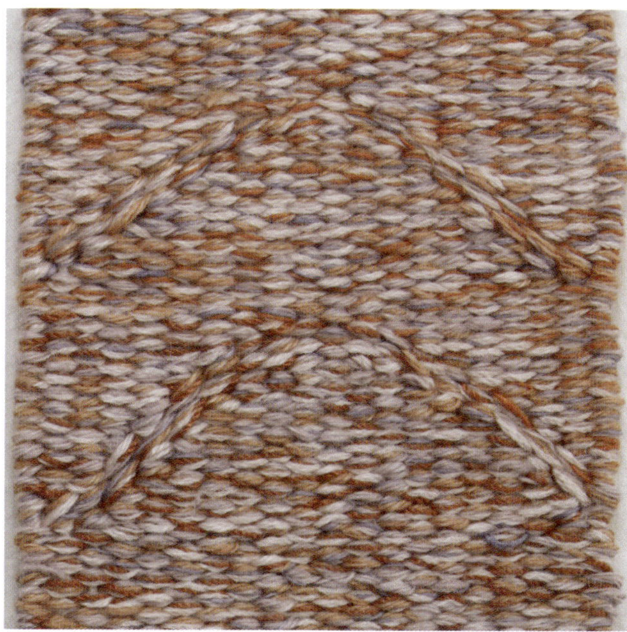

Eccentric outlining. With one weft the curved areas have been formed, then the weft is taken over them for a half or full pass, outlining and returning to the point needed to weave the infill. This subtle detail works well repeated over a bigger area where the pattern becomes more evident.

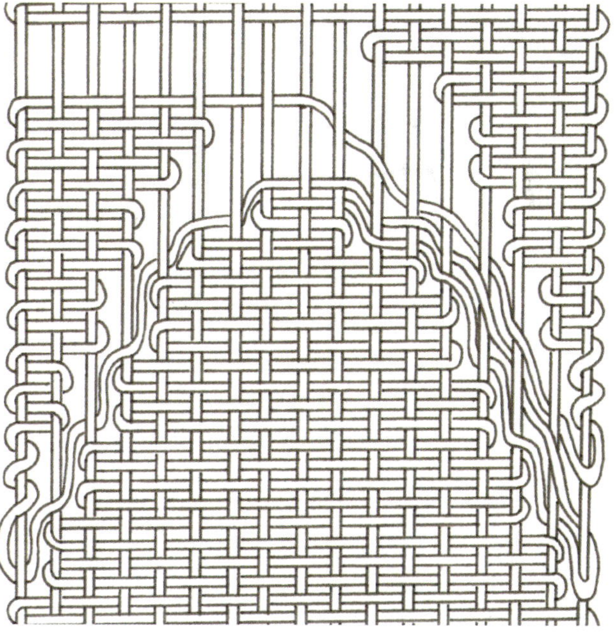

The mound is first made in plain weave, then the weft runs diagonally down the right, back up and over to the left where it infills before passing diagonally back down the right side to infill. The outlining is made visible by the longer diagonal bead. Care is needed to put in enough weft when weaving eccentrically, to avoid it pulling in when beaten down.

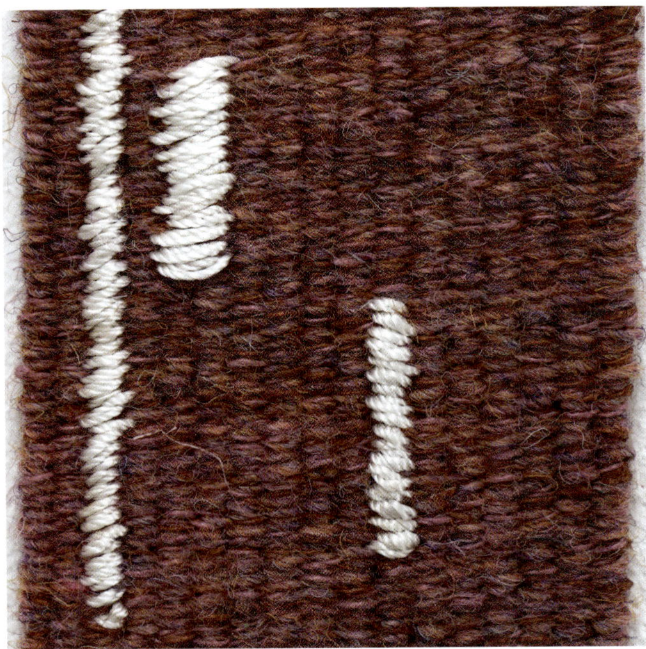

Vertical soumak overlays. A contrasting-coloured weft is wrapped around one or two warps against a background of plain weave, making a prominent mark sitting forward of the surface whilst the background weave continues underneath. The two narrower wraps are made over a single warp in reverse directions, which shows in the shallow slope.

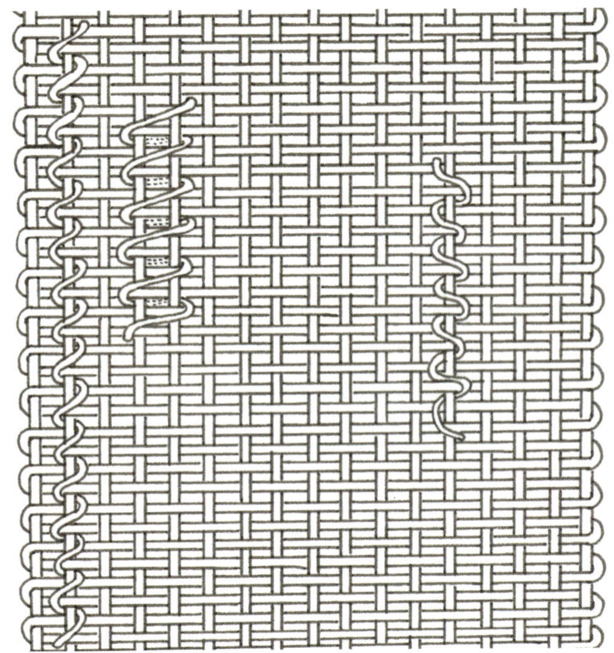

A separate weft for each overlay is introduced from the back. After each pass of plain weave, the overlaying yarn is wrapped around the chosen warp or warps once in the same direction. It is left hanging at the front as the background weave makes another pass. It is finished by simply taking the wrapping weft through to the back.

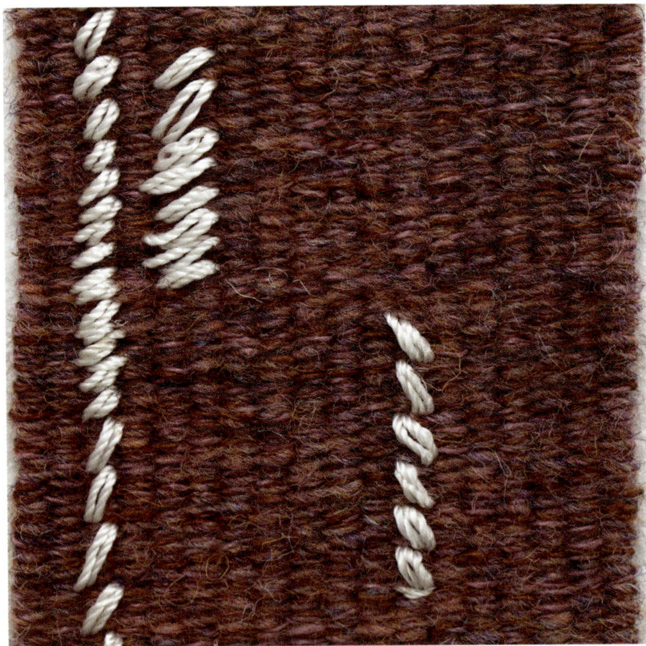

Vertical soumak variation. The wrap is now made with variable numbers of passes of plain weave in between giving longer, more evidently diagonal and freer marks.

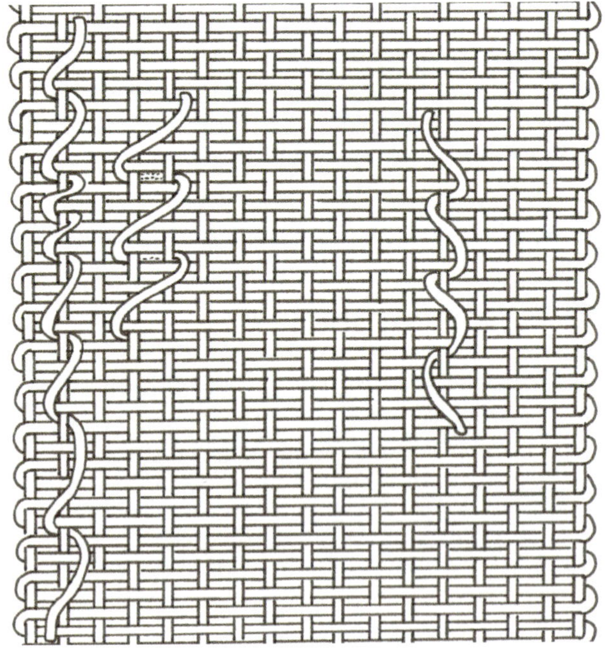

The marks now change throughout their length, winding round the warp after either one, two or three passes of plain weave. The central mark has been made by winding round two warps anticlockwise after two passes of background. The right-hand mark is wrapped round a single warp clockwise after two passes of background.

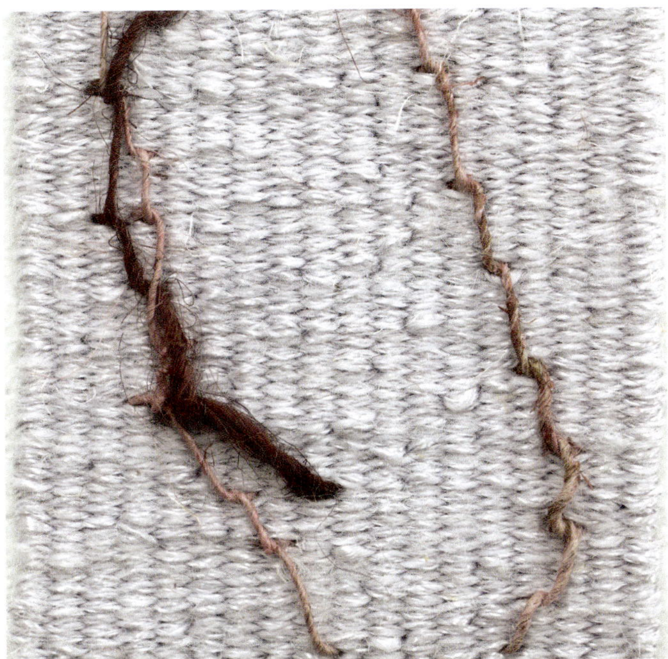

A continuous free soumak overlay. Against a background of plain weave, single strands of nettle yarn in three separate overlays have traced free lines. Despite being a single strand, they are prominent because of the hard spin and robust nature of the yarn, and the length of the wraps made.

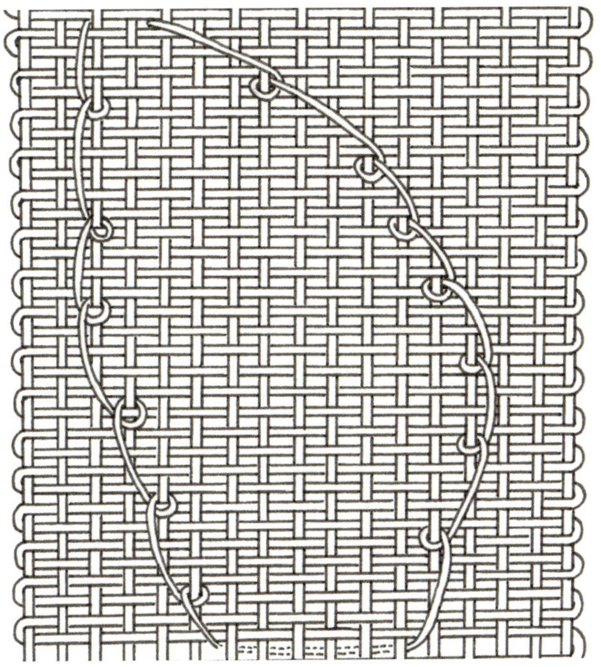

A length of wrapping yarn has been introduced with each end coming through to the front at different points to begin. After a variable number of passes of background weave, the overlay yarn is wrapped around a single warp, either to the left or right. It passes first under then back over below.

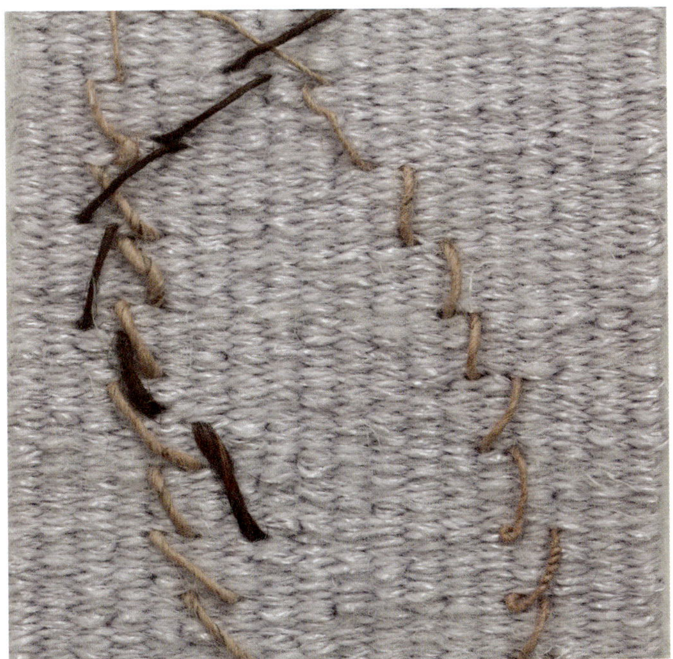

A broken overlaid line. After winding round a warp, the overlay weft simply passes under the warp, without being looped through below. The effect of this is that the individual wraps are no longer continuous but have a space between where the overlaying warp passes under the warp.

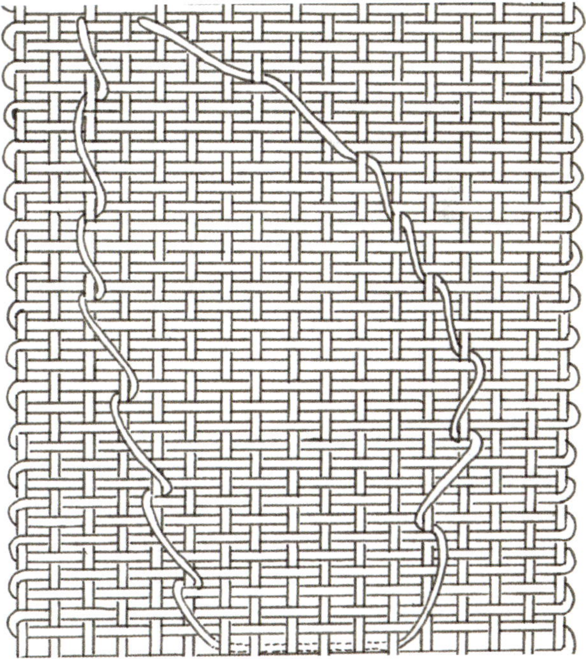

Left hanging at the front, the wrap is brought up after a variable number of background passes. It passes under a warp, either to the left or right consistently, making each wrap detached. The distance between could be increased by passing under more warps, the line breaking into random unconnected marks.

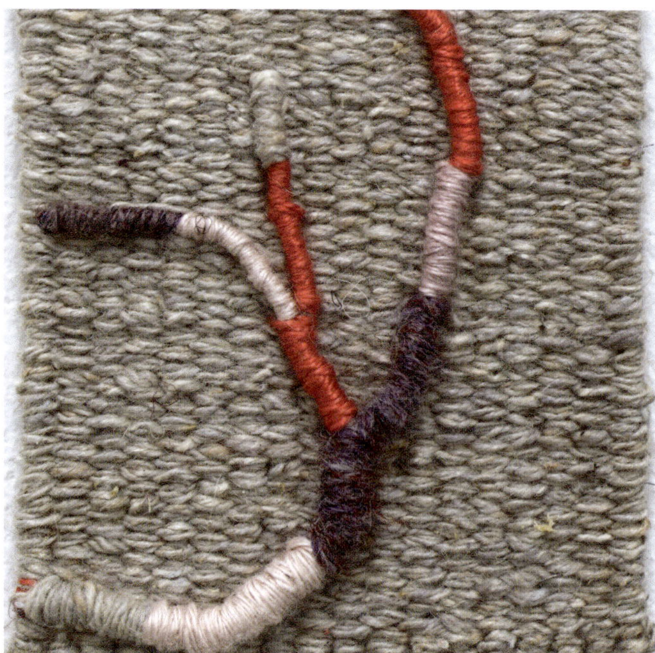

Wraps. This wrap is made with a thick weft bundle which is wrapped with changing strands taken from its core. It can be divided and made to sit freely over the plain weave background to which it is bound at intervals.

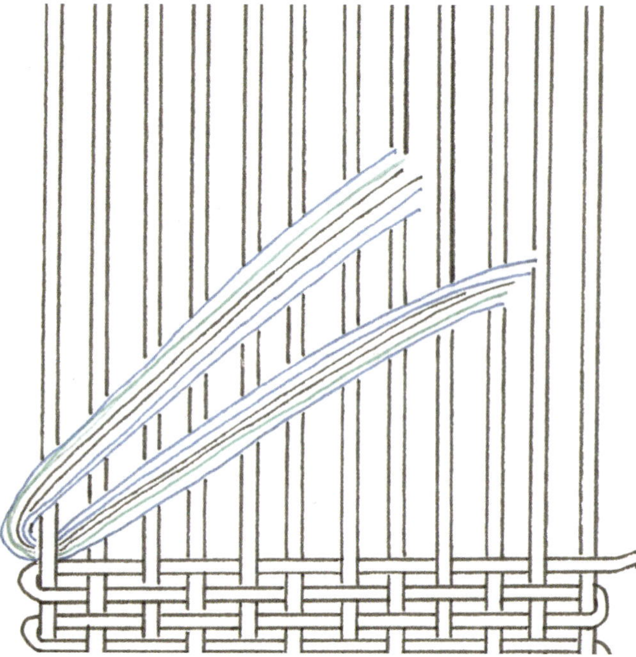

The background weave is first established and the weft paused to the right-hand side, out of the way. A mixed bundle of weft yarns of about 60cm (24in) length is folded in two and looped around a warp. This bundle may be a good deal thicker than one suitable for plain weaving.

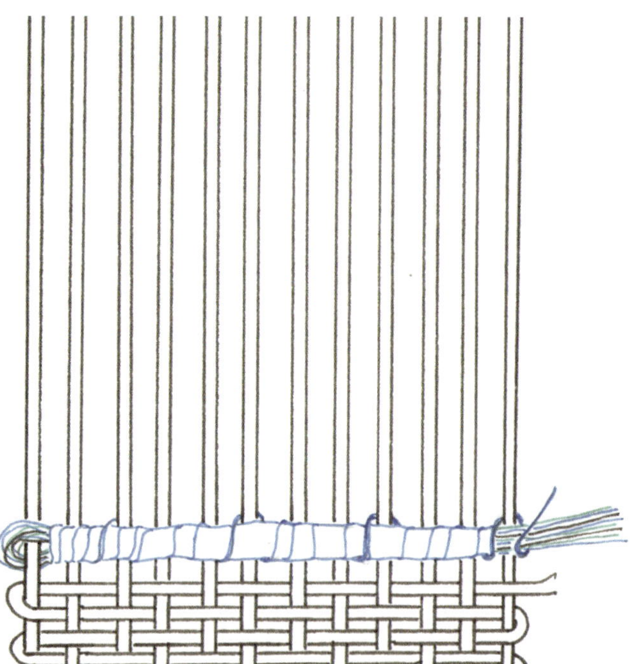

Holding the two ends of this bundle together, a single strand is drawn out and winds tightly round the bundle, forming the core of the wrap. Every third or so warp, the strand wrapping around the bundle also passes behind a warp to tie the wrap to the surface of the weave.

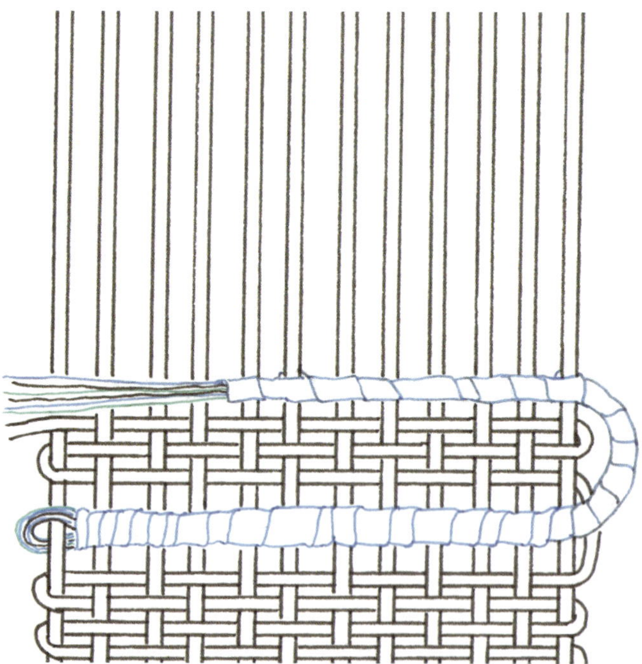

At the edge of the weave the wrap has been paused whilst a section of background weave to the shape which the wrap is to follow has been woven. The wrap then makes a loop to the right-hand side, with the winding around continuing. Returning to the left, it continues, being bound into the weave every few warps.

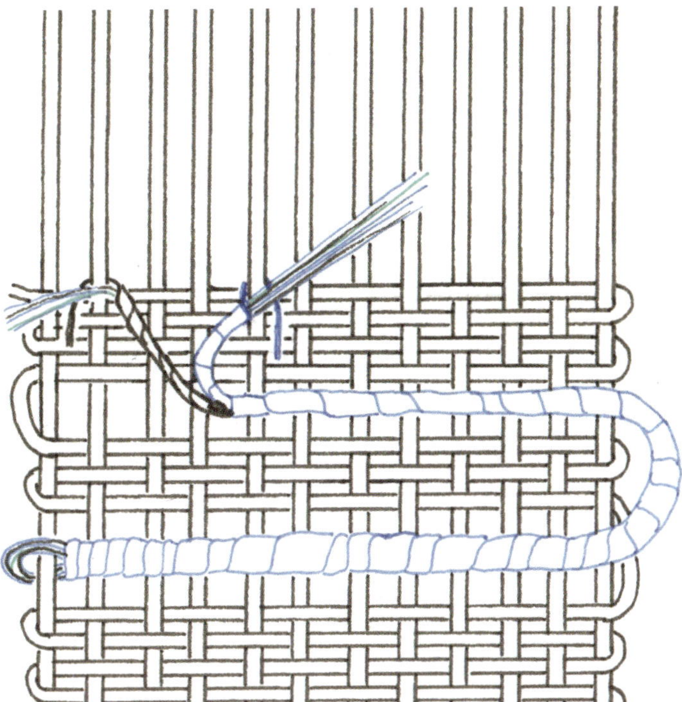

Splitting the wrap. The core of the wrap may be split making two ends which then follow their own direction. A single strand is taken from the new bundle and continues to wrap it. The background weft continues from side to side with the wraps being fastened every centimetre or so to form the desired line.

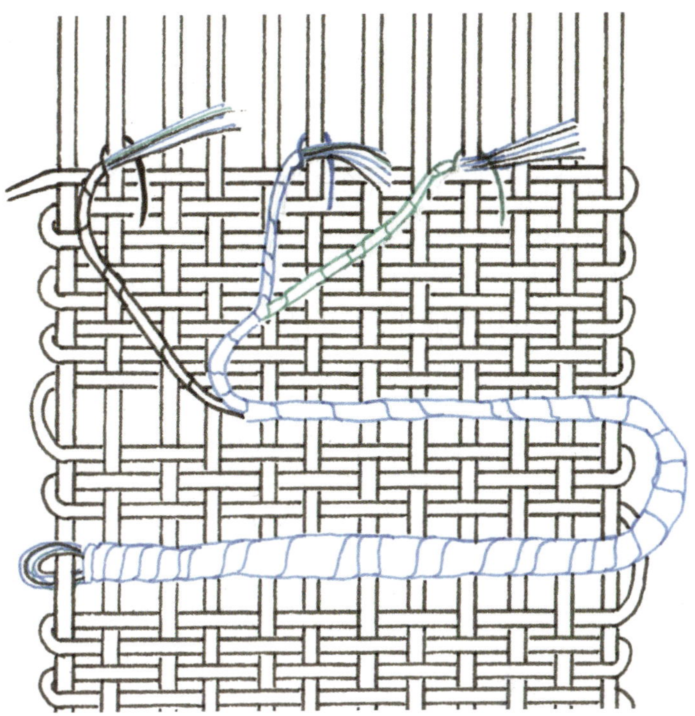

One half of the wrap is split again to give three independent wraps. The background continues to be woven, stopping every few passes to allow the wrapping and securing to warps to continue as desired. After a time, the right-hand branch has been split again and a different colour chosen to wrap with on the right.

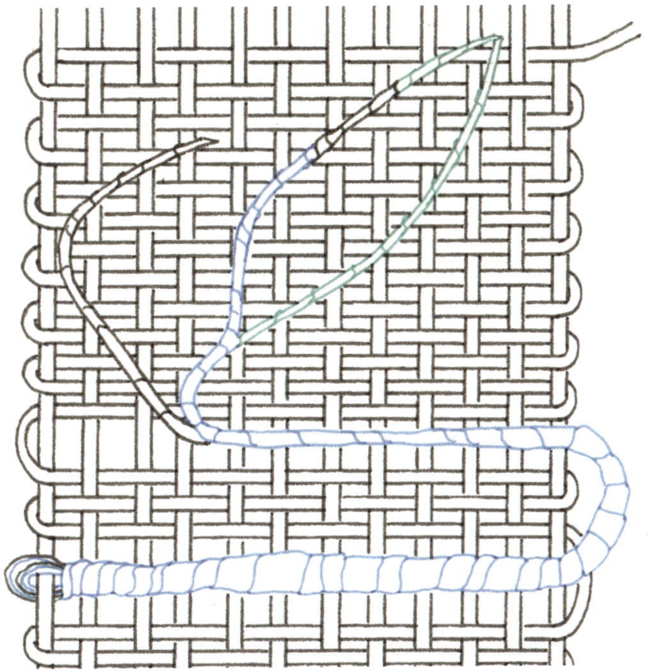

The wrap can move freely over the background with the binding yarn being taken round the warp at intervals. The colour may be altered by taking the wrapping yarn back into the core bundle and selecting a different one. Once complete, a wrap can simply be taken through to the back and secured later by stitching in.

Wraps are one example of a supplementary weft which may be used very freely. Here shown splitting with branches following their own course, they could equally well have been joined back together. Several wraps could be introduced at the same time, and sections of all made to join and divide at will.

The thickness of a wrap may be simply altered by adding strands to or taking from the core bundle. As ever the yarns chosen will affect the physical qualities and the ease of handling. The wrap does not pass over and under warps – it is formed independently of the background weave, despite being woven at the same time.

It is possible to take a wrap out into loops, either to the front or to one side. With the addition of wire to the core a self-supporting structure would be possible. A wrap may pass through to the back of the weave to re-emerge at another point. It could continue on the reverse side, making a double-sided or three-dimensional piece.

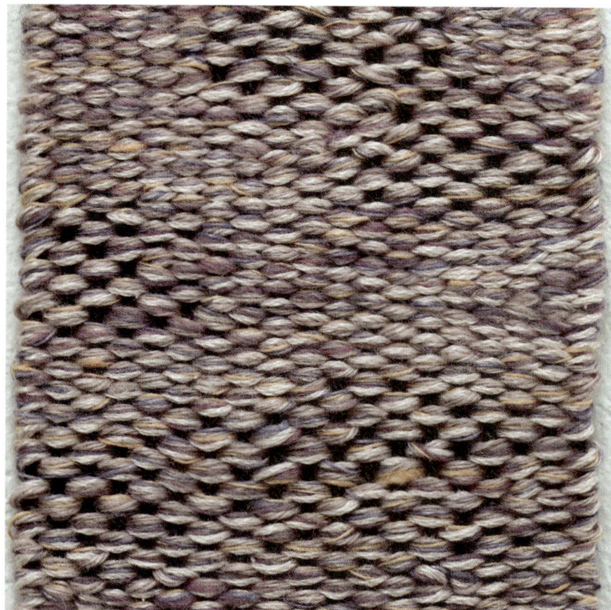

Exposing warps. Here a dark warp is woven with one close-toned weft mix in plain weave throughout. There are areas where the weft has not fully covered the warp, exposing the vertical dark warps. Considered by some to be a tapestry 'sin', exposing warps can offer many interesting weaverly effects.

Two ways to expose the warps are shown here, the first simply beating down very lightly so that the weft does not fully cover the warp. Using a thicker weft or muscular yarn would help with this. The alternative is to leave some passes incomplete, turning mid row so that the warp shows through the unwoven sections when beaten down.

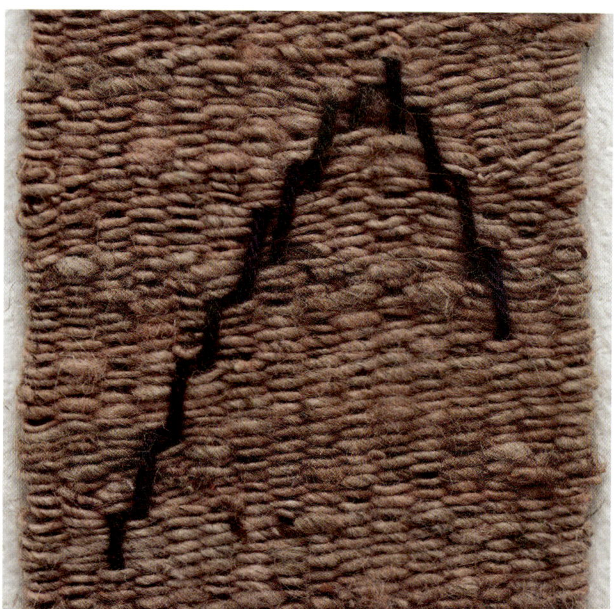

A line made in exposed warp. The dark-coloured warp here shows through in a series of vertical sections which build up to form an arched line. The background weave of nettle yarn continues throughout, showing characteristic irregular thickness and robust texture. The weft has passed under the exposed warp on several successive passes.

Here the plain weave of the background is continuous through the sample, except where a warp is to be exposed. At this point, the weft is simply taken behind three, five or seven warps in place of one. Because the weft continues behind, the exposed warp is pushed forward sitting on the surface rather than bedding in.

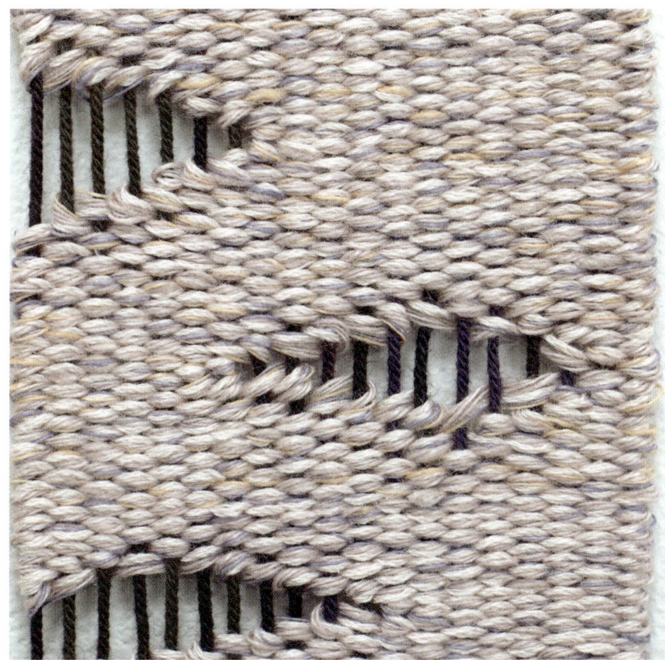

Areas of exposed warps. This background plain weave is interrupted with roughly diamond-shaped areas where the darker-coloured warp remains entirely exposed with no weft visible behind and light visible through the unwoven shapes.

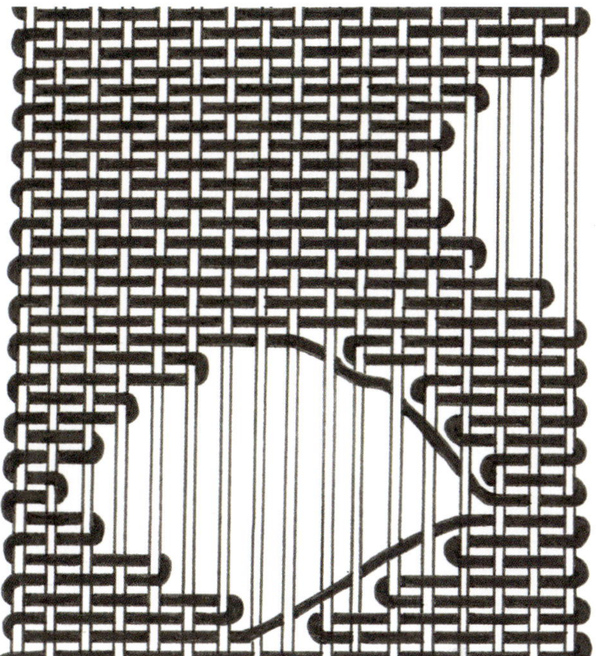

The unwoven areas have been formed by building the negative shape in the background weave, much as when making a solid form except that the warp is then simply left unwoven. Where necessary, the weft has been taken diagonally up or down to the next point it is needed.

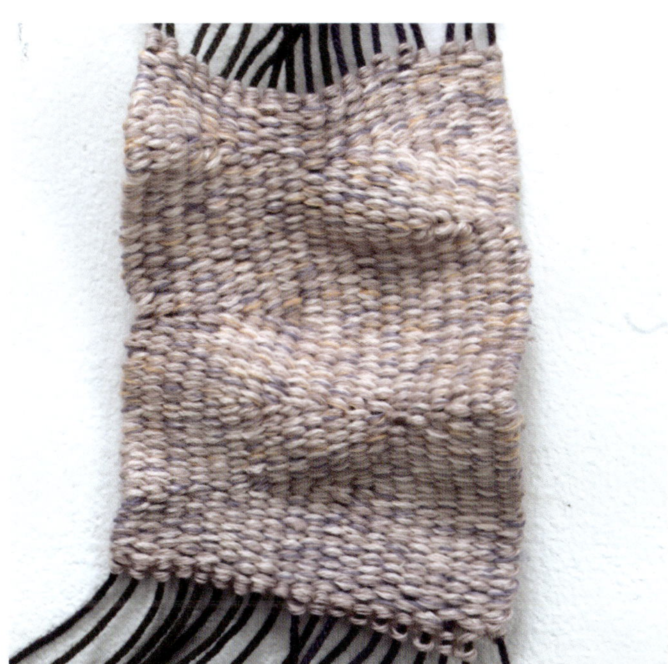

Pulled warps. Here, the same sample as the previous one has been woven. Once cut off the loom, the warps have been pulled through till the exposed areas have closed up. This buckles the surface, pushing the previously exposed area either backwards or forwards from the surface.

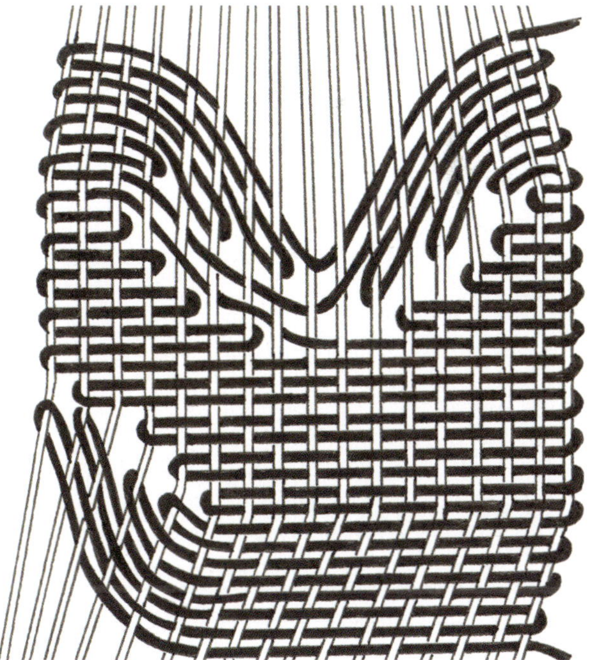

Once cut off the loom, the unwoven area may be closed up by holding the sample firmly and pulling on the warps one by one, starting with the warp where the exposed warps are the closest. Each warp is pulled a little way in turn, working back till the weft has closed over the exposed area.

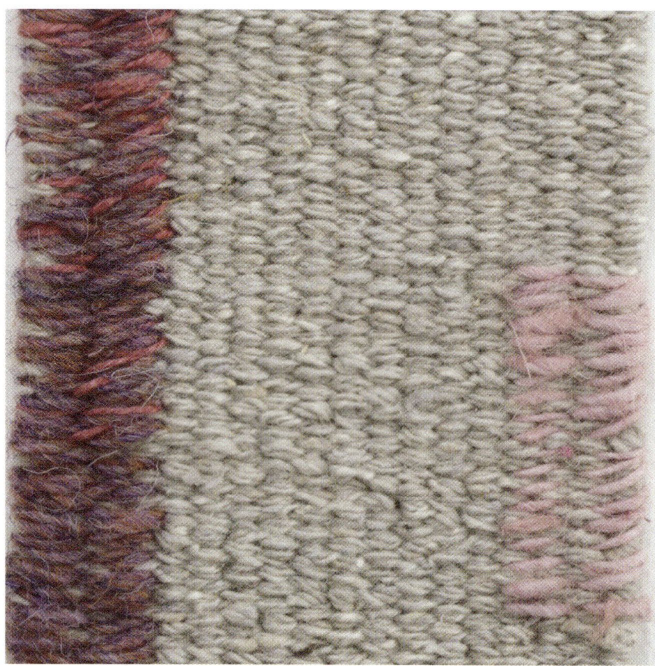

Figure of eight additional weft. An additional weft has been woven in a figure of eight over two under and over two warps at either edge. Here a nettle yarn gives a thickly ribbed mark standing out from the surface of the weave.

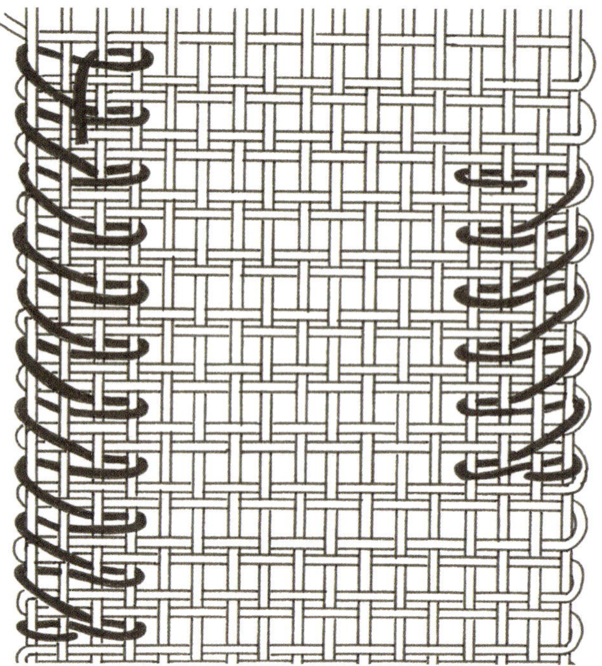

The additional weft introduced from the back between the second and third warp. After each background pass the selvedge weft makes a figure of eight over then under two warps at a time before pausing at the front. This area needs to be packed down hard to keep the weaving level, giving a very firm edge.

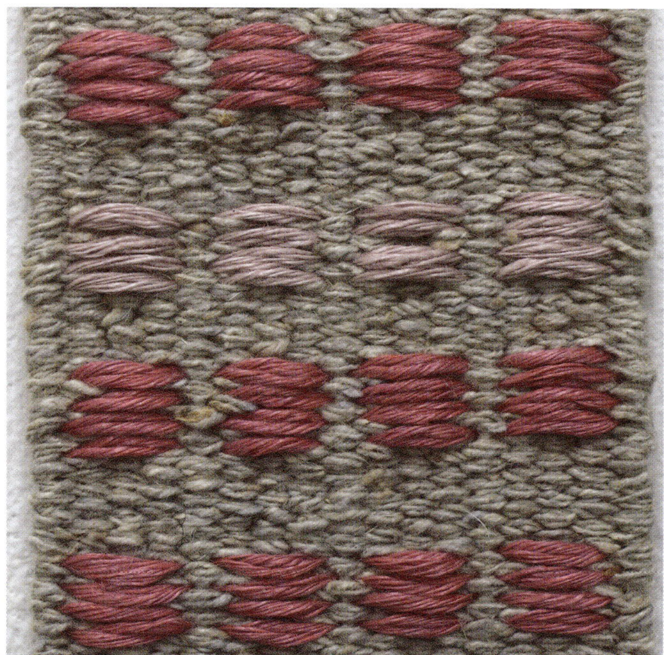

Brocading. Another supplementary weft technique borrowed from loom weaving. Woven concurrently with the background of plain weave, the brocade weft sits on the surface. Here shown in two contrasting colours, and to a pattern, it may also have been formed more freely or organically.

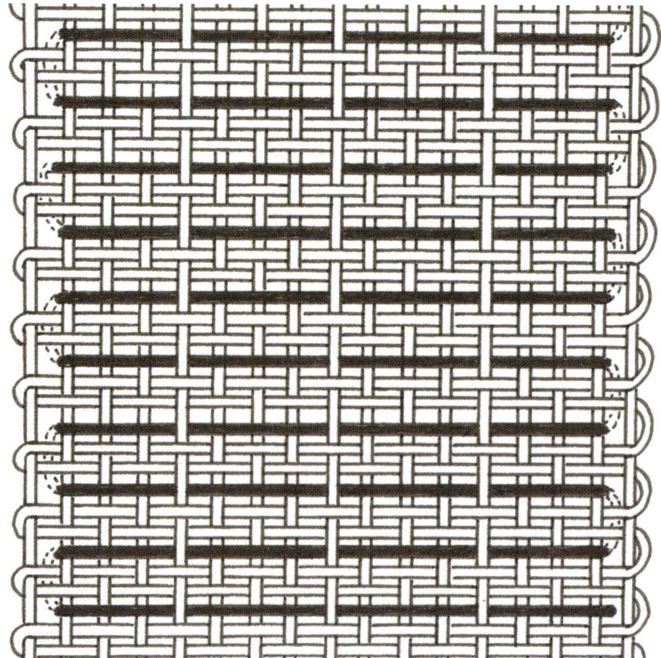

This brocade weft passes over three warps and under one, making four steps across the sample and being taken through to the back after the last. The background then weaves a full pass before pausing at the edge. The brocade weft is brought through to the front and woven back over the same three and under one warp.

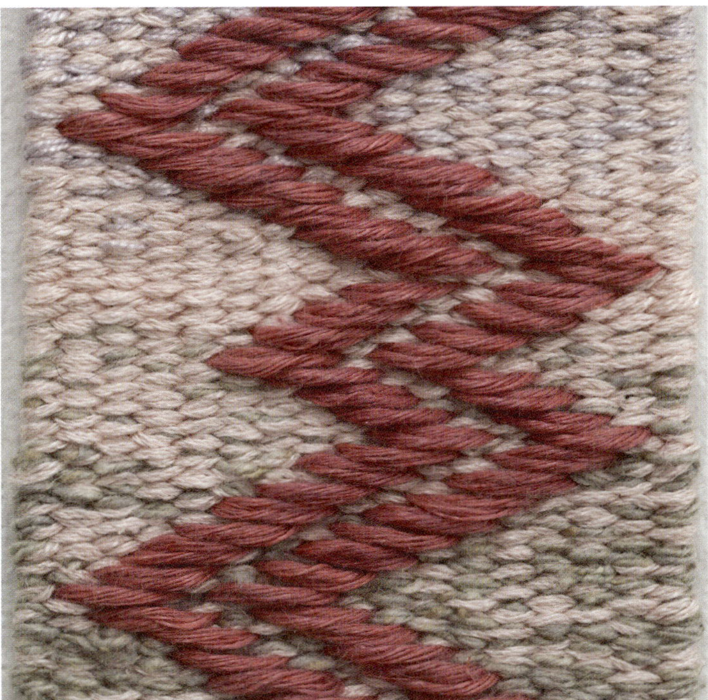

A diagonal brocade. The bold zigzag here stands out, partly due to the contrasting solid colour, and the relatively subdued background, partly because by passing over several warps it now sits forwards of the surface.

The background is of single plain weave with the colour shifting slightly. The cotton brocade weft passes over three warps at a time, stepping sideways by one warp at each pass across the sample, turning just short of the edge to step in the opposite direction. The result is dynamic with a bold zigzag raised mark on the finer background.

Applying techniques creatively

These 'special effects' are a few amongst many more possibilities, and we hope you will see that there are endless ways to apply each of them. We also hope you will enjoy the freedom with which each may be introduced mid weave, allowing for subtle, spontaneous and instinctual changes to be made. This means that with a palette of yarns selected, and the simple outline of a design to follow, it is possible to weave very freely, watching the weave as it develops and responding, rather than slavishly weaving to a predetermined plan. Although it is very much a matter of personality, it is important to work in a way that is true to the medium and makes sympathetic use of the qualities of yarn. Woven tapestry has a language of its own that includes a surface which may be sculpted, or show its underlying structure, and is able to make any number of marks distinctive to the relationship between warp and weft.

The more a tapestry can be formed during the process of weaving, the more chance it has of speaking the authentic language of tapestry. This is very different to any paper medium, and even from other textile media. Use of marks such as those illustrated in this chapter can free the weaver's attention from the need to preplan, leaving them able to progress through the piece, one area rolling on from another.

The temptation to fiddle with fine detail may be lessened as even a design of just a few lines can be brought to life by a few well-chosen additions. It is worth experimenting with these techniques using very different weft choices, at different warp settings, by giving them varying degrees of prominence, applying at random or to a pattern, in isolated marks or overall cover.

There is a possibility with this degree of choice of over embellishing and cluttering a piece, or for the added marks to take over. In making choices it is always good to ask oneself if what you are weaving or about to weave is actually needed. Any detail or change needs a certain amount of space in order to speak, and because of the slowness of the weaving process, it is sometimes difficult to persuade oneself to continue weaving without too much change. Very subtle interventions may be powerful if well placed.

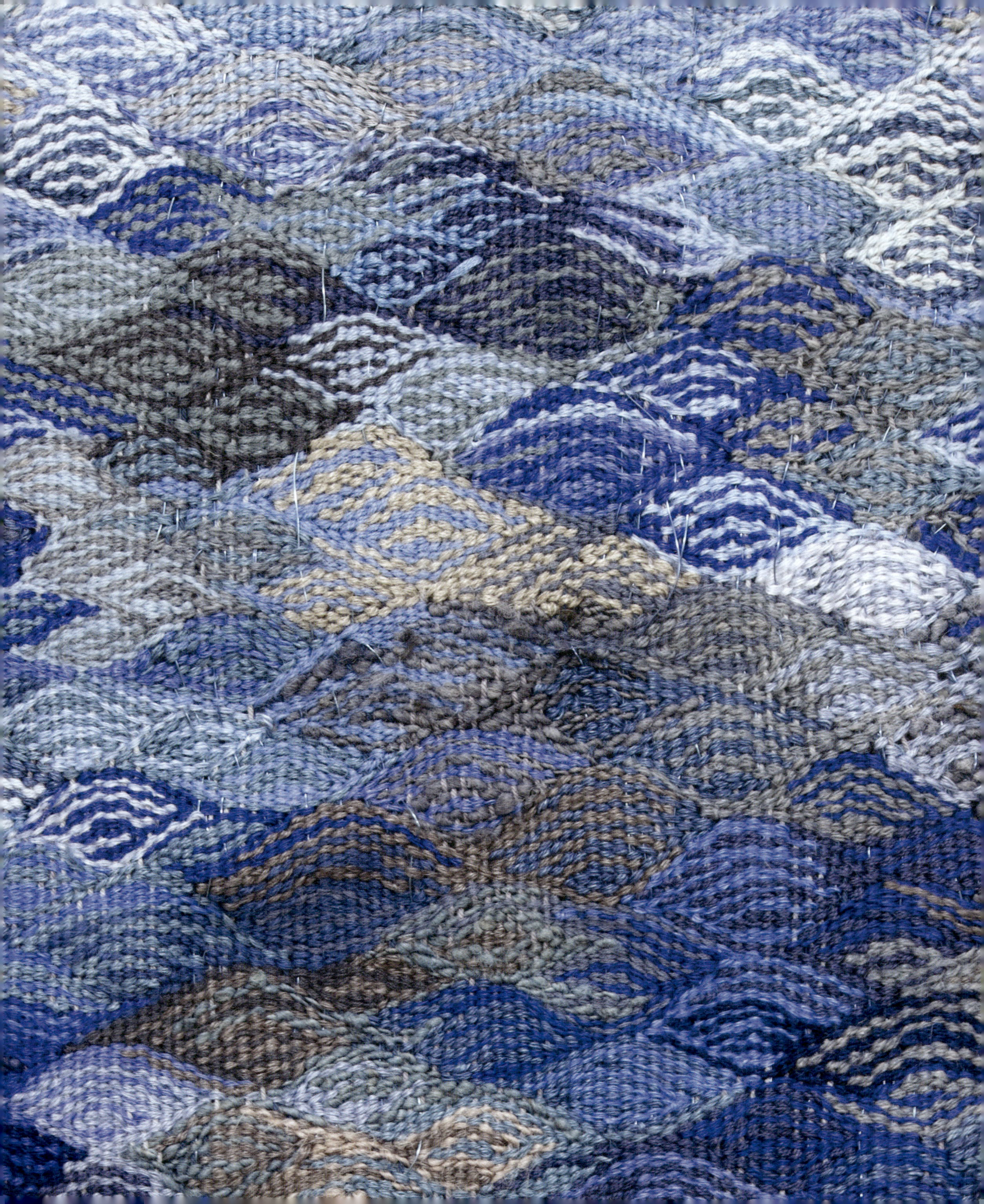

CHAPTER 9

ECCENTRIC WEAVING

Eccentric weave is defined as any weave in which the weft does **not** pass over the warp horizontally, or to put it another way, when the weft is not perpendicular to the warp. Eccentric and plain or horizontal weave may combine quite freely within a piece. It has been used historically since the earliest known Coptic tapestries, and still has a great deal of creative potential left to explore for contemporary weavers.

When woven eccentrically, the weft passes diagonally over the warp at variable angles, which means it can create smooth, flowing lines where straight weave would make a stepped outline. It may be used to outline curved forms made in plain weave or make whole areas with smooth, curving lines.

The visual effect of an area of eccentric weave can be seen from this woven example in which the diagonal section set mid weave is woven at about 45 degrees showing a characteristically elongated bead. Eccentric weave can give a heightened energy and sense of movement, especially when combined with other areas set at opposing angles or used in conjunction with hatching.

This is a relatively spontaneous, playful technique, able to pass over underlying areas of either eccentric or plain weave, and to both form and infill areas freely. There is a limit to how steep an angle it may weave at before the weave becomes loose – generally speaking an angle of up to 45 degrees is a reasonable limit. Weaving at an angle carries a greater risk of pulling in, so care is needed to put in extra weft length to counter this. There is also the risk that eccentrically woven areas will move once cut off the loom and may distort the surface. Weaving adjacent areas at opposing angles will help balance the tension within the piece and reduce this risk. We will consider how to manage the tension when weaving eccentrically, and what the strengths and limitations of this technique are.

Eccentric weaving with jute, wool, nettle and linen weft, cotton and wire warp.

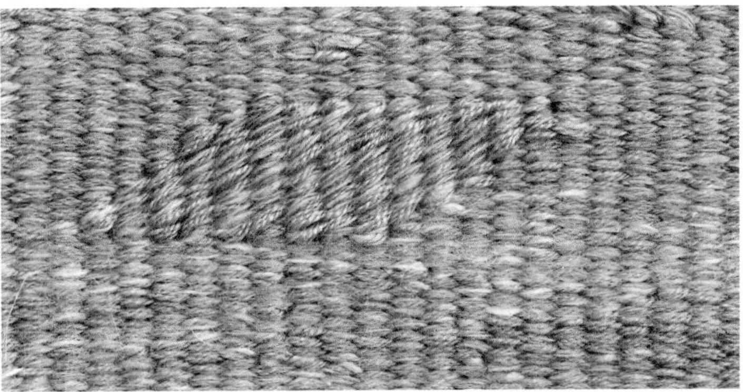

Eccentric weaving within a plain weave. A sloping area of eccentric weave set in a background of plain weave using the same weft mix, showing characteristic diagonal movement and lengthened bead.

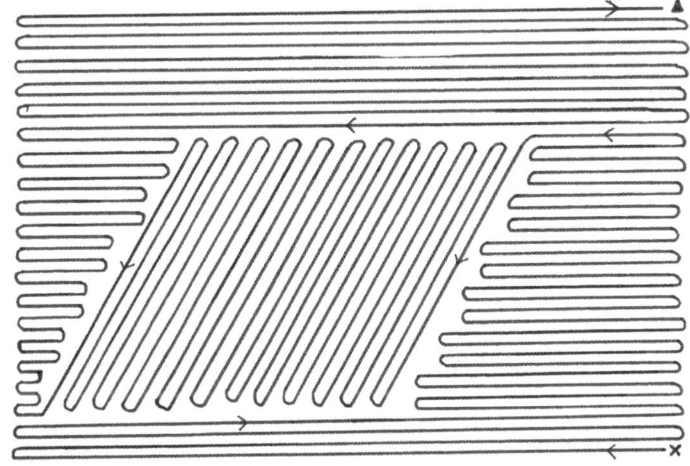

Diagram of eccentric weaving within a plain weave. Here the steep parallel passes of the eccentrically woven area are illustrated. The angle is formed by the right-hand background weft which then slides down the incline. This weft continues by weaving up and down diagonally, stepping by one warp to the left at the top and bottom, on each pass.

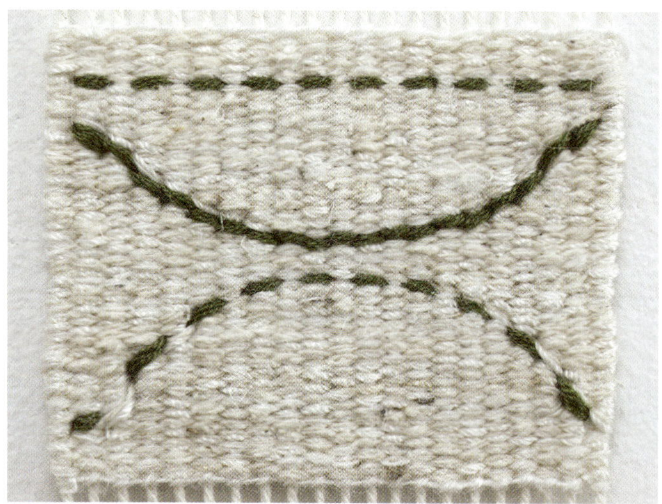

Eccentric pass and half pass outlines. Here a pass and a half pass have been used to outline two curved shapes made in plain weave. This is a very useful technique for smoothing the outline of a curved area. If the curved forms are built using high turns, then the outlining eccentric weft will make low turns and so make the smoothest possible outline. This is opposite to the way a curved form would otherwise be woven, which would be to make low turns to give a smooth line.

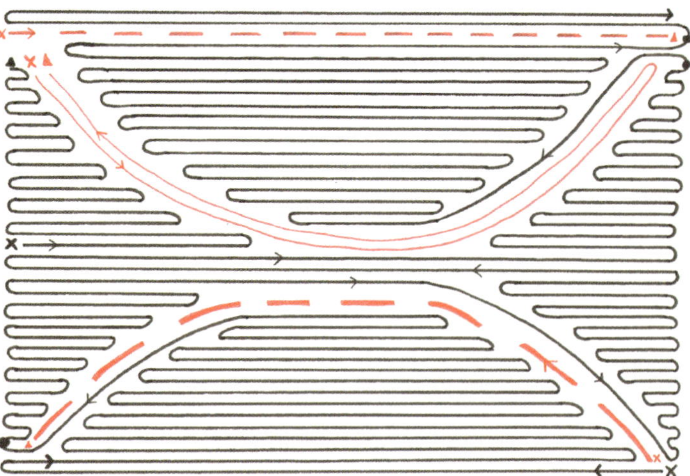

This background has been woven with the weft passing horizontally across the warp, first forming a large mound shape. A half pass in contrasting dark weft then passes over the mound, forming an intermittent line with the bead noticeably elongated as it passes over the warps on the steep sides of the mound. Contrast this with the bead length in the horizontal half pass at the top. The next form, a bowl, is outlined with a full pass, giving a solid line.

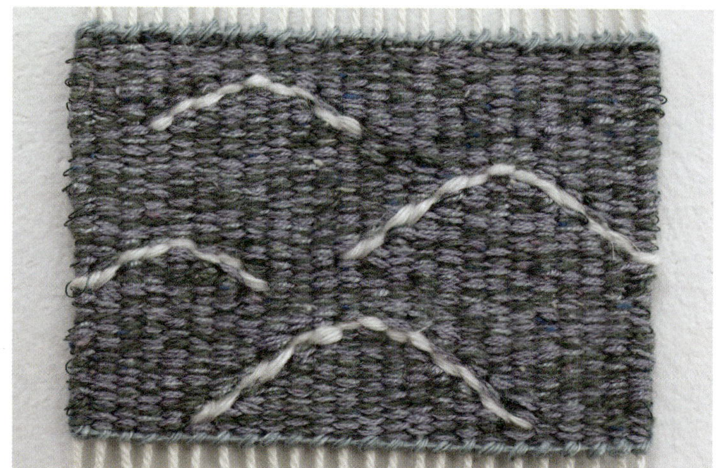

Eccentric outlining. Each of the mound shapes is outlined by an eccentric pass in a contrasting lighter colour. The background and the mound shapes are all woven with the weft perpendicular to the warp except when the weft passes eccentrically from one area to another. By this means, it is possible to weave all the areas of background in this sample with one continuous weft and with only two pauses.

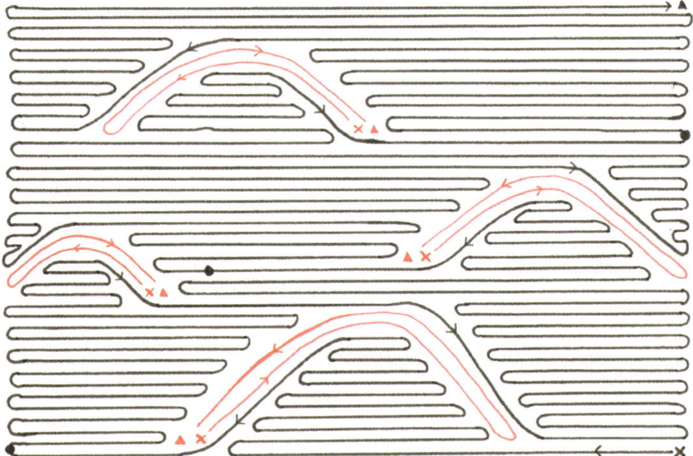

Starting at the bottom right, the background weft first forms a mound mid row then slides eccentrically down it to pause on the left whilst the mound is outlined in the contrasting weft. The single pass finishes on the warp next to the one it started on and so maintains the shed, allowing the background to continue over the top. First the infill then another mound to the left are woven before sliding back down to the bottom right to do likewise, before pausing mid row. Both these two new mounds are then outlined. The same rhythm of forming and outlining continues.

This broad, arched band has been woven eccentrically within a background of plain weave above and below. The altered direction is evident in the angle and length of the bead, especially as the weft passes up and down the sides of the arch. Adding stripes further accentuates the effect and shows how smooth an eccentrically woven curve can be in comparison with a curve formed of many steps, as in plain weave.

The weaving diagram shows that this whole sample is in effect woven continuously. Starting from the bottom right, the weft passes part way along the sample before making horizontal passes of decreasing length to form a mound. The same weft then passes over the mound from side to side creating a band of eccentric weave. Care is needed to allow ample weft length, especially when making eccentric passes over the whole width of the piece. It is important to put in the weft only six to eight warps at a time, raising it into a mound and beating down from the centre outward before moving onto the next few warps. Putting in too little weft will quickly result in the warps drawing together and the sides of the piece pulling in.

Although one colour is exchanged for another to make the stripes, the weaving sequence continues uninterrupted. Once the eccentric band is complete, the same weft infills the left-hand side in plain weave, before passing back over the mound and down the right side which it infills before passing over the whole sample to finish.

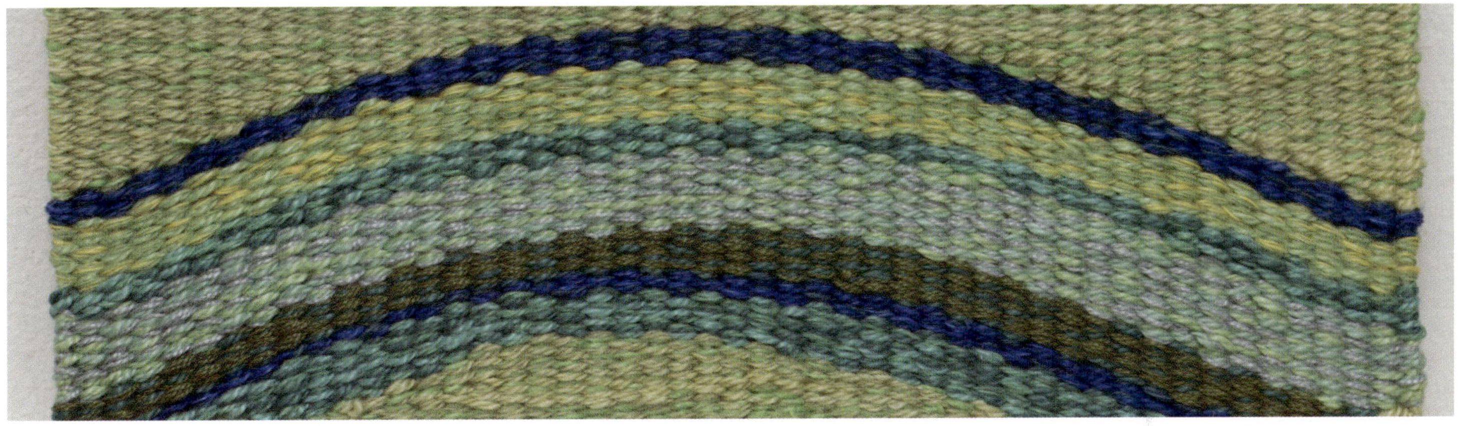

Eccentric passes with one weft changing colours.

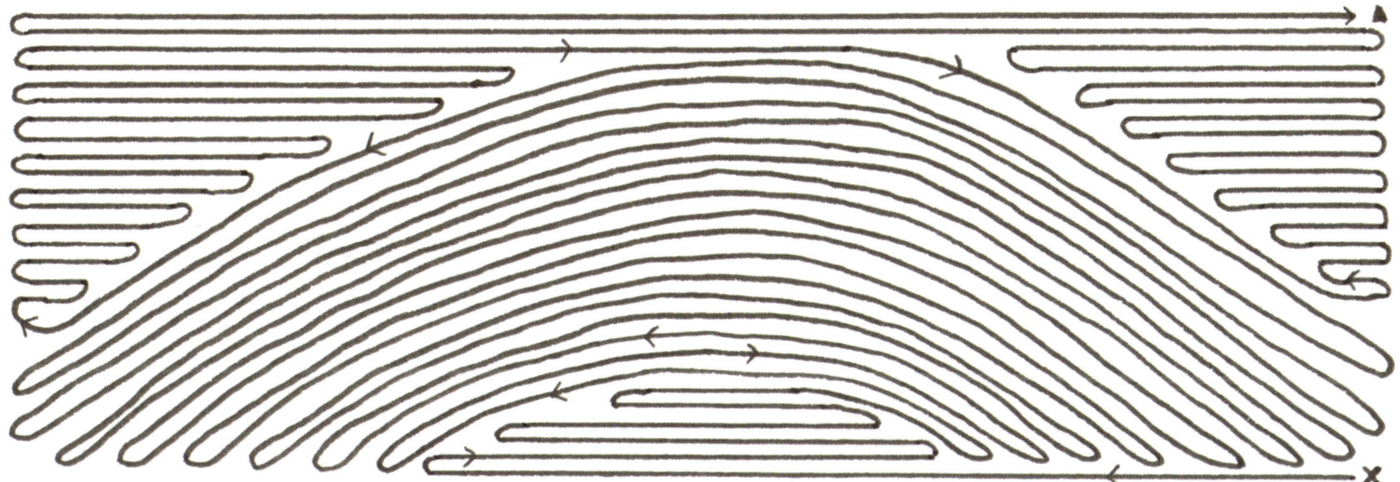

Eccentric passes diagram.

Here, a broad, undulating band of eccentric weave has been set in a background of plain weave. In place of each colour band weaving all the way across as in the previous sample, two wefts now weave, one from either side, and meet in an area of hatching. The mixes are also more varied, with quite similar flecked mixes at the start, through to more contrasting mixes and solid colours towards the top. Now there are two main factors influencing the appearance of the weave. The contrast in colour of the flecked mixes accentuates the elongated bead and direction of weave by comparison with weaving in solid colour. Initially the similar coloured flecked mixes used are not easily distinguished from each other in the weave; the effect is of a gentle undulating flow. Further up, the contrast becomes greater so that the hatching highlights the undulating line of the weave more clearly. The last two mixes of solid contrasting colour hatched together give a bold graphic effect.

In the diagram you will see that the two wefts coloured red and black start from the edges and weave inwards towards each other. The black weft has first formed the two mounds and woven eccentrically over the top of them, making a long then a short pass, before the red is taken up. From there, the two wefts alternate with each other in weaving eccentrically over the mounds. Now instead of weaving continuously, each weft has to pause whilst the other is woven. The meeting points vary on each pass.

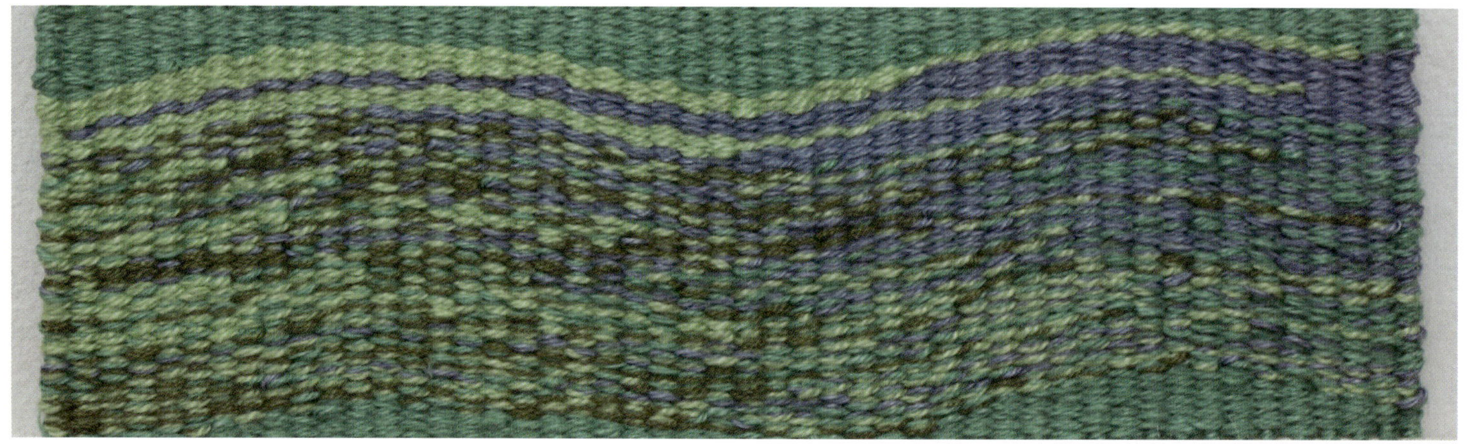

Eccentric hatching with two wefts. 15cm (6in), at 8 epi.

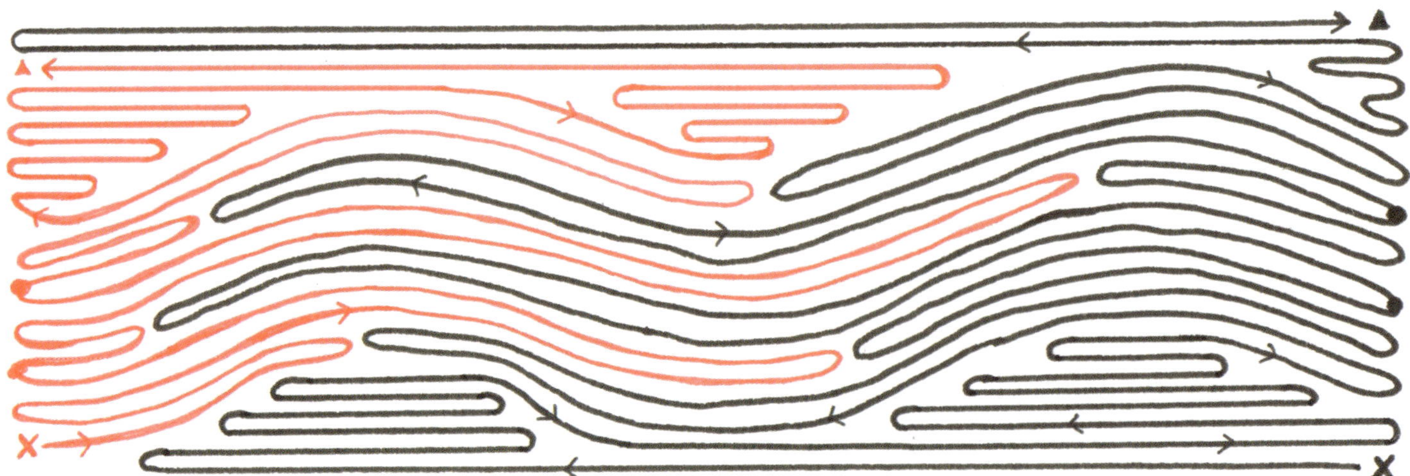

Diagram of the eccentric hatching with two wefts.

Now the weave begins to look more dynamic, the whole piece being woven eccentrically with overlaying areas woven in different directions. The use of two highly contrasting colour mixes hatched together makes the directional lines more graphic. First the central mound is formed, then the right-hand side infilled with an area of steeply sloping straight lines and another of level hatching before the weave slides down to the left in a broad, curved band, with an area of slightly closer toned mixes at the top left to complete.

Although the effect is quite complex, there are still only two wefts used continuously throughout the piece. They start together mid row. The first weaves a pass and a half then pauses (shown as a dot) as far away as you want the second weft to extend. The second weft weaves over the small mound turning where it meets the paused first weft, weaving back to the right edge to pause. Next the black weft passes over the mound; returning to the left side it pauses slightly to the left of where it began. The red weft is picked up and continues to build the mound.

Note, as before, in hatching the two wefts together, they are woven and paused alternately.

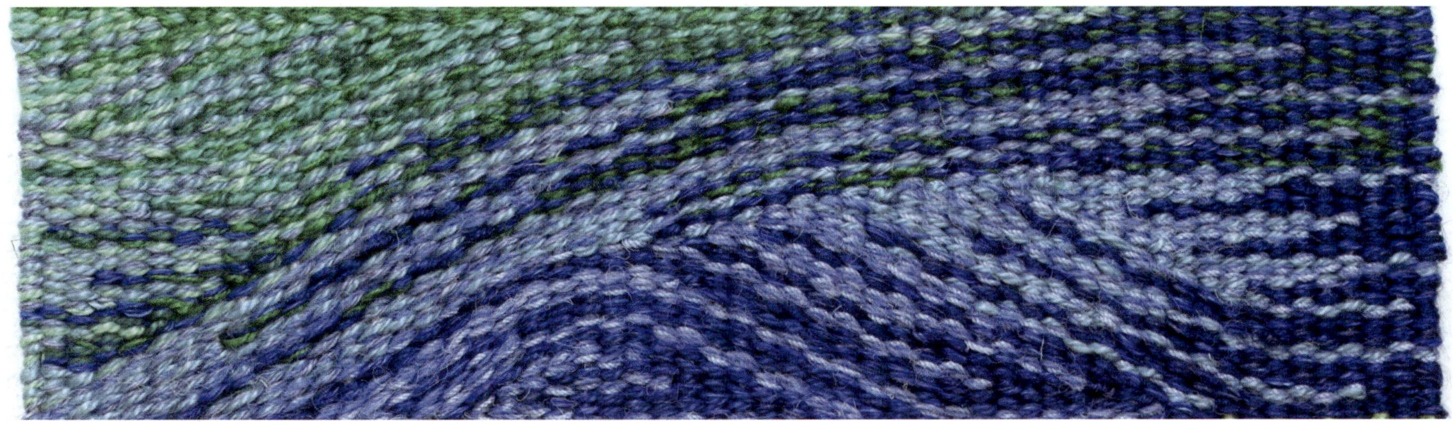

Eccentric hatching in different directions with two wefts. 15cm (6in), at 8 epi.

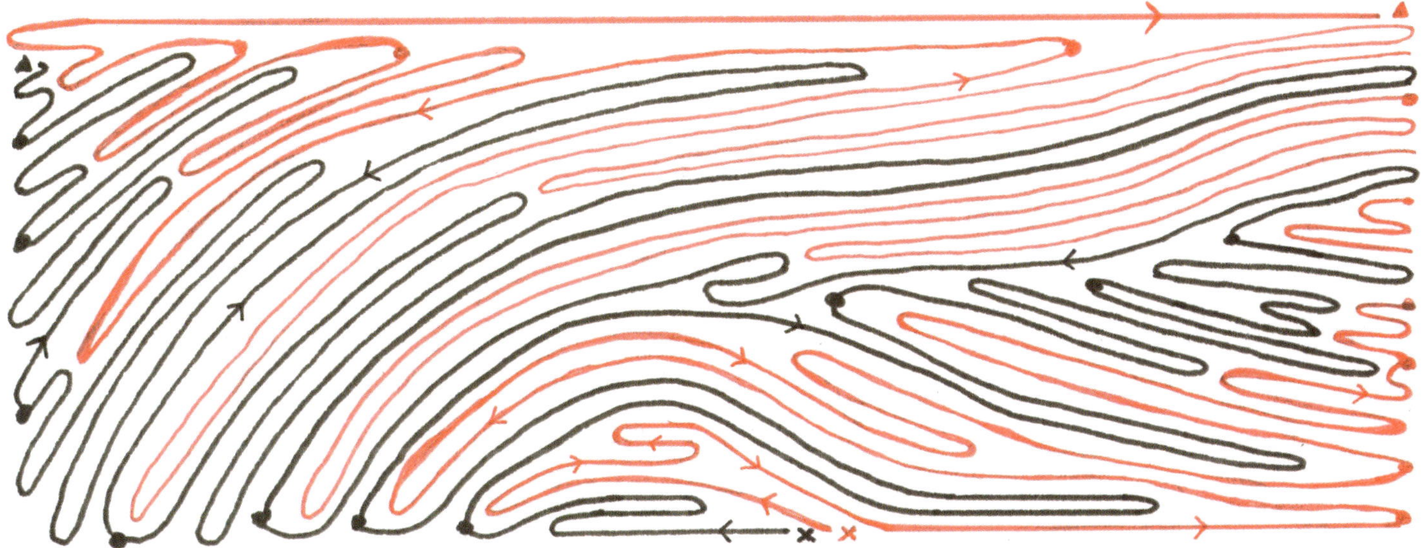

Eccentric hatching diagram.

Here the two eye shapes are formed eccentrically and set in a background of horizontal plain weave using a solid colour mix. In the case of an encapsulated form such as this, the contrast in the rhythm of plain and eccentric weave becomes quite marked, the stripes making it even more so. The use of eccentric weave gives a very smooth outline and makes the fine stripes possible.

The diagram shows how each of the eye forms are woven with only one weft of changing colour, and the whole of the background in a third. Starting from the bottom right, the background weft weaves straight across the piece, builds up the left side, then the middle and lastly the right-hand edge, in horizontal passes of variable length except where passing eccentrically round the eye form to begin the next area of weave. The background extends only to the point where the eye shape turns inward. First one, then the other of the eye forms are then woven. Each of the areas of eccentric weave finishes on the warp next to the warp on which it started. This ensures that the shed is maintained so that the background can be woven over the top.

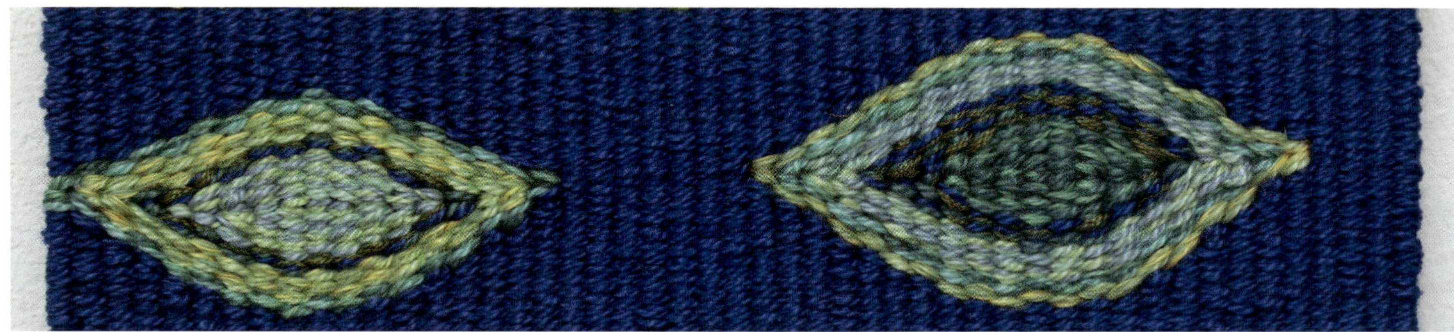

Embedded eccentrically woven form. 15cm (6in), at 8 epi.

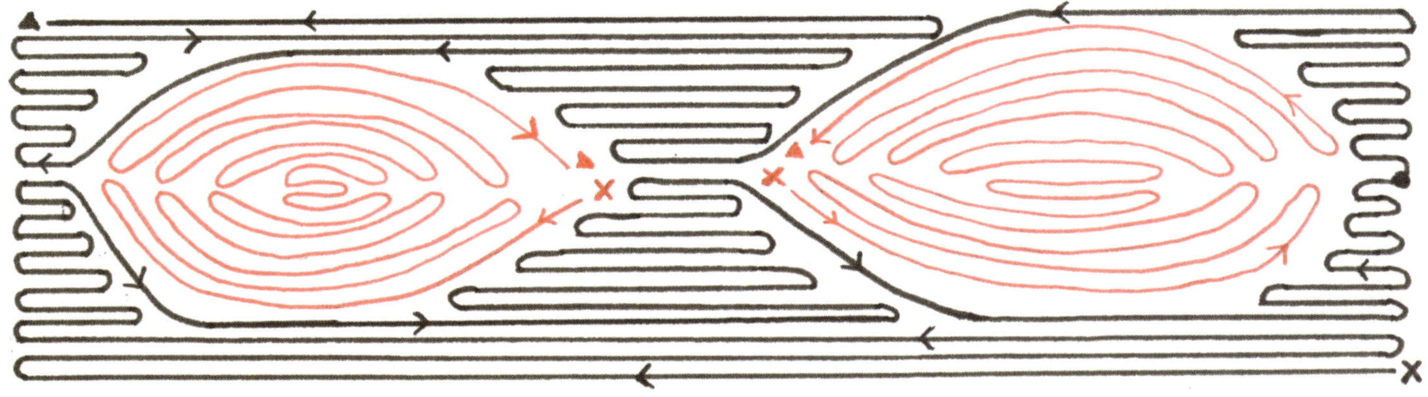

Diagram of the embedded form.

A sample made entirely in eccentric weave, with layers of mounds alternating with their answering forms. There are just two mixes used, both containing strands of contrasting colour which have the effect of highlighting the undulating direction of weave. Using a repeated pattern also gives movement to the piece, showing that even quite a small, repeated mark can give a dynamic effect.

From the diagram you will see that the mounds have all been formed with the same weft. Starting from the bottom right, the weft forms first one then the next mound from the bottom up. The mound is built from the middle, working back and forth eccentrically over part rows of increasing length. This is in contrast to forming in straight weave, where part rows of decreasing length are stacked vertically. Once each mound is completed the weft is taken over the row of mounds to finish where it began on the right-hand side. The infilling weft then starts at the same point, by weaving eccentrically up the outside of the mound and out to the edge in rows of decreasing length before passing over the top and down into the next hollows.

The next layer of mounds starts again on the right side and is formed in the same way – this enables the weft to be floated up from the first row of mounds which is simpler and neater than starting a new one.

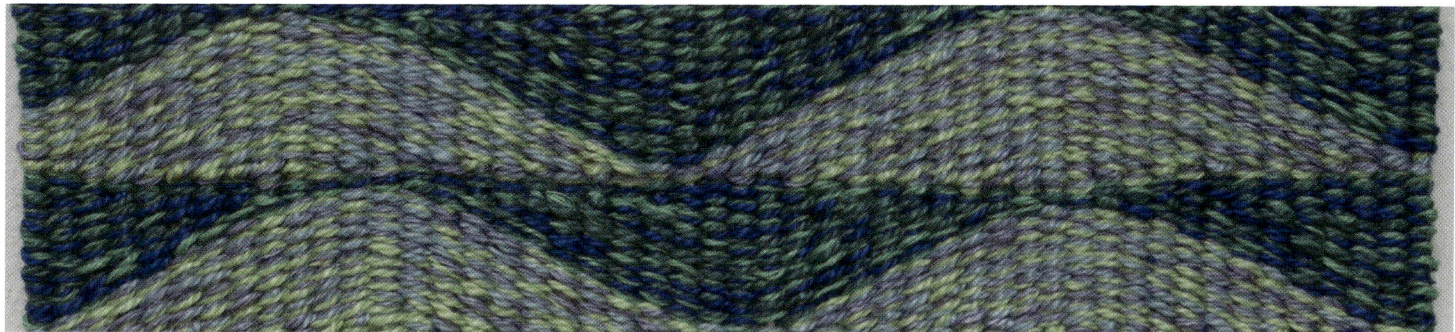

Eccentric wefts forming and infilling mounds. 15cm (6in), at 8 epi.

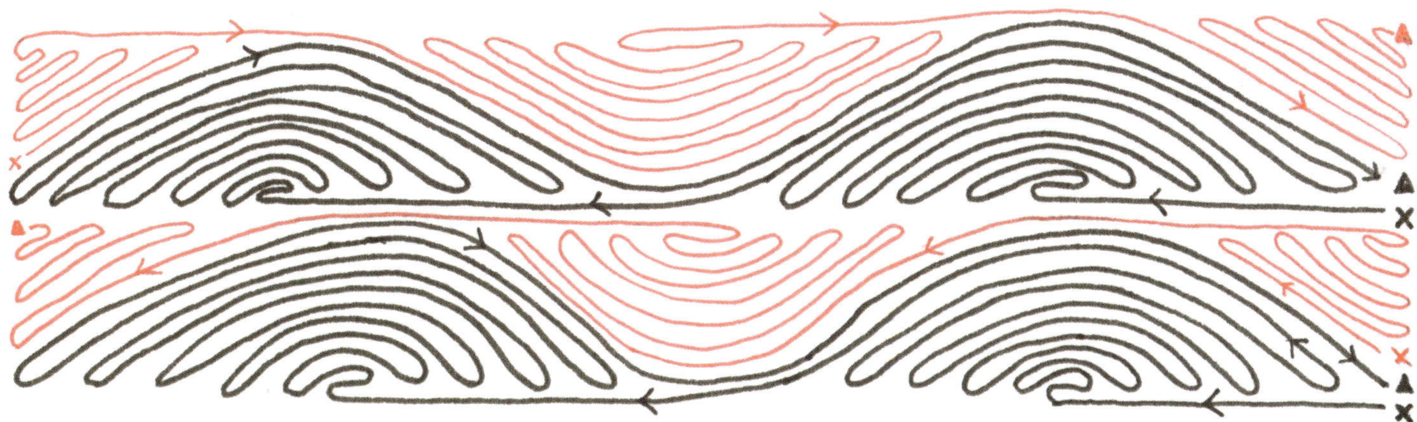

Simplified diagram of wefts forming and infilling.

In this sample, the mound forms are heaped randomly one on top of the other instead of falling in rows as in the previous sample. The mixes are of contrasting colour and tone, again giving a flecked effect which highlights the eccentric movement. Although there are many different mixes, there are only five different colours used.

Eccentric weave offers great freedom and fluidity in the weaving process, so what might appear complex and busy is in practice quite repetitive. The diagram shows the simplicity of the actual weaving. There is only one weft throughout the whole piece which changes colour many times, one weft bundle being finished and another immediately started as if the two were one length. The weft starts at the bottom right and builds up a whole mound before moving along to build another. It then weaves down into the hollow where it builds another mound. The direction of weave is indicated at intervals by an arrow, as this one continuous weft freely forms and infills the mass of mounded forms.

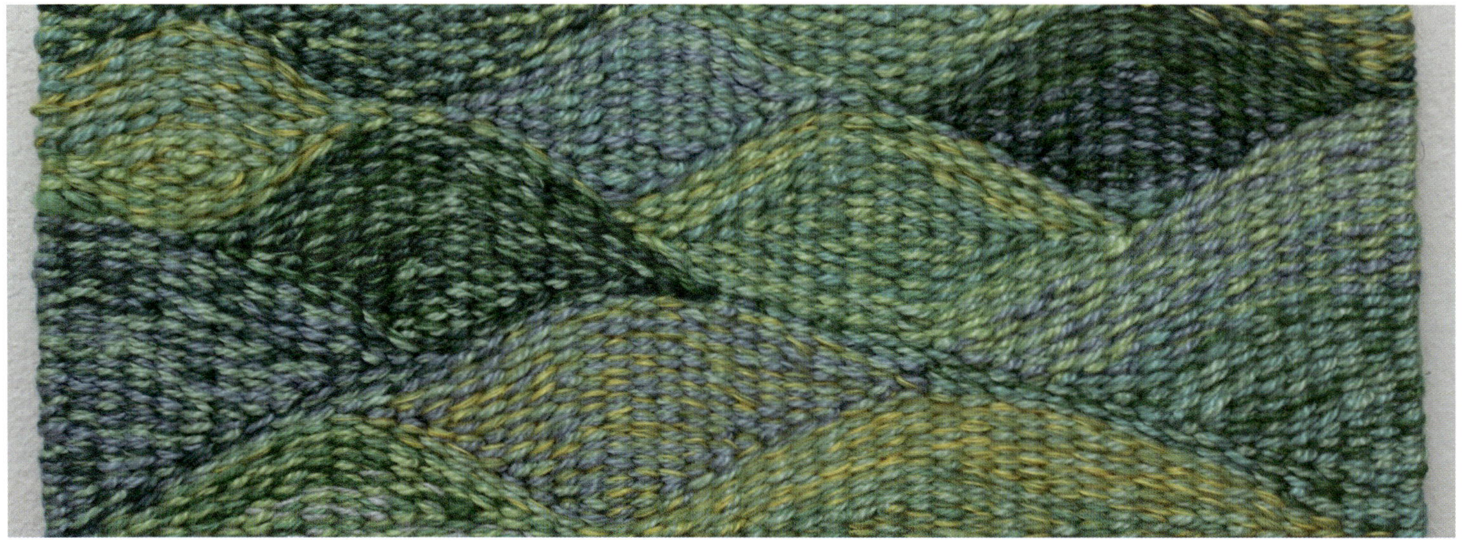

Continuous eccentric weave with one weft. 15cm (6in), at 8 epi.

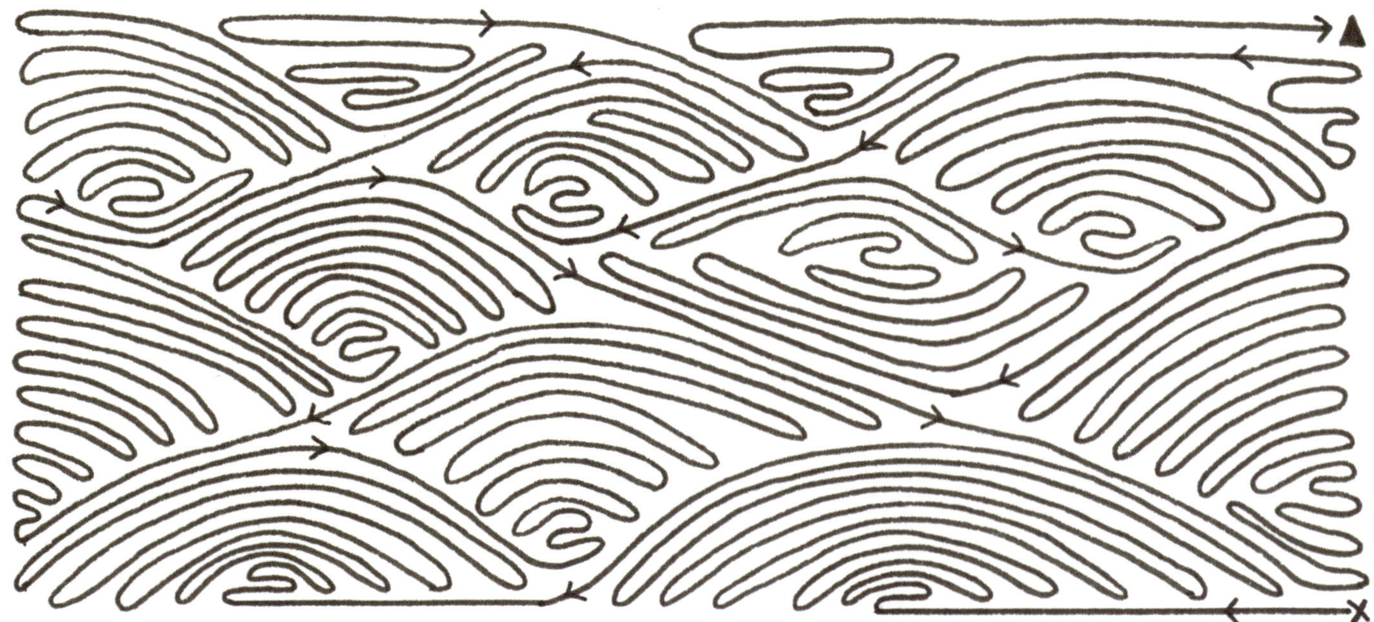

A simplified diagram of the continuous eccentric weave with one weft.

Here, the same pattern of formed and infilled mounds has been used, but the mounds are now woven in alternating passes. By using two contrasting wefts the undulating lines of the weave are highlighted, giving a strongly dynamic effect.

Despite the complex appearance of the weave, there are still only two wefts in play and they remain the same colour throughout. Each weft must pause to allow the other to be woven, the whole piece being worked in an alternating rhythm. The position at which each weft pauses is important to consider since the answering weft must then turn at this point. To weave beyond this point thus crossing the two wefts over would put them out of shed with each other. At times the wefts weave all the way across a mound, at others they meet part way. The shapes shift freely as they are built up by short passes of one or both of the weft colours.

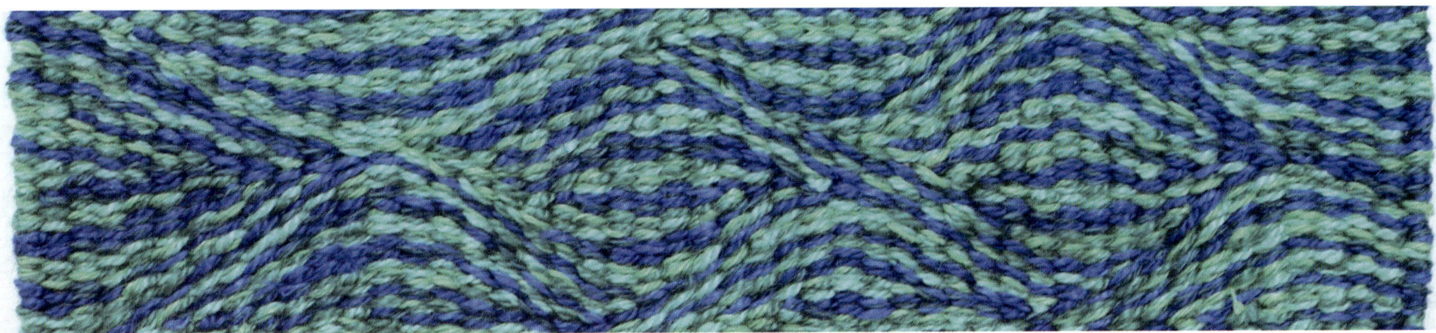

Eccentric weaving with two wefts working together. 15cm (6in), at 8 epi.

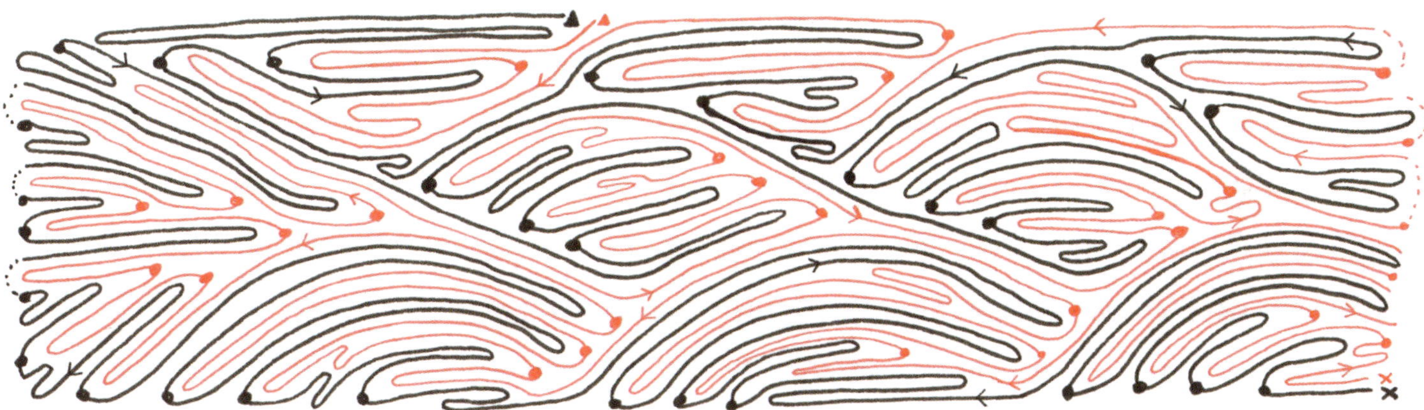

Simplified diagram of two wefts working together.

Continuing to use the mound as a repeated form, apart from the first few passes, this sample is woven entirely in eccentric weave. There are six different weft mixes which change from one mound to the next. The energy of this sample is of an overall flow in which adjacent wefts overlap in perpetual movement.

The drawing shows how all six wefts start on the first row of weaving. In order that they are all able to weave freely over each other, they have been started in pairs on low warps, with one warp left in between. Pairs of wefts make alternating passes, either singly or in multiples, pausing to one side to allow the adjacent weft to overlay.

As ever, it is essential to weave any area ahead of one which overlays it, so that the first pair to start are the green and blue on the left. Before long the red and black need to start, after which point all four wefts build short passes alternating with each other. Wefts are picked up one after another back and forth, alternating across the piece. Once the red and black mound is formed, the final two wefts need to start, after which all six wefts weave back and forth concurrently, overlaying each other in turn.

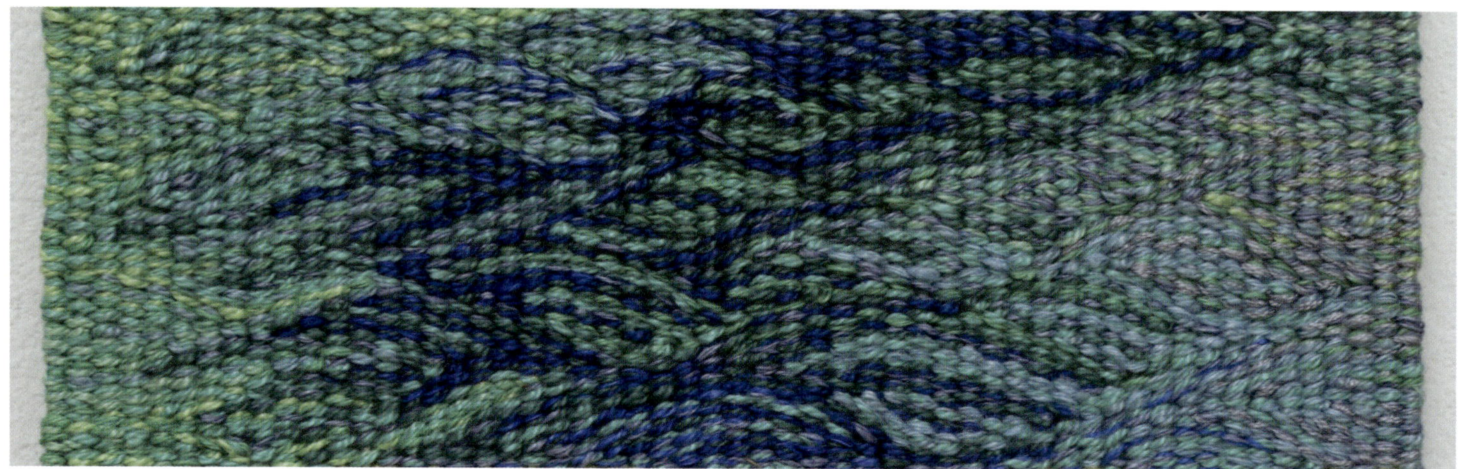

A sample using six eccentric wefts. 15cm (6in), at 8 epi.

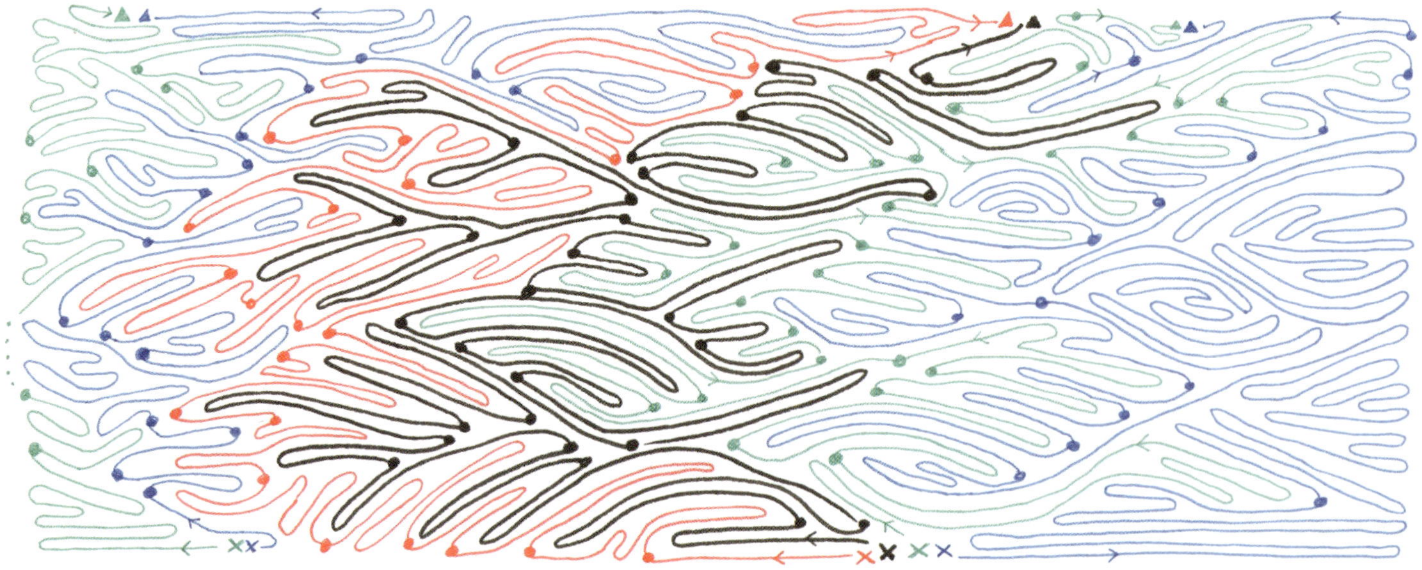

Diagram of how six wefts are woven.

Another pattern made entirely in eccentric weave, this sample returns to using only two wefts. These strongly contrasting wefts in tone and colour make a striking alternating pattern with diagonal bands of gently sloping passes, all leaning to the left, one colour on top of the other. Each band is then outlined eccentrically.

From the drawing you will see that the two wefts have started as ever on adjacent warps, in this case towards the left side. They immediately establish an alternating rhythm of building long and short passes, pausing and being picked up in turn. At the top of the first leftwards leaning area, the black weft was floated up. First the red, then the black weft weave from top to bottom where they immediately restart the alternating rhythm, building up the next sloping band. Again, at the top, both wefts weave down to the bottom and start to build up the next diagonal band. Although there is a definite pattern, it is not rigid.

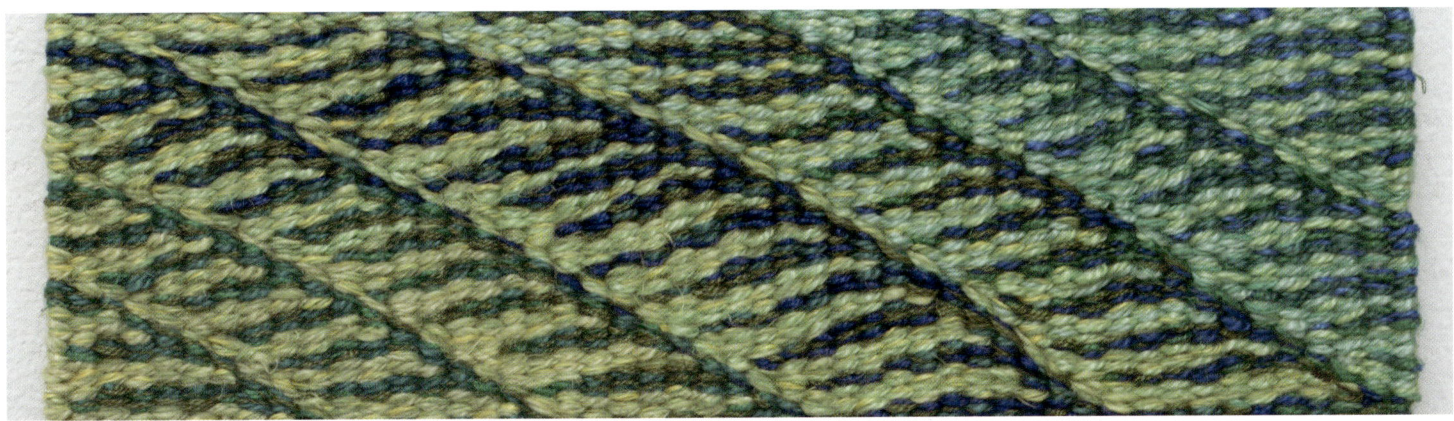

Repeated eccentric weave pattern with two wefts. 15cm (6in), at 8 epi.

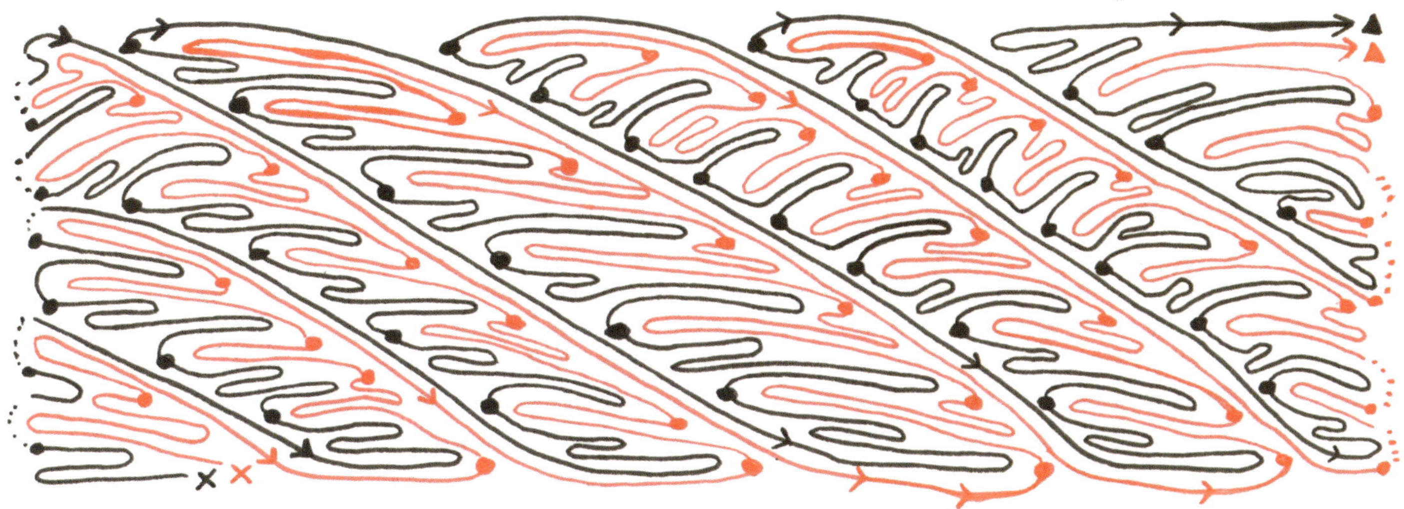

Diagram of the eccentric weave pattern.

This sample is woven more or less eccentrically throughout, the effect being accentuated by the choice of hard cotton and linen wefts. The beads on the sampler are close to vertical and the ribs horizontal, indicating that it was woven on its side as shown in the diagram. This allows the smooth, sinuous lines of the gently sloping areas of plant forms to be readily formed. The simplicity of using just two contrasting solid mixes adds to the clarity of the lines.

Looking at the diagram it is evident that the background has been woven in one weft from start to finish, albeit being paused several times. Each of the plant forms has been woven with a new weft, both started and finished at the left-hand edge.

The background areas of this piece could have been woven in plain weave, perpendicular to the warps, but instead the weft has been taken back and forth at all angles in small areas built one on top of another. The effect is to give movement and energy to the surface, very different to the ordered appearance of plain weave. The plant forms have been woven with the longest passes possible, giving a contrasting, more orderly and directional effect which helps the forms to stand out from the background.

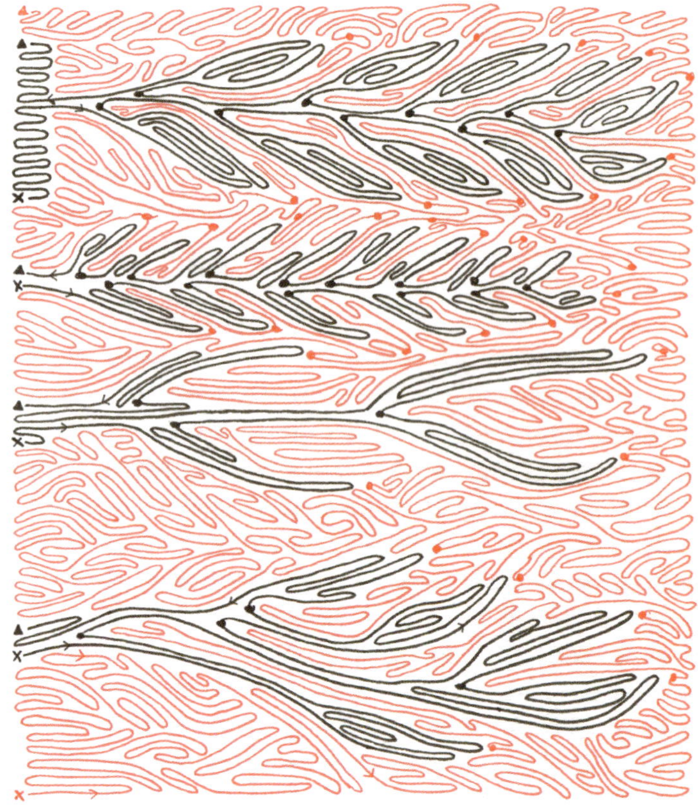

Eccentric forms diagram.

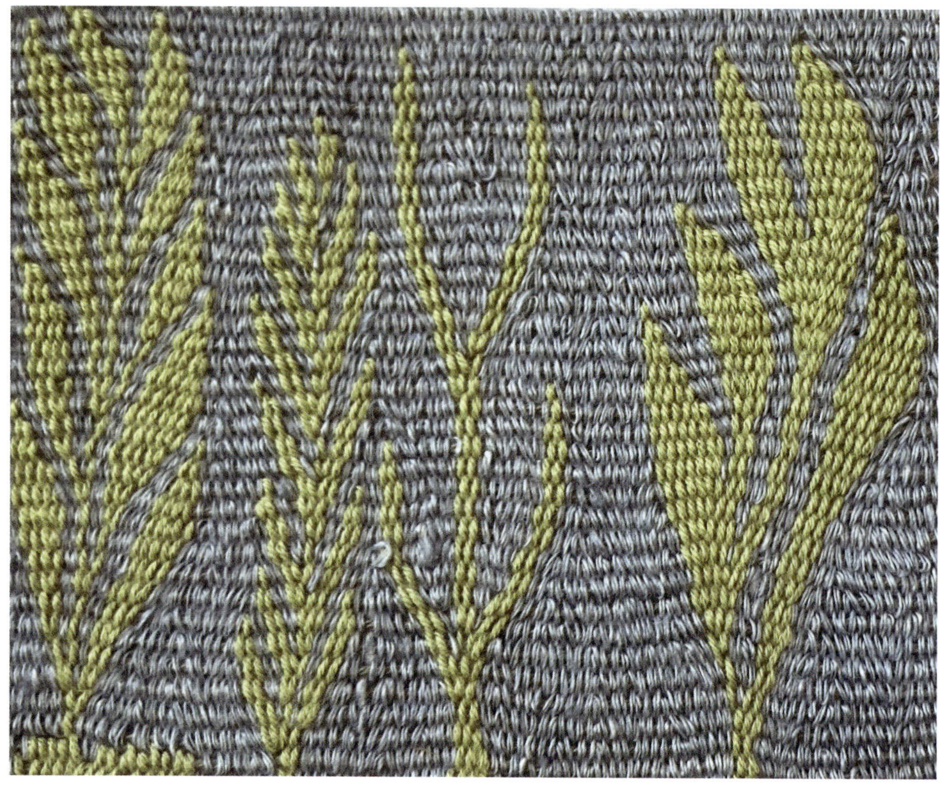

Flowing eccentric forms with two wefts. Coloured cotton fine (12/6) warp, linen and cotton weft. 11 epi.

TIDAL STREAM

As the tides ebb and flow round the Orkney archipelago, the waters are in constant change, often visibly so, reaching speeds of up to 30km/hr. Historically, they dictated travel around the islands, today they are harnessed for electricity generation.

Here eccentric weave is used extensively to portray the direction and speed of the tidal streams at their fastest, from the south and east, to west, six hours after high water. By contrast the solid land and deep sea are woven in the very different rhythm of plain weave.

Combining eccentric weave here with hatching makes for bold dynamic marks. The hatching is deep and does not necessarily follow the convention of making alternating passes. Instead, as with the tidal streams, it gathers and spreads as it flows around the islands.

The angle of weave here has exceeded the suggested maximum 45 degrees quite considerably in places. This means the weft made a very long bead as it passed over the warp and needed to be put in with plenty of length to prevent the warps from pulling together. This is especially the case since the wefts are rayon and linen, neither of which are elastic. This was done in the knowledge that once released from the loom, the natural tension within the eccentric weave would cause the piece to move and take on its own form. This is seen in the undulating surface of the weave in places, and of the whole piece as it hangs. The areas woven at the steepest angle have come forward, whilst others dip backwards. This change happened gradually over the first few months.

This piece demonstrates how eccentric weave has its own tension within a piece. This may be lessened by keeping to shallower angles, by surrounding the eccentric areas with plain weave, or with eccentric weave in the opposing direction. Alternatively, this natural tension could be exploited further to create sculpted tapestries.

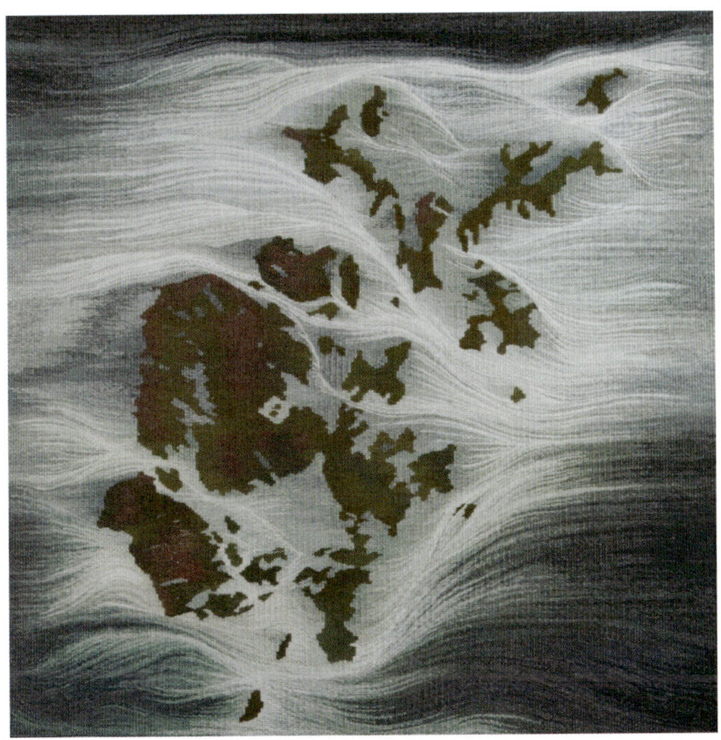

Tidal Stream, Ros Bryant. 80 x 60 cm, woven in wool, linen and rayon.

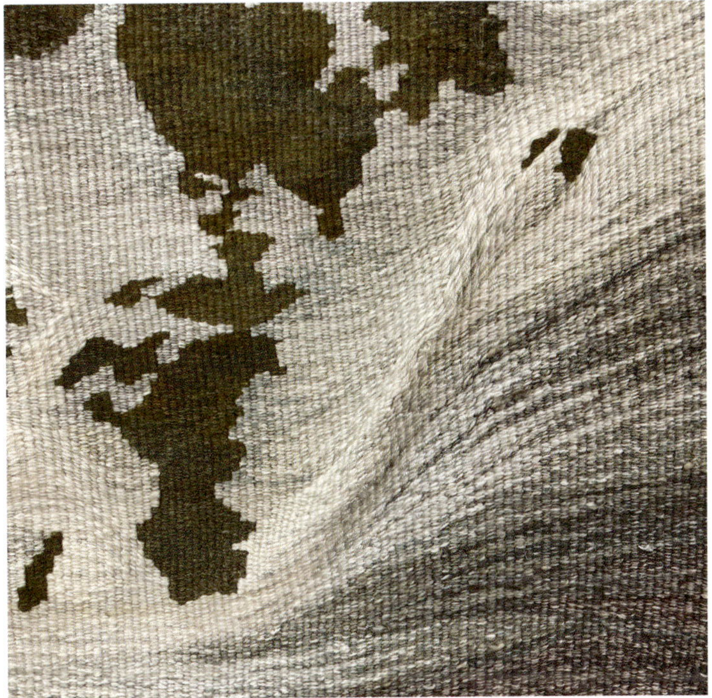

This detail shows the surface of the weave coming forwards because of a combination of high weft volume and extreme angle.

Wedge weave is a form of eccentric weaving used extensively in the Navajo tradition. It differs from other eccentric weave in that areas are formed by making straight eccentric passes in parallel with each other.

The whole of this sample is woven in one continuous weft, with new colours being introduced during the weaving. Instead of weaving horizontally across the warp these stripes have been formed in bands of short passes leaning alternately to left and right, at varying angles. The use of contrasting weft mixes highlights the angle of weave and adds to the overall sense of movement.

The weft starts at the bottom left and immediately passes back over the edge warp. The weft slides diagonally down to take in the second warp, weaving back up at the same angle and turning again on the edge warp before sliding down to take in the third warp. This pattern continues until built up to the desired height, then continues by gaining one warp with each pass along the bottom and reducing by one warp at the top. At the far side, the diagonal passes continue, reducing until turning round a single warp. The next band of weaving starts in the same way, establishing the same pattern of weave now leaning in the opposite direction.

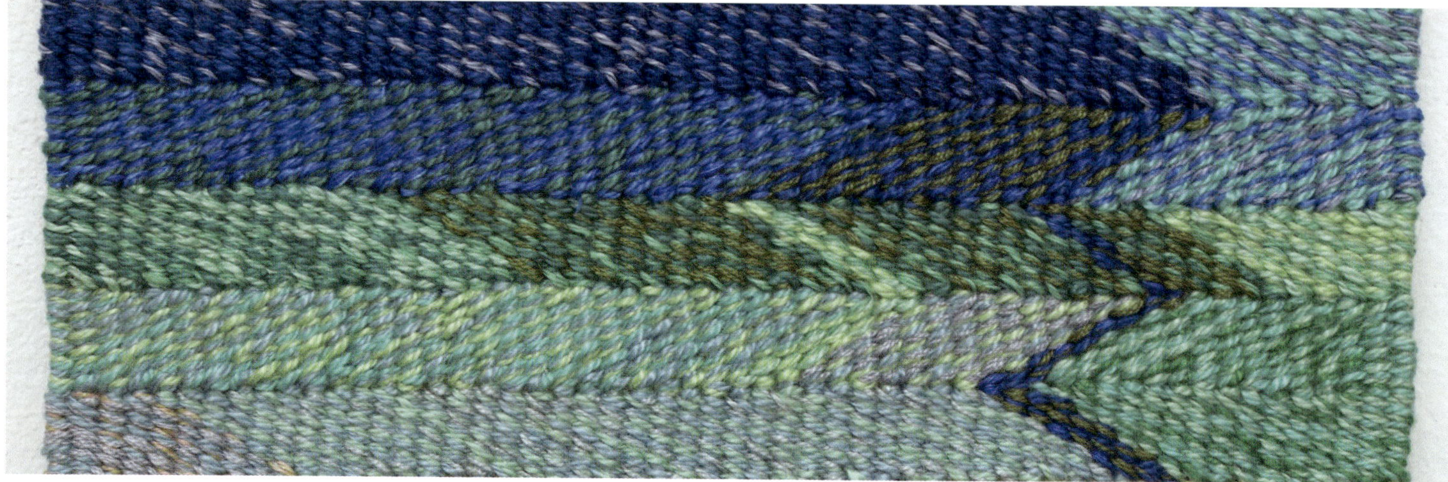

Wedge weave with 55 warps and one weft.

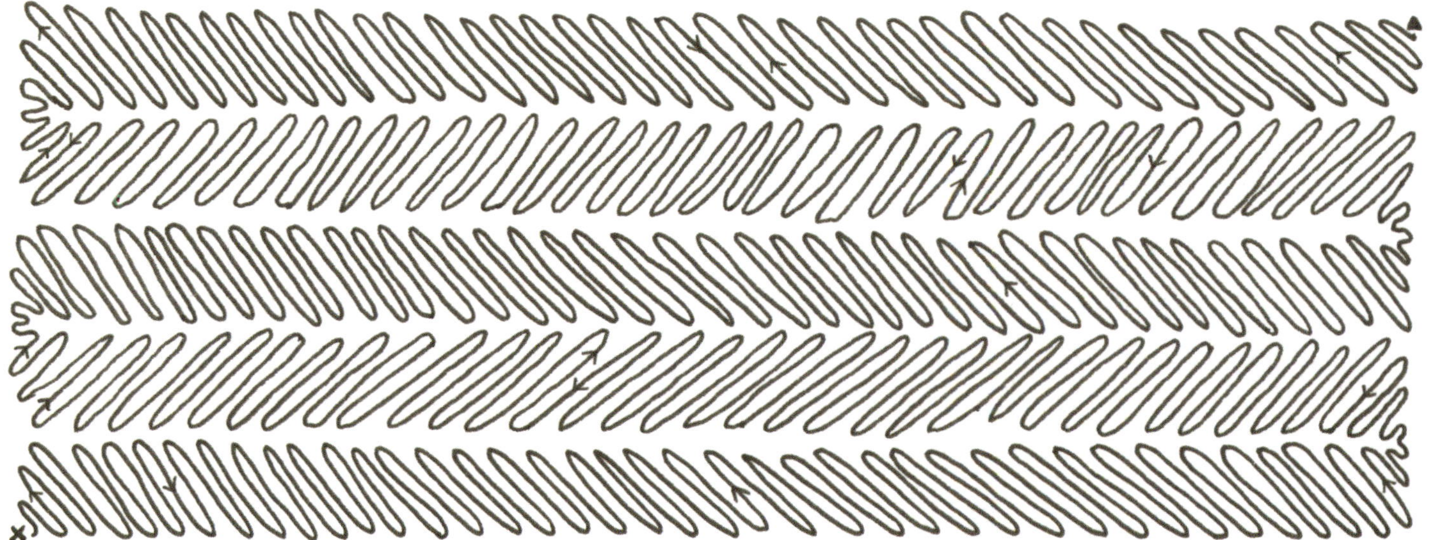

Simplified diagram showing wedge weave.

These hill-like forms have been woven one on top of another at random, each being formed freely in parallel, straight eccentric passes using a single weft mix. Both the weft mix and angle of weave change from each area to the next.

Most of the sample has been formed with one weft which has changed colour for each new form. Likewise, a new angle of weave has been chosen for each of the hill forms. The angle of weave does not dictate the shape of the woven area, indeed some of the hills lean one way whilst the weft leans the opposite way, creating a dynamic, almost three-dimensional effect. The shape of each area is formed simply by the length of the passes used, much as in plain weave except that the same eccentric angle of weave is maintained throughout.

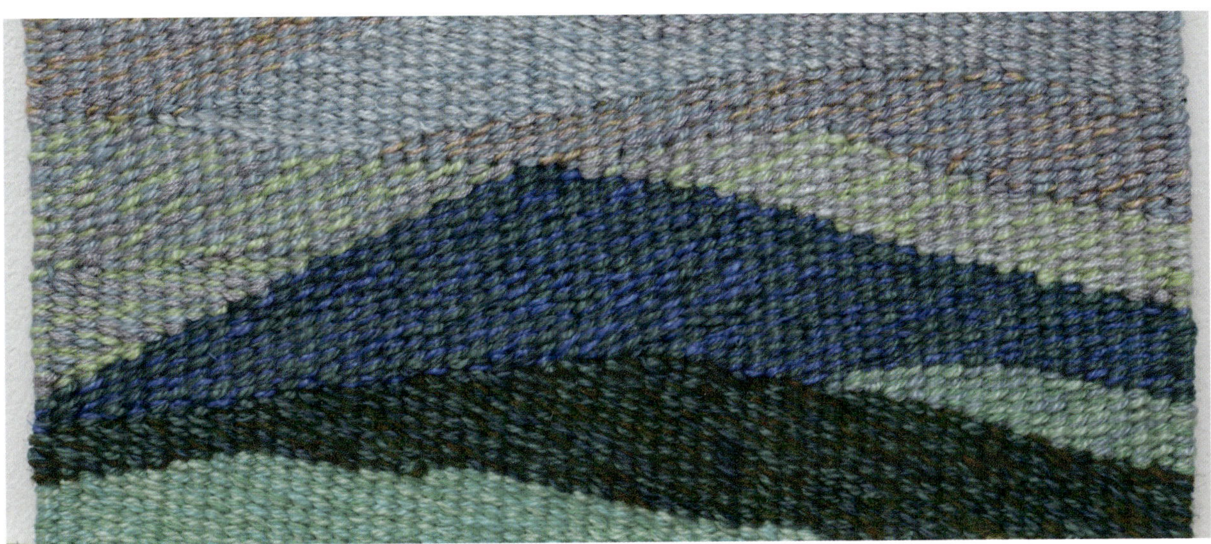

Freely formed wedge weave using 55 warps and two wefts.

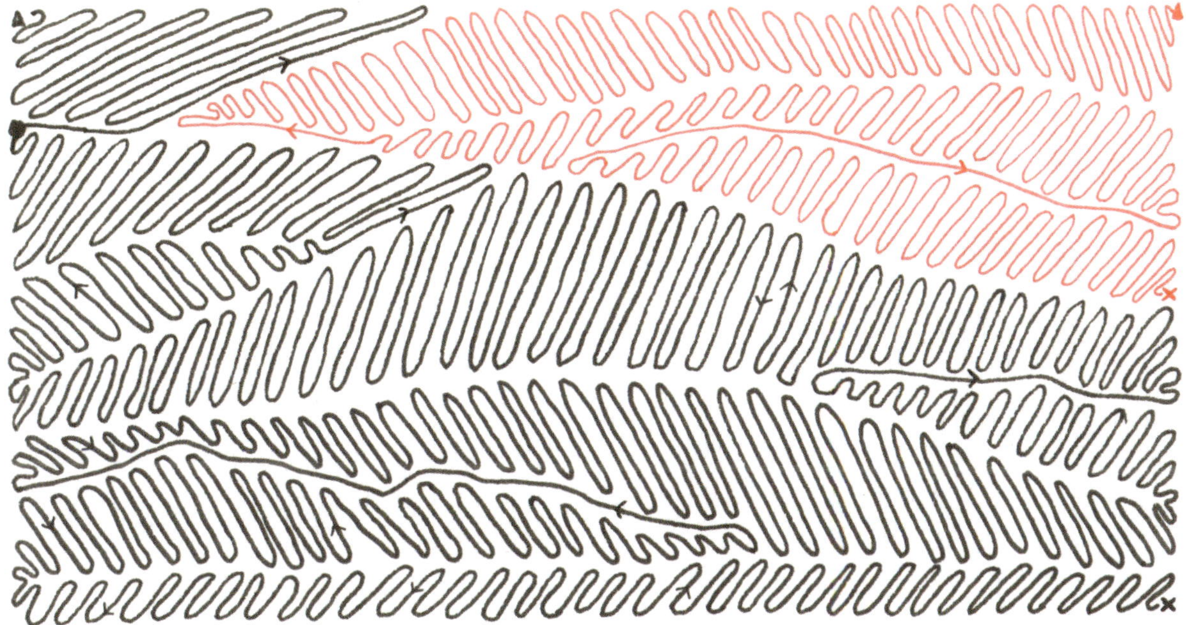

The weaving direction and order of areas woven using only two wefts.

Each of the lozenge shapes in this sample has been formed using straight parallel eccentric passes, or what we have termed a 'free wedge weave'. Each area is woven in one go with a separate, continual weft mix, some of which are more contrasting and so show the angle of weave more clearly. Instead of following a pattern, the direction and angle of weave changes randomly from one form to the next.

By this means, a simple design may be brought to life with directional movement and even the appearance of having three-dimensional form. This is one of many ways in which the structure of warp and weft – far from being constraining – is able to offer tremendous expressive freedom and personality.

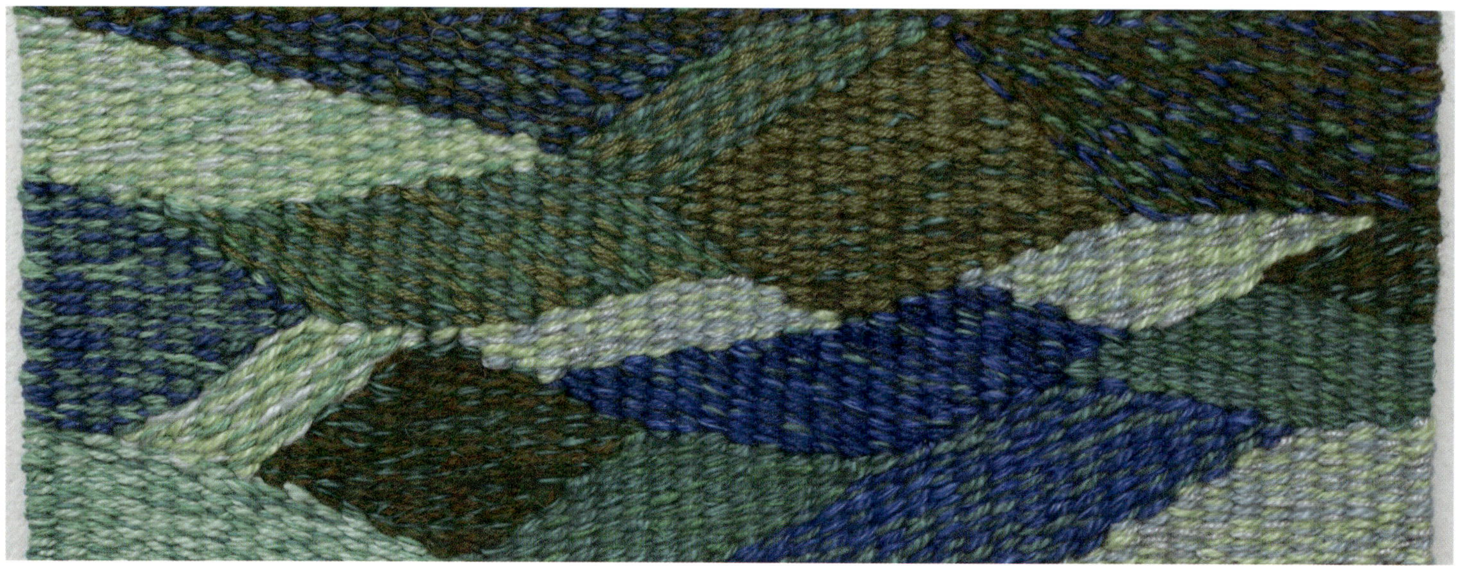

Multiple wedge weave forms using 49 warps and two wefts.

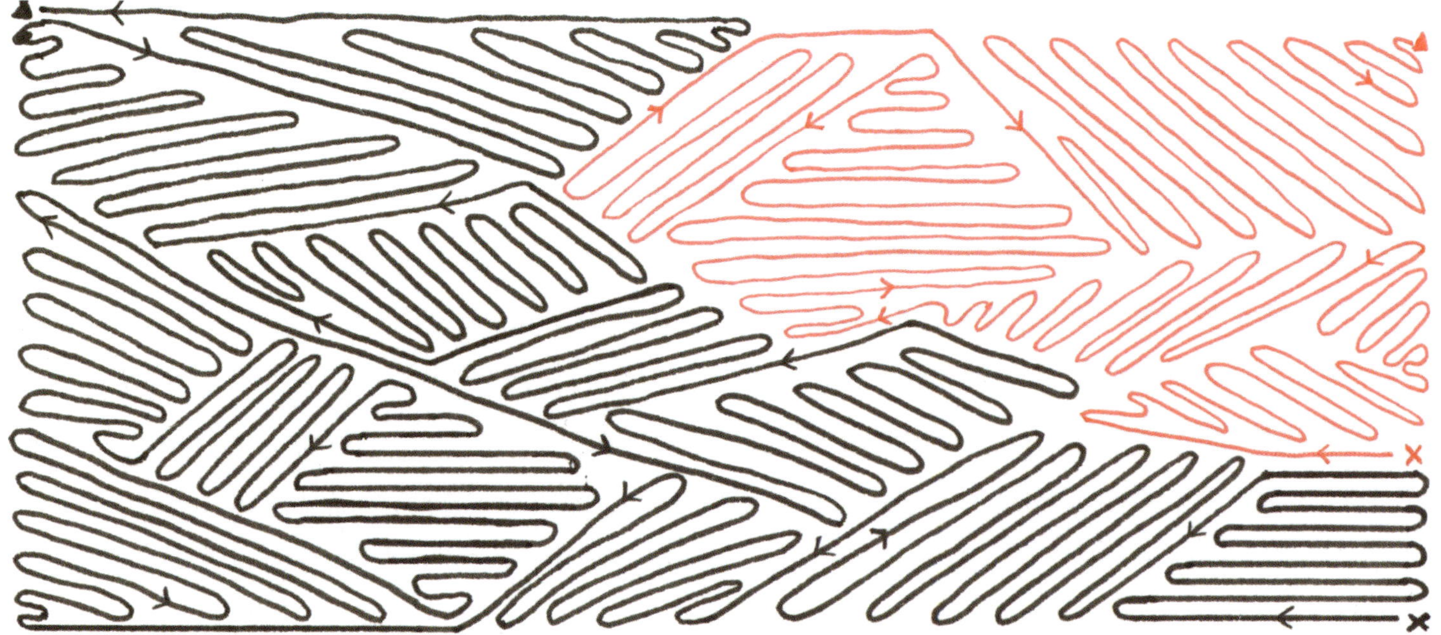

Diagram showing the weft direction in the sampler.

WEDGE WEAVE LANDSCAPE

This image of a Westray beach has been simplified to its main areas, which are then woven in bands of wedge weave. To try this exercise find an image, preferably one with large defined areas. Study the image. Look first at what are the main areas, trying not to become distracted by details. Place tracing paper over the image and trace the main lines. Decide what direction the movement will go, either leaning to the left or right, and variable angles depending on what you see within the image. Next consider the relative tones and colour palette you would like and any textural qualities. Before beginning to weave, it is useful to plan the order in which areas are to be woven and to make careful choices about where to start wefts.

Here is one interpretation of this image in wedge weave using 63 cotton warps. The foreground rocky peninsular has been given the angle and blocky structure characteristic of the Orkney flagstone, with areas partially submerged, with strands of the yarn from the surrounding sea added to the mix. In a landscape where the wind generally keeps the sea and sky in constant movement, wedge weave is ideal to capture the energy of the shifting light, pattern and colour. Most of the sea and the sky mixes change from one directional band to another, some strands common throughout, others changing.

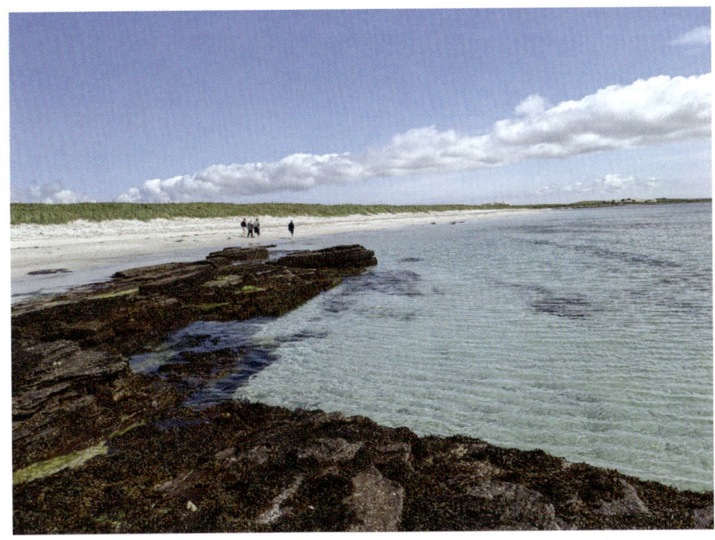

Photograph of a Westray beach.

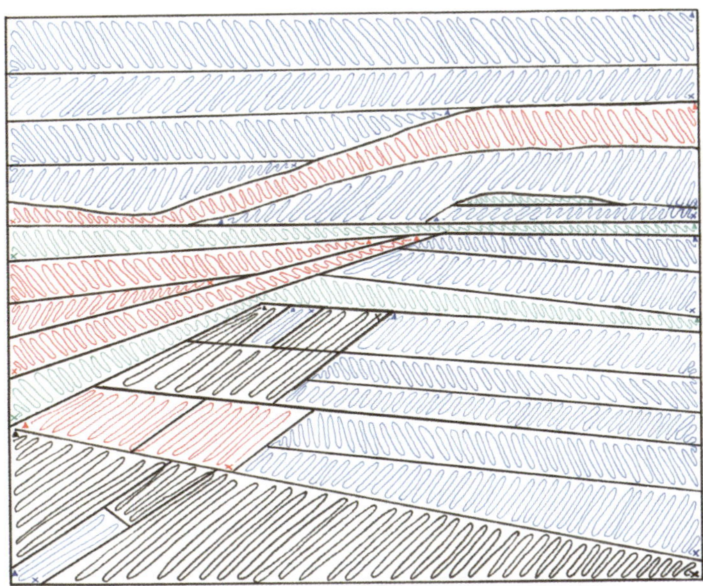

The beach scene interpreted in free wedge weave.

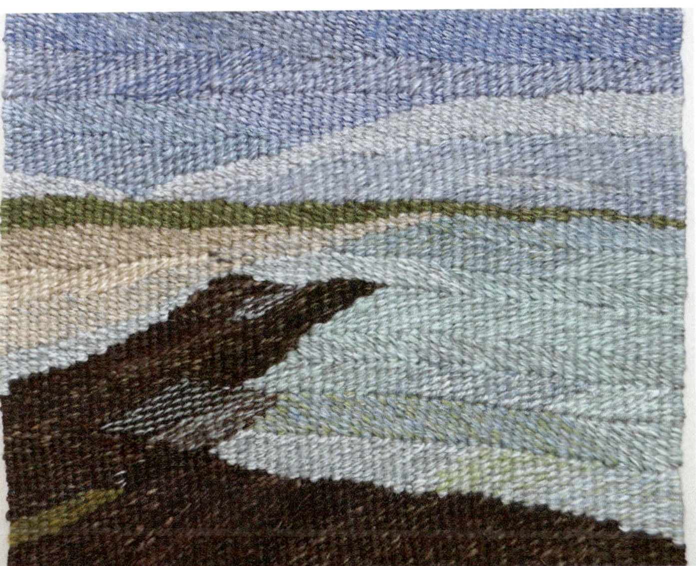

The landscape woven in wedge weave using linen, rayon, wool and silk weft.

CHAPTER 10

MOVING FORWARD

It is our hope that the contents of the previous chapters will have illuminated the way tapestry technique works. If you have been at the loom, we hope you have been able to master the fundamentals of what we believe to be a very exciting art form.

We have aimed to demonstrate tapestry technique in the context of the greatest personal and expressive freedom possible. From here on, the development of a creative voice is largely of an individual journey, more needing to be discovered than taught. We hope to have offered the means and the encouragement to progress in your own journey.

Tapestry is nothing if not slow in the making, and as we hope you will see there is an inexhaustible number of choices to explore. To become fluent takes time at the loom, preferably a great deal of time. There is no reason not to draw on any experience you may have of other media, textile or otherwise in pursuit of making work that is distinctively your own. Whilst respecting the uniqueness of tapestry and sharing a love of its framework, it is our view that there should be no rules beyond that which will or will not work physically. The long history and tradition of tapestry weaving is better used as a springboard rather than a constraint. There is much yet to be discovered in tapestry as an art form which may extend and sustain its place in the contemporary art world.

In this chapter, we lift the lid on a selection of tapestries both of us have made, showing ways in which tapestry is able to express ideas and experiences. They have been chosen with a view to showing just a few of the possible applications of tapestry technique. Warp in particular has more expressive potential than is often realised. Several of the tapestries in this chapter show warp becoming more than just the invisible vehicle for *weft-faced weave.*

Many of the starting points are quite simple, often having come from becoming absorbed in the landscape. Except where marked, the tapestries are Louise's. Notes to each piece explain the techniques used and the handling of materials, most of which will have been covered in more detail throughout the book. We hope that understanding some of our choices will encourage you to move on, and to be adventurous in using the language of woven tapestry to speak of the experiences which excite you.

ASCENDING SNOW MOUNTAIN

On the facing page. 12 epi. Coloured cotton 12/6 warp, cotton, linen, wool, stainless steel and silk weft. Tapestry inspired by Snaefell, the mountain of Louise's native Isle of Man. 18cm × 24cm.

Taking the palette of Snaefell, this miniature piece takes in the wide, unfenced landscape combining a sense of space with intimate detail and constant movement. Colours shift across the piece in forms woven eccentrically at angles verging from level to about 45 degrees. At times a single mix is used, giving a solid area. At others, two colours alternate in flowing lines descriptive of this windswept upland. Light reflects from some areas and is absorbed into the soft surface of others, according to the choice of fibre. Despite there being six or eight mounds from left to right, each only about half an inch or so high, this piece was woven with only two continuous wefts making changes of colour throughout. The restrained palette and repeated technique demonstrate that a tapestry need not be complex to be expressive, in this case capturing the feeling of the moment.

Ascending snow mountain.

TO AND FROM

A walk woven. Using the colours sampled on a walk, simple stripes have become the basis for this piece which turns and returns to the point at which it set out.

Pulled warps and shaped edges

This piece is woven in linen and wool, an epi varying between 10 and 12, and is 30cm (12in) from point to point. In contrast to the warp being the invisible supporter of the weft, this piece is all about warp. To see how it has been made, follow the ribs showing the warp within. From one point to the other you will see that the warp draws together and apart, increases and decreases in number, and turns through 180 degrees.

Woven on a conventional strip of warp, the piece starts and finishes on just three warps, extending to 12 at its widest, decreasing again to finish on three.

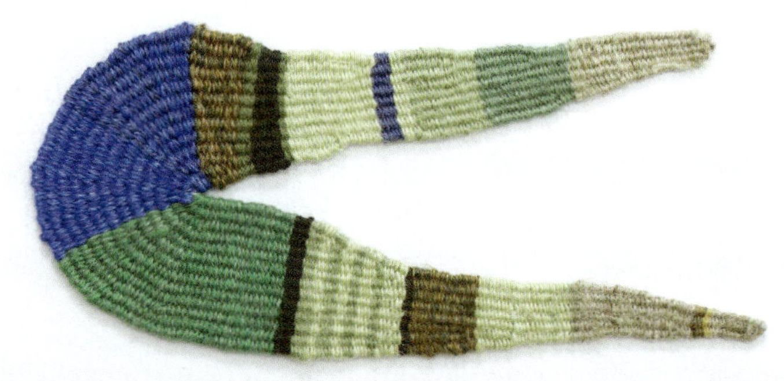

To and From.

The triangular cutouts illustrated are essential to allow the warp to be pulled though once cut off, closing up the gaps and making the turn. During the weaving, these triangular spaces may either be made freehand or formed around a piece of paper cut from the cartoon and inserted into the open shed as a template. Once cut off the loom the templates are removed and the warps are pulled carefully, pushing the weft up to fill the unwoven spaces.

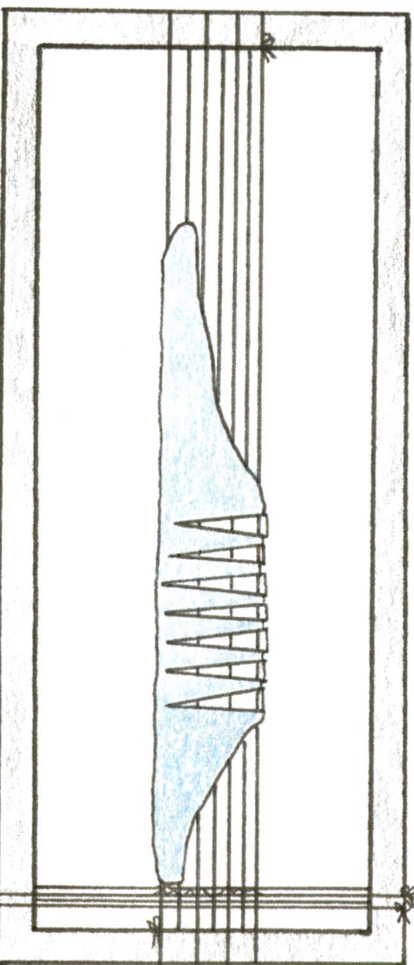

Diagram showing how the tapestry *To and From* was woven.

A FAR AWAY PLACE

25cm × 3cm, woven in linen on 7–12 warps of five colours.

Mongolia. 'A landscape which for me gave calmness and clarity, its vastness suggesting a paring down of information to the essentials.' The hills on the horizon are by no means insignificant but are distanced by miles of open grassland sparsely and simply populated by nomads.

Shaped piece with a continuous edge warp

Unlike the previous example which was weft faced, here the weft is loosely packed down to leave the warps exposed and their colours visible as an under layer.

Woven as a strip, starting and finishing with seven warps, it increases gradually to 12 on the right-hand side during weaving. This becomes the upper side, since the piece was woven to be turned on its side to view. To achieve the smooth outline of the curved edge, a technique was developed. The warp which was the edge warp at the outset has been pulled out to the right-hand side and held there by tying it to the frame. To allow for this, the warp was put on slightly slacker than usual. As extra warps are included then dropped to form the shape, this edge warp is woven in, drawing it to wherever the edge of the piece is. The effect of using a continuous edge warp is to give smoothness, knocking the angles off the long steps made as the number of warps is increased and decreased. This technique was also used in the previous example and the opening page of Chapter 7.

In the illustration, the gap between the warps where the edge warp has been pulled to the side is exaggerated for demonstration. In practice the warps draw back together quite quickly during the weaving, closing up the gap.

Woven with a muscular light green linen, using a mixture of plain and eccentric weave. The weft is one continuous length throughout. In effect this piece departs from two tapestry conventions, in being neither weft faced nor woven with a discontinuous weft.

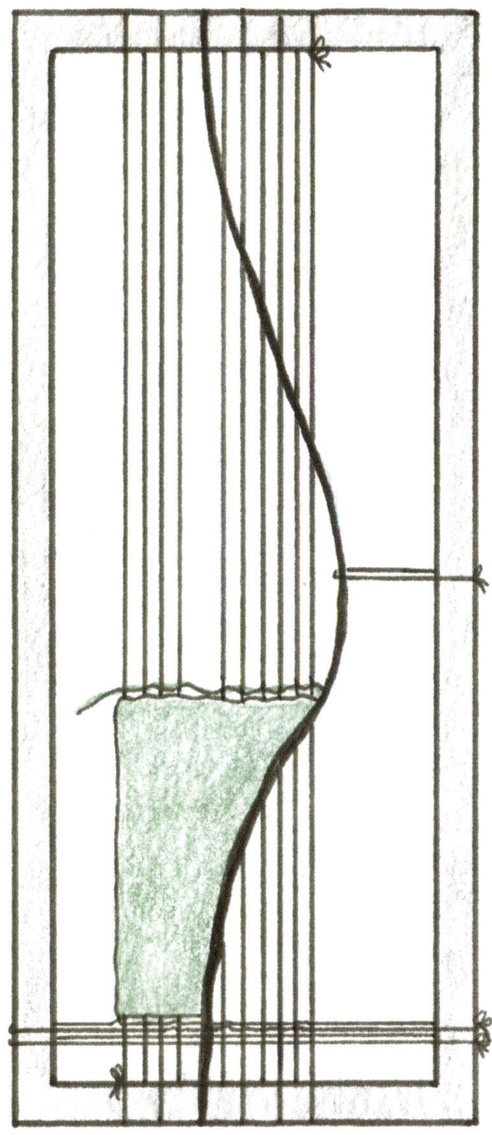

Diagram showing how *A Far Away Place* was woven.

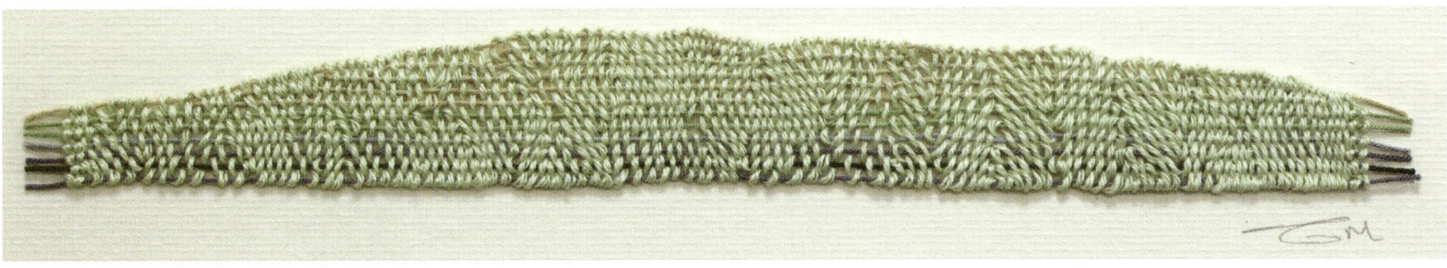

A Far Away Place.

LAND SERIES

14cm × 9cm. 12 epi, woven in linen, cotton and rayon.

Woven in response to time spent in the Gobi Desert, from the colours of earth and marks found in it. 'I choose to colour match directly from the landscape, using yarn where possible. When looking at colour I look for the detail, separating the colours that are within, rather than replicating an overall colour. These become the colours from which I choose to weave. The colour which comes forward may not be the one which was dominant in the landscape.'

Planning shaped pieces

The process of pulling warps is never entirely predictable since the yarns used, each weaver's tension and the scale will all have an effect. However, it is possible to get a good idea of the approximate finished form by using a paper pattern. The round-ended strip illustrated here is the outside shape of the piece, woven on a narrow strip of warp and shaped by adding warps to start and decreasing to finish. The triangular tabs are cut out and set aside in sequence. Next, the paper pattern can be bent into something like the shape the tapestry will take. This only applies where the tabs are cut out right to the last warp, although this technique could be used to plan three-dimensional pieces which would result from cutting out shorter tabs.

As the weaving progresses, the paper pattern forms a guide to where the tabs should be used, sliding the cut-out tab into the open warp and continuing the weave above it.

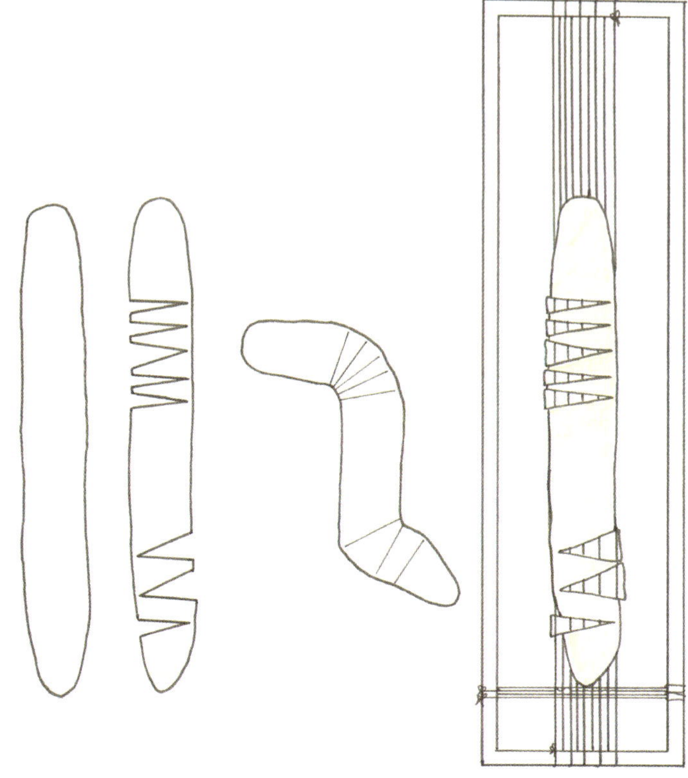

Planning your design.

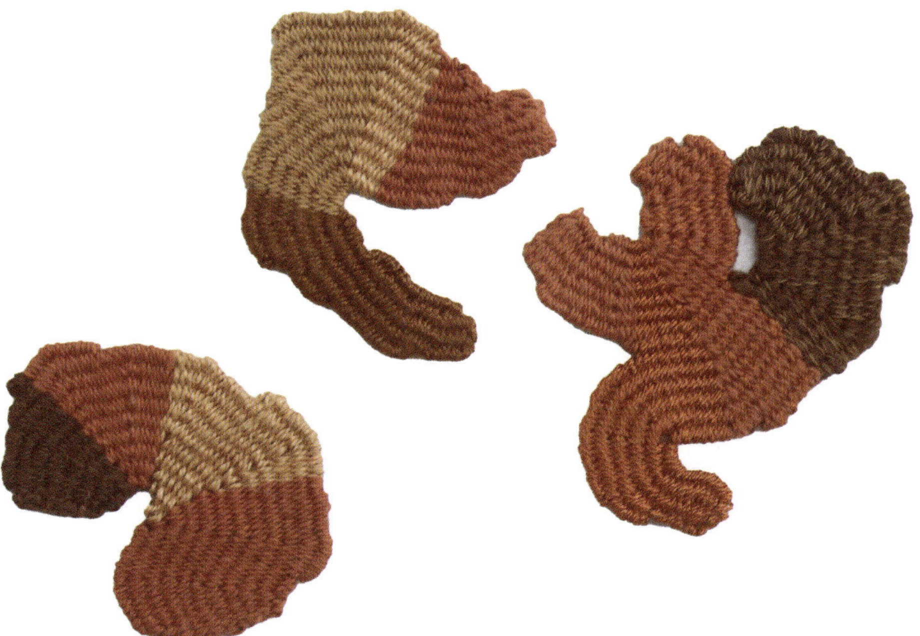

Land series.

PLOUGHED

75cm × 61cm. Coloured cotton 12/6 warp, wool, linen, cotton and silk weft.

A piece which came out of observing changes in the surrounding landscape, in this case Orkney during spring when the fields are being patterned by the plough in preparation for the coming year's barley and new pasture.

Extended warp strip, pulled turns

To understand how this piece is constructed, again follow the warp. The central 'field' shows the warp more or less vertical, deviated slightly to left and right by stripes of eccentric wedge weave.

Woven in one piece on a large scaffolding loom, the long strip to the left-hand side extended straight up from the field shape which occupied the whole width of the warp at the bottom of the loom. The extended strip and the left-hand edge of the field form are woven in four narrow strips which are interlocked together, apart from a small section towards the bottom where a slit has been left for the tip of the extended strip to be later threaded through. The strip narrows to its tip, moving by visible steps, without having been smoothed off by using a continuous edge warp as with *A Far Away Place*.

At the four points where the strip now turns, a large tab was inserted during the weaving. Once complete, the tabs were removed, and the warps pulled to draw the strip up into its finished form. The strip passes behind the corners of the 'field' and is threaded through the slit. The weft throughout the piece has been packed down lightly, allowing for the coloured 12/6 warp to show through.

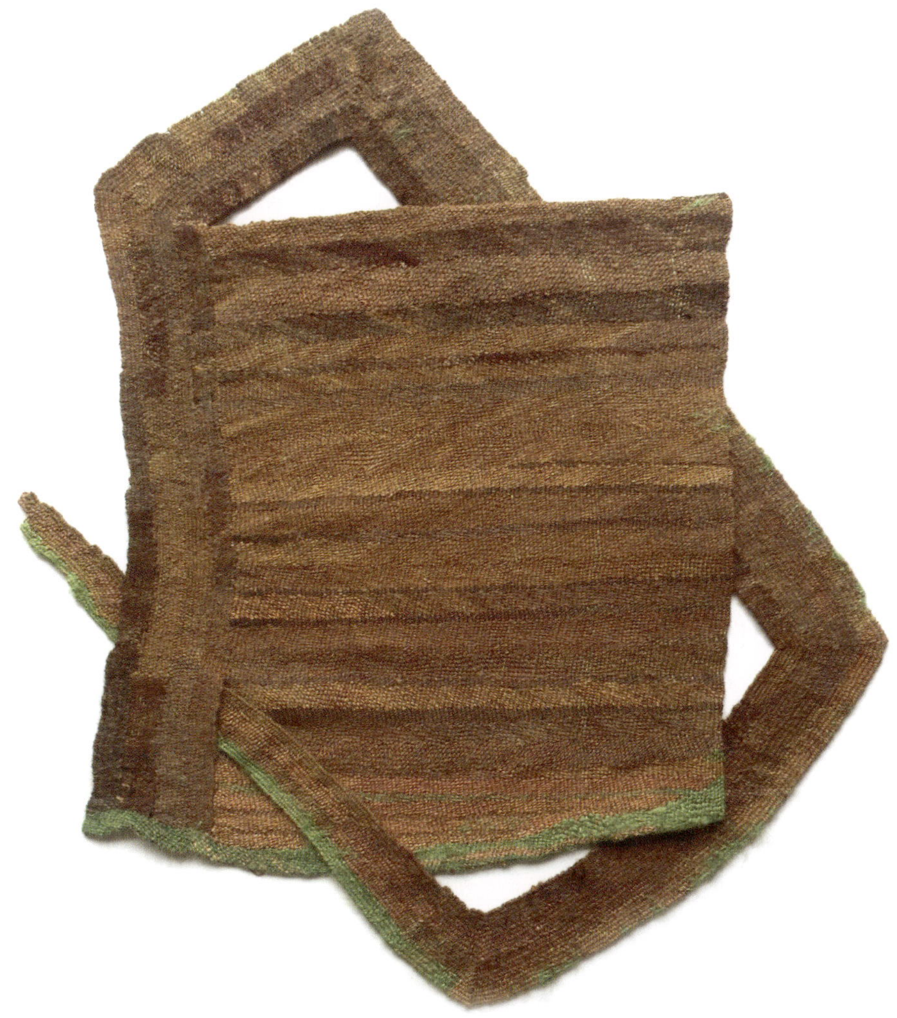

Ploughed.

MEDIEVAL LEAF

10cm × 10cm. 12 epi. Coloured cotton 12/6 warp, wool and cotton weft. From a series of images taken from historic tapestries re-woven with a contemporary interpretation for an exhibition called 'Tapestry Mischief'. This piece also makes mischief with the convention for a tapestry to be properly knotted on and off and the warps sewn invisibly to the reverse side. Here they are allowed to remain free, to tangle and unravel, their colours and disorderliness becoming part of the piece.

Woven with wool and cotton, this leaf is a nod to the leaves found in energetic profusion in the background of medieval tapestries. The leaf image is woven eccentrically throughout, giving smooth lines to the leaf veins. The border of pick and pick follows the same eccentric lines. The warp is of several colours.

When putting on a warp made up of several different lengths, it is important to make sure that they all continue around the frame as if continuous. This means that as one is tied off at the front of the frame, the next is tied on at the back and so on. Care is needed to make sure the tension between warp sections is equal, particularly if using warps of differing weight within a piece.

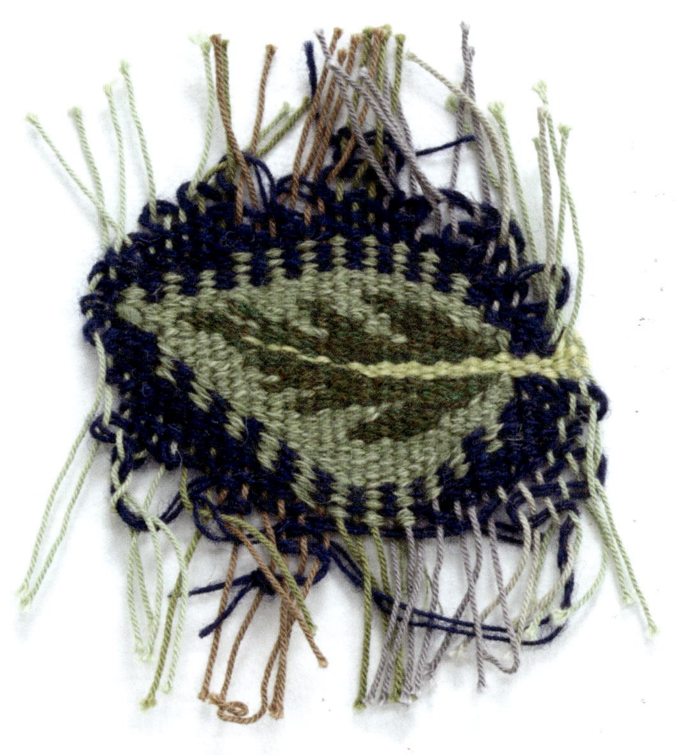

Medieval Leaf.

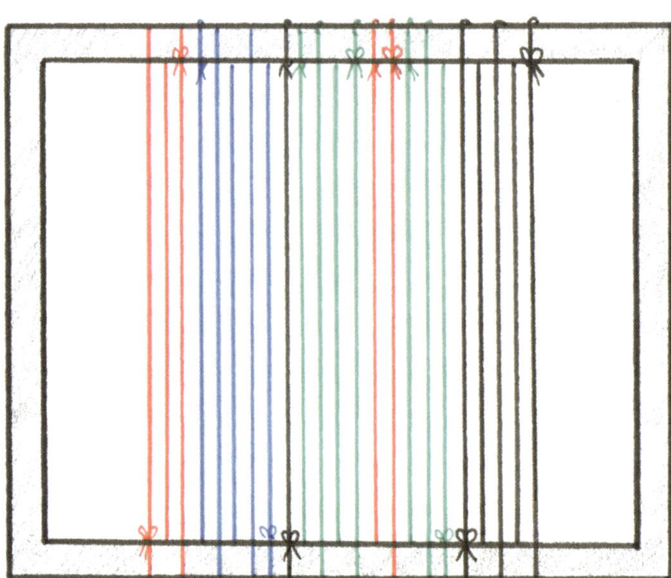

A warped loom using different coloured warps.

LOOKING OUT

Looking out over the Mongolian steppe, vast, unfenced, treeless grassland. 'For me, the framework of warp and weft has long been the place from which expression flows. Now, in the process of absorbing a very different and hugely expansive landscape, it became the foundation from which I was able to make the conscious choice to weave unconsciously.'

A loom warped at a changing epi

14cm × 13cm, woven on coloured cotton 12/6 warp at a variable setting with linen and silk weft.

In order to be free, a palette of yarns was chosen at the outset. To understand the tapestry, follow the warp running left to right. This is another piece woven on its side, which allowed for what have become gently swaying upward marks to be woven smoothly. The warp colours change, becoming increasingly light towards the top. The warp spacing also becomes gradually closer and the weft finer, so that the weave becomes gradually finer and the surface flatter travelling up the piece. Woven in shallow, free eccentric passes, evoking constant gentle movement across the steppe in a kind of 'modern millefleur'.

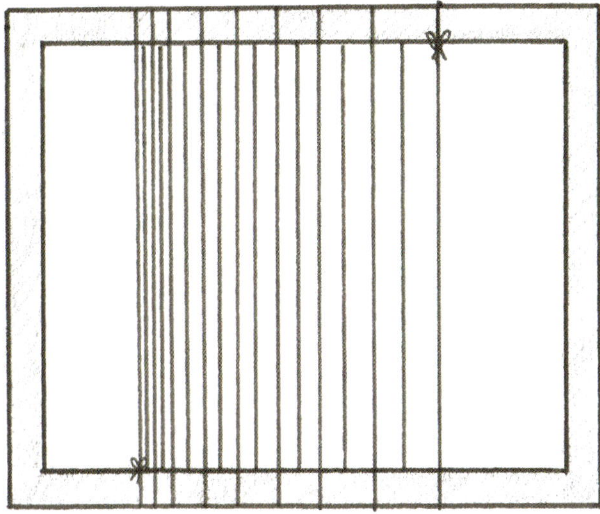

A warped loom with a changing epi.

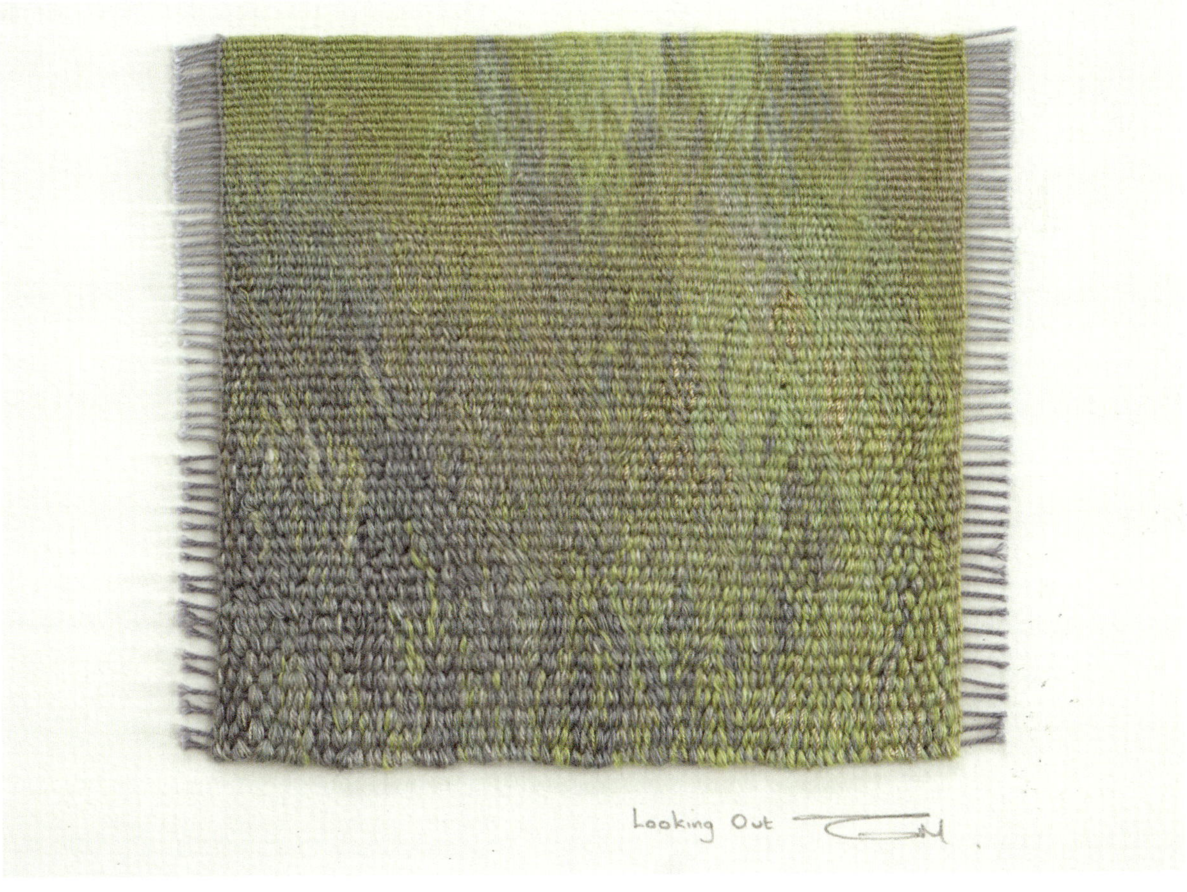

Looking Out.

CIRCUMNAVIGATION

30cm × 8cm, at between 8–14 epi with cotton 12/6 warp. Wool, linen and silk weft.

Standing on Pierowall pier, Westray, taking a 360-degree view from the ground under Louise's feet, over the bay to land beyond, upwards to sky overhead, back down to the sea, returning to the pier. Woven from yarns chosen on site.

A piece shaped by doing just what this book has instructed the reader to avoid – pulling the edges in and pushing them out. As an exercise it is a great way to learn how to control edges, irregular or straight. This has been done by putting in more weft length or thicker mixes with looser turns to push out the edges, or using thinner mixes without raising mounds and making tighter turns to draw them in.

To make a continuous band, the warp has been pulled around the frame, made possible by warping up less tightly than usual with rods put under the warps and pushed round to the ends of the frame. These are removed to slide the warps around and replaced to re-tension. Sticking Sellotape around the ends of the frame also helps the warps to slide. When warping, leave a length of warp about the height of the loom both before tying on and after you have knotted off. These spare warp lengths may be wrapped around the loom at first to keep them away from the weaving, and released in order to pull the warp round to weave the next section. This allows for the weaving to be pulled to the position required with sufficient length to secure the end to the frame.

When weaving, only the warps at the front of the frame are used. The header band and twining are put through the front warps only. When the piece first needs pulling round, they have to be removed. The weaving is stable by then so they are no longer needed. A sheet of card between the front and back warps can help the eye to focus. The final section of weaving completing the loop will need to be woven with a needle. The wefts either need to be laid in or their ends sewn in afterwards to make the piece double sided.

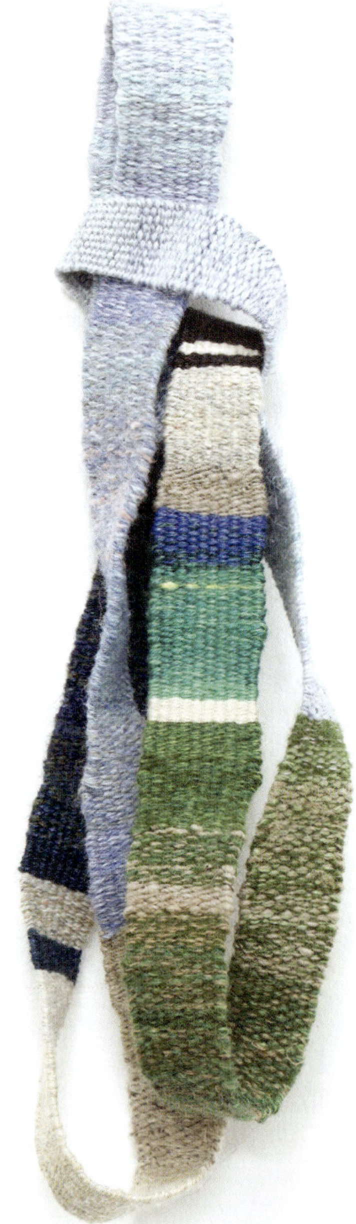

Circumnavigation.

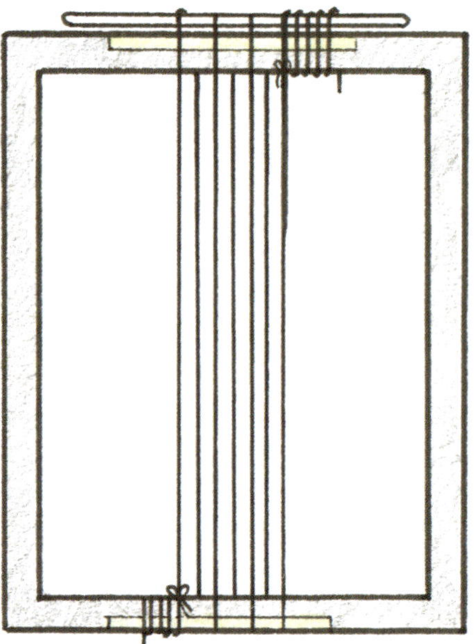

Showing how the loom was set up to create the continuous tapestry.

CAMOUFLAGE

A challenge to replicate a pattern invisibly. Choices of weft weight and yarn, the warp sett and weight, and the direction of weave all needed to be planned before weaving.

White dots on red

12 × 12 cm. 16 episode. Cotton warp, linen and cotton weft.

Woven sideways, this small, rectangular tapestry replicates six full and four half dots. Woven with 15 warps, the whole dots use three warps each. To give the appearance of roundness the full dot was started on the middle of its three warps, on a low warp and finished likewise. To make the piece sit as flat as possible, it was not knotted on and off. The warp and weft ends were all sewn in neatly.

Wavy lines

12 × 12 cm. 12 episode. Cotton warp, wool, linen and cotton weft.

Woven upright in carefully matched coloured wefts and a fine warp to give a thin tapestry that will sit on the background without casting too much of a shadow. In matching the lines of the background at either side, the beating down and number of passes is crucial. Mid row, there is freedom to follow an imagined line between, which has been completed with eccentric outlining.

In both cases a careful cartoon of dots/lines was made and secured behind the warps as a guide. It is crucial when following a cartoon closely to view the warp straight on and not at an angle so that the weave and cartoon match up.

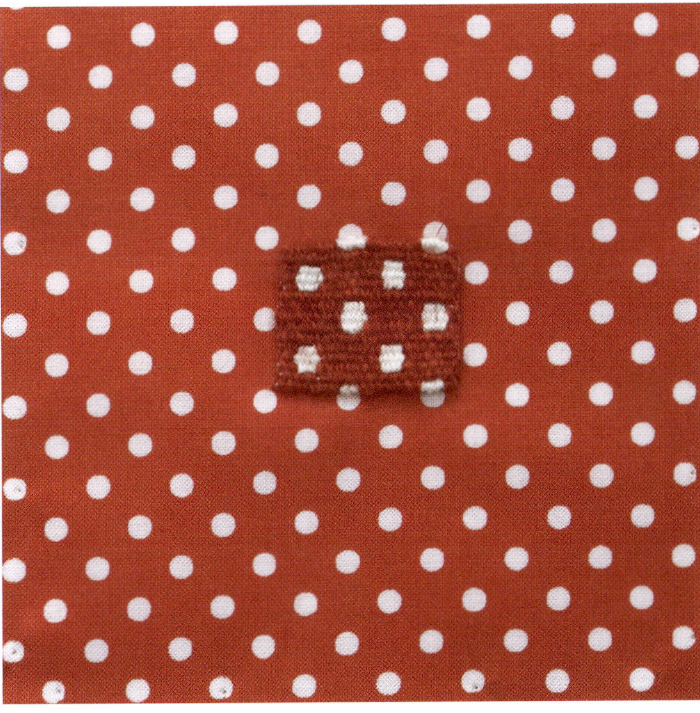

Camouflage series. White dots on red. 12cm × 12cm. 16 epi. Cotton warp, linen and cotton weft.

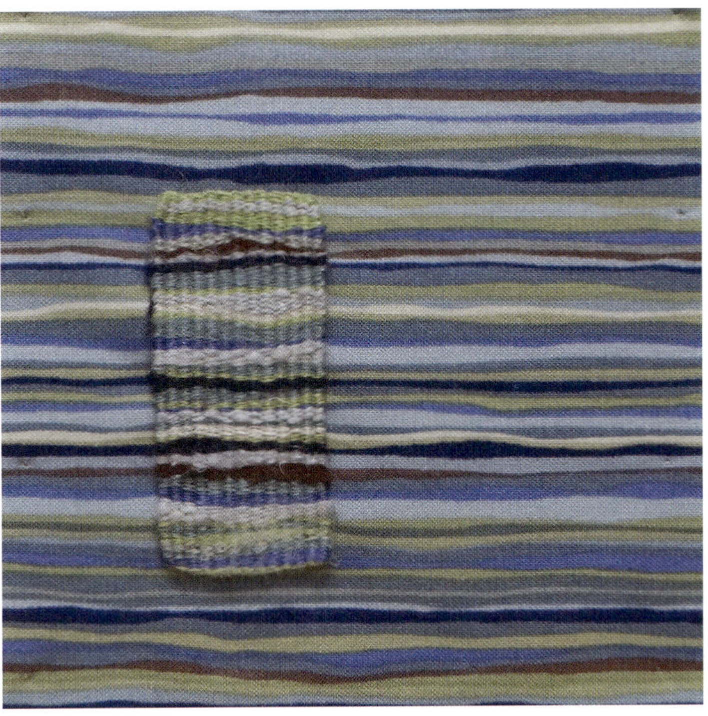

Camouflage series. Wavy lines. 12cm × 12cm. 12 epi. Cotton warp, wool, linen and cotton weft.

CLOSE-E-KEE

'A wallpaper pattern remembered from my Nan's home', woven in double-single weave at 9/18 epi with shantung silk weft.

Double/single weave

In this case the warp is set up for a shed on the double weave since the double weave occupies the larger area. This means that there are two warps around the front then two around the back of the frame alternately. There is no aesthetic difference when woven, only convenience when weaving. It is however important to choose a sett which may be divided into single warps and still be wide enough for the *single weave* areas to be woven. To weave at 9 epi, a medium warp would usually be chosen, and at 18 epi a fine warp. To accommodate both, a fine warp has been chosen.

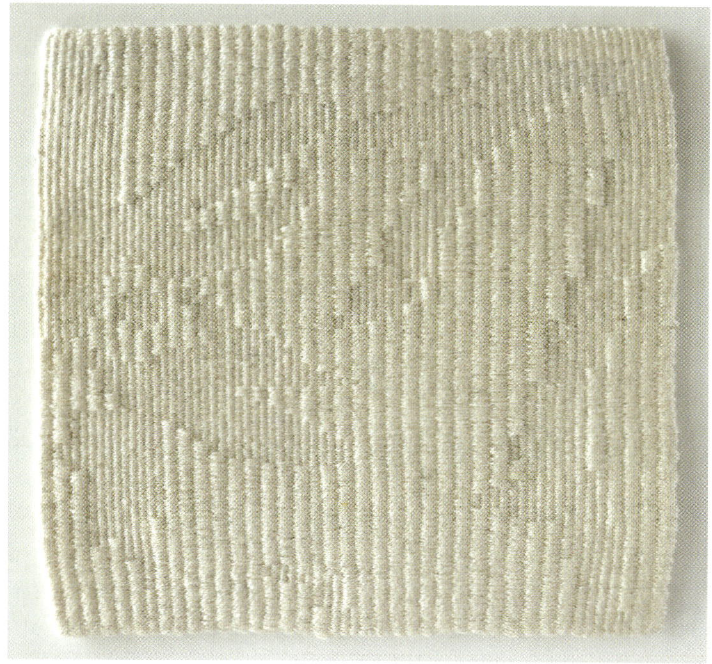

Close-E-Kee.

Warping double begins with putting on a warp as usual. Starting from the same point, a second warp is wound on with each warp falling as closely as possible to the first warps and on the same side at each turn. The header band and twining are put on with the warps grouped in pairs. A double warp may be chosen in place of one, even when not wishing to weave at two different setts, since it gives a flatter bead than a single heavy warp, and therefore a smoother surface.

In this piece, one fine strand of silk was used to knot on, which secured the weave but is not visible. Whilst weaving, the change from double to single weave is made freely, the first row of single after an area of double always needs to be beaten well to force the warps into singles rather than pairs. Double weave will tend to beat down differently to single so care is needed to keep them at an equal level.

The use of the same silk weft in changing colours throughout shows how much variation in warp sett and spacing a given weft can tolerate, though the double weave here is less firm. This is another example where the tapestry convention of discontinuous weft is not followed, since the one weft continues through the whole tapestry, weaving from side to side on each pass.

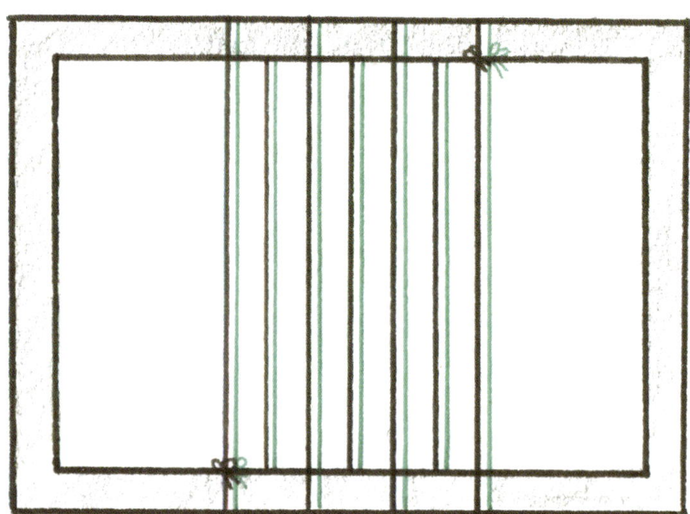

Double warping shown in two colours.

HAW

1.25m × 0.5m, woven over one to five warps at 12 epi. Coloured cotton 12/6 warp, wool, linen, silk, cloth strips, rayon, cotton, nettle and hemp weft.

This tapestry references the colours seen as the light changes on a section of hawthorn trunk, combined with the angle of a traditional laid hedge.

The bead shows that the warp passes through this piece at an angle of about 22 degrees, sloping upwards towards the left. To achieve this, the cartoon was set at an angle behind the warp. Templates were laid into the open shed to form the lower sides with extra angled twining to the lower edges. This means that instead of being woven bottom upwards, the weave is made eccentrically from bottom left to top right.

The weft in the dark areas is much finer, passing over single warps, at times purposefully exposing the coloured warps, whilst the raised areas are formed of much thicker mixes woven over variable numbers of up to five warps at a time to make a deeply contoured surface.

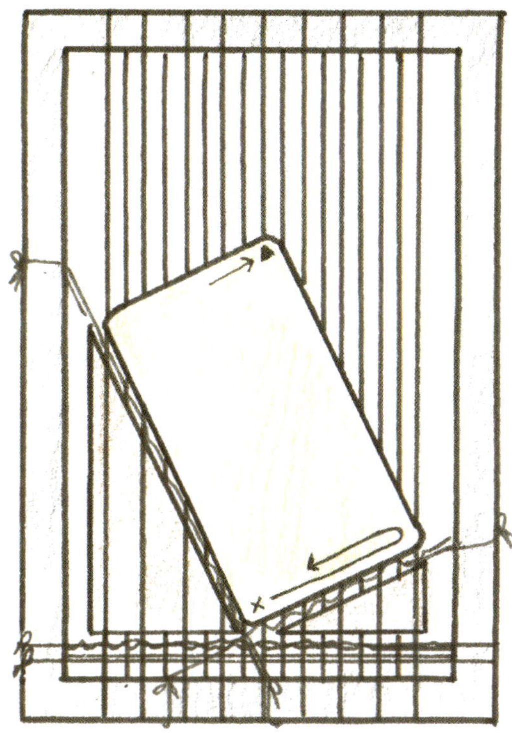

How to set up the loom to make a diagonal warp.

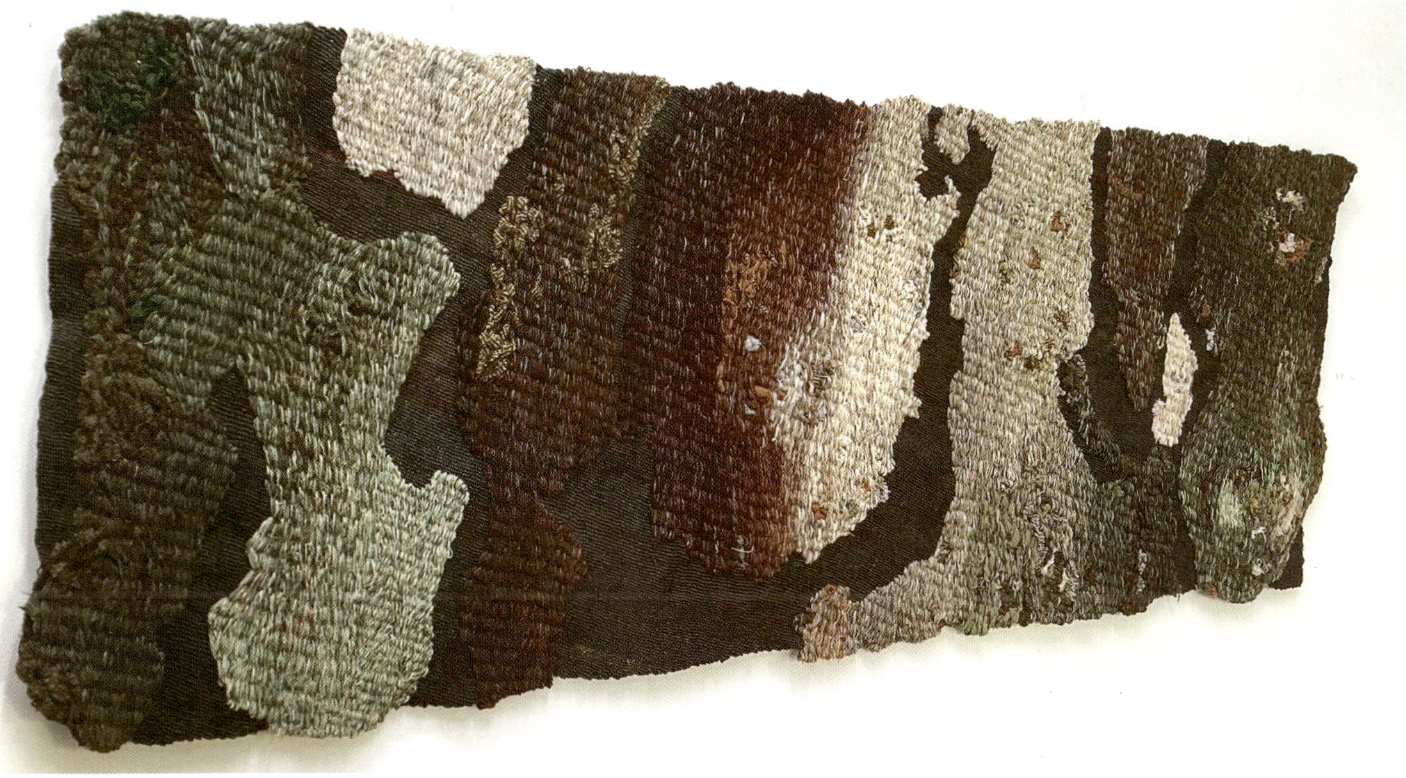

Haw. Commissioning Artist Hermione Spriggs. Woven for Campkin Road Community Centre, Cambridge.

WEATHER WINDOW

Woven in wool, cotton, rayon, at 8 epi, 66 × 90cm.

Boat watching from the island of Cava, Orkney. Wind in Orkney is the norm, high winds and rough seas not unusual. The diminutive landscape is dominated by overarching sky, and sea, so that at times all three feel to be on the move together. This can be both exhilarating and challenging, particularly when on a very small island hoping to get out in a boat.

This piece is woven in a repeated rhythm of motifs formed by using contrasting hatching and steeply eccentric weave. The use of pattern is sympathetic to the constructed nature of woven tapestry. Subtle changes may be made from one repeated motif to the next with powerful effect, in this case that of continuous movement. The use of hatching in this case makes the fairly steep angle of weave possible without distorting the surface. Care was needed throughout to put in sufficient weft not to pull the warps together, particularly when weaving in the less elastic cotton and rayon yarns.

Both the individual forms and their flow across the piece needed to be matched between sections. This was done by weaving all four sections on one warp with the unwoven warps left in between and a template inserted to separate the top and bottom quarters. Adjacent sections were woven concurrently, aiming to match the tension. Care was needed to secure the cartoon and work closely to it, in particular making sure to view the cartoon through the warps at a point exactly level with the weaving rather than from above or below. The initial drawings and the cartoon were one single piece.

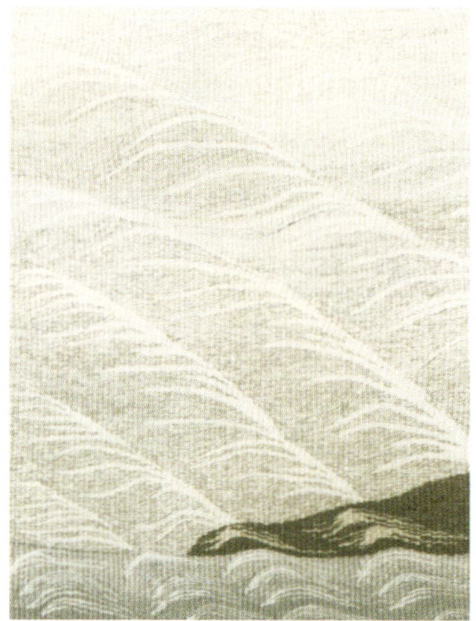
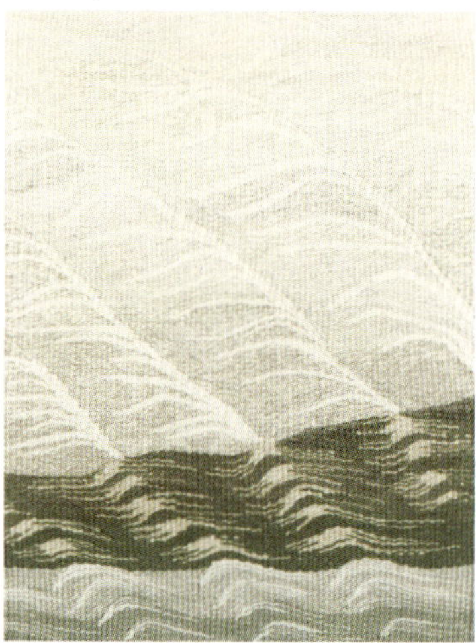
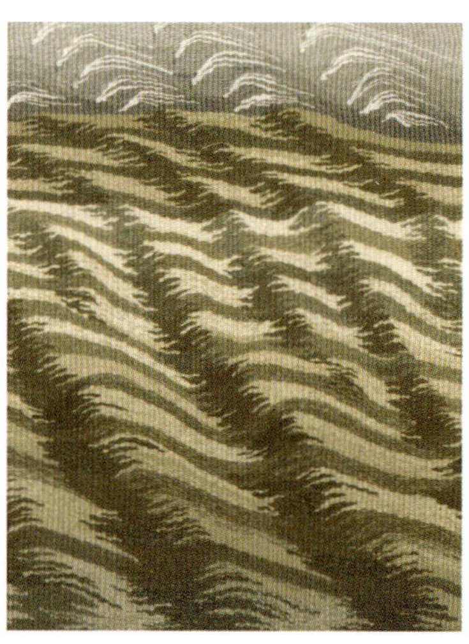
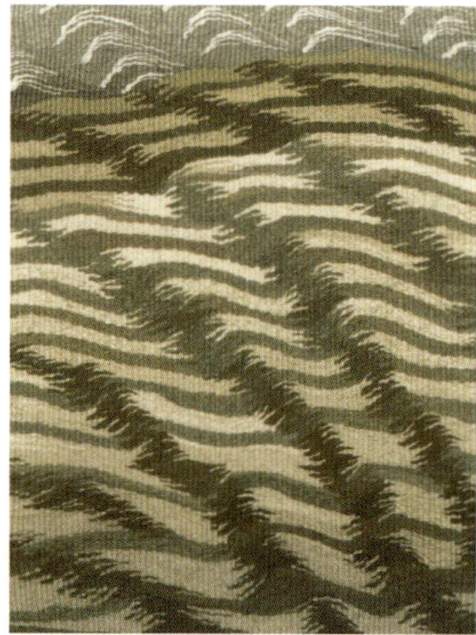

Weather Window, Ros Bryant.

TAKING THE LONG VIEW

2.5m × 1.2m, cotton, silk, rayon on a cotton warp at 8 epi.

Woven following a study of the changing forms which sea and sky take on in response to each other, of the marks which together wind and tide make on the shore and of the sympathetic forms of for example wing, fish or boat designed to move through them. These are marked in direct contrast to the rectangular forms which we choose to construct and inhabit on the land.

The choice to dye my own yarns was a big help with this piece. Particularly useful was the ability to dye several contrasting plant yarns in the same colour. This gave me far greater control over the changing colours and lustres than would have been possible in commercially available dyed yarns. The piece also makes use of ecru, or naturally coloured undyed yarns which have a variable and distinctive quality of colour quite different to dyed yarn.

This piece was a first experience of weaving large scale, made particularly interesting by its dimensions exceeding that of the 2m × 2m (6ft × 6ft) studio in a boat in which it was woven. Weaving in sections meant making meticulous measurements of the lines which continue from one section to the next, particularly as only one could be on the loom at a time. Managing tension to allow for shrinkage once off the loom was crucial, particularly with sections of different length. The height of the loom was also limited by the boat's low head height, so the longer sections were woven on a warp which could be pulled around the loom. To make this, a bar was fastened halfway up the loom to which the warp was first secured. The warping continued around the loom, making a knot on the bar at each turn and tying off on it at the end, so that the warp went around the loom without being fastened to it. Working on a loom with adjustable tension meant this could be released to slide the piece round. Care was needed to tighten to the same tension, judged according to how much the warp bounced when patted.

To form the boat shape a template could have been inserted, but I chose to weave the template as a test piece for the mixes I might use in the weaving. Equipped with a leash bar and bobbins, I found great pleasure – particularly in the areas of hatching – in being able to establish a fluent rhythm of weaving.

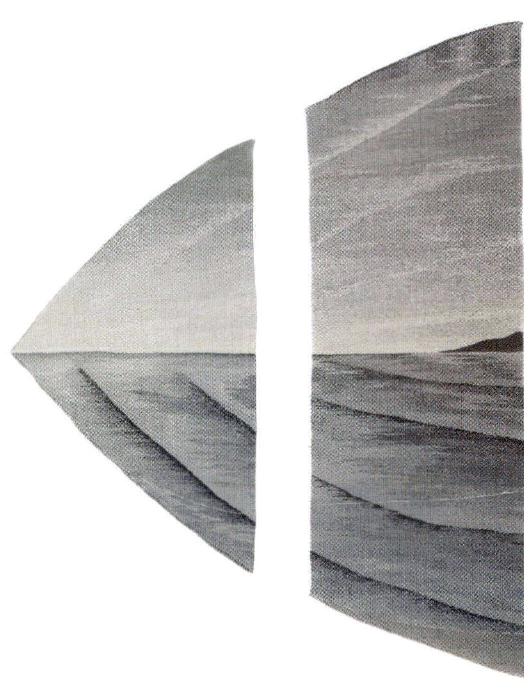
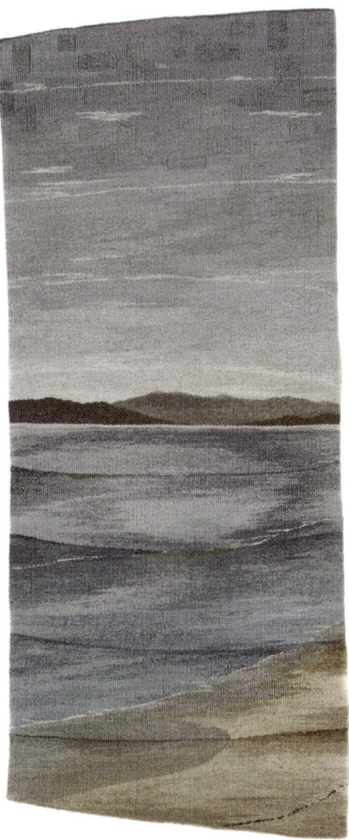
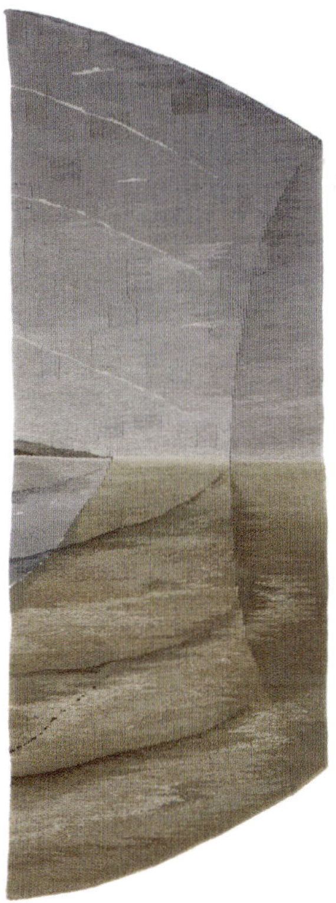

Taking the Long View, Ros Bryant.

QUIRKY PEOPLE SERIES

Since the 1990s Louise has woven 'quirkies', originally responding to treasures found from beach-combing the shores of her native home on the Isle of Man.

Multiple heads and feet woven on a loom

Woven on a warp with an extra row of twining made to the top edge to take away the shed. This makes for a flatter surface, especially when weaving at unconnected points up the warp. The shapes of heads and feet have been woven freehand. They have been started and finished without double half hitches, which would have been visible and clumsy-looking. The weft ends and warps have all been sewn in neatly at the back. The shapes have been bordered by a single strand of cotton stitched around the perimeter with the spare length used to make the legs and neck. The features are made by *couching* down with the same weft and outlining yarns.

Through arranging the woven shapes and choices of treasures gathered from particular times and places, these 'quirky people' come to life.

Cheeky Chappie. Woven heads and feet, china fragment body, embroidered features. Cotton 12/9 medium warp, 10 epi.

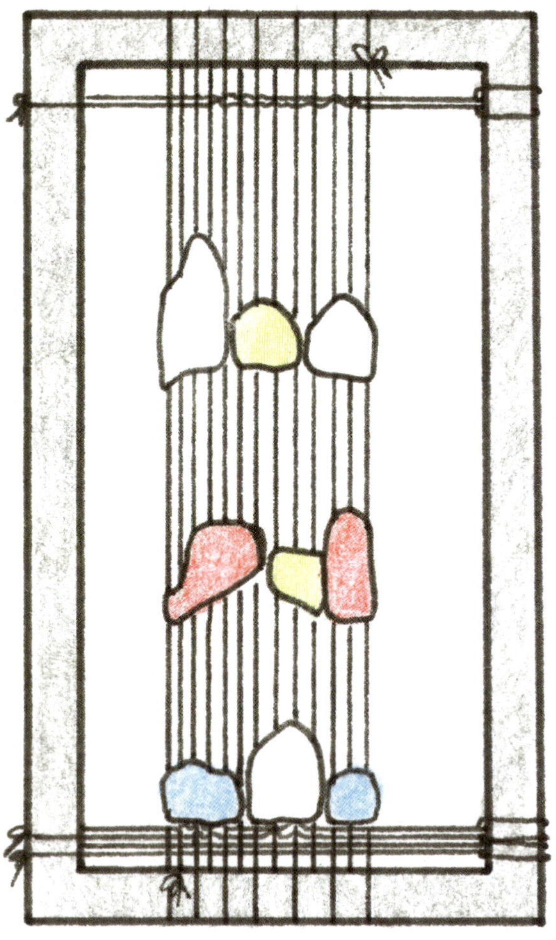

In the case of wishing to make multiple small weavings on one warp as illustrated here, it is very helpful to work with warps that are level all the way up the frame. This has been achieved by putting in another row of twining just below the top bar of the frame.

AFTERWORD – THOUGHTS ABOUT FINDING YOUR OWN VOICE AS A TAPESTRY WEAVER

Your eye and hand are unique. Only you can make your best work, and the same goes for all of us. Be true to your own instinct and ideas, and beware not to be swayed by whatever anyone else writes, says or weaves!

By far the best way to learn to weave is to weave, weave, weave. Feel the yarn, how it grips the warp, how yarns blend or conflict with each other, absorb or reflect the light, whether they feel to be 'your' yarns… Tapestry is a constructed hands-on medium which works best when hand, eye and imagination work together.

A good deal of this book has been given to the business of technical 'correctness'. Our experience is that becoming fluent allows the weaving to flow, so that the structure may become a source of new ideas, not an obstacle. Woven tapestry has its own unique language, because of – not despite – being woven. Mastery of the basic technique does take time and focussed attention for which we have urged readers to find the patience. It is well worth trying different materials, scale and warp settings to find how you work best.

Since tapestry may only be woven from bottom to top, it demands a particular dialogue between observing what has already been woven and reacting to it. Even the most experienced of weavers cannot know entirely how a piece will progress, and if they could there would seem little point in actually weaving it.

The choice to design at the loom or on paper is a very personal one. Either way, there will be constant choices to make which can take all the concentration the weaver can give.

Tapestry is slow. We offer no apology for this – weaving time can be a privileged space in which to savour the experience, idea or place that took you to the loom at the outset. There will always be surprises and welcoming them may make the work come alive and lead onto new questions and discoveries. There is a particular balance to be found in knowing when to run with the unexpected, and when something isn't working. If a mix or a mark really is not sitting well, then going back and taking it out may be the best way forward.

Consider every mark, ask whether it is needed. There is great impact to be gained by restraining yourself to what you really want to see in a piece which may be lost by fussing or embellishing. Woven tapestry has the capacity for amazing photo realism, but it can offer far more than that. There is a visual, tactile and structural language of warp and weft which is unique to woven tapestry. The choices it offers are beyond any of us to explore in a lifetime. The most exciting tapestries are those which embrace the integrity of weave. Learn to see the world in weave, and to work in an authentically weaverly way.

Be adventurous, take risks, think beyond the grid of warp and weft, treat it as a vehicle not a cage. There can be no failure in experimenting, you will always learn something from an experiment, even if it's that you don't wish to repeat it. If you've seen something woven, then it's already been woven, why replicate what others have done? Instead, ask how you might take an idea further, make it in another way.

Here's to all the tapestries yet to be woven, and in particular to yours.

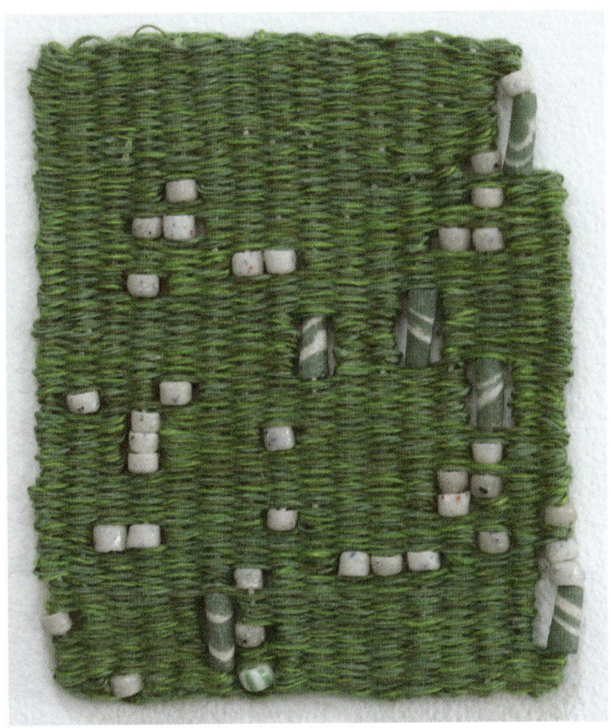

Cotton warp with Ghanaian glass beads, linen weft. 6 epi. 7cm × 8.5cm.

INDEX

First published in 2025 by
The Crowood Press Ltd
Ramsbury, Marlborough
Wiltshire SN8 2HR

enquiries@crowood.com
www.crowood.com

British Library Cataloguing-in-Publication Data
A catalogue record for this book is available from the British Library.

For product safety-related questions, contact:
productsafety@crowood.com

ISBN 978 0 7198 4565 9

Typeset by Envisage IT
Cover design by Sergey Tsvetkov
Printed and bound in India by Parksons Graphics

Acknowledgments
We are grateful to our friends and families for their encouragement and understanding during the writing of this book. In particular we thank John Martin for photography, Irene Cockett for photography and Sarah Pitts for technical support.

Thanks also to the island of Westray, Orkney for space and quietness in which to work.